アドベンチャー

日本語2

ADVENTURES IN JAPANESE 2

TEXTBOOK

HIROMI PETERSON & NAOMI HIRANO-OMIZO

Illustrated by Michael Muronaka & Emiko Kaylor

Cheng & Tsui Company

12 11 10 09   3 4 5 6 7 8 9 10

First Edition 1998
Second Edition 2004

Published by
Cheng & Tsui Company
25 West Street
Boston, MA 02111-1213 USA
Fax (617) 426-3669
www.cheng-tsui.com
"Bringing Asia to the World"™

Adventures in Japanese Vol. 2 Textbook, Third Edition:
        Paperback ISBN: 978-0-88727-577-7
        Hardcover ISBN: 978-0-88727-578-4

The *Adventures in Japanese* series includes textbooks, workbooks, teacher's handbooks, audio CDs,
software, and hiragana/katakana workbooks. Visit www.cheng-tsui.com for more information.

Binding is suitable for heavy classroom use per NASTA book manufacturing standards (MSST).

Printed in the United States of America

ADVENTURES IN JAPANESE 2
CONTENTS

FOREWORD

As a recent author of an elementary Japanese textbook for college students I am keenly aware of the difficulty of writing an elementary textbook. It is time-consuming, energy-consuming and creativity-consuming. Writing an elementary Japanese textbook for high school students must be much harder than writing the counterpart for college students, because it involves a host of age-adequate considerations peculiar to high school students.

Adventures in Japanese has been prepared by highly experienced and knowledgeable high school teachers of Japanese, Hiromi Peterson and Naomi Hirano-Omizo, who know exactly what is teachable/learnable and what is not for high school students. They know how to sustain the students' interest in the Japanese language and its culture by employing so many age-adequate, intriguing activities with a lot of fun illustrations. The grammar explanations and culture notes provide accurate and succinct pieces of information, and each communicative activity is well designed to assist the students in acquiring actual skills to use grammar and vocabulary in context. In short, *Adventures in Japanese* is an up-to-date high school Japanese textbook conceived and designed with a proficiency-based approach. Among many other things, it comes with a teacher's handbook which is intended to help a novice high school teacher of Japanese teach Japanese in a pedagogically correct manner from day one.

I am pleased that at long last we have a high school textbook that is both learnable and teachable, and very importantly, enjoyable. I endorse *Adventures in Japanese* wholeheartedly.

Seiichi Makino
Professor of Japanese and Linguistics
Department of East Asian Studies
Princeton University

TO THE STUDENT

Welcome to the second volume of *Adventures in Japanese*! We hope you enjoyed learning from the first volume of the series.

In Volume 1, you learned how to express your basic needs in Japanese. Your dialogues were centered around Ken and Emi. In Volume 2, dialogues continue to center on Ken. You will also be introduced to Mari, a student from Japan who shares many new cultural insights on her country. This provides many opportunities to compare Japanese and American customs. We hope your experience with Volume 2 will be as fulfilling and enjoyable as your encounter with Volume 1.

While your studies this year will take you a step further, our overall goals remain the same:

1. To create a strong foundation of the Japanese language through the development of the four language skills: speaking, listening, reading, and writing.
2. To strengthen, in particular, students' conversational skills.
3. To deepen students' understanding of the Japanese people and culture through the study of the language and the many aspects of the Japanese culture.
4. To encourage a rediscovery of the students' own language and culture through the study of Japanese language and culture.
5. To shape culturally sensitive, globally aware, responsible world citizens.

In addition, we note here that through these goals, this text addresses many of the National Standards for Japanese Learning, which revolve around the 5 C's: communication, cultures, connections, comparisons and communities. Through the content of the textbook lessons, homework assignments, classroom activities (individual, group, and presentational), lab activities, assessment exercises and projects, students have ample opportunities to communicate in various modes and gain knowledge and understanding of Japanese culture by demonstrating their understanding of the practices, products and perspectives of the Japanese. Certain activities in the text provide opportunities for students to connect with other disciplines, such as weather related activities, geography and measurement. Through the activities provided by the text and by the teacher in the classroom, students also frequently compare the nature of their own language and the Japanese language, as well as derive a better understanding of "culture" through comparison of their own culture and the culture of Japan. In several activities, students are able to communicate to others in the community using Japanese. They are provided with ample tools and practice to enjoy and enrich their personal lives through Japanese.

Let us examine more specifically how you will fulfill these goals in Volume 2.

Topics

Topics for Volume 2 were again carefully selected and arranged so that you will be able to make maximum use of Japanese after completing the course. Many lessons present opportunities for Ken (and you) to go out into the community and use Japanese where you are likely to encounter the language, (e. g., at a Japanese restaurant, speaking with a Japanese student, at a part-time job, when giving directions). As in Volume 1, topics that are part of your daily school life are included, (e. g., illness, sports such as basketball, Japanese class: self-introduction, school rules, driving). Numerous lessons in Volume 2 now allow you to compare and contrast Japanese and American customs and ways of thinking (e. g., school rules, driving, Japanese restaurant, working part-time, New Year's). One lesson, a simplified traditional Japanese folk tale (The Mouse Wedding), gives a good illustration of the values of the Japanese. You will also find that your lessons are arranged in such a way that you will often be studying a topic that is time-appropriate. (Some lessons that coincide with appropriate times of the year are New Year's, Basketball Game, and Mother's Day).

Tasks

At the beginning of each lesson, you will find two tasks that you will be expected to successfully complete by the end of the lesson. We hope that this will give you a better idea of the objectives of each lesson. It also provides you with a guide for preparing for your end-of-the-lesson evaluation.

Dialogues

At the beginning of each lesson, you will find a sample dialogue with illustrations. You will be expected to study the dialogue, then carry out the dialogue with a partner using the illustrations as cues.

Some of the dialogues in this volume are presented in both the formal and informal style. At this level, you are expected to learn the formal style only. The informal style and male/female speech forms will be introduced in Volume 3. However, it is provided in this text as it a more natural speaking style which you may also find interesting to study. The formal (sometimes referred to as polite) style is used in situations when one speaks with persons with whom one is not very familiar. The informal style is used when the speaker perceives his relationship with the listener(s) as being relatively close. The informal style is slightly different for male and female speakers. Further explanation will follow in Volume 3.

Vocabulary

As in Volume 1, the vocabulary words and expressions presented in Volume 2 are those that students use frequently in selected situations. While vocabulary items are limited to 30 - 40 per lesson, students will find that they are extremely practical and more than sufficient to successfully communicate their thoughts. One of the features of this text that we expect to be helpful to you, the student, is the list of previous vocabulary, expressions and grammatical forms that reappear in the current lesson. You should always study these lists to refresh your memory.

Grammar

The grammatical structures in this volume build upon those you have learned in Level One. We have tried to use short grammatical explanations that are clear and simple for you to understand. Verb conjugations are introduced in a systematic way, so that you will be able to progress smoothly from one form to the next. By the end of this volume, you should have the grammatical capability to describe an ongoing state or action, to grant or ask for permission, to prohibit actions, to express your intentions, to state your obligations, to express your ability or potential to do something, to give conditions, to compare things or actions, to express expectation or supposition, to describe the act of doing and receiving favors and much, much more!

Writing

By the end of Volume 1, you were expected to have mastered both *hiragana* and *katakana*, as well as 17 basic *kanji*. In Volume 2, you will be introduced to eight new *kanji* per lesson on the average. By the end of Volume 2, you will have learned 122 *kanji*. The sequence of *kanji* introduction was planned carefully, so that you will first recognize basic *kanji* parts, then advance to more complicated ones. Another feature of this text that makes it easy and fun to learn from is the *kanji* section, which introduces each *kanji* and its origin, or its "story," through pictures. The *kanji* illustrations are also accompanied by English explanations.

Kanji may at first appear complicated, but you will soon begin to see a pattern in the combinations, and will no doubt eventually appreciate *kanji* as much as the Japanese. Learning *kanji* requires diligent and frequent practice. Only through constant practice will you be able to learn and remember *kanji*.

Wakachigaki (spacing between word units) is used in this volume to make reading easier. At more advanced levels, spacing is often not provided. Authentic reading materials also generally do not provide spacing. When you write Japanese at this level, you may choose to write Japanese with or without spacing between words.

Culture
Culture is introduced directly through the lessons, e. g., comparisons of Japanese and American school rules, driving, restaurant etiquette, holidays, etc. The folk tale is a lesson on traditional Japanese values. Your teacher will surely also supplement the text with more cultural information or activities in class.

Japanese Culture Corner
After every odd-numbered lesson, there is a list of questions relating to aspects of Japanese culture. Use whatever resources you have available to you -- friends, relatives, the internet, books, e-mail -- to discover more about Japan!

Fun Corner
Japanese crafts and games are fun and fascinating! In the Fun Corner, you will have the opportunity to learn how to make *origami*, play games, cook, and even exercise to music! Have fun!

Review Questions
After every even-numbered lesson, there is a list of about 30 commonly asked questions related to the topics covered in the lesson. Ask your partner these questions in Japanese, and your partner should answer you without looking at the textbook. Take turns asking and answering questions. Pay attention to speed, intonation, and pronunciation. This portion of the lesson is included in the review tape for listening practice. You may practice your answers using the tape.

Before you begin using this text, we recommend that you study its format and discover all of the supplementary information included. You will find that knowing the contents of this text will be helpful to you in your year's study of Japanese 2.

As we have stated in the previous volume, the key to success in the early years of foreign language study is frequent and regular exposure to the language. Take advantage of the class time you spend with your teacher, use your lab time effectively, and most important, keep up with your work. Learn your material well, don't hesitate to try it out, and most of all, enjoy yourself! がんばりましょう！

TO THE TEACHER

In addition to the background provided in the "To the Student" section, we want to present you with the following additional information about this volume. As mentioned in the earlier section, the curriculum that one establishes around *Adventures in Japanese* closely follows the National Standards of Japanese. Beyond using this textbook, we highly recommend integrating ancillaries such as the audio CDs and CD-Roms and suggestions provided in the teacher's handbook in your curriculum. In particular, we regard the completion of projects as essential to meeting the specifications of the national standards. The projects can easily be modified to suit your students' needs and your preferences, but used as is, they are collectively designed to meet all of the standards. In meeting the standards, using *Adventures in Japanese* also better prepares the students for many of the expectations of the Advanced Placement program. Again, we emphasize that in order for students to be best prepared for APs and for meeting the expectations of the national standards, we recommend incorporating the materials provided in the ancillaries, specifically the audio CDs and the teacher's handbook.

For additional ideas and activities, please consult the *Adventures in Japanese* website for teachers at http://www.punahou.edu/aij. Teachers are invited to submit their own supplementary activities to this website for sharing.

We now present the following examination of the national standards and how they are met in the curriculum that is built around Volume II of *Adventures in Japanese*. While this is not an exhaustive discussion, it will inform you, the teacher, about how standards can be met as one teaches from this volume.

I. Communication: Communicate in Japanese.

1.1 Interpersonal Communication. *Students engage in conversations, provide and obtain information, express feelings and emotions, and exchange opinions.* Students will speak consistently in class for every lesson as they practice with the vocabulary and grammar activities in the text in pairs or in small groups. These exercises elicit information, feelings, emotions and opinions about matters ranging from school rules to eating at restaurants, to illnesses, special celebrations, working part-time, and sports. During oral assessments, they will demonstrate their abilities to speak with proficiency using tasks provided at the start of each lesson or responding to a series of questions from their classmates or teacher. While using Volume II, students also communicate interpersonally through writing, as they learn to write a New Year's card to send to a Japanese friend of relative and a Mother's Day card which eventually may presented to the student's mother, grandmother or another "mother" who may appreciate a note of gratitude in Japanese. They may interview native speakers or communicate through e-mail to obtain information about matters relating to schools, food and cooking, or any topic that is listed in the Japanese Culture Corner section of alternative lessons.

1.2 Interpretive Communication. *Students understand and interpret written and spoken language on a variety of topics.* Students engage in activities that regularly require them to actively listen and read, comprehend, then demonstrate their understanding. For example, their daily class interactions with classmates and teacher which are based on pair activities or group activities require strong listening skills. Students who are required to complete the exercises for each lesson on the audio CDs and CD-Roms gain excellent practice in listening comprehension. Students also regularly practice their reading as they read dialogues and narratives. Students are given an opportunity to read a traditional Japanese folk tale, *Nezumi no Yomeiri*, in this volume. Students may be asked to read simple and authentic sources of information from the internet to answer questions from the Culture Corner section of each odd-numbered lesson.

1.3 Presentational Communication. *Students present information, concepts and ideas to an audience of listeners or readers on a variety of topics.* Short recitations and presentations are a regular part of class activities. Lessons 11 and 12 provide students with an opportunity to present a traditional Japanese folktale to an audience. In the course of the year, students will also have opportunities to engage in projects, such as a cooking project, which will require them to present a cooking demonstration in Japanese.

II. Cultures: Gain Knowledge and Understanding of Japanese Culture.

2.1 *Students demonstrate an understanding of the relationship between the practices and perspectives of Japanese culture.* Students are given ample opportunities to investigate, think about, and discuss common Japanese practices and perspectives through the Culture Corner sections of the lessons. In several lessons, students are introduced to dialogues in the informal style of speech so they may recognize how a difference in speech style reflects relationships between speakers in Japan. The numerous lessons on food, eating, presentation and methods of preparation encourage students to think about these practices and their connection to the Japanese lifestyle. In the lessons on schools, driving, and the basketball game, students learn through the culture notes about the emphasis Japanese place on promptness and following rules. They learn to deduce why these values are important to the Japanese. Students may also engage in traditional Japanese activities such as *rajio taisoo, hanafuda, fukuwarai,* storytelling and *nengajoo* making which help them better understand traditional practices and why they continue to survive in contemporary Japan.

2.2 *Students demonstrate an understanding of the relationship between the products and the perspectives of Japanese culture.* Volume II provides ample opportunities for students to learn about the daily life of Japanese. Ken ventures out into communities that immerse him in culturally authentic experiences. For example, Ken learns about a variety of Japanese foods and how they are presented, prepared and eaten. Recipes are provided so students may actually prepare many of the foods. A special "fun" corner in this volume allows students to fold *origami* pieces and design and create New Year cards so they can appreciate the precise art of crafting in the Japanese culture.

III. Connections: Connect with other disciplines and acquire information.

3.1 *Students reinforce and further their knowledge of other disciplines through the Japanese language.* In Volume II, students are able to further their understanding of other disciplines, mainly social studies (sociology, geography, economics, etc.), home economics, drama, art, music, and physical education. The Culture Corner touches on many aspects of social studies as it allows students to investigate many probing questions about Japanese society, geography and economics in English and Japanese from various sources. Lesson 1 offers a thorough look at the map of Japan and a detailed lesson on calisthenics done to music. The opportunity to connect to P. E. reappears in the lesson on the basketball game. Numerous cooking opportunities in several lessons offer strong connections with home economics, and the many craft opportunities connect to art. Several songs with Japanese lyrics give the musically talented an opportunity to boast their strengths while drama enthusiasts will enjoy the chance to share their talents in the skit *Nezumi no Yomeiri*.

3.2 *Students acquire information and recognize the distinctive viewpoints that are only available through Japanese language and culture.* In this volume, students are introduced to the system of speech styles which differentiate speakers' relationships to their listeners. Through the lesson on restaurants and shopping, students are also given their first taste of *keigo,* as honorific and humble forms appear in interactions between waiter/shop clerk and customer. Some of the probing questions in the Culture Corner also reveal to students similar and contrasting viewpoints and values of the Japanese. Volume II also introduces sprinklings of proverbs that reveal much about the thinking of Japanese.

IV. Comparisons: Develop Insight into the Nature of Language and Culture.

4.1 *Students demonstrate understanding of the nature of language through comparison of the Japanese language and their own.* In almost all of their encounters in a Japanese language class, students are exposed to comparisons and contrasts between Japanese and their own language. For example, they learn that verbs in English and Japanese do not translate equally. In Japanese, the word *yaku* carries the multiple meanings of "bake, grill, roast, fry, burn, toast, char," while the English verb "to wear" translates differently depending on where or how one wears clothing or accessories. As mentioned earlier, they are introduced to informal and formal speech styles, and honorific speech. Perhaps the best example of a unique Japanese linguistic feature that students must demonstrate an understanding of, appears at the end of the text in the form of verbs of giving. This is one of the best illustrations of how language reflects the perspectives of culture.

4.2 *Students demonstrate understanding of the concept of culture through comparisons of Japanese culture and their own.* In this volume, students have increased opportunities to compare aspects of Japanese culture with their own. The numerous cultural notes on topics such as school practices, driving, restaurant etiquette and food preparation, shopping, transportation and holiday celebrations offer rich cultural comparisons to students. For example, students read about department stores in Japan and learn about the diversity of customer services offered and the extreme politeness and service-orientedness of the employees at Japanese department stores. How and why are there such differences in such practices in Japan and America? Such questions arise naturally, but are re-emphasized in the questions posed in the Culture Corner.

V. Communities: Participate in Multilingual Communities at Home and Around the World.

5.1 *Students use Japanese both within and beyond the school setting.* In this volume, students are able to share aspects of language and culture in multiple ways. They are able to share their language skills by sending out New Year's greetings to friends or relatives, or participate in New Year's card contests. In a similar way, they share their more advanced language skills through their Mother's Day messages on cards they have designed. Students may share their speaking skills by performing the skit *Nezumi no Yomeiri* to peer or younger audiences at school or in the community. Students also enjoy sharing their culinary and language skills as they prepare foods such as *oyako donburi* and *sukiyaki* for their families.

5.2 *Students show evidence of becoming lifelong learners by using Japanese for personal enjoyment and enrichment.* Using lessons they have studied in Volume II, students are able to take with them cultural and linguistic lessons into their later lives. For example, students will likely engage in activities such as the *hanafuda* card game or *origami* folding well into their adult lives. Should students travel to Japan, knowledge they have gained about Japanese foods, restaurants, shopping, geography and transportation will contribute to a much more enjoyable and enriching experience. One of the greatest moments of satisfaction for a foreign language student is to be unexpectedly stopped one day and asked for directions by a speaker of the foreign language the student is studying. In Volume II, students are equipped with this skill, and hopefully will gain confidence to assist foreign visitors at home in this way, even years after leaving the classroom. Finally, students completing this volume will likely feel comfortable preparing Japanese foods for themselves, friends and family after their own cooking experiences with Japanese foods in their classes.

We hope that the preceding information has provided you, the teacher, with suggestions on how *Adventures in Japanese, Volume II* may help your students meet national language standards and better prepare them for Advanced Placement exams.

The ultimate goal of the authors of this text however, is one that supersedes meeting national standards or succeeding at AP exams. Our aim is to nurture students who grow to love the language and culture of Japan. We want to see our students integrate some aspect of Japan, its culture and language into their lives so they may eventually contribute to a stronger relationship between our nations. We hope that with their appreciation of the power of understanding many languages and cultures, they will be better prepared to someday lead us to a more peaceful and harmonious world.

ACKNOWLEDGMENTS

Adventures in Japanese was developed thanks to the efforts and contributions of our colleagues at Punahou School and beyond, input and feedback from the hundreds of students who have spent time in our classrooms, and the support of the administration and staff at Punahou School. We gratefully express our appreciation to all who contributed in any way, even if we may have failed to mention them below.

First and foremost, a warm thanks to all of our students who have contributed directly and indirectly to the development of the text. They have provided us with a purpose, motivated us, taught us, given us ideas and suggestions, and encouraged us in many ways.

We acknowledge Professor Seiichi Makino of Princeton University, who has written the foreword, conducted workshops for us and offered us much support and encouragement throughout the project. We thank Professor Masako Himeno of the University of the Air in Japan for her guidance over many portions of the text and for her valuable suggestions and support. We express our gratitude to our illustrators, former Punahou student Michael Muronaka and former colleague Emiko Kaylor. Our thanks are extended to present and former Japanese language colleagues at Punahou School who contributed to the writing of the text, to the creation of supplementary materials, or gave suggestions for improving the text. They include Junko Ady, Jan Asato, Linda Fujikawa, Carin Lim, Kazuko Love, Naomi Okada, Carol Shimokawa, Michiko Sprester, Misako Steverson, Rae Tadaki, and Hiroko Kazama. We express our gratitude to our colleague Jan Asato and Punahou graduate Brandon Yoshimoto for producing the CD-Roms for Volume II. We also acknowledge Janice Murabayashi, a former Social Studies colleague, for writing the questions on Japanese culture and Kathy Boswell, a former English colleague, for naming our text. Our gratitude is also extended to Sarah Sugimoto for writing the *hanafuda* fun corner and Fusako Takishita for the instructions for the Mother's Day card. We also thank the Chuugoku Shinbun newspaper company, Shinji Nakatani, Jan Asato, Kayo Nakai, Phyllis Sano and Kofu Kogyo High School for providing the photos, the Keirin Chinese restaurant and Kazuko Muneyoshi for their cooperation to take photos. We thank Wes Peterson for generously sharing his technological expertise and support throughout the project.

We also thank Carol Loose, Michelle Morikami, Linda Palko Rucci, Martha Lanzas, Susan Oi, and the staff at the Punahou Visual Production Center for their years of assistance with the compilation of the text. In addition, we recognize the late Mike Dahlquist, Celia Calvo and the staff at the Punahou ITV (Instructional Television) for their help in the production of many of the preliminary audio materials.

Our gratitude is also extended to Harry Kubo, Kazuo Ogawa, Junko Ady, Keiko Kaneko and Masaru Ishikawa, who produced the final version of the audio tapes. We extend our thanks to Mr. Takuroo Ichikawa for the use of the tape of his musical presentation. Our appreciation is also extended to faculty member Junko Ady for sharing her vocal talents for the songs on tape and CD, and to Amy Mitsuda, Music School Director at Punahou, for her keyboard accompaniment, and Jeff Ady for his guitar accompaniment.

We thank all of the administrators at Punahou School for their assistance in our textbook effort.

Finally, we express our appreciation to our families for their unwavering support of our efforts in the development of *Adventures in Japanese*.

Hiromi Peterson and Naomi Hirano-Omizo

Useful Expressions

1. いい(お)てんきですねえ。

The weather is nice!

2. あめですねえ。

It's raining (a lot)!

3. (お)げんきですか。

How are you? [lit., Are you fine?]

This expression is used only when one meets a person after not seeing him/her for several days or more.

4. はい、げんきです。

Yes, I am fine.

Notice that the polite prefix "お" is removed here, since the speaker is talking about himself.

5. ぐあいが わるいです。

I feel sick.

6. ねむいです。

(I) am sleepy.

7. つかれて います。

(I) am tired.

8.  すみません。もういちど おねがいします。

Excuse me.　　One more time please.

もう means more, いちど means one time, おねがいします is commonly used when one asks a favor of someone.

1

9.

すみません。ゆっくり　おねがいします。

Excuse me.　　Slowly, please.

ゆっくり means "slowly; leisurely."

10.

ちょっと　まって　ください。

Please wait a minute.

11.

すみません。　おそく　なりました。

I'm sorry to be late. [lit., I am sorry. I have become late.]

12.

Tree は　にほんごで　なんと　いいますか。

How do you say "tree" in Japanese?

にほんご means "Japanese language," で means "by means of," なん means "what," と is a particle used for quotations, いいます means "say" and か is a particle that marks questions.

13. わすれました。

I forgot.

14. なくしました。

I lost (it).

15. ええと...／あのう...

Let me see... Well...

When you need time to think, or to pause, these expressions may be used to "buy time."

2

16.

おてあらい／（お）トイレへ　いっても
いいですか。
May I go to the bathroom?

17.

ロッカーへ　いっても　いいですか。
May I go to the locker?

18.

（お）みずを　のんでも　いいですか。
May I get a drink of water?　[lit. "May I drink water?"]

19.

えんぴつを　かして　ください。
Please lend me a pencil.

20.

すみません。しつもんが　あります。
Excuse me, I have a question.

21.

（かみ）を　ください。
Please give me (some paper).

3

TEACHER'S DIRECTIONS

1. かいてください。
Please write.

2. よんでください。
Please read.

3. みてください。
Please look.

4. きいてください。
Please listen.

5. すわってください。
Please sit down.

6. たってください。
Please stand up.

7. だしてください。
Please turn in (something).

8. みせてください。
Please show me (something).

9. あけてください。
Please open it.

10. しめてください。
Please close it.

11. しずかにしてください。
Please be quiet.

12. でんきをつけてください。
Please turn on the light.

13. でんきをけしてください。
Please turn off the light.

14. よくできました。
Well done!

By the end of this lesson, you will be able to communicate the information below in the given situations.

【 II -1 タスク 1 】

Interview your partner, then introduce your partner to your class. Find out, then share information about your partner's:

    (1) name.

    (2) age.

    (3) grade.

    (4) family.

        a. siblings (names, ages, grades, etc.).

        b. parents (jobs, etc.).

    (5) interests.

【 II -1 タスク 2 】

You meet a new friend who just arrived from Japan. Briefly introduce yourself, then find out:

    (1) where your friend is from.

    (2) when your friend came to (your city).

    (3) whether your friend has brothers/sisters.

    (4) information about siblings (ages, grades, etc.)

    (5) what your friend likes/dislikes.

    (6) what sorts of things he/she would like to do during his/her stay.

一課

【 お話 】

<Ken meets Mari, a Japanese student, at school for the first time.>

ケン：はじめまして。ケンです。どうぞ　よろしく。お名前は？

まり：まりです。はじめまして。どうぞ　よろしく。日本語が
　　　上手ですねえ。

ケン：いいえ、下手です。日本語が　少し　わかりますから、ゆっくり
　　　話して　ください。

まり：はい、わかりました。

ケン：まりさんは　日本の　どこから　来ましたか。

まり：東京から　来ました。

ケン：いつ　来ましたか。

まり：八月二十日に　来ました。

ケン：そうですか。兄弟は　何人　いますか。

まり：二人　います。姉と　兄です。

ケン：まりさんは　何年生ですか。

まり：高校一年生です。

ケン：どんな　事が　好きですか。

まり：スポーツや　音楽が　好きです。

ケン：そうですか。ここで　どんな　事を　したいですか。

まり：友達を　たくさん　作りたいです。

Hiragana is used for *KUN* (Japanese) readings and *katakana* for *ON* (Chinese) readings.

1. 一　one　　ひと　　一つ〔ひとつ〕one (general object)

　　　　　　　イチ　　一月〔いちがつ〕January

　　　　　　　☆　　　一日〔ついたち〕the first day of the month

2. 二　two　　ふた　　二つ〔ふたつ〕two (general objects)

　　　　　　　ニ　　　二月〔にがつ〕February

　　　　　　　☆　　　二日〔ふつか〕the second day of the month

3. 三　three　みっ　　三つ〔みっつ〕three (general objects)

　　　　　　　　　　　三日〔みっか〕the third day of the month

　　　　　　　サン　　三月〔さんがつ〕March

4. 四　four　　よ（っ）四つ〔よっつ〕 four (general objects)

　　　　　　　　　　　四日〔よっか〕the fourth day of the month

　　　　　　　よん　　四本〔よんほん〕four (long objects)

　　　　　　　シ　　　四月〔しがつ〕April

5. 五　five　　いつ　　五つ〔いつつ〕five (general objects)

　　　　　　　　　　　五日〔いつか〕the fifth day of the month

　　　　　　　ゴ　　　五月〔ごがつ〕May

6. 六　six　　　むっ　　六つ〔むっつ〕six (general objects)

　　　　　　　☆　　　六日〔むいか〕the sixth day of the month

　　　　　　　ロク　　六月〔ろくがつ〕June

7. 七　seven　なな　　七つ〔ななつ〕seven (general objects)

　　　　　　　なの　　七日〔なのか〕the seventh day of the month

　　　　　　　シチ　　七月〔しちがつ〕July

8. 八　eight　やっ　　八つ〔やっつ〕eight (general objects)

一課

		よう	八日〔ようか〕the eighth day of the month
		ハチ	八月〔はちがつ〕August
9.	九 nine	ここの	九つ〔ここのつ〕nine (general objects)
			九日〔ここのか〕the ninth of the month
		キュウ	九十〔きゅうじゅう〕ninety
		ク	九月〔くがつ〕September
10.	十 ten	とお	十日〔とおか〕the 10th day of the month
		ジュウ	十月〔じゅうがつ〕October
11.	月 moon	ガツ	一月〔いちがつ〕January
		ゲツ	月曜日〔げつようび〕Monday
12.	日 sun, day	ひ	その日〔ひ〕that day
		び	月曜日〔げつようび〕Monday
		か	十四日〔じゅうよっか〕the 14th of the month
		ニチ	日曜日〔にちようび〕Sunday
13.	火 fire	カ	火曜日〔かようび〕Tuesday
14.	水 water	みず	お水〔みず〕water
		スイ	水曜日〔すいようび〕Wednesday
15.	木 tree	き	おおきい木〔き〕a big tree
		モク	木曜日〔もくようび〕Thursday
16.	金 gold	かね	お金〔かね〕money
		キン	金曜日〔きんようび〕Friday
17.	土 soil	ド	土曜日〔どようび〕Saturday

Let's review previous vocabulary!

A. めいし Nouns

1. にほんご	Japanese language		11. おんがく	music
2. にほん	Japan		12. ここ	here
3. 八月〔はちがつ〕	August		13. ともだち	friend
4. 二十日〔はつか〕	20th		14. えいご	English
5. きょうだい	siblings		15. どこ	where?
6. あね	(own) older sister		16. いつ	when?
7. あに	(own) older brother		17. なんにん	how many (people)?
8. こうこう一ねんせい	first year high school student		18. なんねんせい	what grade?
9. こと	thing (intangible)		19. どんな	what kind of?
10. スポーツ	sports			

B. どうし Verbs

20. thing が わかります 〔G1 わかって〕　to understand (thing)
21. はなして 〔G1 はなします〕　to talk
22. きました 〔IR きて〕　came
23. います 〔G2 いて〕　to exist, to have (for animate objects)
24. したいです 〔IR します／して〕　want to do
25. つくりたいです 〔G2 つくります／つくって〕　want to make

C. -な けいようし NA Adjectives

26. じょうず	skillful	28. すき	to like
27. へた	unskillful		

D. ふくし Adverbs

29. すこし	a little	31. たくさん	a lot, many
30. ゆっくり	slowly		

E. じょし Particles

32. から	from	34. (time) に	on; in
33. (language) で	in (a language)	35. A や B	A and B, etc.

F. Counters

36. 二人〔ふたり〕   two (persons)

G. Others

37. そして   And

H. Expressions

38. はじめまして。   How do you do?

39. どうぞ よろしく。   Glad to meet you.

40. わかりました。   I understand. I get it.

41. おなまえは？   What is your name?

42. そうですか。   Is that so?

I. ぶんぽう Grammar

43. Sentence 1 + から、 Sentence 2。   Sentence 1, <u>so</u> Sentence 2.

きょう にほんから きましたから、えいごが よく わかりません。

I came from Japan today, so I do not understand English well.

44. Verb (TE form) + ください。   Please do ～ .

ゆっくり <u>はなして ください</u>。   Please speak slowly.

45. Verb (Stem form) + たい（ん）です。   I want to do ～ .

ともだちを つくり<u>たいです</u>。   I want to make friends.

【アクティビティー】

A. ペアワーク

Interview your partner in Japanese using the cues below. Take notes in Japanese. Introduce your partner to your class based on the information you received from him/her.

Introduce yourself.	
（お）なまえ？	渡部 麻衣子
なんさい？	十三 さい
なんねんせい？	日本語学校に 七 ねんせい
とくいな こと？	さんすう，バレー
にがてな こと？	日本語学校の しゅくだい
すきな たべもの？	あまいもの
きらいな たべもの？	ピーマン，ねぎ
たんじょう日？	一月二十五日
ことし どんな ことを したいですか。	

一課

【単語】

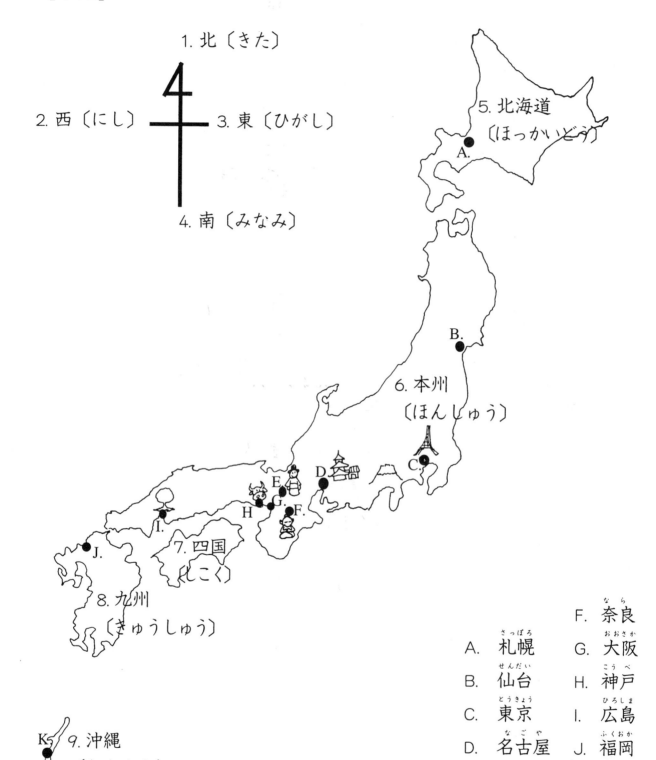

1. 北〔きた〕

2. 西〔にし〕　3. 東〔ひがし〕

4. 南〔みなみ〕

5. 北海道〔ほっかいどう〕

A.

B.

6. 本州〔ほんしゅう〕

D.

E.

G.

H.

F.

C.

I.

J.

7. 四国〔しこく〕

8. 九州〔きゅうしゅう〕

K. 9. 沖縄〔おきなわ〕

F. 奈良〔なら〕

A. 札幌〔さっぽろ〕　G. 大阪〔おおさか〕

B. 仙台〔せんだい〕　H. 神戸〔こうべ〕

C. 東京〔とうきょう〕　I. 広島〔ひろしま〕

D. 名古屋〔なごや〕　J. 福岡〔ふくおか〕

E. 京都〔きょうと〕　K. 那覇〔なは〕

A. ペアワーク

Copy and cut out the cards on the bottom of the next page. Place the stack of cards upside down. Flip one card at a time and place it in the correct block on this map. You have one minute only. The winner is the person who has the most correct answers.

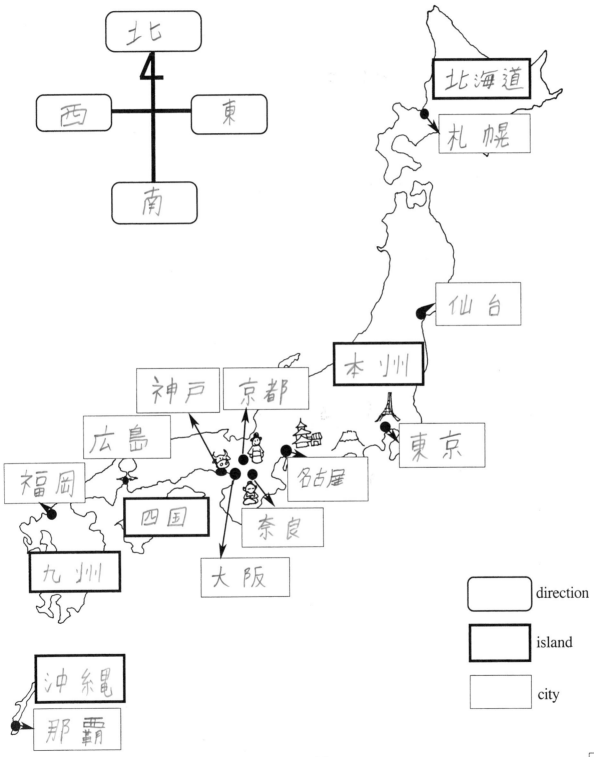

北

西　東

南

北海道

札幌

仙台

本州

神戸　京都

広島

東京

福岡

名古屋

四国

奈良

九州

大阪

沖縄

那覇

☐ direction

☐ island

☐ city

一課

B. グループワーク

List as many things (festivals, foods, tourist spots, etc.) you can think of that are associated with each of the places listed below.

1. 札幌〔さっぽろ〕	うし
2. 仙台〔せんだい〕	さくら
3. 東京〔とうきょう〕	はらじゅく
4. 名古屋〔なごや〕	しゃちほこ
5. 京都〔きょうと〕	てら
6. 奈良〔なら〕	しか
7. 大阪〔おおさか〕	おおさかべん
8. 神戸〔こうべ〕	こうべぎゅう
9. 広島〔ひろしま〕	ばくだん
10. 福岡〔ふくおか〕	ラーメン
11. 那覇〔なは〕	ドーナツ

C. クラスワーク

Find pictures in magazines of as many of the famous things you listed above and decorate the classroom bulletin board. Label them by city, or place them on a map of Japan.

- -

Copy and cut these cards out along the lines for Exercise A.

東〔ひがし〕	本州〔ほんしゅう〕	仙台〔せんだい〕	大阪〔おおさか〕
西〔にし〕	四国〔しこく〕	東京〔とうきょう〕	神戸〔こうべ〕
南〔みなみ〕	九州〔きゅうしゅう〕	名古屋〔なごや〕	広島〔ひろしま〕
北〔きた〕	沖縄〔おきなわ〕	京都〔きょうと〕	福岡〔ふくおか〕
北海道〔ほっかいどう〕	札幌〔さっぽろ〕	奈良〔なら〕	那覇〔なは〕

【文法】

---

* A. Verb (Stem form) ＋ たいです。   want to do ～

               たくないです。   do not want to do ～

The noun that English speakers consider the direct object of this sentence may take either を or が. This construction is used most commonly when the subject is first person, "I" or "We." It is also used to ask another person, usually a person of equal or lower status, if he or she would like to do something. It is not considered polite to use this to superiors, especially if one does not know the person well.

---

1. クッキーを or が　たくさん　食べたいです。　I want to eat lots of cookies.
2. 日本へ　行きたいです。　I want to go to Japan.
3. コーヒーは　飲みたくないです。　I do not want to drink coffee.

---

* B. Something ＋ が ＋ ほしいです。   want (something)

     Something ＋ は ＋ ほしくないです。   do not want (something)

The particle that follows the noun one wants is が. The particle は may be used in sentence ending with a negative. This construction is not commonly directed to superiors as a question, as it is considered impolite to be so direct.

---

* Previously introduced.

1. 車が　ほしいです。　I want a car.
2. 赤い　ぼうしは　ほしくないです。　I do not want a red hat.

【アクティビティー】

A. ペアワーク

     Ask your partner if he/she wants to do the following things this year.

     Ex. 質問：「ことし　バスケットが　したいですか。」

          答え：「はい、したいです。」or「いいえ、したくないです。」

しつもん	はい	いいえ
1. ことし　にほんへ　いきたいですか。		
2. ことし　よく　べんきょうしたいですか。		
3. ことし　あたらしい　ともだちを　つくりたいですか。		

一課

B. クラスワーク

The teacher prepares side A and side B for each pair of students. One student reads the beginning of the sentences in A1 (# 1 ～ 6). The partner listens and, using the B sheet, finds the phrase that best completes the sentence. Students switch sheets for A2 (# 7 ～ 12).

A1	B
1. あした　フットボールの しあいが　ありますから、	a. こんばん　べんきょうします。
2. つかれていますから、	b. たべたいです。
3. あした　しけんが　ありますから、	c. かちたいです。
4. うたを　うたいたいですから、	d. くすりを　のみたいです。
5. あしたは　ははの たんじょう日ですから、	e. うちへ　かえって、ねたいです。
6. きのうの　えいがは　とても おもしろかったですから、	f. お水を　のみたいです。

A2	
7. のどが　かわきましたから、	g. カラオケに　いきましょう。
8. わたしの　ショーツは　とても ふるいですから、	h. プレゼントを　あげたいです。
9. とても　さむいですから、	i. しごとを　したいです。
10. にほんへ　いきたいですが、 お金が　ありませんから、	j. また　みたいです。
11. おなかが　ぺこぺこですから、	k. あたらしいのが　ほしいです。
12. あたまが　いたいですから、	l. あたたかい　ジャケットが ほしいです。

【文法】

* A. This construction is used to conjoin two or more simple sentences into one. The tense of the entire sentence is determined by the tense of the final sentence. The particle と cannot be used to conjoin sentences.

　　Sentence 1 [Verb (TE form)]、　Sentence 2。　　　　　S1 and S2.

　　Sentence 1 [- I Adjective (-くて)]、　Sentence 2。　　S1 and S2.

　　Sentence 1 [Noun / NA Adjective] ＋ で、　Sentence 2。　S1 and S2.

1. 毎日　六時に　起きて、学校へ　行きます。　I get up at six o'clock and go to school.

2. 日本語の　授業は　おもしろくて、楽しいです。
　　　　　　　　　　　　Japanese class is interesting and enjoyable.

3. あの　先生は　やさしくて、いいです。　That teacher over there is kind and (she is) good.

4. 兄は　大学生で、今　サンフランシスコに　います。
　　　　　　　　My older brother is a college student and is in San Francisco now.

5. 母は　テニスが　好きで、父は　ゴルフが　好きです。
　　　　　　　　　My mother likes tennis and my father likes golf.

* B. Verb (TE form) ＋ ください。　　　　　Please do ～ .
　This construction is used when one politely requests a favor.

1. ちょっと　待って　ください。　　　　Please wait a minute.

2. お金を　かして　ください。　　　　Please lend me some money.

3. ここに　来て　ください。　　　　Please come here.

* C. Verb (TE form) ＋ も　いいです（か）。　　You may; May I ～?
　This construction is used to ask for or grant permission. This construction, when used in a statement form, is not generally used directly to superiors.

* Previously introduced.

1. トイレに　行っても　いいですか。　　May I go to the bathroom?

2. お水を　飲んでも　いいです。　　You may drink water.

3. 宿題を　あとで　出しても　いいですか。　　May I turn in my homework later?

一課

【 🧑‍🤝‍🧑 アクティビティー】

A. ペアワーク

Ask your partner about what he/she has done today. Write down the answers.

Ex. 質問：「今朝　何時に　起きましたか。」

答え：「～時に　起きました。」

質問：「起きて、（それから）何を　しましたか。」

答え：「起きて、朝御飯を　食べました。」

質問：「朝御飯を　食べて、（それから）何を　しましたか。」　　etc.

1. ___7___ じに　おきました。
2. あさごはんを　たべました。
3. はを みがきました。
4. コンタクトを 入れました。
5. ようい しました。
6. 学校 へ 行きました。

B. ペアワーク

Ask your partner's opinions about the things listed below. Your partner should answer using <u>two</u> descriptive words.

Ex. 日本の　車

質問：「日本の　車は　どうですか。」

答え：「小さくて、ちょっと　高いです。」

1. にほんごの　じゅぎょう	かんたんです。
2. にほんごの　きょうしつ	人が いっぱいです。
3. あなたの　へや	ここちが いいです。
4. この　がっこう	みんな やさしいです。
5. カフェテリアの　たべもの	あったかそうです。

C. ペアワーク

Ask your partner the following questions. Your partner should answer in one sentence.

Ex. 質問：「何才ですか。何年生ですか。」
　　答え：「私は　〜才で、〜年生です。」

1. なんさいですか。なんねんせいですか。	私は十三才で、七年生です。
2. がっこうの　ピザは　いくらですか。 　　ホットドッグは　いくらですか。	三ドルです。
3. どんな　ことが　とくいですか。 　　どんな　ことが　にがてですか。	さんすうが とくいで、しゃかいが にがてです。
4. どんな　たべものが　すきですか。 　　どんな　たべものが　きらいですか。	あまいものが すきで、ピーマン、ねぎ、いろいろ きらいです。
5. じゅうしょは　どこですか。 　　でんわばんごうは　なんばんですか。	ないしょ♡

D. ペアワーク or クラスワーク

Play Simon Says with your partner or your class. You may use some of these examples.

1. 立って　ください。
2. 座って　ください。
3. 〜に　名前を　書いて　ください。
4. 〜を　読んで　ください。
5. 〜を　開けて　ください。
6. 〜を　閉めて　ください。
7. 〜を　貸して　ください。
8. 〜へ　行って　ください。
9. ここへ　来て　ください。
10. 〜を　見せて　ください。
11. 〜を　出して　ください。
12. 〜さんに　〜を　あげて　ください。
13. 寝て　ください。
14. 起きて　ください。

E. ペアワーク

You are a student and your partner is a teacher. Ask permission to do the following things.

Ex. 質問：（お）トイレへ　行っても　いいですか。

答え：はい、いいです。 or いいえ、だめです。

1. いま　お水を　のんでも　いいですか。	はい、いいです。
2. いま　ポテトチップスを　たべても　いいですか。	はい、いいです。
3. いま　ロッカーへ　いっても　いいですか。	はい、いいです。
4. きょうしつで　ねても　いいですか。	はい、いいです。
5. いま　クラスを　おわっても　いいですか。	はい、いいです。

F. ペアワーク

Put up pictures of various celebrities somewhere at the front of your classroom. At your seat, mentally select one of the celebrities. Do not reveal your celebrity to your partner, but describe your celebrity using at least two descriptive (い adjective or な adjective) words in one sentence. Your partner will try to guess who your celebrity is. Take turns.

JAPANESE CULTURE 1: 日本のまち Cities in Japan

Find the answers from books, by talking to friends, or by using the Internet.

1. South of Tokyo in a city called Kamakura is a famous statue of Buddha. Try to draw it here:

2. Which city in Japan hosts a famous snow and ice festival?

札幌

3. What is the old name for Tokyo?

江戸

4. Which city is famous for its hand-massaged, beer-fed cattle (which makes for very expensive beef!)?

神戸

5. Which ancient capital is famous for its shrines, temples (including one gilded with 24-karat gold), and *geisha* district?

京都

6. What city hosted the 1998 Winter Olympics?

名古屋

7. Name the two cities that were hit by American nuclear bombs in 1945.

広島と長野

8. What is the second largest city in Japan?

大阪

9. Find out something famous about Nara, Sendai, Fukuoka, or Naha.

10. Which city in Japan would you most like to visit? Why?

東京

一課

Rajio Taiso

 Rajio taiso or "radio exercises" are calisthenics performed to music. They originated after World War II to encourage cooperation and unity. The custom of lining up together in neat rows for daily morning exercises continues today at schools and at certain companies. Originally, people gathered around their radios or piped the radio music over public address systems into playgrounds or playing fields where the exercises took place. Today, one can still observe this morning ritual as one goes by schools, parks, or companies. However, one is also able to tune in to early morning television broadcasts every day and do the exercises in the privacy of their own homes.

 There are several versions of *rajio taiso* with which most Japanese are familiar. The instructions called out as part of the lyrics, give cues as to which exercise to do and how to do them. The exercises include familiar ones such as "jumping jacks," "windmill," and "toe touching."

Senior citizens in Japan gather at a park for *rajio taiso* at 6:30 a.m.

ラジオたいそう

	Beginning position	Intermediate steps	Ending position
1		Stretch arms out up in front; gently lower, extending out to the sides.	
2		Bend knees and swing arms outward while lifting heels.	
3		Swing arms out, rotate arms in a forward circle; then rotate arms in a backward direction.	
4		Extend arms straight out; then extend arms backward and upward (V slant) with the chest out.	

一課

	Beginning position	Intermediate steps	Ending position
5		Bend arms overhead (with the upper body) and to the side two times; left, then right.	
6		Relax and bend forward touching the ground three times; straighten up; bend back with hands on waist.	
7		Loosely swing arms while twisting body; left, right, left, right. Then fling arms in an upward left slant two times. Repeat on the right side.	
8		Put left foot out to the side while putting arms on shoulder; stand on toes while extending arms up; return hands to shoulder; bring left foot back and arms down. Repeat with right foot.	

	Beginning position	Intermediate steps	Ending position
9		 Bend towards left, touch the ground two times, then straighten up and bend back; repeat on right side.	
10		 Swing arms and body, making a big circle starting from the left; repeat by reversing direction.	
11		 Jump lightly with both feet together, then do two jumping jacks, extending arms out, down, out, down.	
12		 (Repeat Exercise # 2.) Bend knees and swing arms outward while lifting heels.	

一課

	Beginning position	Intermediate steps	Ending position
13		(Repeat Exercise # 1.) Stretch arms upward and gently lower to the sides.	

By the end of this lesson, you will be able to communicate the information below in the given situations.

【 II -2 タスク 1 】

Interview your friend in Japanese. Provide:
 (1) name.
 (2) age.
 (3) grade.
 (4) interests.
 (5) place of birth.
 (6) where your family lives now.
 (7) father's place of employment.
 (8) mother's place of employment.
 (9) siblings (ages, marital status, occupation, residence).
(10) anything else of interest.

【 II -2 タスク 2 】

Ask your friend about his/her house. Discuss:
 (1) location.
 (2) color.
 (3) size: big or small.
 (4) impression: good or bad.
 (5) how many rooms?
 (6) his/her room and its contents.
 (7) pets? What kind?
 (8) how many cars?
 (9) relative location of the home to a landmark.
(10) anything else of interest.

【お話】

<Mari introduces herself in the classroom.>

　自己紹介します。私は　林まりです。十六才で、高校一年生です。趣味は
スポーツで、特に　野球が　好きです。東京で　生まれました。家族は
東京に　住んで　います。父は　銀行に　勤めて　いて、母は　デパートで
働いて　います。姉は　もう　結婚して　いて、赤ちゃんが　います。
赤ちゃんは　まだ　一才です。姉は　今　仕事を　して　いません。兄は
大学四年生で、りょうに　住んで　います。毎日　本屋で　アルバイトを
して　います。

　皆さんは　スミスさんを　知って　いますか。私は　今　スミスさんの
家に　ホームステイを　して　います。スミスさんに　ついて　少し　話し
ます。家は　とても　広くて、きれいです。家族は　車を　二台　持って
います。部屋の　中に　きれいな　ベッドや　机が　あります。白い　猫が
一匹　いて、いつも　ドアの　所に　寝て　います。家の　前に　公園が
あります。そして、公園に　プールが　あって、私は　毎日　プールで
泳いで　います。私は　泳ぐのが　大好きです。

　どうぞ　よろしく　お願いします。

Let's review previous vocabulary!

A. めいし　Nouns

1. 十六さい　　　　　　　　16 years old
2. こうこう一年生〔いちねんせい〕　high school sophomore
3. スポーツ　　　　　　　sports
4. やきゅう　　　　　　　baseball
5. とうきょう　　　　　　Tokyo
6. かぞく　　　　　　　　family
7. ちち　　　　　　　　　(own) father
8. はは　　　　　　　　　(own) mother
9. デパート　　　　　　　department store
10. あね　　　　　　　　　(own) older sister
11. いま　　　　　　　　　now
12. だいがく四〔よ〕ねんせい　college senior

13. 毎日〔まいにち〕　every day
14. ほんや　　　　　bookstore
15. みなさん　　　　everybody
16. スミスさん　　　Mr./Ms. Smith
17. わたし　　　　　I
18. うち　　　　　　home
19. くるま　　　　　car
20. へや　　　　　　room
21. ベッド　　　　　bed
22. つくえ　　　　　desk
23. ねこ　　　　　　cat
24. ドア　　　　　　door

B. どうし　Verbs

25. はなします〔G1 はなして〕　to talk; to speak
26. あります〔G1 あって〕　to exist, to have (for inanimate objects)
27. いて〔G2 います〕　to exist, to have (for animate objects)
28. ねて〔G2 ねます〕　to sleep

C. -い けいようし　I Adjectives

29. ひろい　　　spacious
30. しろい　　　white

D. -な けいようし　NA Adjectives

31. すき　　　like
32. きれい　　pretty, clean
33. だいすき　　like very much, love

E. ふくし　Adverbs

34. もう + Aff.　already
35. すこし　　a little
36. いつも　　always

F. Counters

37. 一〔いっ〕さい   one year old   39. 一〔いっ〕ぴき   one (small animal)
38. 二だい   two (cars)

G. Others

40. そして   and

H. Expressions

41. どうぞ よろしく おねがいします。 Glad to meet you. [lit., Please take good care of me.]

I. ぶんぽう Grammar

42. Noun / NA-Adjective で、～。   ～ and ～.
　しゅみは スポーツで、やきゅうが すきです。

                                  My hobby is sports and I like baseball.

43. Verb (TE form)、～。   ～ and ～.
　プールが あって、毎日〔まいにち〕 およぎます。

                                  There is a pool and I swim (there) every day.

44. I Adjective (TE form -くて)、～。   ～ and ～.
　うちは ひろくて、きれいです。   The house is spacious and pretty.

【会話】　ケン：まりさんは 今 どこに 住んで いますか。
　　　　　まり：私は スミスさんの 家に 住んで います。

【文型】

Verb (TE form) ＋います	is doing ～ [continuation of an action]
Verb (TE form) ＋います	[state]

【単語】

1. (Place で) 生まれました
[G2 うまれる／うまれて]
was born (in ～)

2. (Place に) 住んで います
[G1 すむ／すみます]
live (in), reside (in)
すみます means "will live", "will reside."
(future only)

3. (Place に) 勤めて います
[G2 つとめる／つとめます]
is employed (at ～)

4. (Place で) 働いて います
[G1 はたらく／はたらきます]
is working (at ～)

二課

5. (Place で)(アル)バイト(を)して　います
　　[Ir.(アル)バイト(を)する／します]
　　　is working part-time [for students]

6. (Person と)結婚(を)して　います
　　[Ir. けっこん(を)する／します]
　　　　is married (to 〜)

7. 持って　います
　[G1 もつ／もちます]
　　have, possess, hold, carry

Both あります and もっています may both mean "possess." もっています, however, is used when the possesser is animate and the possessed thing is inanimate.

8. 知って　います　　　　知りません
　　[G1 しる／します]
　　know　　　　　　　　do not know

しります means "to get to know" and しっています expresses "know." "Do not know" is しりません. しっていません is never used.

9. 習って　います
　[G1 ならう／ならいます]
　　　is learning

10. ホームステイを　します
　　　[G1 する／して]
　　　will do a homestay

【*オプショナル単語】
1. *べっきょして　います　　　　　　* is separated
2. *りこんして　います　　　　　　　* is divorced
3. *どくしんです　　　　　　　　　　* is single

二課　　　　　　　　　36

【漢字】

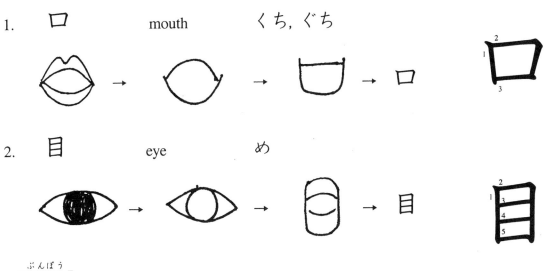

1. 口　　　　mouth　　　　くち, ぐち

2. 目　　　　eye　　　　め

【文法】

A. Verb TE form ＋います。

The Verb -て　います form combines the TE form of verbs and います, which may conjugate in any way. The TE form of あります and います cannot be used in this way. The interpretation of this construction varies depending on the verb which appears in the -て form.

The verbs appearing in this pattern may mean:

1) An action is / is not / was / was not occurring, or continuing.

Ex. のんで　います　　　　　is drinking
のんで　いません　　　　is not drinking
のんで　いました　　　　was drinking
のんで　いませんでした　　was not drinking

2) As a result of an action, a state exists. Often verbs that do not express continuity cannot take on this meaning.

Ex. しにます　　　　will die　　　　しんで　います　　　　is dead
しります　　　　will get to know　　しって　います　　　know
☆ The negative of しっています is not しっていません, but is しりません.
けっこんします　will marry　　　けっこんして　います　is married
もちます　　　　will carry　　　もって　います　　　have, possess, is carrying
つとめます　　　will be employed　つとめて　います　　is employed
すみます　　　　will live　　　　すんで　います　　　live/ reside, is living/ residing

1. 「今　何を　して　いますか。」　　　　"What are you doing now?"
「お昼御飯を　食べて　います。」　　　　"I am eating lunch."

2. 姉は　結婚して　います。　　　　My older sister is married.

37

二課

3. 今 お金を 持って いません。   I do not have any money now.

4. 「この 人を 知って いますか。」   "Do you know this person?"

   「いいえ、知りません。」   "No, I do not know him/her."

---

* B. 「もう お昼御飯を 食べましたか。」   "Have you already eaten lunch?"

   「いいえ、まだです。」   or   "No, not yet."

   「いいえ、まだ 食べて いません。」   "No, I have not eaten yet."

---

* Previously introduced.

1. 「この 漢字を もう 習いましたか。」   "Have you already learned this *kanji*?"

   「いいえ、まだ 習って いません。」   "No, I have not learned it yet."

【 ● ぶんかノート】

Part-time Jobs in Japan

    The number of students and housewives who work part-time has increased tremendously over the past decade or two. High school students, who until recently rarely held afternoon or weekend jobs, now commonly work part-time. More high school girls hold part-time jobs than boys, since more boys are pressured to study hard or attend cram schools (called *juku*) in preparation for college entrance exams. This trend has affected participation in one of the major forms of socialization in Japanese high schools, the clubs, which traditionally meet after school and on weekends.

【 アクティビティー】

A. ペアワーク

Interview your partner and take notes in Japanese.

1. どこで うまれましたか。	
2. いま どこに すんで いますか。	
3. おとうさんは どこに つとめて いますか。	
4. いま アルバイトを して いますか。	
5. どこで はたらきたいですか。	
6. いま １００ドルを もって いますか。	
7. かんじを ひゃく しって いますか。	

B. ペアワーク: Information gap game

On this and the next page, you will find two identical pictures with some different names missing on each. Look at one picture as your partner looks at the other. Complete your picture by asking your partner what each person whose name appears in the box is doing. Your partner's picture will have the answers to your questions. Write the names in the correct bracket. Take turns. After you are both finished asking questions, compare the names in the two pictures. Are they accurate?

Person A asks: 「～さんは　いま　なにを　して　いますか。」

1. ゆきお	2. いちろう	3. だいすけ	4. けんじ	5. としかず
6. しんいち	7. あきら	8. まこと	9. けんた	

バイクに　のります [G1] to ride a motor bike, うんてん（を）します to drive [IR]

二課

Person B asks: 「～さんは　いま　なにを　して　いますか。」

1. えみこ	2. さちこ	3. みちこ	4. ゆか	5. あい
6. まゆみ	7. なおみ	8. ゆうこ	9. シロ	

バイクに　のります [G1] to ride a motor bike,　うんてん（を）します to drive [IR]

【会話（かいわ）】　ケン：鉛筆（えんぴつ）は　どこに　ありますか。

　　　　　　まり：机（つくえ）の　下（した）に　ありますよ。

【文型（ぶんけい）】

Topic は Something の Position に　います／あります。

Something の Position に Subject が　います／あります。

【単語（たんご）】

1. 上（うえ）

on, above, on top of

2. 下（した）

under, below

3. 中（なか）

inside

4. 外（そと）

outside

5. 前（まえ）

in front of

6. 後ろ（うしろ）

back, behind

7. 右（みぎ）

right side

8. 左（ひだり）

left side

9. そば

by, nearby

10. 間（あいだ）

between

11. となり

next (to)

二課

12. 近く〔ちかく〕
vicinity; nearby

13. 遠く〔とおく〕
far away

14. 所〔ところ〕
place
ドアのところに　います。

【*オプショナル単語】
1. *横〔よこ〕　　　　　* side
2. *向こう〔むこう〕　* beyond
3. *手前〔てまえ〕　　* this side
4. *近所〔きんじょ〕　* neighborhood
5. *真ん中〔まんなか〕* middle

【漢字】

1. 人　person　　ひと　あの　人 that person

ニン　三人〔さんにん〕 three people

ジン　アメリカ人 American

☆　一人〔ひとり〕 one (person)

二人〔ふたり〕 two (persons)

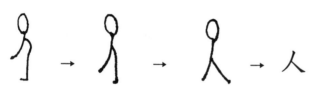

2. 本　origin, book　もと　山本〔やまもと〕さん, 中本〔なかもと〕さん,
川本〔かわもと〕さん, 木本〔きもと〕さん

ホン　本を　よむ to read a book

日本〔にほん or にっぽん〕 Japan

ポン　　一本〔いっぽん〕 one (long object)

ボン　　三本〔さんぼん〕 three (long objects)

The base of a tree is its origin.　Books are made from felled trees.　The trunk of the tree is long and cylindrical.

【文法】

A.	Topic は	Location				います。 [for animate objects]
		Noun の	Position		に	
			うえ	above		
			した	below		
			なか	inside		
			そと	outside		
			まえ	front		あります。 [for inanimate objects]
			うしろ	back		
			みぎ	right		
			ひだり	left		
			そば	nearby		
			となり	next		
			あいだ	between		

Location		に	Subject が	います。 [for animate objects]
Noun の	Position			あります。 [for inanimate objects]

This is an expansion of the previous N1 は Place に あります／います and Place に Noun が あります／います patterns.　In this new construction, the exact position of an object in relation to another object or place can be expressed.　It is important to learn that words that indicate position (e. g., front, back, etc.) are considered <u>nouns</u> in Japanese and are to be treated as such.

1. 猫が　車の　上に　います。　　　　The cat is on the car.

2. 家の　外に　木が　たくさん　あります。　There are many trees outside (my) home.

43

二課

3. 私の　後ろに　ジョン君が　います。　　　John is behind me.

4. 学校の　そばに　病院が　あります。　　　There is hospital near the school.

5. 家は　本屋と　パン屋の　間に　あります。　　　My house is between the bookstore and the

bakery.

B.	Location	に	います。	[for animate objects]
	Noun　の　ところ		あります。	[for inanimate objects]

When one indicates the existence of an object at a certain location, one simply uses the place word に + existence verb. When one needs to indicate the existence of an object at a location which is <u>not</u> a place, e. g., a person (doctor) or thing (door), however, then one must attach の　ところ after the person or thing to create a "place word" as the location of existence.

1. 犬が　ドアの　ところに　います。　　　The dog is where the door is.

2. 宿題は　先生の　ところに　あります。　　　The homework is at the teacher's (place).

3. 一時に　あの　木の　ところで　待って　いますよ。

At 1 o'clock, I will be waiting where the tree is (by the tree).

【 ● ぶんかノート】

1. First Names

In Japan, first names are not used as frequently as in the West. First names are used to call only those one is extremely close to, i.e., younger family members and very good friends. One would never call a superior by his first name. Last names and/or titles are used instead. If first and last names are given, the family name generally appears before the personal name. Japanese do not usually have middle names.

Children are normally given their names by parents or other family members. Some considerations are made in selecting names, including birth order, matching the first and family names in meaning, sound and number of *kanji* character strokes, and birthdate. Perhaps more common, however, is the selection of names for their auspicious meanings and happy associations.

2. A Japanese Proverb 「石の　上にも　三年」

いし means "a stone." This proverb means that (sitting) on a stone for three years makes everything possible. If you sit on the stone three years, even the stone becomes warm. This proverb is used to express that perseverance overcomes all things.

【👤👤アクティビティー】

A. ペアワーク

One partner draws three objects in the top two pictures without showing his/her partner what or where he/she has drawn them. His/her partner does the same for the bottom two pictures. Describe your pictures to your partner, who will draw in the objects as you describe them to him/her. After both partners have completed their pictures, compare pictures and see how well you have communicated.

二課

B. ペアワーク

You will find two incomplete pictures in this exercise. You will take one picture and your partner will take the other. Complete both of your pictures by asking your partner for the items listed under the heading "Find." Draw in the items according to the locations your partner gives you. After you are both finished asking questions, compare your pictures. Are they accurate?

Ex. 「～は　どこに　あります／いますか。」

Your picture:

Find
ごみばこ
ごきぶり
バット
はな
おとこのこ
いぬ
25セント
本

Partner's picture:

Find

ギター
ねこ
ボール
木
ぼうし
おんなのこ
ードル

C. ペアワーク

Ask what each person/animal is doing now and where it is being done.

Ex. 「～は 今 どこで 何を して いますか。」

ジョン	
バーバラ	
ケン	
いぬ	
ねこ	

二課

2課－3 : THE BABY IS STILL ONE.

【会話】　ケン：赤ちゃんは　いくつですか。

　　　　まり：まだ　一才です。

【文型】

Verb Dictionary form	
まだ＋ Affirmative predicate。	still
＊まだ＋ Negative predicate。	(not) yet
もう＋ Negative predicate。	(not) any more
＊もう＋ Affirmative predicate。	already

＊ Previously introduced.

【単語】

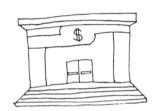

1. 家〔いえ〕　　2. 銀行〔ぎんこう〕　　3. 公園〔こうえん〕　　4. 寮〔りょう〕
　　house　　　　　　bank　　　　　　　　park　　　　　　　　dormitory

5. 赤〔あか〕ちゃん　　6. ～ちゃん　　　　　7. まだ＋ Aff.　　8. もう＋ Neg.
　　baby　　　　　　Used instead of ～さん when　　still　　　　(not) any more
　　　　　　　　　addressing or referring to young,
　　　　　　　　　small, cute animals or children.

二課
48

9. ～について

about ～

10. しょうかい(を)します
[Ir. する／して]

to introduce

11. じこしょうかい(を)します
[Ir. する／して]

to do a self-introduction

【*オプショナル単語】

1. *アパート   * apartment
2. *マンション   * condominium
3. *郵便局（ゆうびんきょく）   * post office
4. *ガソリンスタンド   * gas station
5. *教会（きょうかい）   * church
6. *映画館（えいがかん）   * movie theater
7. *ホテル   * hotel
8. *パン屋（や）   * bakery

【漢字】

1. 今　now　いま　今、一時です。It's 1 o'clock.

今田〔いまだ〕さん

コン　今月〔こんげつ〕this month

今週〔こんしゅう〕this week

☆　今日〔きょう〕today

今年〔ことし〕this year

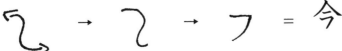

Now, three people are deciding whether to come or go.

二課

2. 年　year　　とし　　今年〔ことし〕this year

毎年〔まいとし〕every year

ネン　毎年〔まいねん〕every year

来年〔らいねん〕next year

去年〔きょねん〕last year

一年〔いちねん〕one year

四年生〔よねんせい〕fourth grader

一九九九年〔せんきゅうひゃくきゅうじゅうきゅう

ねん〕the year 1999

年

第 → 季 → 年 → 年

Once a year, people cut the rice that was born from the earth.

【文法】

A.	まだ + Affirmative predicate。	still
	もう + Affirmative predicate。	already
	*まだ + Negative predicate。	(not) yet
	*もう + Negative predicate。	(not) any more

　　　* Previously introduced.

1. 赤ちゃんは　まだ　一才です。　　　　The baby is still one.

2. 私は　まだ　十五才です。　　　　　　I am still 15 years old.

3. 私は　もう　お昼を　食べました。　　I already ate my lunch.

4.「お兄さんは　まだ　サンフランシスコに　住んで　いますか。」

　　　　　　　　　　　　　"Is your older brother still living in SF?"

　「いいえ、兄は　もう　サンフランシスコに　住んで　いません。」

　　　　　　　　　　　"No, my older brother is not living in SF any more."

5. 私は　もう　高校一年生です。　　　　I am already a high school sophomore.

6.「もう　宿題を　しましたか。」　　　　"Have you done your homework already?"

　「いいえ、まだ　して　いません。」　　"No, I have not done it yet."

二課　　　　　　　　　　50

1. **Group 1 verbs**

Group 1 verbs are identified by the verb stem, which is the verb form that remains after dropping -ます. If there are more than two *hiragana* characters remaining in the verb stem after dropping the ます and the final sound of the verb stem is an -i ending sound, the verb can usually be categorized as a Group 1 verb. To obtain the dictionary form, change the -i ending verb stem to its corresponding -u sound. See the chart below for examples.

[☐ -i ます]

	MASU form	Meaning	Dictionary form
[み]	のみます	to drink	のむ
	よみます	to read	よむ
	やすみます	to rest, be absent	やすむ
[に]	しにます	to die	しぬ
[び]	あそびます	to play	あそぶ
[い]	あいます	to meet	あう
[ち]	かちます	to win	かつ
[り]	わかります	to understand	わかる
	しります	to get to know	しる
	かえります	to return (place)	かえる
	あります	to be (inanimate)	ある
	がんばります	to do one's best	がんばる
	はしります	to run	はしる
[き]	ききます	to listen, hear	きく
	かきます	to write	かく
	いきます	to go	いく
	あるきます	to walk	あるく
[ぎ]	およぎます	to swim	およぐ
[し]	はなします	to talk, speak	はなす

2. **Group 2 verbs**

Group 2 verbs can be identified by a verb stem (verb without ます) that ends in an "-e sounding" *hiragana* or a verb stem that contains only one *hiragana*. See the examples below. A few special verbs do exist. They must simply be learned as special verbs. Group 2 dictionary verb forms are created simply by replacing -ます with る.

二課

	MASU form	Meaning	Dictionary form
[☐ -e ます]	みえます	can be seen	みえる
	きこえます	can be heard	きこえる
	たべます	to eat	たべる
	まけます	to lose	まける
[One *hiragana*]	みます	to see, watch	みる
	います	to be (animate)	いる
	ねます	to sleep	ねる
[Special verbs]	おきます	to get up	おきる

3. **Group 3 Irregular verbs**

Only きます, します and a noun ＋します verbs belong to this group. Memorize the individual dictionary forms as they do not follow any rules.

MASU form	Meaning	Dictionary form
きます	to come	くる
します	to do	する
べんきょう（を）します	to study	べんきょう（を）する
タイプ（を）します	to type	タイプ（を）する
りょこう（を）します	to travel	りょこう（を）する
かいもの（を）します	to shop	かいもの（を）する
しょくじ（を）します	to have a meal	しょくじ（を）する
れんしゅう（を）します	to practice	れんしゅう（を）する

【 ● ぶんかノート】

Birthdays

Traditionally, Japanese babies were considered to be a year old at birth, as it was thought that their lives began at conception. This practice can be seen at times of major birthday celebrations such as the やくどし, which actually marks the 42nd birthday, but is celebrated when one becomes 41.

やくどし is one of the major birthday celebrations of a Japanese male. The 42nd year of a man's life is believed to be a dangerous one, because 42, when read in Japanese, is しに, a form of the verb to die, しにます. One celebrates this birthday in order to chase all of the bad spirits of that year away. Another significant birthday celebrated by males is the 60th, or かんれき. It is believed that a man enters his second cycle of life at 60, since he has completed the five celestial symbols (earth, gold, fire, water, and wood) of the 12 animal years of the Chinese zodiac. Since he becomes a "child" again, he is dressed in a red children's vest and a red cap at his birthday party. Although not celebrated to the extent of the 42nd and 60th, the 25th birthday is also significant for a male, as it is the age at which he reaches manhood.

For woman, the most celebrated birthday is the 33rd. This is when she is considered to be at her peak. It is also a time she makes special efforts to ward off bad spirits, however, since 33 sounds somewhat similar to the Japanese word さんざん, which means misery. The eighteenth birthday is another significant birthday for Japanese women.

【👩👧アクティビティー】

A. ペアワーク

One partner asks the questions listed in the left column. The second partner should answer the questions using the information in the right column. Switch roles for the second set of questions and answers.

Who?	My older brother:
Name?	His name is Mike.
Age?	He is 20 years old.
Which college?	He goes to college in California.
Does he live in a dormitory?	He still lives in a dormitory.
Does he have a car?	He does not have a car.
Does he want to buy a car?	He wants to buy a car.
Is he working part-time?	He is working part-time at bookstore.

Who?	My older sister:
Name?	Her name is Lisa.
Age?	She is 25 years old.
Married?	She is married.
Baby?	She has a baby.
Age of baby?	Her baby is still one.
Where does she live?	She lives by a park.
Job?	She is not working now.

二課

B. ペアゲーム： Tic-Tac-Toe Game
Play Tic-Tac-Toe with your partner by changing the -*masu* form to the correct dictionary form in the square that you choose. The answers are on the next page.

a.

のみます	しにます	みます
おきます (to get up)	ねます	かちます
やすみます	はなします	かきます

b.

います	きます (to come)	かえります
あいます	よみます	たべます
いきます	わかります	します

c.

しります	まけます	ききます
あります	かいもの（を）します	はしります
がんばります	べんきょう（を）します	りょこう（を）します

a.

のむ [のみます]	しぬ[しにます]	みる [みます]
おきる [おきます]	ねる [ねます]	かつ[かちます]
やすむ [やすみます]	はなす [はなします]	かく [かきます]

b.

いる [います]	くる [きます]	かえる [かえります]
あう [あいます]	よむ [よみます]	たべる [たべます]
いく [いきます]	わかる [わかります]	する [します]

c.

しる [しります]	まける [まけます]	きく [ききます]
ある [あります]	かいもの（を）する [かいもの（を）します]	はしる [はしります]
がんばる [がんばります]	べんきょう（を）する [べんきょう（を）します]	りょこう（を）する [りょこう（を）します]

【会話】　ケン：まりさんは　何を　するのが　好きですか。

まり：私は　泳ぐことが　特に　好きです。

【文型】

| Verb Dictionary form | ＋ の／こと　が　好きです。 | I like to do 〜. |
| Verb Dictionary form | ＋ の／こと　は　楽しいです。 | It is fun to do 〜. |

【単語】

1. 特〔とく〕に

especially

2. 両親〔りょうしん〕／御両親〔ごりょうしん〕

(one's own) parents　　(someone else's) parents

3. 正〔ただ〕しい

[い Adjective]

is correct

5×6=25

4. ちがいます

[G1 ちがう]

is wrong, to differ

5. 質問〔しつもん〕

[Noun]

question

しつもんを　します

[IR する]

to ask a question

6. 答〔こた〕え

[Noun]

answer

こたえます

[G2 こたえる]

to answer

二課　　　　56

【*オプショナル単語】

1. *そふ   * (one's own) grandfather

2. *そぼ   * (one's own) grandmother

【漢字】

1. 私   I, me   わたくし   私は 中本です。 I am Nakamoto.

                            わたし*

    * WATASHI is not a proper reading in formal writing, but has come into general use colloquially.

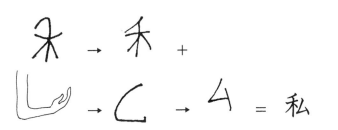 

The harvested grain I am holding in my arm is mine.

2. 曜   day of the week   よう   日曜日 〔にちようび〕 Sunday

                                     月曜日 〔げつようび〕 Monday

                                     火曜日 〔かようび〕 Tuesday

                                     水曜日 〔すいようび〕 Wednesday

                                     木曜日 〔もくようび〕 Thursday

                                     金曜日 〔きんようび〕 Friday

                                     土曜日 〔どようび〕 Saturday

                                     何曜日 〔なんようび〕 What day of the week?

二課

【文法】

> A. Verb Dictionary form ＋ の／こと　が　好きです。
>
> 　　Verb Dictionary form ＋ の／こと　は　楽しいです。
>
> This construction is used to describe or comment upon some action or state. The action or state being described is used in its verb dictionary form, followed by の or こと, which nominalizes the verb form. の or こと are nouns which literally mean　"(the) act (of)."

1. 母は　歌を　歌うのが　好きです。　　　　　　My mother likes to sing.

2. 日本語を　勉強するのは　楽しいです。　　　Studying Japanese is fun.

3. 私は　本を　読むのが　嫌いです。　　　　　I dislike reading books.

4. 朝　七時に　学校へ　来るのは　大変です。　It is difficult to come to school at 7:30.

5. 日本語を　書くのは　むずかしいです。　　　Writing *kanji* is difficult.

【 ● ぶんかノート】

1. Swimming

Swimming is a popular pastime in Japan today. Swimming clubs have proliferated throughout the country. During the summer, public pools are jammed full of people, with little space for actual swimming. During the summer months, people also flock to the shore. Swimming in Japan has its origins as a martial art. *Samurai* were trained to swim while carrying weapons, to move underwater, and to swim silently.

2. A Japanese Proverb　「となりの　花は　赤い」

となり means "next door" or "neighbor." This proverb means that the neighbor's flowers are red. Its equivalent in English is "The grass is greener on the other side of the fence." This proverb suggests that once one owns something (even if it previously looked attractive), it loses its appeal and other things become more attractive.

【👩👩アクティビティー】

A. ペアワーク

Interview your partner using the cues below. Check the appropriate column according to your partner's answer. After asking the 10 questions, find out which activity your partner thinks is especially fun and especially uninteresting. Circle those activities.

Ex. 歌を　歌います

「歌を　歌うのは　楽しいですか。つまらないですか。」

しつもん	たのしい	つまらない
1. ダンスを　します		
2. にほんごを　ならいます		
3. ともだちと　はなします		
4. ほんを　よみます		
5. コンピューターゲームで　あそびます		
6. えいがを　みます		
7. はしります		
8. およぎます		
9. かんじを　かきます		
10. がっこうへ　きます		

「何を　するのが　特に　楽しい／つまらない　ですか。」

B. ペアワーク

Interview your partner about activities his/her family member likes or dislikes.

Ex. 「お父さんは　何を　するのが　好きですか。」

人	すきな　こと	きらいな　こと
おとうさん		
おかあさん		
Partner		

二課

質問しよう！　答えよう！

Ask your partner these questions in Japanese.
Your partner should answer in Japanese.

1. Where were you born?

2. Where are you living now?

3. Is your father working at a bank?

4. What kind of person do you want to marry?

5. Are you working at a part-time job now?

6. What do you have in your hand now?

7. Do you know my address and telephone number?

8. Please introduce yourself.

9. Who is sitting by you?

10. Is there a park near your house?

11. Do you write with your right hand or left hand?

12. What is by the door?

13. What is in front of your house?

14. What is inside your room?

15. Which bank do your parents go to?

16. Do you want to live in a college dormitory?

17. What do you want to do this weekend?

18. Do you like to swim?

19. Are you still a freshman?

20. Have you eaten lunch already?

21. Do you like to play with babies?

22. Do you want to have a homestay in Japan?

23. When do you want to travel to Japan?

24. What part (=where) of Japan do you want to visit (=go)?

25. Where is Hokkaido? Do you know?

26. Where is Sendai? Do you know?

27. Where is Hiroshima? Do you know?

28. Where is Tokyo? Do you know?

29. Where is Okinawa? Do you know?

30. Do you like to study the Japanese language?

二課

ひこうき

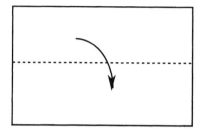 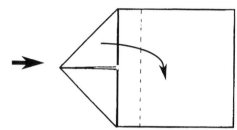

1. Take a rectangular sheet of paper, hold it across with the shorter edges at the left and right. Fold in half lengthwise. Reopen the paper so the center crease runs horizontally.

2. Fold the upper left corner to the center. Do the same with the lower left corner.

3. Fold the pointed edge of the paper forward and crease vertically about an inch from the base of the triangle, as shown in the illustration.

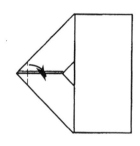 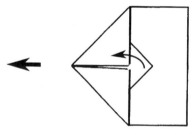 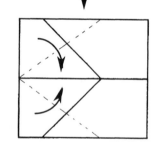

6. Next, fold the left most tip of the triangle forward and down.

5. Fold the small protruding triangle forward and toward the left against the large triangle base.

4. Fold the left upper and lower corners down to center line again.

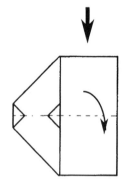 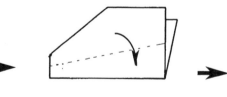 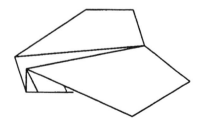

7. Fold in half, bringing the top half forward.

8. Make the wings by folding downwards at a slight angle as shown.

9. Spread the wings and fly!

二課

By the end of this lesson, you will be able to communicate the information below in the given situations.

【II-3 タスク1】

A Japanese student is visiting an American school. He/She asks many questions about the American school's dress code. Answer the questions based on your school's rules.

Japanese student:

(1) Ask the American student whether he/she thinks his/her school rules are strict or liberal.

(2) Answer. Ask if it is okay to wear T-shirts to school.

(3) Ask if it is okay to wear shorts.

(4) Ask if boys can have long hair. Also ask if boys can wear pierced earrings.

(5) Answer "yes," but not in school. Ask if girls can wear short skirts.

(6) Ask if it is okay to wear sunglasses.

(7) Ask if it is okay to wear hats in class.

American student:

(1) Give your opinion. Ask if Japanese schools are strict.

(2) Answer based on your school's rules.

(3) Answer based on your school's rules.

(4) Answer based on your school's rules. Ask if boys wear earrings in Japan.

(5) Answer based on your school's rules.

(6) Answer based on your school's rules.

(7) Answer based on your school's rules.

【II-3 タスク2】

The Japanese student asks about the American student's school library. The American student answers based on facts.

Japanese student:

(1) Ask where the school library is.

(2) Ask what is needed to borrow books.

(3) Ask from what time to what time the library is open.

(4) Ask if the following acts are okay in the library:
   a. Eating, drinking
   b. Chewing gum
   c. Talking to friends
   d. Listening to a CD player
   e. Sleeping

American student:

(1) Describe where the library is in relation to other school buildings.

(2) Answer based on facts.

(3) Answer based on facts.

(4) Answer based on your library's rules. Ask if the Japanese student thinks the rules are strict.

三課

三課

【会話】

<学校で>

まり：ケンさん、この 学校の きそくに ついて 聞いても いいですか。

ケン：はい、どうぞ。

まり：ケンさん、学校で Tシャツを 着ても いいんですか。

ケン：はい、いいんですよ。

まり：ショートパンツを はいても いいんですか。

ケン：ええ、かまいません。でも、ショートパンツは 短くては
　　　いけません。

まり：あの 男の 生徒は ピアスを して いますが、いいんですか。

ケン：はい、かまいません。でも、小さいのだけ いいんです。

まり：アメリカの 学校の きそくは 本当に 自由ですねえ。
　　　ところで、図書館は どこですか。

ケン：図書館は あの 白い 建物です。見えますか。

まり：あ、はい、はい、見えます。本を 借りに 行きたいんですが、何が
　　　いりますか。

ケン：証明書が いります。それから、図書館の きそくは とても
　　　きびしいですから、気を つけて 下さい。図書館の 中で
　　　ぜったい 話しては いけません。

まり：どうも ありがとう。

ケン：一時に 門の ところで 会いましょう。
　　　お昼を 食べに 行きましょう。

まり：あ、いいですねえ。でも、一時半でも いいですか。

ケン：ええ、一時半でも いいですよ。 じゃ、また あとで。

Let's review previous vocabulary!

A. めいし Nouns

1. がっこう	school	
2. おとこ	male	
3. 小〔ちい〕さいの	small one	
4. アメリカ	America	
5. としょかん	library	
6. どこ	where?	
7. たてもの	building	

8. 本〔ほん〕	book
9. 何〔なに〕	what?
10. 中〔なか〕	inside
11. 一時〔いちじ〕	one o'clock
12. ところ	place
13. おひる（ごはん）	lunch

B. どうし Verbs

14. いきたいんです〔G1 いく／いきます／いって〕　want to go
15. 〜が　いります〔G1 いる／いって〕　need 〜
16. はなして〔G1 はなす／はなします〕　to talk, to speak
17. たべ〔G2 たべる／たべます／たべて〕　to eat [stem form]
18. いきましょう〔G1 いく／いきます／いって〕　let's go

C. -い けいようし I Adjectives

19. いい	good, okay	21. しろい	white	
20. みじかい	short [for length]	22. きびしい	strict	

D. ふくし Adverbs

23. とても　very

E. Others

24. でも	However	25. それから	and then, in addition

F. Expressions

26. あ、はい　はい。　Oh, yes, yes.
27. どうも　ありがとう。　Thank you very much.
28. あ、いいですね。　Oh, that sounds good.
29. じゃ、またね。　Well, see you again.

G. ぶんぽう Grammar

30. Sentence 1 + が、 Sentence 2。　　　　　　　　　　Sentence 1, but Sentence 2.

　　日本ごは　むずかしいですが、おもしろいです。

　　　　　　　　　　　　　　　　　　　　The Japanese language is difficult, but it is interesting.

31. Sentence 1 + から、 Sentence 2。　　　　　　　　Sentence 1, so Sentence 2.

　　おなかが　すきましたから、たべましょう。　I am hungry, so let's eat.

32. Verb (Stem form) + たい（ん）です。　　　　　I want to do 〜 .

　　今　たべたいんです。　　　　　　　　　　　　I want to eat now.

　　　　　　　[ん is inserted when one explains to the listener what one wants to do.]

【お話】　ケンさんは　白い　シャツを　着て、青い　ズボンを
はいて　います。　そして、黒と　赤の　ぼうしを
かぶって　います。

【文型】

"wear"	シャツを	きて　います	wear a shirt
	くつを	はいて　います	wear shoes
	イヤリングを	して　います	wear earrings
	ぼうしを	かぶって　います	wear a hat
	サングラスを	かけて　います	wear sunglasses

【単語】

1. きて　います
[G2 きる／きます]

wear [above the waist or on the entire body]

2. はいて　います
[G1 はく／はきます]

wear [below the waist]

3. して　います
[IR する／します]

wear [accessories]

4. かぶって　います
[G1 かぶる／かぶります]

wear [on, or draped over the head]

5. かけて　います
[G2 かける／かけます]

wear [glasses]

6. 服〔ふく〕

clothing

三課

7. Ｔ〔ティー〕シャツ	8. ズボン	9. ショートパンツ or ショーツ	10. セーター
T-shirt	pants	shorts	sweater

11. ワンピース	12. スカート	13. せいふく	14. くつ下 or ソックス	15. ゆびわ
dress	skirt	uniform	socks	ring

16. めがね	17. サングラス	18. ネックレス	19. イヤリング	20. ピアス
eyeglasses	sunglasses	necklace	earrings	pierced (earrings)

【*オプショナル単語〔たんご〕】

1. *水着〔みずぎ〕   * bathing suit
2. *アクセサリー   * accessories; jewelry
3. *ブレスレット   * bracelet
4. *ユニホーム   * sports uniform
5. *ストッキング   * stockings
6. *サンダル   * sandals
7. *ぞうり   * slippers, flip flops
8. *ジャケット   * jacket

9. *せびろ or スーツ   * suit

10. *こん（いろ）   * navy blue [a common color for Japanese uniforms]

11. *ぬぐ [G1 ぬぎます]   * to take off [articles used with verbs きる, はく, かぶる]

12. *はめる [G2 はめます] * to insert; fit on to (something) [i.e., rings and gloves]

13. *とる [G1 とります]   * to take off [articles used with verbs する, かける, はめる]

【漢字】

1. 上   above   うえ   上田〔うえだ〕さん

                                     目上〔めうえ〕の人 superiors

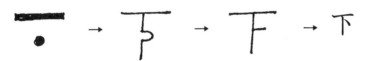

2. 下   below   した   木下〔きのした〕さん

                          くだ   食べて　下さい。Please eat.

一 → 下 → 下 → 下

【文法】

    A. Verbs of wearing

The Japanese verb "to wear" varies according to where or how one wears the item on one's body.

きます is used to describe things worn above the waist or on the entire body.

      きます   will wear (above the waist, or on the entire body)

      はきます   will wear (below the waist)

      します   will wear (accessories)

      かぶります will wear (on or draped over the head)

      かけます   will wear (glasses)

With verbs of wearing, the MASU form is an imperfect tense which means that an action will take place in the future. -ています is used to describe one's present state or a habitual state, or that the action of wearing is occurring at the present moment.

      きます   will wear   きて　います   is wearing or wears

      きません   will not wear   きて　いません is not wearing or does not wear

三課

1. 父は　青い　シャツを　着て　います。　　My father is wearing a blue shirt.

2. あの　生徒は　黒いズボンを　はいて　います。　　That student is wearing black pants.

3. 姉は　白い　ネックレスを　して　います。　　My older sister is wearing a white necklace.

4. 弟は　いつも　ぼうしを　かぶって　います。　　My younger brother always wears a hat.

5. 母は　めがねを　かけて　います。　　My mother is wearing glasses.

B. * Review of Colors

い Adjectives		Noun	
しろい	is white	しろ	white
くろい	is black	くろ	black
あかい	is red	あか	red
あおい	is blue	あお	blue
きいろい	is yellow	きいろ	yellow
ちゃいろい	is brown	ちゃいろ	brown
		みどり	green
		むらさき	purple
		ピンク	pink
		グレイ	gray
		きんいろ	gold
		ぎんいろ	silver

Usage:

a white shirt　　　しろい　シャツ　or　しろの　シャツ

a black and white shirt　　しろと　くろの　シャツ

【 ● ぶんかノート】

1. The Japanese Uniform

The uniform is standard among most schools, particularly public schools, in Japan. Uniforms are more common at the junior high school and high school levels than at the elementary level. It is a way to identify students in general, but is also a way to deter students from bad behavior, since they can easily be identified by the uniforms they wear. It is not uncommon to see students wearing their uniforms to school or other functions even on days when they are not attending classes. Some schools now hire top fashion designers to design their uniforms to satisfy the tastes of today's highly fashion-conscious teens. Generally, however, uniforms tend to remain conservative in style, and are usually black, navy blue, or gray. Uniforms are not limited to students, but are also commonly worn by workers in banks, department stores, certain companies, and service-type employees.

2. The Japanese Summer and Winter Uniforms

In Japan, most school students have two sets of school uniforms: a summer uniform (なつふく) and a winter uniform (ふゆふく). All students switch from one uniform to the other on pre-determined days in May or June and October.

Summer uniform (なつふく)

Winter uniform (ふゆふく)

【アクティビティー】

A. ペアワーク

Ask your partner if any of your classmates is wearing the following items. Your partner should respond based on the facts.

Ex. 白_{しろ}い　Ｔシャツ

質問_{しつもん}：「だれが　白_{しろ}い　Ｔシャツを　着_きて　いますか。」

答え_{こた}：「〜さんが　白_{しろ}い　Ｔシャツを　着_きて　いますよ。」

or 「〜さんです。」

or 「だれも　着_きて　いません。」 No one is wearing (it).

1. しろい　Ｔシャツ		6. あおい　シャツ	
2. ぼうし		7. しろい　ソックス	
3. めがね		8. サングラス	
4. とけい		9. ピアス	
5. くろい　くつ		10. せいふく	

73

三課

B. クラスワーク

Your teacher will give each student a sheet of paper. On it, write your name and describe what you are wearing today from head to toe, using color descriptions for each item. Use one sentence only to describe everything. The teacher will collect the self-descriptions from each student and read them at random. Try to guess who is being described. After all of the descriptions are read, check for correct answers. Students who correctly identify all of their classmates are the winners.

1.	13.
2.	14.
3.	15.
4.	16.
5.	17.
6.	18.
7.	19.
8.	20.
9.	21.
10.	22.
11.	23.
12.	24.

C. クラスゲーム "Fashion Rainbow"

Make a circle using one less chair than the number of participating students. One student who is "It" must stand in the center of the circle. "It" describes something that people wear. (See examples below.) Students who fit the description must leave their chairs and quickly sit in another open chair. During that time, "It" can move to one of the empty chairs and sits down. The student who is left without a chair becomes the new "It." If one becomes "It" three or more times, the student must return all the chairs to the original classroom configuration.

Ex. 「しろい　くつを　はいて　います。」
　　「あおい　シャツを　きて　いません。」
　　「めがねを　かけて　います。」
　　「ぼうしを　かぶって　いません。」

３課ー２: MAY WE WEAR A HAT?

【会話】 まり：教室で ぼうしを かぶっても いいですか。

ケン：いいえ、かぶっては いけません。

【文型】

Verb (TE form)		＋も	いいです。	Permission
い Adjective (TE form ーくて)			かまいません。	may, is allowed
Noun	＋で	＋は	だめです。	Prohibition
な Adjective			いけません。	may not, should not

【単語】

1. 規則〔きそく〕

rule, regulation

2. 自由〔じゆう〕
   [な Adj.]
free, liberal

3. いけません

won't do, must not do

4. かまいません

I do not mind if ...

5. たばこを すいます
   [G1 すう／すって]
to smoke cigarettes

6. ガムを かみます
   [G1 かむ／かんで]
to chew gum

7. ごみを すてます
   [G2 すてる／すてて]
to litter, to throw away garbage

三課

8. うんてん（を）します
[IRする／して]
to drive

9. Person に 会^あいます
[G1 あう／あって]
to meet someone

10. Person に 聞^ききます
[G1 きく／きいて]
to ask someone

11. ぜったい(に)
absolutely

【*オプショナル単語^{たんご}】

1. *まんが   * comics
2. *まやく   * drugs
3. *アルコール, おさけ   * alcohol
4. *ピストル   * gun
5. *ナイフ   * knife
6. *けしょうを　します   * to wear makeup
7. *マニキュアを　します   * to polish one's nails

【漢字^{かんじ}】

1. 大　　big　　おお　　　　　大きい　人 a big person, 大下〔おおした〕さん,
　　　　　　　　　　　　　　　大月〔おおつき〕さん
　　　　　　タイ　　　　　　　大変〔たいへん〕 hard, difficult, very
　　　　　　ダイ　　　　　　　大学〔だいがく〕 college, 大好き like very much

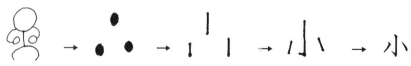

大

2. 小　　small　　ちい（さい）　小さい　人 a small person
　　　　　　ショウ　　　　　　　小学生 elementary school student
　　　　　　　　　　　　　　　小学校 elementary school

小

三課　　　　　　　　　　　76

When you go to a ticket window in Japan, you will see these *kanji* with prices listed after them.
What do you think these *kanji* mean?

大人 小人

What do you think the following *kanji* mean?

大火〔たいか〕 大水〔おおみず〕 大木〔たいぼく〕

Guess the meaning of these *kanji*.

太 (skinny or fat?) 犬 (dog or cat?)

【文法】

A. Verb TE form	＋も いいです／かまいません。
い Adjective （－くて）	＋も いいです／かまいません。
Noun / な Adjective ＋ で	＋も いいです／かまいません。

This sentence construction allows the speaker to ask for, or grant permission to do, something. The verb - て form is followed by the particle も, then いいです or かまいません. いいです is translated as "all right if," or "may," and is often equated with "don't mind if." The question form is usually used to receive permission from superiors. This pattern is not generally used for granting permission to persons who are superior.

1. この 学校では Tシャツを 着ても いいです。

You may wear T-shirts at this school.

2. 「ショートパンツを はいても いいですか。」 "May I wear shorts?"

「はい、かまいません。」 "Yes, I don't mind."

3. プレゼントは 高くても かまいません。 I don't mind if the present is expensive.

4. パーティーは 一時でも いいです。 I don't mind if the party is at 1 o'clock.

B. Verb TE form	＋は だめです／いけません。
い Adjective （－くて）	＋は だめです／いけません。
Noun / NA Adjective ＋ で	＋は だめです／いけません。

This sentence construction expresses prohibition. It is used by superiors to inferiors, e.g., teachers to students, parents to children. The verb - て form is followed by the particle は, then いけません, or だめです. いけません is often translated "must not" while だめです is translated "it is not good if . . ." だめです is perceived as a stronger expression than いけません.

1. 図書館で 話しては だめです。 You must not talk in the library.

2. 教室で 食べては いけません。 You must not eat in the classroom.

77

三課

3. ショートパンツは 短くては いけません。   Shorts should not be (too) short.

4. この 本では だめです。   This book will not do.

【 ● ぶんかノート】

Japanese School Regulations

Japanese school regulations are much stricter than those in America. Dress codes are generally much more confining. Rules for uniforms, hair length and style, skirt length, color of socks, accessories, and use of makeup, including nail polish, are strictly enforced. Besides rules such as no smoking, drinking, etc., which exist in American schools, other rules regarding truancy, tardiness, and general misbehavior are applied much more severely in Japan than in America. In the classroom, one is not allowed to eat, drink, or chew gum. One does not move freely about the classroom without permission from the teacher. It is uncommon for students to ask their teachers if they may leave the room to get a drink of water or to use the restroom.

【 アクティビティー】

A. ペアワーク

One student takes the role of a parent and the other, the role of a child. The child asks the parent if he/she may do the following things. The parent responds by either permitting or prohibiting it.

Ex. こども：「アルバイトを しても いいですか。」

おとうさん／おかあさん：

「ええ、アルバイトを しても いいです／かまいません。」

or 「いいえ、アルバイトを しては だめです／いけません。」

1. アルバイトを しても いいですか。	
2. 金曜日の よる ともだちの うちへ いっても いいですか。	
3. 100ドルの シャツを かっても いいですか。	
4. おさけを すこし のんでも いいですか。	
5. よる ともだちと でんわで はなしても いいですか。	
6. うちの くるまを うんてんしても いいですか。	
7. しゅうまつ うちで パーティーを しても いいですか。	
8. 土曜日に ともだちが うちへ きても いいですか。	
9. 土曜日の よる うちで ダンスを しても いいですか。	

B. ペアワーク

You are planning to have a party at your partner's house. Ask your partner whether the following things should be allowed.

Ex. 質問：「パーティーは　十二時でも　いいですか。」

答え：「はい、十二時でも　いいです／かまいません。」

or 「いいえ、十二時では　だめです／いけません。」

1. パーティーは　十二じでも　いいですか。	
2. パーティーは　日曜日でも　いいですか。	
3. パーティーは　おそくても　いいですか。	
4. パーティーで　おさけを　のんでも　いいですか。	
5. パーティーは　うるさくても　いいですか。	
6. パーティーで　カラオケを　しても　いいですか。	

C. ペアワーク

Ask your partner about Japanese class rules. Your partner should answer based on the facts.

Ex. 質問：「日本語の　クラスで　食べても　いいですか。」

答え：「はい、食べても　いいです。」

or 「いいえ、食べては　いけません。」

1. 日本ごの　クラスで　たべても　いいですか。	
2. 日本ごの　クラスで　ガムを　かんでも　いいですか。	
3. 日本ごの　クラスで　ぼうしを　かぶっても　いいですか。	
4. 日本ごの　クラスで　えいごを　はなしても　いいですか。	
5. 日本ごの　クラスで　サングラスを　かけても　いいですか。	
6. 日本ごの　クラスで　ソーダを　のんでも　いいですか。	
7. 日本ごの　クラスで　うるさくても　いいですか。	
8. 日本ごの　クラスで　ねても　いいですか。	

三課

【会話】　まり：図書館へ　何を　しに　行きますか。

　　　　　ケン：本を　借りに　行きます。

【文型】

Place へ／に	Verb (Stem form) に	Direction verb 。	
海へ	泳ぎに	行きます。	I will go to the beach to swim.

【単語】

1. 借ります

[G2 かりる／かりて]

to borrow, rent (from)

2. 気を　つけて

[G2 気を　つける／気を　つけます]

to be careful

3. 映画館

〔えいがかん〕

movie theater

4. 証明書

〔しょうめいしょ〕

I.D.

5. 運転免許

〔うんてんめんきょ〕

driver's license

6. パスポート

passport

7. ところで

by the way

【*オプショナル単語】

1. *お金を　だします	* to withdraw money (e.g., from a bank)
2. *ゆうびんきょく	* post office
3. *ゆうびんを　出します	* to mail
4. *きって	* postage stamp
5. *きょうかい	* church
6. *おいのりを　します	* to pray
7. *どうぶつえん	* zoo
8. *どうぶつ	* animal

【漢字】

1.　夕　early evening　　　ゆう　　　夕方　late afternoon, early evening

2.　何　what　　　なに　　　何人〔なにじん〕　What nationality?

なん　　　何人〔なんにん〕　How many people?

何月〔なんがつ〕　　What month?

何曜日〔なんようび〕　　What day of the week?

何日〔なんにち〕　　What day of the month?

man carrying luggage

What is the luggage the man is carrying?

三課

【文法】

> A. Verb (STEM form) ＋ に　Direction verb。
> いきます
> きます
> かえります
>
> This pattern expresses going, coming, or returning somewhere for the purpose of doing something. The place of destination is followed by に or へ, followed by the purpose (a verb stem form, or a noun). The purpose is followed by the purpose particle に, which is then followed by any of the three directional verbs.

1. 友達の　うちへ　勉強しに　行きます。　　　　I will go to my friend's house to study.

2. ここへ　本を　借りに　来ました。　　　　　I came here to borrow a book.

3. 父は　お昼御飯を　食べに　うちへ　帰りました。

My father returned home to eat lunch.

> When a verb is of the noun ＋ を　します type, the noun may replace the verb stem as the purpose. There is no change in meaning. See examples below.

1. 勉強を　しに　行きます。　　　　　　　　I will go to study.

   or 勉強に　行きます。　　　　　　　　　I will go to study.

2. 食事を　しに　行きます。　　　　　　　　I will go to eat.

   or 食事に　行きます。　　　　　　　　　I will go to eat.

【 ● 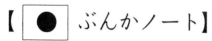 ぶんかノート】

Libraries in Japan

　Japan boasts the highest literacy rate in the world. Until the mid-1960's, however, there were not many public libraries in Japan. Historically, libraries were only open to the aristocracy. There was also a traditional emphasis that one should own one's own books. This probably explains the fact that there are so many bookstores in all parts of Japan even today.

三課　　　　　　　　82

【アクティビティー】

A. ペアワーク

Ask your partner if he/she goes to the following places. If so, ask your partner the purpose for which he/she goes there.

Ex. 図書館
とょかん

Aさん：「ところで、〜さんは 図書館へ 行きますか。」
                              とょかん い

Bさん：「はい、行きますよ。」
                い

Aさん：「何を しに 行きますか。」
                い

Bさん：「宿題を しに 行きます。」
         しゅくだい   い

図書館　　　　　銀行　　　　　本屋　　　　　映画館
とょかん　　　　ぎんこう　　　ほんや　　　　えいがかん

スーパー　　　　　　　　　　　　　　　　　　　公園
                                                        こうえん

スタジアム　　　　デパート　　　　大学　　　ともだちのうち
                                          だいがく

三課

B. ペアワーク

You want to do the following things. Ask your partner what you need to do them.

Ex. 図書館で　本を　借りたいんです。

質問：図書館で　本を　借りたいんですが、何が　いりますか。

答え：証明書が　いりますよ。

1. としょかんで ほんを かりたいんです。	2. スキーを したいんです。	3. 日本に りょこう したいんです。	4. くるまを うんてんしたい んです。
5. バスケットの しあいを　みに いきたいんです。	6. レンタル ビデオを かりたいんです。	7. マクドナルドで アルバイトを したいんです。	8. いい だいがくへ いきたいんです。

【会話】　まり：運転しても　かまいませんか。

ケン：はい、かまいませんよ。

【文型】

おすしを　たべませんか。	Don't you eat *sushi*? [**Negative question**]
<u>はい</u>、たべません。	Yes (= I agree), I don't eat (it).
<u>いいえ</u>、たべます。	No (= I disagree), I eat (it).
いい<u>ん</u>ですか。	Is it really all right?
～だけ	only ～

【単語】

1. ～が　見〔み〕えます
～ can be seen, visible

2. ～が　聞〔き〕こえます
～ can be heard, audible

3. 門〔もん〕
gate

4. 本当〔ほんとう〕に
really, truly
[Adverb]　ほんとう is a noun and means truth.

5. 本当〔ほんとう〕ですか。
Is it true/real?

6. ～だけ
only ～
だけ replaces を、が、は and
is used with へ、に、で, etc.

85

三課

【漢字】

1. 中　　inside, middle　　なか　　中本〔なかもと〕さん

　　　　　　　　　　　　　　　　中口〔なかぐち〕さん

　　　　　　　　　　　　　　　　今中〔いまなか〕さん

　　　　　　　　　　チュウ　　中学〔ちゅうがく〕 junior high school

　　　　　　　　　　　　　　　　中学生〔ちゅうがくせい〕

　　　　　　　　　　　　　　　junior high school student

　　　　　　　　　　　　　　　　中国〔ちゅうごく〕 China

　　　　　　　　　　　　　　　　中国人〔ちゅうごくじん〕Chinese citizen

2. 外　　outside　　そと　　家の　外〔いえの　そと〕 outside the house

　　　　　　　　　ガイ　　外国〔がいこく〕 foreign country

　　　　　　　　　　　　　　外国人〔がいこくじん〕 foreigner

　　　　　　　　　　　　　　外国語〔がいこくご〕 foreign language

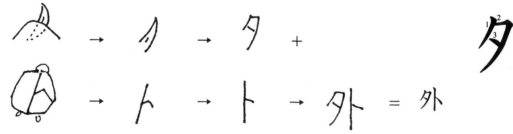

In ancient China, fortunes were told by throwing tortoise shells into the fire, then reading the shape of the cracks on the shell. How is this related to "outside"? It is because fortune telling was practiced outside in the early evening.

【文法】

A. Negative Question

　　　「食べませんでしたか。」「はい、食べませんでした。」

The Japanese negative question is answered differently from English. The Japanese answer affirmatively or negatively to the stated form of the verb rather than to the action implied. For example, in responding to the question 「きのう　うみへ　いきませんでしたか。」, the response would be, "Yes, I agree with your assumption that I didn't go to the beach." and say 「はい、いきませんでした。」. If he did go to the beach, he would respond, "No, I disagree with your assumption that I didn't go to the beach, I went." and say 「いいえ、いきました。」.Do not confuse this form with the negative invitation form. When responding to an invitation, one would answer as one would in English.

1. 「わかりませんか。」 　　　　　　　　　"Don't you understand it?"

　「はい、わかりません。」 　　　　　　"No, I do not understand it."

2. 「中国語を　話しませんか。」 　　　　"Don't you speak Chinese?"

　「ええ、話しません。」 　　　　　　　"No, I don't speak (it)."

3. 「昨日　海に　行きませんでしたか。」 "Yesterday, didn't you go to the beach?"

　「はい、行きませんでした。」 　　　　"No, I didn't go."

4. 「英語で　話しては　いけませんか。」 "Mustn't I speak in English?"

　「ええ、だめです。」 　　　　　　　　"No, it is no good."

B. 〜だけ　　　　only 〜
　　だけ replaces を, が, は and is used with other particles like へ, で, に, から.

1. ピアスを　一つだけ　しても　いいです。　　You may wear only one pierced earring.

2. 小さいのだけ　しても　いいです。　　　　　You may wear only a small one.

3. 女の　生徒だけ　ぼうしを　かぶっても　いいです。

　　　　　　　　　　　　　　　　Only female students are allowed to wear hats.

4. ケンさんは　学校でだけ　勉強します。　　Ken studies only at school.

三課

C. 「いい**ん**ですか。」

The -n desu ending is frequently used in speaking. When it appears in a question form, it serves the purpose of inviting an explanation from the listener. When used in a statement form, it suggests that the speaker feels obligated to explain himself.

1. 結婚を　したい**ん**です。　　　I (really) want to get married.
2. 今晩　映画に　行きたい**ん**です。　　I really want to go to a movie.
3. この　車を　運転しても　いい**ん**ですか。　May I really drive this car?

【 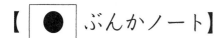 ぶんかノート】

In-school and out-of-school shoes

When one goes to school in Japan, one must remove one's shoes, place them in cubbyholes near the entrance, then change into special shoes to be worn inside the school only. At the end of the school day, one changes back to one's regular shoes. Recently, problems have developed with this system. Students who come to school with expensive shoes find that their shoes disappear from the cubbyholes. Teachers therefore, discourage students from wearing expensive shoes to school.

【アクティビティー】

A. ペアワーク

Sketch of a view of the outdoors from one of the windows of your home in the first frame below. Describe the view to your partner who will draw the view in the second frame below on his paper according to the description you give. Switch. Compare sketches and see how well you communicated with one another.

「まどから　〜が　みえます。」

[View from a window of your home]　　　[View from a window of your partner's home]

B. ペアワーク

Ask your partner the following negative questions. The partner should answer based on the facts.

Ex. 質問：「きのう　おすしを　食べませんでしたか。」
　　答え：「はい、食べませんでした。」or「いいえ、食べましたよ。」

1. きのう　おすしを　たべませんでしたか。 	2. きのう　日本ごの　しゅくだいを　しませんでしたか。	3. きのう　テレビを　みませんでしたか。
4. けさ　あさごはんを　たべませんでしたか。	5. あなたの　テキストを　かりても　かまいませんか。	6. いま　たべても　かまいませんか。
7. あなたに　十ドル　かしませんでしたか。	8. ちゅうがく一ねんせい　ではありませんか。	9. 今日は　金曜日では　ありませんか。

三課

C. ペアワーク

Ask your partner the following questions. Your partner should answer based on the facts. Use だけ appropriately in your responses.

Ex. 質問：「今　何人の　人が　スカートを　はいて　いますか。」

答え：「三人だけ　です。」

1. 今　何人の　人が　スカートを　はいて　いますか。		
2. うちに　くるまが　何だい　ありますか。		
3. 今　お金を　いくら　もって　いますか。		
4. 今　えんぴつを　何本〔なんぼん〕　もって　いますか。		
5. 今　きょうしつで　何人の　人が　めがねを　かけて　いますか。		
6. 今　きょうしつに　せんせいが　何人　いますか。		

D. ペアワーク

You suggest doing the following activities with your friend/partner. You ask what time and where you will meet. Your friend suggests the time and the location. Decide on a mutually agreeable time and place. Fill in the spaces below with the appropriate information.

Ex. お昼御飯を 食べたいです。

Ａさん：お昼御飯を 食べに 行きましょう。

Ｂさん：はい、行きましょう。

Ａさん：何時に 会いましょうか。

Ｂさん：十二時半に 会いましょう。

Ａさん：どこで 会いましょうか。

Ｂさん：門の ところで 会いましょう。

	1. えいがを みたいです。	2. フットボールの しあいを みたいです。	3. バスケットを したいです。	4. およぎ たいです。	5. たんじょう日の プレゼントを かいたいです。
Suggested activity					
Meeting time					
Meeting place					

三課

Find the answers from books, by talking to friends, or by using the Internet.

1. What process must Americans go through to get into college or university? What must Japanese students do?

2. How much does it cost for an American to go to a public school? To a private school? What are public and private tuition costs in Japan?

3. What kinds of extracurricular activities are popular in American schools? In Japanese schools?

4. What is a *juku*? Is there an American equivalent?

5. What are the advantages and disadvantages of the Japanese educational system? Of the American educational system?

6. Which educational system appeals to you more? Why?

7. See if you can write to a Japanese pen pal online or through the mail, and practice your language skills together.

HANAFUDA

Background

Hanafuda, the only traditional table game to have originated in Japan, continues to be enjoyed by both males and females, young and old, throughout the country. Although its popularity has waned somewhat in recent times, it is a game played by children and older people for fun. Unlike *go*, *shogi*, and *mah-jong*, which originated in China, *hanafuda* is a uniquely Japanese creation that evolved from the *kai-awase* (matching pictures on shells game) and playing cards introduced by the Portuguese in the late 1500's. Quintessentially Japanese in its stylized depiction of the seasons, the colorful cards bear pictures of Japanese flora, fauna, *tanzaku* (strips of paper for writing poems), and Japanese symbols of good luck. *Hanafuda* is a perfect illustration of the Japanese obsession with love of the seasons.

Cards

A *hanafuda* deck consists of 48 cards. There are 12 different suits, four cards in each. Each suit bears a seasonal flower or plant representing one of the 12 months of the year. Each card has a face value that falls into one of four different categories: Light beams-20 points, animals-10 points, *tanzaku* or *tan* (red or blue strips of paper)-5 points, and *kasu* (junk)-1 point. There is one red and black colored junk card of the *yanagi* or *ame* suit sometimes called the *gaji*. The *gaji* acts like a joker and can take any card of any suit. Also included with each deck is a blank card that can be used to replace a lost or bent card.

The Game

There are numerous ways of playing and scoring *hanafuda*, and they vary from region to region in Japan. Therefore, to avoid squabbling late into the game, it is best to establish the rules beforehand. The five most common ways of playing are: *Bakappana* (Matching Flowers or Fool Flowers), *Hachi-hachi* (Eighty-eight), *Koi-koi* (Come on), *Kabu* (Nine), and *Mushi* (Honeymoon *Hanafuda*). Because the rules and scoring become increasingly difficult variations of the game, it is highly recommended that beginners start out by playing the basic *Bakappana* game in order to get familiarized with the different suits and points. Although *Hachi-hachi* is the most popular and interesting method of playing, it is also the most complicated. For simplicity's sake, we will explain *Bakappana* , the "Fool's method," in this text.

Points

Each card has a face value of 1, 5, 10, or 20 points. However, the points of the cards increase in bonus combinations called *yaku* (see page 98). Playing with *yaku* requires more skill and adds excitement to the game.

Players

The standard and most recommended number of players is three, although it is possible to play with two to seven participants. If there are four or six players, you can play in pairs seating partners alternately.

三課

Dealing

The dealer or *oya* is determined by having each player draw one card at the beginning. The one whose card represents the earliest month of the year becomes the *oya*. Other players arrange themselves in order of the months chronologically to the right. (You can also draw to see who has the highest point card.) The *oya* shuffles, cuts once and deals the cards counterclockwise in the combinations listed below. The remainder of the deck becomes the *yama* (mountain) in the middle of the table.

    For 2 players: 8 cards each, 8 cards face up on table

        3 players: 7 cards each, 6 cards on table

        4 players: 5 cards each, 8 cards on table

        5 players: 4 cards each, 8 cards on table

        6 players: 3 cards each, 12 cards on table

        7 players: 3 cards each, 6 cards on table

Players should not touch their cards until all have been dealt.

Note: It is possible to trade hands with the *oya* before the game starts. The object of the game is to get the most points.

Rules and Procedure

The *oya* begins by trying to match a card from his/her hand with any card of the same suit facing up on the table. He/she then draws a card from the *yama*. If he/she is able to make another match with a card on the table, he/she may draw again. If not, then it is the turn of the player on his/her right. A player can continue to draw from the *yama* until he/she can no longer make a match. If on your turn, you cannot make a match, you may discard your least important card and draw one from the *yama*. Those familiar with "Go Fish" should understand the basic concept of the game. Remember all cards taken must remain face up for everyone to see. Beginners should go for the highest point cards instead of trying to hold out for *yaku* combinations. Sometimes three cards of the same suit will be dealt face up on the table. When this occurs, the player holding the missing card can take all three.

Reminder: the *gaji* acts as a wild card and can take any card from any suit. The game ends when all the cards have been played. Each player adds up his/her score, remembering to add extra points for *yaku* combinations. The total number of points possible is 264. The player with the most points becomes the new *oya*.

Have fun!

花札〔はなふだ〕

1. 一月：松〔まつ〕 "Pine"

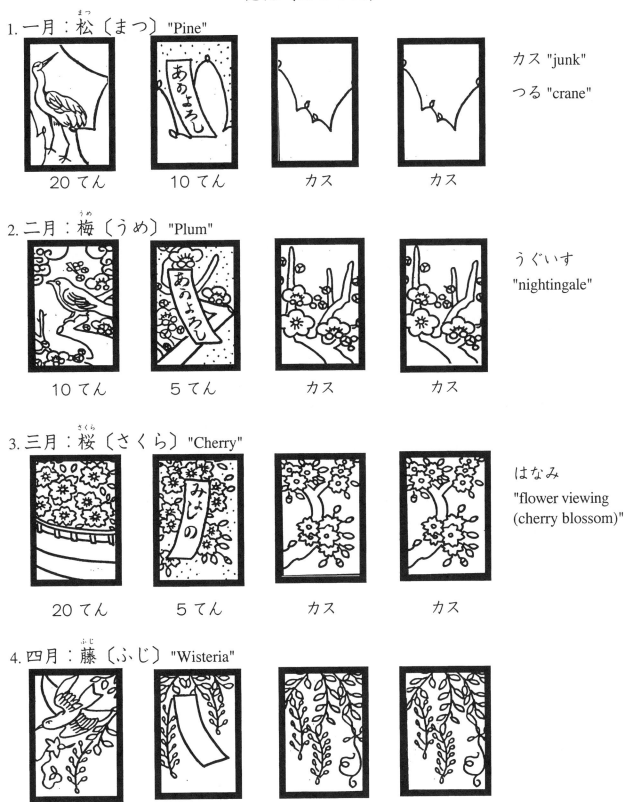

| 20 てん | 10 てん | カス | カス |

カス "junk"

つる "crane"

2. 二月：梅〔うめ〕 "Plum"

| 10 てん | 5 てん | カス | カス |

うぐいす
"nightingale"

3. 三月：桜〔さくら〕 "Cherry"

| 20 てん | 5 てん | カス | カス |

はなみ
"flower viewing
(cherry blossom)"

4. 四月：藤〔ふじ〕 "Wisteria"

| 10 てん | 5 てん | カス | カス |

三課

5. 五月：あやめ "Iris"

    10 てん   5 てん   カス   カス

6. 六月：ぼたん "Peony"

ちょう
"butterflies"

    10 てん   5 てん   カス   カス

7. 七月：はぎ "Bush clover"

いのしし "boar"

    10 てん   5 てん   カス   カス

8. 八月：すすき "Pampas" or ぼうず "Bald head"

つきみ
"moon viewing"

    20 てん   10 てん   カス   カス

三課

9. 九月：菊〔きく〕 "Chrysanthemum"

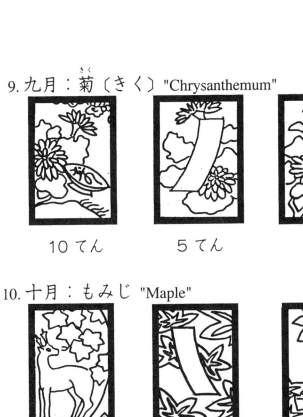

さかずき
"rice wine cup"
寿〔ことぶき〕
"longevity"

10てん　　5てん　　カス　　カス

10. 十月：もみじ "Maple"

しか "deer"

10てん　　5てん　　カス　　カス

11. 十一月：やなぎ "Willow" or 雨〔あめ〕 "Rain"

かえる "frog"

つばめ "swallow"

がじ "joker"

20てん　　10てん　　5てん　　カス & がじ

12. 十二月：きり "Paulownia"

ほうおう
"phoenix"

20てん　　10てん　　カス　　カス

三課

やく　Bonus Combinations

1. 五光〔ごこう〕１００てん
Five Light Beams - 100 Points

まつ　　きり　　ぼうず　　さくら　　あめ

2. 四光〔しこう〕５０てん
Four Light Beams - 50 Points

まつ　　きり　　ぼうず　　さくら

3. 三光〔さんこう〕３０てん
Three Light Beams - 30 Points

まつ　　きり　　ぼうず

4. 梅松桜　３０てん
〔うめ・まつ・さくら〕
Plum, Pine, Cherry - 30 Points

5. 猪鹿蝶　１００てん
〔いの・しか・ちょう〕
Boar, Deer, Butterfly - 100 Points

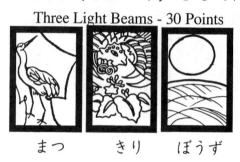

6. のみ [はな見で一ぱい] ３０てん
Drinking Sake while Viewing Cherry Blossoms - 30 Points

のみ [月見で一ぱい] ３０てん
Drinking Sake while Viewing the Moon - 30 Points

7. 赤短〔あかたん〕３０てん
Red Strips with Words - 30 Points

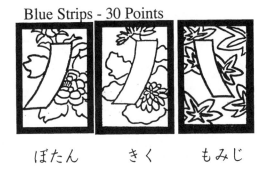

まつ　　　うめ　　　さくら

8. 青短〔あおたん〕３０てん
Blue Strips - 30 Points

ぼたん　　　きく　　　もみじ

9. 草三短〔くささんたん〕３０てん
Red Strips - 30 Points

ふじ　　　あやめ　　　はぎ

10. 六短〔ろくたん〕　３０てん

Six Cards [Any six cards except red rain.] - 30 Points

11. 七短〔ななたん〕　５０てん

Seven Cards [Any seven cards except red rain.] - 50 Points

12. カス十枚〔カスじゅうまい〕５０てん

Ten Junk Cards - 50 Points

三課

梅
Plum flowers

桜
Cherry blossoms

By the end of this lesson, you will be able to communicate the information below in the given situations.

【Ⅱ-4　タスク1】

Two friends are talking. Friend B has just received his/her driver's license. Friend A asks many questions about it.

Friend A:
(1) Ask your friend if he/she really has a driver's license.
(2) Ask to see the driver's license.
(3) Ask who taught your friend how to drive.
(4) Ask how the driving test was, and whether or not it was difficult to get a license.
(5) Answer appropriately. Ask your friend whether his/her driving is safe.

Friend B:
(1) Answer yes, and ask your friend if he/she wants to see it.
(2) (Show the license to your friend).
(3) Answer appropriately.
(4) Give your opinion. Ask if your friend will also get a license.
(5) Give your opinion.

【Ⅱ-4　タスク2】

Two friends plan to go see a movie. Friend B offers to drive. Friend A feels a little nervous, and can't help but give a lot of advice.   Friend B, who is trying to be a careful driver, also makes many requests.

Friend A:
Warn your friend:
(1) to be careful.
(2) not to speed.
(3) not to turn the corner (so) quickly.
(4) to stop for the yellow light.
(5) not to stop suddenly.

Friend B:
Ask your friend:
(1) not to forget his/her seat belt.
(2) not to chew gum in the car.
(3) not to talk loudly (to you).
(4) not to listen to loud music.
(5) not to worry about your driving.

四課

四課

【 会話 - Formal 】

＜学校の　門の　ところで＞

まり：ケンさんは　もう　運転しても　いいんですか。

ケン：はい、ぼくは　先月　運転免許を　取りました。

まり：見せて　下さい。わあ、すごいですねえ。

ケン：さあ、自動車に　乗って　下さい。お昼を　食べに　行きましょう。

まり：大丈夫ですか。　ちょっと　こわいですねえ。

ケン：心配しないで　下さい。　シートベルトを　して　下さい。

　　　さあ、出かけましょう。

＜道で＞

まり：危ない！　信号は　黄色でしたよ。行っては　いけませんよ。

ケン：大丈夫ですよ。

まり：あっ、ケンさん、角を　速く　まがらないで　下さいよ。

ケン：ごめんなさい。

まり：あれは　救急車ですか。

ケン：そうです。あそこに　パトカーや　警官も　いますね。事故ですよ。

まり：気を　つけて　下さいね。

　　　あまり　スピードを　出さないで　下さい。

ケン：はい、レストランに　着きましたよ。

まり：ケンさん、急に　止まらないで　下さいよ。

ケン：ごめんなさい。さあ、速く　降りて　下さい。

【会話 - Informal】

＜学校の　門の　ところで＞

まり：ケンさんは　もう　運転しても　いいの？

ケン：うん、ぼく　先月　運転免許を　取ったんだよ。

まり：見せて。わあ、すごいわねえ。

ケン：さあ、自動車に　乗って。お昼を　食べに　行こう。

まり：大丈夫？　ちょっと　こわいなあ。

ケン：心配しないで。シートベルトを　して。さあ、出かけよう。

＜道で＞

まり：危ない！　信号は　黄色だったわよ。行っちゃ　いけないわよ。

ケン：大丈夫だよ。

まり：あっ、ケンさん、角を　速く　まがらないでよ。

ケン：ごめん。

まり：あれ、救急車？

ケン：そうだ。あそこに　パトカーや　警官も　いるね。事故だよ。

まり：気を　つけてね。あまり　スピード　出さないで。

ケン：はい、レストランに　着いたよ。

まり：ケンさん、急に　止まらないでよ。

ケン：ごめん。さあ、速く　降りて。

Let's review previous vocabulary!

A. めいし   Nouns

1. 学校〔がっこう〕   school
2. もん   gate
3. ところ   place
4. ぼく〔せん〕   I [used by males]
5. 先月〔せんげつ〕   last month
6. うんてんめんきょ   driver's license

7. 自動車〔じどうしゃ〕   car
8. おひる   lunch
9. あれ   that one over there
10. あそこ   over there
11. レストラン   restaurant

B. どうし   Verbs

12. うんてんして〔IR うんてんする／うんてんします〕   drive
13. とりました〔G1 とる／とって〕   took
14. 食〔た〕べに〔G2 たべる／たべます／たべて〕   to eat [purpose]
15. 行〔い〕きましょう〔G1 いく／いきます／いって〕   let's go
16. 行〔い〕って〔G1 いく／いきます〕   go
17. います〔G2 いる／いて〕   be, exist

C. -い けいようし   I Adjectives

18. すごい   terrific, terrible (Used to describe the extreme)

D. ふくし   Adverbs

19. もう + Aff.   already
20. ちょっと   a little

21. あまり + Neg.   (not) very

E. じょし   Particles

22. A や B   A and B and alike

23. も   also

F. Expressions

24. わあ   Wow!!
25. さあ   Well . . .

四課   106

26. 大〔だい〕じょうぶですか。　　　　　Is it okay?/ Are you okay?

27. 大〔だい〕じょうぶですよ。　　　　　It's okay.

28. あっ　　　　　　　　　　　　　　　　Oh!

29. ごめんなさい。　　　　　　　　　　　I'm sorry.

30. そうです。　　　　　　　　　　　　　That's right.

G. ぶんぽう　Grammar

31. Verb TE form + も　いい（ん）ですか。　　　Is it alright if 〜?

　　としょかんで　たべても　いいんですか。　Is it alright if I eat in the library?

32. Verb TE form + 下さい。　　　　　　　　Please do 〜.

　　たべて　下さい。　　　　　　　　　　Please eat it.

33. Verb TE form + は　いけません。　　　You must not 〜.

　　としょかんで　たべては　いけません。　You must not eat in the library.

【会話】　まり：今、図書館へ　行く？

ケン：ううん、今　行かない。でも、あとで　行くよ。

【文型】

Formal Speech Style	→	Informal Speech Style	
Verbs: 行きます。	→	行く。	will go / be going
行きません。	→	行かない。	will not go / is not going
行きますか。	→	行く？✔	Will you go? / Are you going?
行って　下さい。	→	行って。	Please go.
い Adjectives: あついです。	→	あつい。	It is hot.
あつくないです。	→	あつくない。	It is not hot.
あついですか。	→	あつい？✔	Is it hot?

【単語】

1. うん

Yes. (Informal)

2. ううん

No. (Informal)

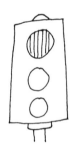

3. しんごう

traffic lights

赤　黄色　青

4. あか, きいろ, あお

red, yellow, green

あお is used to describe the green color of traffic lights.

5. パトカー

police car

6. 救急車〔きゅうきゅうしゃ〕

ambulance

います is used instead of あります to describe a moving car that is occupied.

四課

108

7. けいかん
   police officer

8. おしえる
   [G2 おしえます／おしえて]
   to teach

【＊オプショナル単語<ruby>単語<rt>たんご</rt></ruby>】

1. ＊おまわりさん　　　　　＊police officer
2. ＊こうばん　　　　　　　＊police box
3. ＊サイレン　　　　　　　＊siren (sound)
4. ＊オートバイ　　　　　　＊motor bike

【<ruby>漢字<rt>かんじ</rt></ruby>】

1. 行　go　　　　い（く）　　　行きます go
　　　　　　　　　コウ　　　　　旅行〔<ruby>旅<rt>りょ</rt></ruby>こう〕します travel
　　　　　　　　　　　　　　　　銀行〔<ruby>銀<rt>ぎん</rt></ruby>こう〕 bank

北 → 仒 → 行 → 行

To go along the intersection.

2. 来　come　　　き（ます）　　来て　下さい。Please come.
　　　　　　　　　　　　　　　　よく　<ruby>出来<rt>て</rt></ruby>ました。 did well
　　　　　　　　　く（る）　　　来る come
　　　　　　　　　こ（ない）　　来ないで　下さい。Please do not come.
　　　　　　　　　ライ　　　　　来年〔らいねん〕 next year
　　　　　　　　　　　　　　　　来月〔らいげつ〕 next month
　　　　　　　　　　　　　　　　来週〔らい<ruby>週<rt>しゅう</rt></ruby>〕 next week

四課

grain

The time to harvest rice is coming.

【文法】

> A. Verb NAI form : Informal negative nonpast form
>
> "do not do ～," "will not do ～," "is not going to do ～"
>
> The formal negative nonpast form is -ません. Its informal equivalent is the NAI form. The NAI form is used in informal situations, such as when one talks with family or close friends. The meaning of a sentence remains the same whether one uses formal or informal endings. The NAI form may also be used preceding extenders in certain sentence patterns, as in the -ない ＋ でください negative request pattern, which means, "Please do not do (such and such)."

1. **Group 1 verbs**

Group 1 verbs are identified by the verb stem, which is the verb form that remains after dropping -ます. If there are more than two *hiragana* characters remaining in the verb stem after dropping the ます and the final sound of the verb stem is an -i ending sound, the verb can usually be categorized as a Group 1 verb. To obtain the NAI form, change the -i ending sound of the verb stem to the corresponding -a ending sound, then attach the -ない. See the chart below for examples.

[☐ ☐ -i ます]

	MASU form	Meaning	Dictionary form	NAI form
	-i		-u	-a
[み]	のみます	to drink	のむ	のまない
	よみます	to read	よむ	よまない
	やすみます	to rest, be absent	やすむ	やすまない
[に]	しにます	to die	しぬ	しなない
[び]	あそびます	to play	あそぶ	あそばない
[い]	あいます	to meet	あう	あわない
[ち]	かちます	to win	かつ	かたない
[り]	わかります	to understand	わかる	わからない
	しります	to get to know	しる	しらない
	かえります	to return (place)	かえる	かえらない

四課　　　　　　　　　　110

[り]	あります	to be (inanimate)	ある	ない *
	がんばります	to do one's best	がんばる	がんばらない
	はしります	to run	はしる	はしらない
[き]	ききます	to listen, hear	きく	きかない
	かきます	to write	かく	かかない
	いきます	to go	いく	いかない
	あるきます	to walk	あるく	あるかない
[ぎ]	およぎます	to swim	およぐ	およがない
[し]	はなします	to talk	はなす	はなさない

* ない is the NAI form of あります. It is an exception.

2. Group 2 verbs

Group 2 verbs can be identified by a verb stem (verb without ます) that ends in an "-e sounding" *hiragana* or a verb stem that contains only one *hiragana*. See examples below. A few special words do exist. They must simply be learned as special verbs. Group 2 verb's NAI forms are created simply by adding ない after removing the - ます.

	MASU form	Meaning	Dictionary form	NAI form
[□ -e ます]	みえます	can be seen	みえる	みえない
	きこえます	can be heard	きこえる	きこえない
	たべます	to eat	たべる	たべない
	まけます	to lose	まける	まけない
[One *hiragana*]	みます	to see, watch	みる	みない
	います	to be (animate)	いる	いない
	ねます	to sleep	ねる	ねない
[Special verbs]	おきます	to get up	おきる	おきない
	かります	to borrow	かりる	かりない
	おります	to get off, to get out	おりる	おりない

3. Group 3 Irregular verbs

Only きます, します and a noun + します verbs belong to this group. You must memorize the NAI form individually, as they do not follow rules.

MASU form	Dictionary form	NAI form
きます to come	くる	こない
します to do	する	しない
べんきょう(を)します to study	べんきょう(を)する	べんきょう(を)しない
タイプ(を)します to type	タイプ(を)する	タイプ(を)しない
りょこう(を)します to travel	りょこう(を)する	りょこう(を)しない
かいもの(を)します to shop	かいもの(を)する	かいもの(を)しない
しょくじ(を)します to have a meal	しょくじ(を)する	しょくじ(を)しない
れんしゅう(を)します to practice	れんしゅう(を)する	れんしゅう(を)しない

B. Informal Conversation

When Japanese talk with family and friends, they use the informal speech style. Use of the informal style indicates that the relationship between the speaker and listener is close. The dictionary form is an informal style of -ます. The NAI form is an informal style of -ません. A question may be formed in informal speech by ending the informal sentence with a rising intonation.

	Formal Speech Style	→	Informal Speech Style	
Verbs:	行きます。	→	行く。	will go / be going
	行きません。	→	行かない。	will not go / is not going
	行きますか。	→	行く？	Will you go? / Are you going?
	行って　下さい。	→	行って。	Please go.
い Adjectives:	あついです。	→	あつい。	It is hot.
	あつくないです。	→	あつくない。	It is not hot.
	あついですか。	→	あつい？	Is it hot?

1. 「行く？」   "Are you going?"

   「うん、行く。」   "Yes, I will go."

2. 「今　お昼御飯　食べる？」   "Are you going to eat lunch now?"

   「ううん、今　食べない。」   "No, I am not eating now."

3. 「そのコーヒー　熱い？」   "Is that coffee hot?"

   「ううん、あまり　熱くないね。」   "No, it is not very hot, is it?"

【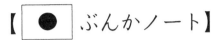 ぶんかノート】

1. あお

The word あお in Japanese may mean either blue or green. In very early times, blue and green were perceived by the Japanese as a single color. The color of the ocean, which is arguably blue or green, is described as あお. The Japanese refer to the color of young sprouting leaves as あお. The color of the traffic light which English speakers call "green," is called あお by Japanese. The color あお can also connote immaturity in Japanese. A new, immature rookie is referred to as being あお. あお can also imply paleness. When one is ill, one's face is described as becoming あお.

2. Traffic Sounds

The traffic sounds in Japan differ from those you might hear in the United States. Generally, the sounds are higher pitched, and more melodic. At major crosswalks in Japan, the visual signals indicating "cross" are accompanied by a twittering sound so that blind persons can tell when they may cross the streets. During political campaigns, silence is also broken by the noisy, blaring messages of political candidates as they drive through the streets. In residential neighborhoods, one can also occasionally hear cars announcing that the "tissue exchange" man is in the vicinity for those who want to exchange old newspapers, rags, etc., for boxes of tissue.

四課

【🧑🧑アクティビティー】

A. ペアワーク

You have your learner's permit and are taking driving lessons from a driving instructor. You are the driver and your partner is the instructor. As you are driving, you see/hear the things below, and verbalize what you see to the instructor. The instructor gives you directions on what to do. Perform the actions after you hear the instructions.

Ex. You: しんごうが あかです。

Instructor: とまって 下さい。[とまる to stop]

1. しんごうが あおです。	
2. うしろに けいかんが みえます。	
3. きゅうきゅうしゃが きこえます。	
4. パトカーが うしろから 来て います。	
5. 子どもが くるまの まえを あるいて います。	
6. しんごうが きいろです。	

B. ペアワーク

Carry on the following conversation in the informal speech style.

1. まり：ケンさん、今 お昼御飯を 食べますか。

　ケン：いいえ、今 食べません。

　まり：いつ 食べますか。

　ケン：一時ごろに 食べます。

　まり：この おむすびを 食べて 下さい。

　ケン：どうも ありがとう。

2. ベン：明日 ぼくの うちで ビデオを 見ませんか。

　エミ：はい、いいですね。 何の 映画ですか。

　ベン：スーパーマンの 映画です。

　エミ：私は スーパーマンの 映画は 見たくないです。

　ベン：そうですか？ 残念ですねえ。

C. ペアワーク：Tic-Tac-Toe ゲーム

Play Tic-Tac-Toe. Change the -ます form to the correct -ない form. The answers are on the next page.

a.

のみます	しにます	みます
おきます	ねます	あそびます
やすみます	はなします	はきます

b.

まちます	来ます	まがります
あいます	よみます	たべます
行きます	とまります	します

c.

かいます	まけます	ききます
あります	かきます	はしります
わすれます	およぎます	うんてん（を）します

四課

[こたえ]

a.

のまない [のみます]	しなない [しにます]	みない [みます]
おきない [おきます]	ねない [ねます]	あそばない [あそびます]
やすまない [やすみます]	はなさない [はなします]	はかない [はきます]

b.

またない [まちます]	来（こ）ない [来ます]	まがらない [まがります]
あわない [あいます]	よまない [よみます]	たべない [たべます]
行かない [行きます]	とまらない [とまります]	しない [します]

c.

かわない [かいます]	まけない [まけます]	きかない [ききます]
ない [あります]	かかない [かきます]	はしらない [はしります]
わすれない [わすれます]	およがない [およぎます]	うんてん（を）しない [うんてん（を） します]

【会話】

Formal style:　　まり：ケンさん、そんなに　スピードを　出さないで　下さい。

　　　　　　　　　ケン：心配しないで　下さい。

Informal style:　まり：ケンさん、そんなに　スピードを　出さないで。

　　　　　　　　　ケン：心配しないで。

【文型】

Verb (NAI form) ＋で　下さい。　　　　Please do no do ～.
うるさい　　is noisy　[い Adjective]　　→　うるさく　　noisily, loudly [Adverb]
きれい　　　is pretty, neat [な Adjective]　→　きれいに　　neatly [Adverb]

【単語】

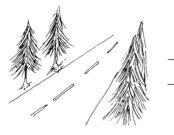

1. 道〔みち〕

street, road

2. 角〔かど〕

corner

3. 速く〔はやく〕

fast, quickly

4. 早く〔はやく〕

early

5. 急〔きゅう〕に

suddenly

きゅう is a な adjective
meaning "urgent."

6. を

through, along

7. けっして＋ Neg.

never

8. Place に/で　止まる
[G1 とまります]

to stop

四課

9. Placeで／を　曲がる
[G1 まがります]
to turn at/ along (place)

10. スピードを　出す
[G1 だします]
to speed

11. 心配(を)　する
[Ir. しんぱい(を) します]
to worry

【*オプショナル単語】

1. *かぎ　　　　　　　　　　　* key
2. *歩行者〔ほこうしゃ〕　　* pedestrian
3. *こうさてん　　　　　　　* intersection
4. *アルコール, さけ　　　　* alcohol
5. *ビール　　　　　　　　　* beer
6. *まやく　　　　　　　　　* drugs
7. *ちゅうしゃ（を）します　* to inject

【漢字】

1.　子　　child　　　こ　　　子ども child

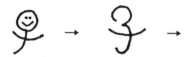

2.　車　　vehicle　　　くるま　　車に　のる。ride in a car
　　　　　　　　　　シャ　　　自動車 car, 自転車 bicycle, 電車 electric train,
　　　　　　　　　　　　　　　外車〔がいしゃ〕foreign imported car

【文法】

A. Verb NAI form ＋ で 下さい。　　Please do not do ~. [Negative request]

The polite negative imperative pattern is used when one politely asks the listener not to do something. It is translated as "please don't do . . ." The extender で 下さい is attached to the verb -NAI form.

---

1. 宿題を 忘れないで 下さい。　　　　　Please don't forget (your) homework.

2. 教室で ぼうしを かぶらないで 下さい。　　Please don't wear (your) hat in the classroom.

3. 英語で 話さないで 下さい。　　　　　Please don't speak in English.

B. Adverbial usage of adjectives

Some adverbs are derived from -い adjectives and -な adjectives. Observe how each type is derived below.

* Remember! Adverbs describe verbs, adjectives and other adverbs, while adjectives describe nouns.

a. -い Adjective (-い)		→	-い Adjective (- く) [Adverb]	
はやい	is fast, is early	→	はやく	fast, quickly, early
おそい	is slow, is late	→	おそく	slowly, late
いい	is good	→	よく	well
うるさい	is noisy	→	うるさく	noisily

b. -な Adjective		→	-な Adjective ＋ に [Adverb]	
しずか	is quiet	→	しずかに	quietly
じゆう	is free, is liberal	→	じゆうに	freely
きれい	is pretty, is clean	→	きれいに	neatly
きゅう	is urgent, is sudden	→	きゅうに	suddenly

When -い Adjectives become adverbs, the final い is dropped and replaced by く. When -な Adjectives become adverbs, に is added to the adjective. -く and に are never used together.

---

1. 速く 運転しないで 下さい。　　　Please do not drive fast.

2. 今日は おそく 起きました。　　　I got up late today.

3. 図書館では 静かに 勉強して 下さい。　Please study quietly in the library.

4. ここでは 自由に 話しても いいです。　You may talk freely here.

5. よく 出来ました。　　　　　You did well. [lit., It is well done.]

四課

【 ● ぶんかノート】

初心者マーク
Shoshinsha maaku
"new, first-time driver's mark"

1. Driver's Licenses

In Japan, driver's licenses are issued to persons 18 or older. One must be 20 to drive a heavy truck. Motorcycle licenses can be obtained at the age of 16. Most Japanese now enroll in driving school, as one does not have to take a road test if one has received certification from an accredited driving school. The courses, however, are rigorous and costly.

New drivers must attach a yellow and green arrow-shaped sticker on visible parts of the car to alert others on the street that they are still inexperienced drivers. This sticker is called the "初心者マーク *Shoshinsha maaku*" or the "new, first-time driver's mark."

2. Traffic Signs

a. Pedestrian crossing zone

f.  No entry for vehicles

b. Crossing by pedestrians prohibited

g.  Pedestrians only

c.  Road closed

h. Pedestrians & bicycles only

d.  Stop

i. No parking from 8:00 to 20:00 (8 a.m. to 8 p.m.)

e. Maximum speed (50 km per hour)

j. Parking zone

【アクティビティー】

A. ペアワーク

You are at the locations below, and you or your partner are breaking the rules established for that area. You are warned politely of your unacceptable behavior. You apologize and promise never to do it again.

　　Ex. You are eating.

　Supervisor: ここで　食(た)べないで　下さい。

　　　You: ごめんなさい。けっして　もう　ここで　食(た)べません。

a. としょかんで:

A student and a librarian

1. コーラを のまないで 下さい。	2. うるさく しないで 下さい。	3. ごみを すてないで 下さい。
4. ガムを かまないで 下さい。	5. はしらないで 下さい。	6. ぼうしを かぶらないで 下さい。

四課

b. 日本語の　教室で：

A student and a teacher.

1. たべないで　下さい。	2. のまないで　下さい。	3. ガムを　かまないで　下さい。
4. えいごで　はなさないで　下さい。	5. ぼうしを　かぶらないで　下さい。	6. あるかないで　下さい。
7. ねないで　下さい。	8. えいごの　本を　よまないで　下さい。	9. ＣＤを　きかないで　下さい。

c. 車の　中で:

Your friend is driving and you are
worried about his/her driving.

1. きゅうに　とまらないで　下さい。

2. かどを　きゅうに
　　まがらないで　下さい。

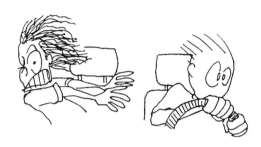

3. うるさい　おんがくを
　　きかないで　下さい。

4. きいろの　しんごうで
　　とまって　下さい。

5. スピードを　ださないで　下さい。

6. まえを　よく　みて　下さい。

7. 大きい　こえで
　　うたわないで　下さい。

四課

d. 車の　中で：

You are driving a car and your friend
does things which annoy you.

1. まどを　あけないで　下さい。 	2. うるさい　おんがくを 　きかないで　下さい。 
3. シートの　うえに　ごみを 　すてないで　下さい。 	4. しんぱいしないで　下さい。  

四課　　　　　124

【会話】

Formal style:	まり：警官も　パトカーも　いますね。
	ケン：交通事故でしょう。
	まり：こわいですねえ。
Informal style:	まり：警官も　パトカーも　いるね。
	ケン：交通事故だろう。
	まり：こわいわねえ。

【単語】

1. あぶない
   [いAdj.]
   is dangerous

2. あんぜん
   [なAdj.]
   is safe

3. こわい
   [いAdj.]
   is scary

4. こうつうじこ

   traffic accident

5. vehicle に　乗る
   [G1 のります]
   to ride (vehicle)

6. vehicle から/を　おりる
   [G2 おります]
   to get off, to get out (vehicle)

7. シートベルトを　する
   [IR します]
   to wear a seat belt

125

四課

  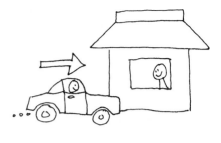

8. place から　出^てかける

[G2 でかけます]

to go out

Used only to describe a person who is leaving.

9. place を／から　出^てる

[G2 でます]

to leave (a place)

10. place に　着^つく

[G1 つきます]

to arrive (at a place)

【*オプショナル単語^{たんご}】

1. *じこを　おこす　　　　　　　　　* to cause an accident

2. *ドア　　　　　　　　　　　　　　* door

3. *うんてんしゅ or ドライバー　　　* driver

【漢字^{かんじ}】

1. 学　　study　　　ガク　　　学生〔がくせい〕 student

小学生〔しょうがくせい〕 elementary school student

中学生〔ちゅうがくせい〕 junior high school student

大学〔だいがく〕 college

ガッ　　学校〔がっこう〕 school

Children study under the roof of the school, which displays the school emblem.

四課　　　　　　　　　　126

2. 校　　school　　コウ　　学校〔がっこう〕school

中学校〔ちゅうがっこう〕junior high school

小学校〔しょうがっこう〕elementary school

高校〔こうこう〕high school

高校生〔こうこうせい〕high school student

In the wooden school house, six students sit with their legs crossed.

【 ⬤ ぶんかノート】

Police

Just as in English, there are many words in Japanese for the word "police." Those most commonly accepted are けいかん, けいさつ, じゅんさ, and おまわり(さん). As in America, Japanese police officers travel in many different types of vehicles. Police cars are generally black and white. Because of the narrow streets, many Japanese police officers use bicycles.

パトカー Police car

【アクティビティー】

A. ペアワーク

You are going to a party and you take your friend with you. You drive to your friend's house with your parents' car to pick him/her up. Your friend asks you many questions. You answer.

1. 本とうに　うんてんめんきょを　もって　いますか。	
2. うんてんめんきょを　みせて　下さい。	
3. うんてんめんきょを　いつ　とりましたか。	
4. だれが　あなたに　うんてんを　おしえましたか。	
5. うんてんの　しけんは　むずかしかったですか。	
6. あなたの　うんてんは　あんぜんですか。	

B. ペアワーク

Your Japanese friend from Tokyo is coming to your town for the first time. You discuss your friend's arrival at the airport over the phone.

1. 何日（なんにち）に　来ますか。	
2. どの　エアーラインに　のって　来ますか。	
3. ひこうきは　何じに　とうきょうを　でますか。	
4. 何じに　ここの　くうこう (airport) に　つきますか。	
5. にもつ (luggage) が　たくさん　ありますか。	
6. ゲートで　あいましょうか。	
7. 私の　日本ごが　わかりましたか。	
8. あなたが　来るのを　たのしみに　して　います。	

C. ペアワーク

You are a driver's education teacher. You give your student instructions as you go out on the road.
Your student repeats what he/she is supposed to do. Act out.

Ex. 先生：さあ、車に　乗って　下さい。
　　生徒：はい、車に　乗ります。

1. かりめん(permit)を　みせて　下さい。	
2. 車に　のって　下さい。	
3. シートベルトを　して　下さい。	
4. 行って　下さい。	
5. きいろの　しんごうで　とまって　下さい。	
6. つぎの　かどで　ひだりに　まがって　下さい。	
7. スピードを　ださないで　下さい。	
8. まえを　よく　みて　下さい。	
9. がっこうへ　かえって　下さい。	
10. よく　できました。　学校に　つきましたね。	X
11. 車から　おりて　下さい。	

D. ペアワーク

You are driving with a friend and run into many traffic jams. Your partner asks you about each traffic problem you encounter. You explain what you see from your window. Create a short conversation appropriate to the situation.

> Choices: 交通事故, パレード, 映画のロケ (movie location), 工事 (construction), 火事 (fire)

Ex.

Partner: 人が たくさん いますね。
何ですか。
You: 工事ですね。
Partner: 何を 作って いますか。
You: 何でしょうか。大きい 建物ですね。
Partner: 気を つけて 下さいね。
You: はい、ゆっくり 行きましょう。

1.

2.

3.

4.

【単語】

1. スクールバス

school bus

2. うんてんしゅ
or ドライバー

driver

3. かぎ

key

4. ビール

beer

5. アイスクリーム
ice cream

6. ポテトチップス
potato chips

7. ゆか
floor

8. けんか（を）する
[IR します]

to have a fight

9. Place に　入る
[G1 はいります／はいって]
to enter (a place)

10. Place を　出る
[G2 でます／でて]
to leave (a place)

11. 出す
[G1 だします／だして]
to extend out, submit, take out
まどから　てをだす means
"stick one's hand out of the window."

四課

【漢字】

1. 見　　look, see　み（る）　　　見ます look

　　多 → 貝 → 見 → 見　　　　　見

A person standing sees well with his big eyes.

2. 良　　is good　　よい　　　　良くないです is not good

　　偵 → 良 → 良 → 良　　　　　良

a grain of rice and a person (This *kanji* alone means "good.")

3. 食　　eat　　　　　た（べる）　　食べましょう。 Let's eat.
　　　　　　　　　　ショク　　　　食事を　します to have a meal
　　　　　　　　　　　　　　　　　夕食〔ゆうしょく〕supper
　　　　　　　　　　　　　　　　　外食〔がいしょく〕eating out

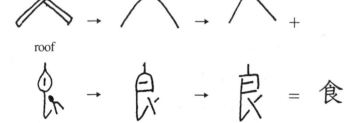

roof

A good thing for a person to do in his house is to eat rice.

【 ● ぶんかノート】

Buses

Riding the bus in Japan is not very different from doing so in America. There is an extensive system of bus routes in Tokyo that takes riders to and from large train stations and other major stops. When there is a standard bus fare, riders board at the front and insert their coins in the fare box or show their passes to the driver. If fares vary depending on distance, one boards at the back, takes a ticket, then gives the driver the correct fare and ticket as one exits the bus. For this system, the current fare, by ticket number, is shown at the front of the bus. Buses that are operated only by the driver only are called ワンマンバス (one-man bus).

四課

132

【アクティビティー】

A. グループワーク（４人〜５人）

Form groups of four or five. Assign one student to be a school bus driver, one to be a chaperone, and the rest of the group to be passengers. Each person on the bus is doing something wrong. Members of the group must politely ask each other not to do these things. The teacher prepares the signs for each of the bad behaviors listed below and shows one sign at a time. The group responds by acting out the behavior, indicated by the sign and requests that the offender stop the bad behavior. The person apologizes for his/her bad behavior.

Ex. drinking

「のまないで　下さい。」　　「ごめんなさい。」

The school bus driver:

1. is speeding.

2. turned the corner (too) quickly.

3. stopped suddenly.

The chaperone:

1. closed all the windows.

2. is smoking.

3. is drinking beer.

The passengers are:

1. throwing litter out the window.

2. eating ice cream.

3. talking loudly.

4. chewing gum.

5. standing.

6. writing on the window.

7. lying on the floor.

8. sticking their hands and faces out of the window.

9. singing loudly.

10. fighting.

Ask your partner these questions in Japanese.
Your partner should answer in Japanese.

1. May I ask you a question?

しつもんを きいても いいですか

2. Are your school rules strict?

あなたの 学校の きそくは きびしいですか

3. Do you like to wear a uniform?

せいふくを きるのは すきですか

4. What kind of clothing do you wear to school?

どういう ふくを 学校へ きていくのですか

5. Do you always wear a necklace?

いつも くびわ ネックレスを つけているのですか

6. Are students allowed to wear hats in your Japanese classroom?

きょうしつで せいとは ぼうしを かぶっていても いいのですか

7. Are students allowed to chew gum in your Japanese classroom?

きょうしつで せいとは ガムを かんでいても いいのですか

8. I want to go to the library to borrow books. What do I need?

としょかんへ いきたいのですが、なにか ひつようですか

9. Is eating allowed in the library?

としょかんで 食べても いいですか

10. Do you smoke?

たばこを すいますか

11. Do you sometimes litter?

あなたは ときどき ごみを すてていますか

12. By the way, do you already have a passport?

ところで、パスポートは もう もっているのですか

13. At what age can Americans drive cars?

アメリカ人は なんさいで 車を うんてんできるのですか

14. Do you already have a driver's license?

もう うんてんめんきょは もっているのですか

15. From whom do you want to learn to drive? / From whom did you learn to drive?

だれに うんてんを ならいたいですか / だれに うんてんを おしえてもらったの

16. Do your parents drive safely?

あなたの おやは あんぜん うんてん を しますか

17. Do your parents usually go through yellow lights?

あなたの おやは ふつう きいろい しんごうでも とおりますか

18. Do your parents drive fast?

あなたの おやは うんてん はやいですか

19. Are there lots of traffic accidents (in your city)?

いっぱい こうつうじこ は ありますか

20. Do you always wear a seatbelt?

いつも あなたは シートベルト を しますか

21. What kind of car does your family have?

あなたの かぞくは どの 車を もっていますか

22. By the way, what are you afraid (scared) of?

ところで、あなたは なにが こわいですか

23. With whom do you fight?

だれと けんかを しますか

24. How many keys do you carry?

カギ は なんこ もって いますか

25. What (do you do that) worries your parents?

おやは なにに しんぱい しますか

26. What time did you leave home this morning? And what time did you arrive at school?

けさ 何時に でかけましたか。何日寺に 学校へ つきましたか

27. What can be seen from the window of your room (at home)?

へや の まどから 何が 見えますか

28. What time does your father/mother usually leave home in the morning?

いつも 父や 母は 何時に いえを 出ますか。

29. Don't you mind even if the exam is tomorrow?

あした が しけん でも かまわないのですか

30. Don't you mind if the exam is very difficult?

しけん が むずかしくても かまわないのですか

GOOD JOB ☺

四課

てっぽう

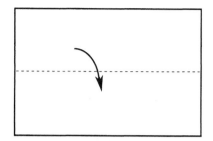

1. Take a rectangular sheet of paper. Fold in half lengthwise, crease, and open.

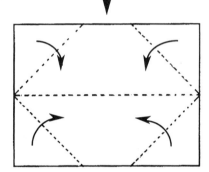

2. Fold each corner forward to the center crease.

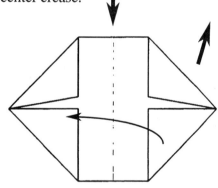

3. Fold in half vertically.

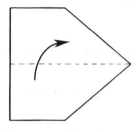

4. Fold in half horizontally.

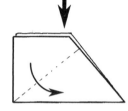

5. Fold the top left corner down, crease.

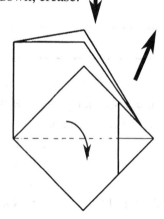

6. Open along the creased edge to form a partial square as shown in the illustration.

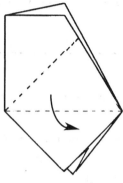

7. Turn to reverse and repeat the procedure to form a square.

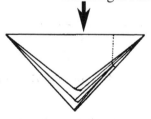

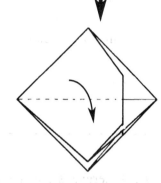

8. Fold in half lengthwise.

9. Hold at the right open corner.

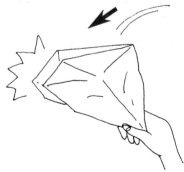

10. Swing downward with a quick snapping motion. The てっぽう should pop loudly!

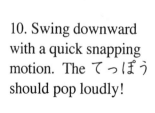

By the end of this lesson, you will be able to communicate the information below in the given situations.

【 II -5 タスク１】

A customer goes to a small Japanese restaurant for lunch. The waiter/waitress takes the order.

Waiter/Waitress:
(1) Welcome the customer and show him/her a seat, then give him/her a menu.
(2) Ask for his/her order.
(3) Bring his/her order. After the customer finishes, ask if he/she will have anything else.
(4) Direct the customer to the register. Tell him/her the total.
(5) Thank the customer and ask him/her to come again.

Customer:
(1) Look at the menu and pick an item that sounds delicious.
(2) Order a meal and drink.
(3) Say that you're full and ask for the check.

(4) Hand over the appropriate amount of money.
(5) Thank the waiter/waitress for the meal.

【 II -5 タスク２】

An American student and Japanese student go to a Japanese restaurant in the U.S. for dinner. They sit down at a table and look over the menu.

Japanese Student:
(1) Announce that you are very hungry. Decide on two dishes from the menu. Ask your friend what he/she would like to try.
(2) Use the appropriate expression before your meal. You are surprised because your food is so delicious. Ask your friend if he/she wants to try some.
(3) After you finish eating, use the appropriate after-meal expression.
(4) Thank your friend. Offer to leave the tip. Ask what percent (of the check) you should leave as a tip.

American Student:
(1) Decide on one dish from the menu. When the waiter/waitress comes, give your order and also ask for tea.

(2) Politely decline by making an excuse.

(3) Comment that you are very full. Offer to pay for both meals.
(4) Answer that a 15% tip is fine.

五課

139

五課

【会話 - Formal style】

＜レストランで＞

まり：あの　テーブルに　行きましょう。

ケン：ちょっと、ちょっと、まりさん、それは　いけません。
　　　　ここで　待って　いなければ　なりません。

ウェイトレス：いらっしゃいませ。　何人様ですか。

ケン：二人です。予約は　して　いないんですが...

ウェイトレス：けっこうですよ。どうぞ、こちらへ。メニューを　どうぞ。
　　　　＜After a while＞ 御注文は？

まり：私は　にぎりずしに　します。

ケン：ぼくは　お腹が　ペコペコですから、肉うどんと　親子どんぶりに
　　　　します。

ウェイトレス：ほかに　何か？

ケン：それだけです。

＜The waitress brings the food and they start eating.＞

ケン：いただきます。うどんは　はしで　食べなければ　なりませんか。

まり：いいえ、おはしで　食べなくても　いいんですよ。ケンさん、
　　　　にぎりずしを　一つ　食べて　みませんか。おいしいですよ。

ケン：いいえ、けっこうです。ぼくは　魚が　好きじゃないんですよ。
　　　　＜After the meal＞ ごちそうさま。おいしかったですね。おなかが
　　　　いっぱいです。今日は　ぼくが　ごちそう　しますよ。

五課　　　　　　　　　　　　140

まり：ありがとう。じゃ、私が　チップを　払いましょう。いくらぐらい
　　　置かなければ　なりませんか。

ケン：だいたい　十五パーセントぐらいです。

　　　<He calls the waitress.> すみません、お勘定を　お願いします。

ウェイトレス：ありがとう　ございました。あちらの　レジで　お願いします。

ケン：あっ、まりさん、さいふを　忘れました。すみませんが、お金を
　　　貸して　下さい。明日　返しますから。

まり：はい、はい。

141　　　　　　　　　　　　　　　　　　　　　　　　　五課

【 会話 - Normal style 】

<レストランで>

まり：あの　テーブルに　行こう。

ケン：ちょっと、ちょっと、まりさん、それは　だめだよ。

ここで　待って　いなきゃ　いけないよ。

ウェイトレス：いらっしゃいませ。　何人様ですか。

ケン：二人です。予約は　して　いないんですが...

ウェイトレス：けっこうですよ。どうぞ、こちらへ。メニューを　どうぞ。

<After a while> 御注文は？

まり：私は　にぎりずし。

ケン：ぼくは　おなかが　ペコペコだから、肉うどんと　親子どんぶり。

ウェイトレス：ほかに　何か？

ケン：それだけです。

<The waitress brings the food and they start eating.>

ケン：いただきます。うどんは　はしで　食べなきゃ　いけない？

まり：ううん、おはしで　食べなくても　いいのよ。ケン、にぎりずしを

一つ　食べて　みない？　おいしいわよ。

ケン：ううん、いらない。ぼくは　魚が　好きじゃないんだ。

<After the meal> ごちそうさま。おいしかったね。おなかが

いっぱいだ。今日は　ぼくが　ごちそう　するよ。

まり：ありがとう。じゃ、私が　チップを　払おうね。いくらぐらい

置かなきゃ　いけない？

ケン：だいたい　十五パーセントぐらいだよ。

<He calls the waitress.> すみません、お勘定、お願いします。

ウェイトレス：ありがとう　ございました。あちらの　レジで　お願いします。

ケン：あっ、まりさん、さいふを　忘れた。ごめん、お金を　貸して。

明日　返すから。

まり：も～う。

Let's review previous vocabulary!

A. めいし Nouns

1. レストラン	restaurant	8. おなか	stomach
2. それ	that	9. （お）はし	chopsticks
3. ここ	here	10. さかな	fish
4. 何人〔なんにん〕さま	how many (people)? [polite]	11. 今日	today
5. 二人	two (people)	12. いくらぐらい	about how much?
6. 私	I	13. お金	money
7. ぼく	I [used by males]	14. あした	tomorrow

B. どうし Verbs

15. 行きましょう〔G1 行く／行って〕 — let's go
16. いけません — won't do
17. わすれました〔G2 わすれる／わすれて〕 — forgot
18. かして　下さい〔G1 かす／かします〕 — please lend

C. -い けいようし I Adjectives

19. いい	good	21. おいしい	delicious, tasty
20. おいしかった	was delicious, was tasty		

D. -な けいようし NA Adjectives

22. すきじゃないんです — do not like

E. Expressions

23. ちょっと、ちょっと	Just a minute, just a minute.
24. おなかが　ペコペコです。	I am terribly hungry.
25. いただきます。	[Expression used before a meal.]
26. いいえ、けっこうです。	No, thank you.
27. ごちそうさま。	[Expression used after a meal.]
28. ありがとう。	Thank you.
29. じゃ、	Then,
30. おねがいします。	Please do it.
31. ありがとう　ございました。	Thank you very much. [for something done in the past.]
32. すみませんが...	Excuse me, but . . .
33. はい、はい。	Okay, okay.

F. ぶんぽう Grammar

34. Sentence 1 + から、 Sentence 2。　　Sentence 1, so Sentence 2.

おなかが　ぺこぺこですから、はやく　食べたいです。

I am very hungry, so I want to eat early.

【会話】

Formal style:　　まり：う〜ん . . .　おいしそうですねえ。

ケン：何に　しますか。

まり：私は　にぎりずしに　します。

ケン：ぼくは　親子どんぶりに　肉うどんを　食べます。

Informal style:　　まり：う〜ん . . .　おいしそうねえ。

ケン：何に　する？

まり：私　にぎりずしに　するわ。

ケン：ぼくは　親子どんぶりに　肉うどんだ。

【文型】

おいし＋そうです。	looks delicious
something　に　します。	will have something ./ decide on something .
something　に　something	〜 and 〜 [A particle to combine two or more nouns.]

【単語】

1. う〜ん
Yummm . . .

2.（おいし）そうです
looks (delicious)

3. 〜に　します
decide on 〜

4. 〜に　〜
〜 and 〜 (as a set)

五課

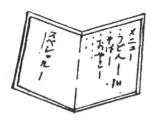

5. メニュー

menu

6. うどん

thick white noodles in broth

7. 肉〔にく〕うどん

うどん topped with beef

8. ざるそば

buckwheat noodles
(grey)
Served cold.

9. ラーメン

Chinese noodle soup
(yellow)
Also called ちゅうかそば.

10. 親子〔おやこ〕どんぶり

chicken and egg over a
bowl of steamed rice.
おや means "parent" and
子 means "child."

11. とんかつ

pork cutlet

12. カレーライス
or ライスカレー
or カレー

curry rice

13. (お)みそしる

soup flavored with
miso (soy bean paste).

五課

14. 焼き肉〔やきにく〕

meat grilled over a fire

やきます means to cook or to grill.

15. 焼き鳥〔やきとり〕

grilled skewered chicken

16. にぎりずし

sushi rice shaped in bite-sized rectangles topped with fish, roe, shellfish, vegetables, or egg. にぎります means "to grasp."

【*オプショナル単語】

1. *ぎょうざ

* Japanese pot stickers

2. *焼きそば

* fried noodles

3. *そうめん

* thin white noodles served cold

【漢字】

1. 川 river 　かわ 　川口〔かわぐち〕さん
　　　　　　　　がわ 　小川〔おがわ〕さん

五課

2. 山　　mountain　　やま　　山口〔やまぐち〕さん,山本〔やまもと〕さん,

　　　　　　　　　　　　　　　大山〔おおやま〕さん,小山〔こやま〕さん,

　　　　　　　　　　　　　　　中山〔なかやま〕さん,山下〔やました〕さん

　　　　　　　　サン　　富士山〔ふじさん or ふじやま〕Mt. Fuji

3. 出　　go out　　で（る）出かけます leave,出て　下さい。Please get out.

　　　　　　　　　　　　　よく　出来ました。did well,出口〔でぐち〕exit

　　　　　　　だ（す）出して　下さい。Please turn it in.

　　　　　　　　　　　スピードを　出す speed up

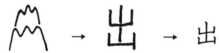

A series of mountain peaks coming out of the earth.

【文法】

A. Noun + に　します　　　　　　　　　　decide on ～

This construction is used when the subject chooses an item, or decides on a certain item. This is often used in restaurants or while shopping, or other situations that require selecting one thing over others.

---

1. ぼくは　ピザと　コーラに　します。　　　　I will have pizza and a coke.

2. 私は　おすしに　しましょう。　　　　　　(I guess) I'll have *sushi*.

3.「何に　しますか。」　　　　　　　　　　"What will you have?"

　「そうですねえ...　肉うどんに　します。」　"Let me see . . . I'll have beef *udon*."

B. い Adjective [Stem form] 　　　+ そうです。　　looks, appears

　　な Adjective 　　　　　　　　　+ そうです。

　　　　Verb [Stem form] 　　　　　+ そうです。

This construction is used to describe the appearance of the subject under discussion. It suggests that the speaker is unsure of his/her statement, which is based on his/her observations or inferences.

五課　　　　　148

いいです becomes よさそうです which means "looks good." ないです becomes なさそうです which means "looks like there is not/does not exist." Only certain verbs can be used with そうです. Nouns are not used with そうです.

1. 今日は　あつそうですねえ。　　　　　　It looks hot today, doesn't it?

2. あの　学生は　頭が　よさそうですね。　That student over there looks smart, doesn't he?

3. この　レストランは　静かそうですねえ。This restaurant looks quiet, doesn't it!

4. あの　人は　テニスが　上手そうですねえ。That person looks skillful at tennis!

5. あの　人は　お金が　なさそうです。　That person looks like he doesn't have any money.

6. 今日は　雨が　ふりそうですねえ。　　It looks like it will rain today.

7. あかちゃんが　なきそうです。　　　　The baby looks like she will cry.

C. Noun に　Noun　　　" ~ and ~ "

The particle に may be used to combine two or more nouns that are usually considered part of a set.
に implies that one or more than one object has been added to the first object.

1. 朝ご飯は　毎日　パンに　コーヒーです。　Every day, my breakfast is bread and coffee.

2. 「何を　買いましたか。」　　　　　　"What did you buy?"

「シャツに　ズボンに　ぼうしを　買いました。」"I bought a shirt, pants, and a hat."

【 ● ぶんかノート】

1. *Zarusoba*

Zarusoba is a favorite noodle dish. During the summer, it can be found at almost any Japanese restaurant. The noodles are made from a combination of buckwheat and wheat flour, and have a grayish brown color. They are served cold on a bamboo mat in a square or round lacquered box. Thin strips of *nori* (dried seaweed) are sprinkled over the noodles.

A soy-based dipping sauce accompanies the noodles in a small dish. Condiments such as minced *negi* (green onions) and *wasabi* (horseradish) are served alongside the dipping sauce in tiny dishes.

To eat the noodles, one may add the desired condiments to the dipping sauce. One then dips bite-sized amounts of noodles into the broth with chopsticks and eats with a slurping sound. At certain restaurants, the broth in which the *soba* was boiled is provided in a small, often square teapot-looking container. It may be added to the dipping sauce, then drunk as a broth after the meal.

Zarusoba

五課

メニュー

あさごはん （月曜日から土曜日まで午前11時まで）

ホットケーキ	３００円	フレンチトースト	３００円
バタートースト（ジャムつき）	２００円	ハムとコーンのオムレツ	５００円
モーニングセット（トースト、ミニサラダ、ゆでたまご、コーヒーつき）			４００円

お食事 （毎日まで午前11時から）

セットにはスープかミニサラダと、ライスかパンと、
アイスクリームかシャーベットと、コーヒーかこうちゃが　つきます。

ステーキ	１０００円	ステーキセット	１３００円
ハンバーグ	８００円	ハンバーグセット	１１００円
コロッケ	６００円	コロッケセット	９００円
カキフライ	９００円	カキフライセット	１２００円
ライス	１５０円	パン	１５０円

スープとサラダ

コーンスープ	３００円	今日のスープ	３００円
グリーンサラダ	３００円	ツナサラダ	３５０円

ピザとパスタとカレー

ツナとコーンのピザ	５００円	チーズピザ	４００円
ハムとパイナップルのピザ	５００円		
スパゲッティーミートソース	６００円	和風たらこスパゲッティー	６００円
スパゲッティーボンゴレ	６００円		
ビーフカレー	６００円	チキンカレー	６００円

うどん、そば、ラーメン、やきそば

肉うどん	４５０円	月見うどん	４００円
ざるそば	３５０円	きつねうどん	３５０円
ラーメン	３５０円	やきそば	４００円

和食
定食はごはんとみそしるとつけものつきです。

とんかつ	７００円	とんかつ定食	１０００円
てんぷら	７００円	てんぷら定食	１０００円
さしみ	８００円	さしみ定食	１１００円
すし　（１０こ）	９００円	すし定食	１２００円
焼き鳥　（５本）	６００円	焼き鳥定食	９００円
焼き肉	７００円	焼き肉定食	１０００円
みそしる	２００円	ごはん	１００円

どんぶり

親子どんぶり	６００円	牛どん	７００円
天どん	７００円	かつどん	７００円

デザート

プリン	３５０円	アイスクリーム	３５０円
シャーベット	３５０円	チーズケーキ	３５０円
チョコレートケーキ	３５０円	チョコレートサンデー	６００円
いちごパフェ	５５０円	あんみつ	５００円

お飲み物

アメリカンコーヒー	３５０円	コーヒー	３５０円
アイスコーヒー	３５０円	紅茶	３５０円
ミルク	３００円	トマトジュース	３５０円
オレンジジュース	４００円	コーラ	３５０円
ウーロン茶	３５０円	ココア	４００円
クリームソーダ	４５０円	レモンスカッシュ	４００円

五課

2. おすしのバラエティー：Varieties of *Sushi*

にぎりずし

hand-molded *sushi*

ちらしずし

loose garnished *sushi*

まきずし

rolled *sushi*

いなりずし

cone *sushi*

てまきずし

hand-rolled *sushi*

【👩👩アクティビティー】

A. ペアワーク

Look at the *sushi* menu and ask your partner the following questions. Write your partner's answers.

Ex. Which looks delicious?

質問：「どれが　おいしそうですか。」

答え：「～が　おいしそうです。」

1. どれが　たかそうですか。	にぎりずし
2. どれが　やすそうですか。	まきずし
3. どれが　おいしそうですか。	てまきずし
4. どれが　すきですか。	いなりずし
5. どれが　きらいですか。	ちらしずし

B. ペアワーク

Ask your partner what he/she will have today from the menu on the previous pages. Write your partner's response.

質問：「何に　しますか。」

答え：「そうですねえ...　私は　～に　します。」

何に　しますか。
そうですねえ...　私は　にぎりずしに　します。

C. クラスワーク - うた

おやこどんぶり

津川 主一 作詩
作曲者不詳

五課

【会話】

Formal style:　　ケン：うどんは　はしで　食べなければ　なりませんか。

　　　　　　　　　まり：いいえ、おはしで　食べなくても　いいんですよ。

Informal style:　ケン：うどんは　はしで　食べなきゃ　いけない？

　　　　　　　　　まり：ううん、はしで　食べなくても　いいのよ。

【文型】

Verb [NAI form] (ーな)ければ　なりません いけません	have to do ~
Verb [NAI form] (ーな)くても　いいです かまいません	do not have to do ~

【単語】

1. チップ
tip

2. テーブル
table

3. (お)かんじょう
a check; bill

7.		%
	1	いっパーセント
	2	にパーセント
	3	さんパーセント
	4	よんパーセント
	5	ごパーセント
	6	ろくパーセント
	7	ななパーセント
	8	はっパーセント
	9	きゅうパーセント
	10	じ(ゅ)っパーセント
	?	なんパーセント

4. レジ
cash register

5. だいたい
generally, approximately [Adv.]

6. なりません
(it) won't do

五課

8. 食べなければ　なりません

[G2 食べる]

have to/ should eat

lit., If (you) do not eat, it won't do.

9. 食べなくても　いいです

[G2 食べる]

do not have to/ no need to eat

lit., Even if (you) do not eat, it is okay.

10. 予約(を)　します

[IR よやく(を)　する]

to make a reservation

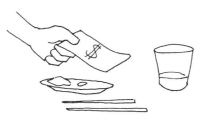

11. 注文(を)　します

[IR ちゅうもん(を)　する]

to order

12. 置きます

[G1 おく]

to put, leave

13. 払います

[G1 はらう]

to pay

【＊オプショナル単語】

1. ＊とりけします [G1 とりけす]　　＊ to cancel

1. 先　　first, previous　　セン　　　　　　　先生 teacher, 先月〔せんげつ〕last month,

先週 last week

と　→　ρ　→　ノ　＋

※　→　土　→　土　＋

⺍　→　ル　→　儿　＝　先

First, the teacher points the way to go on the ground.

2. 生　　be born　　　　う（まれる）　　生まれました was born

person　　　セイ　　　　　先生〔せんせい〕teacher

学生〔がくせい〕college student

生徒〔せいと〕 pre-college student

と　→　ρ　→　ノ　＋

※　→　生　→　主　＝　生

Sprouts point upward from layers of earth.

【文法】

> A. Verb NAI form (ーな)ければ　なりません
> 　　　　　　　　　　　　いけません
>
> This construction is used when one wants to express "have to (do)" or "must (do)." It is constructed by dropping the final -i of the verb NAI form and adding the extender - *kereba narimasen* or - *kereba ikemasen*.

1. 今　授業に　行かなければ　なりません。　　　I have to go to class now.

2. 明日までに　この　本を　読まなければ　なりません。

I have to read this book by tomorrow.

3. 早く　帰らなければ　いけませんよ。　　　　I have to return home early, you know.

4. 明日　試験が　ありますから、勉強しなければ　なりません。

Since I have a test tomorrow, I have to study.

B. Verb NAI form (ーな)くても　いいです

かまいません

This is the negative equivalent of the previously introduced permission pattern. It is formed by taking the verb NAI form, dropping the final -い, and adding ーくても　いいです／ーくても　かまいません. It is literally translated as "it is all right even if (you) don't," but is also often used in situations where English speakers would say "(you) don't have to." This pattern would be an appropriate negative reply to a question asked in the なければ　なりませんか pattern.

　　Ex.「あした　行かなければ　なりませんか。」　"Do I have to go tomorrow?"

　　　「いいえ、行かなくても　いいですよ。」　"No, you don't have to go."

---

1. お昼ご飯を　食べなくても　いいです。　　I don't have to eat lunch.

2. 明日　学校へ　来なくても　いいです。　　You don't have to come to school tomorrow.

3. 「今日　出さなければ　なりませんか。」　"Do (we) have to turn (it) in today?"

　「いいえ、今日　出さなくても　かまいません。」

"No, I don't mind if you don't turn it in today."

4. 漢字で　書かなくても　いいです。　　It is all right even if you don't write with *kanji*.

【 ● ぶんかノート】

1. *Tempura*

The popular Japanese food known as *tempura* is said to have originated with the Portuguese missionaries who arrived in Japan during the latter part of the 16th century. Japanese often use fish, shrimp, squid, and vegetables (e.g., eggplant, green peppers, sweet potatoes, pumpkin, green beans, mushrooms, lotus root, carrots, etc.) to make these deep-fried fritters. When eaten, *tempura* is dipped in a soy-sauce-based broth. Grated *daikon* (winter radish) and grated ginger may be added to the dipping sauce for greater flavor. Often the word *tempura* is written in Japanese as 天ぷら, though it is not related to "heaven" in any way. *Tempura* lovers, however, will tell you that well-made てんぷら is heavenly to eat!

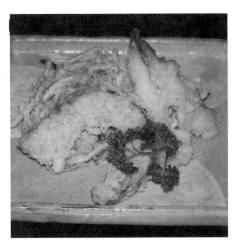

五課

2. Chopstick Etiquette

Chopsticks are versatile eating utensils. Once one has mastered their use, one must be careful to observe chopstick etiquette. Here are some "don'ts" to remember:

One must **not**:

1. vertically roll chopsticks between one's open palms.
2. rub chopsticks against each other (to remove splinters).
3. vertically stick one's chopsticks into a bowl of rice.
4. lay chopsticks along the right or left of one's dishes as one would do with spoons, forks or knives. They should be placed parallel to the edge of the table horizontally below the dishes closest to the person eating the meal. The pointed end of the chopsticks should rest on a はしおき, or chopstick rest. This chopstick rest is often a small ceramic, glass or wooden piece. It may be simple, or be fashioned into the shape of an animal, food, flower, etc.
5. pass food to or from another person from chopstick to chopstick.
6. stab one's food with the chopsticks.
7. bite or suck the chopsticks.
8. use chopsticks to slide dishes across the table.

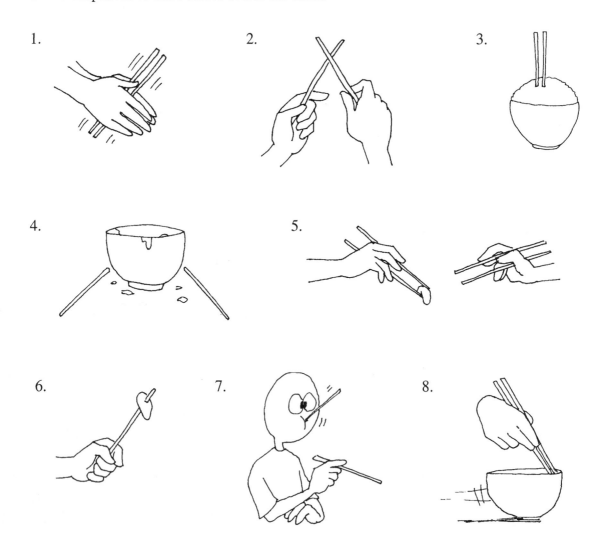

【😊😊アクティビティー】

A. ペアワーク

This is your schedule for today. Fill in the blanks with times that are appropriate for you. Ask your partner about his/her schedule for today, then jot down the answers in the second block below. After you have finished asking each other questions, compare your answers and see how successfully you have communicated with one another.

My schedule for today: Write your schedule.
私は　今日 ＿＿＿＿＿＿に　起きなければ　なりませんでした。
私は　今日 ＿＿＿＿＿＿に　うちを　出なければ　なりませんでした。
私は　今日 ＿＿＿＿＿＿に　学校へ　来なければ　なりませんでした。
私は　今日 ＿＿＿＿＿＿に　家へ　帰らなければ　なりません。
私は　今日 ＿＿＿＿＿＿に　寝なければ　なりません。

Your partner's schedule: Ask your partner for his/her schedule and write the answers below.
Ex.「～さんは　今日　何時に　起きなければ　なりませんでしたか。」
＿＿＿さんは　今日 ＿＿＿に　起きなければ　なりませんでした。
＿＿＿さんは　今日 ＿＿＿に　うちを　出なければ　なりませんでした。
＿＿＿さんは　今日 ＿＿＿に　学校へ　来なければ　なりませんでした。
＿＿＿さんは　今日 ＿＿＿に　家へ　帰らなければ　なりません。
＿＿＿さんは　今日 ＿＿＿に　寝なければ　なりません。

五課

B. ペアワーク

Ask your partner these questions. Your partner gives complete answers based on fact.

Ex. 質問：「今日　日本語の　宿題を　しなければ　なりませんか。」

答え：「はい、しなければ　なりません。」

or 「いいえ、しなくても　いいです。」

しつもん	はい	いいえ
1. 今日　日本ごの　しゅくだいを　しなければ　なりませんか。		
2. 今日　ばんごはんを　うちで　食べなければ　なりませんか。		
3. 日曜日に　きょうかい(church)へ　行かなければ　なりませんか。		
4. 今日　はやく　うちへ　かえらなければ　なりませんか。		

C. ペアワーク

You are in Japan. Your Japanese friend takes you to a Japanese restaurant. You are worried about what to do there and ask many questions. Your Japanese friend answers your questions.

Ex. 質問：「くつ下を　はかなければ　なりませんか。」

答え：「はい、はかなければ　なりません。」

or 「いいえ、はかなくても　いいです。」

しつもん	はい	いいえ
1. レストランの　よやくを　しなければ　なりませんか。		
2. たたみに　すわらなければ　なりませんか。		
3. おはしで　たべなければ　なりませんか。		
4. チップを　あげなければ　なりませんか。		
5. おかんじょうは　キャッシュで　はらわなければ　なりませんか。		

5課－3: LET'S TRY TO EAT.

【会話】

Formal style: まり：リサさん、にぎりずしを　一つ　食べて　みませんか。

リサ：いいえ、けっこうです。私は　魚が　にがてなんです。

Informal style: まり：リサさん、にぎりずし　一個　食べて　みない？

リサ：ううん、けっこう。私　魚が　にがてなの。

【文型】

Verb (TE form) ＋ みます。	will try doing ～
みましょう。	Let's try doing ～
みませんか。	Would you like to try doing ～? [Invitation]
みて　下さい。	Please try doing ～. [Request]
みたいです。	I want to try doing ～.

【単語】

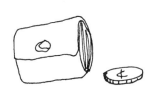

1. さいふ
wallet

2. (食べて) みます
will try (eating)

5. General counter

Used for small objects that take the ひとつ, ふたつ series, but used more conversationally.

1	いっこ
2	にこ
3	さんこ
4	よんこ
5	ごこ
6	ろっこ
7	ななこ
8	はっこ
9	きゅうこ
10	じ(ゅ)っこ
?	なんこ？

3. ごちそう(を) する
[IR ごちそう(を) します]
to treat (someone) to a meal

4. 返します
[G1 かえす]
to return (something)

五課

【漢字】

1. 父　father　　　ちち　　　　　　　父 one's own father
　　　　　　　　　　とう　　　　　　　お父さん someone else's father

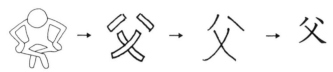

A Japanese father with upright shoulders sits cross-legged.

2. 母　mother　　　はは　　　　　　　母 one's own mother
　　　　　　　　　　かあ　　　　　　　お母さん someone else's mother

A mother's job is to caress her baby with her two arms as she breastfeeds it.

【文法】

A. Verb TE form ＋みます

This pattern is constructed by taking the verb in its TE form and attaching みます or other conjugated forms of みます. It means "try and do...." It is generally used in a context where the subject will "do something and find out (something about it)." The *kanji* 見 is not used for this みます because this みます means "to try," not to see with one's eyes.

食べて　みます。	I'll try eating.
食べて　みましょう。	Let's try eating./ Let me try eating.
食べて　みませんか。	Would you like to try eating (it)? [Invitation]
食べて　みて　下さい。	Please try eating. [Request]
食べて　みたいです。	I want to try eating.

1. おすしを　食べて　みましょう。　　　　Let's try eating *sushi*.

2. この　ドレスを　着て　みます。　　　　I will try wearing this dress.

3. この　くつを　はいて　みて　下さい。　Please try wearing these shoes.

4. 私は　来年　日本へ　行って　みたいです。　I want to try going to Japan next year.

【 ● ぶんかノート】

1. What Does -やき Mean?

   Many foreigners are familiar with the word "*teriyaki*." The word "*yaki*," which comes from the verb "*yakimasu*" or "*yaku*," means "to burn, bake, roast, toast, broil, grill, char, or fry." Any food prepared in these ways often includes the word "*yaki*," e.g., *yakisoba, misoyaki, yakiniku, shioyaki, sukiyaki, yakitori*, etc. Can you think of any others? The left radical of the *kanji* for *yaki* (焼), which is the fire radical, also clearly tells us the meaning of this character.

2. Tipping in Japan

   It is not customary to tip in Japan. Recently, however, some restaurants or other service-oriented businesses may indicate to customers that a tip is already included in the bill.

【 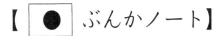 アクティビティー】

A. ペアワーク

   You see something and share your impression of it with your friend. Your friend suggests that you try it.

   Ex. This cake looks delicious.

   You: 「この　ケーキは　おいしそうですねえ。」

   Your friend: 「そうですねえ。じゃ、食べて　みましょう。」

1.

   looks delicious
   おいし（い）

2.

   looks interesting
   おもしろ（い）

3.

   looks cheap
   やす（い）

4.

   looks good
   いい or よ（い）

五課

5.
looks fun
たのし（い）

6.
looks delicious
おいし（い）

7.
looks cold
つめた（い）

8.
looks expensive
たか（い）

B. ペアワーク

You are working at a store and want to sell the items below to a customer. You recommend that the customer try them. The customer (your partner) decides to try them and comments on them. Switch roles.

Ex. くつ

Clerk:　「この　くつは　とても　いいですよ。はいて　みませんか。」

Customer:　「じゃ、ちょっと　はいて　みましょう。
　　　　　　あ、ちょっと　小さいですね。」

1.チョコレート	
2.ジュース	
3.ペン	
4.サングラス	
5.ＣＤプレーヤー	
6.コンピューター	
7.車	
8.ぼうし	

5課－4：WELCOME!

【会話】

Formal style:

ウェイトレス：いらっしゃいませ。何人様ですか。

ケン：二人です。

ウェイトレス：どうぞ　こちらへ。メニューを　どうぞ。

【単語】

1. ウェイター
waiter

2. ウェイトレス
waitress

3. こちら, そちら, あちら, どちら？
here, there, over there, where?
Polite equivalent of ここ, そこ, あそこ, どこ.

4. いらっしゃいませ。
Welcome.

5. どうぞ　こちらへ。
This way, please.

6. ごちゅうもんは？
May I take your order?
[lit., What is your order?]

7. ほかに　何か？
Anything else?

8. それだけです。
That's all.
[lit., It is only that.]

9. すみません。
Excuse me.
[to get someone's attention]

五課

【漢字】

1. 毎　every　　マイ　　　　毎日 every day, 毎月〔まいつき〕every month,
　　　　　　　　　　　　　　　　毎年〔まいねん or まいとし〕every year,
　　　　　　　　　　　　　　　　毎週 every week, 毎食〔まいしょく〕every meal

Mother points out the one correct way every time.

2. 書　write　　か（く）　　書いて　下さい。Please write.
　　　writing　ショ　　　　教科書 textbook, 辞書 dictionary, 図書館 library,
　　　　　　　　　　　　　　書道 calligraphy

You write with a brush using your five fingers during the day.

【 🔴 ぶんかノート】

Western Food in Japan

ステーキ

ハンバーグ

スパゲッティ

五課　　　　　　　　　　　166

コロッケ croquettes

サラダ

スープ

When one dines in Japan and orders "American food" at a Japanese-owned restaurant, the foods will often appear as they do above. The food is somewhat "Japanized." Portions are smaller and are presented in a very appealing way.

【アクティビティー】

A. ペアワーク

Role play with your partner. (ウェイ represents a waiter or a waitress and きゃく is a customer.)

1. ウェイ：いらっしゃいませ。何人様^{さま}ですか。

   きゃく：一人です。

   ウェイ：どうぞ　こちらへ。メニューを　どうぞ。

   <After a while.>

   ウェイ：御注文^{ごちゅうもん}は？

   きゃく：ラーメンと　ギョウザに　します。

   ウェイ：ほかに　何か？

   きゃく：それだけです。

2. きゃく：すみません。お勘定^{かんじょう}を　お願^{ねが}いします。

   ウェイ：ありがとう　ございました。あちらの　レジで　お願^{ねが}いします。

3. ケン／まり：いただきます。

   <Ken eats Chinese noodles and Mari eats sushi.>

   まり：おすし、一つ　どうぞ。

   ケン：ありがとう。でも、けっこう。ぼく、おなかが　いっぱい。

   ケン／まり：ごちそうさま。

Find the answers from books, by talking to friends, or by using the Internet.

1. In a traditional Japanese restaurant, where would you find the menu?

2. Many Japanese restaurants display plastic models of their dishes in their windows. What do you think of this practice? Should U.S. restaurants adopt this practice?

3. Name different types of major dishes available at the Japanese restaurant in your area (if there is one!).

4. In traditional Japanese restaurants, restaurants serve only very specific things, such as *sushi* or *yakitori*. Thus, you would not be able to go to a *sushi-ya* and order *udon* or curry rice. Is there any equivalent in terms of American food?

5. What kinds of foods can be found in a traditional Japanese breakfast?

6. Why are Japanese as a whole healthier than Americans? How is their diet different?

7. How much does a box of corn flakes cost in America? How much does a box of corn flakes cost in Japan?

8. Is it common practice to tip waiters or waitresses in Japan?

FUN CORNER 5: おや子どんぶり OYAKODONBURI

A simple but favorite dish of the Japanese is *oyakodonburi*. It is a complete meal contained in a deep, large bowl filled partially with rice and topped with cooked chicken, vegetables, eggs, and broth. The dish is served in the bowl with a matching lid, which helps to conserve the heat and keeps the food steaming until ready to be eaten. *Oyako* means "parent and child." This, of course, refers to the fact that this dish contains both chicken (parent) and egg (child). *Donburi* is the word for the bowl that holds this dish, but also refers to any dish served in this deep bowl. Other favorite *donburi* dishes include *tanindonburi* and *katsudon*. In contrast to the chicken and egg, the main ingredients of tanin *donburi* are beef and egg. The combination of these two unrelated ingredients resulted in an appropriate name for this dish, as the word *tanin* means "unrelated" or "outsider." *Katsudon* is prepared in much the same way as *oyakodonburi* and *tanindonburi*, but its main ingredient is pork cutlet. *Donburi* dishes, called *donburimono*, are generally served with soup and pickled vegetables.

Let's try and make some delicious *oyakodonburi* for lunch or dinner!

Ingredients:

4 servings of cooked rice (to lightly fill four *donburi* bowls)

3/4 pound of chicken (breast or thighs)

4 pieces of dried mushroom

several stalks of watercress

4 eggs

small, thinly sliced *nori** for garnish (optional)

Broth:

1/4 cup soy sauce

1/4 cup *mirin***

1 3/4 cups water

五課

Preparation:

1. Soak mushrooms in water ahead of time.
2. Slice chicken into thin pieces.
3. Wash watercress thoroughly and cut into 1 1/2 inch pieces.
4. Beat eggs well in a container. When serving in individual bowls, separate eggs into four portions.
5. After mushrooms have softened, remove stems and cut into small pieces.

Preparing the broth and cooking:

1. Quickly boil all broth ingredients together.
2. Remove from heat.
3. Add chicken and mushrooms and let boil.
4. Immediately lower heat and remove scum that may have surfaced to the top of the broth.
5. Cook for 2 - 3 minutes.
6. Separate into four equal portions. Cook a portion at a time hereafter.
7. Pour one portion of beaten egg over the cooked mixture and let cook over low heat for 20 - 30 seconds.
8. Fill the *donburi* bowl about 2/3 full with hot rice.
9. Gently pour mixture over rice.
10. Garnish with slivers of *nori*. (Optional)
11. Cover with lid if available and serve hot.

いただきましょう!!!

* *nori* - thin, seasoned seaweed
* *mirin - a sweet cooking seasoning containing corn syrup, water, rice wine and vinegar.
   May substitute 3 tablespoons of rice wine with 1 tablespoon of sugar.

My child made *oyakodonburi* at home!

_____
Your parent's signature.

五課   170

By the end of this lesson, you will be able to communicate the information below in the given situations.

【 II -6 タスク1】

Student A has been absent from school for a week. Student B is worried and calls to ask how he/she is.

Student A:
(1) You answer the phone.
(2) Acknowledge that it is you.
(3) Say that you caught a cold and have a high fever.

(4) Tell your friend that you plan to turn in the report next week.

Student B:
(1) Identify yourself and ask for your friend.
(2) Ask what happened.
(3) Express sympathy. Remind your friend that there is an English report that is supposed to be turned in tomorrow.
(4) Say that it can't be helped, and tell your friend to take care of him/herself.

【 II -6 タスク2】

Student A is still absent from school and is worried about his/her school work. He/she calls the teacher at home.

Student A:
(1) Call the teacher's residence and ask for your teacher by name (politely).
(2) Identify yourself.
(3) Explain that you could not study at all because you have been sick for four days.
(4) Answer yes. You had a sore throat and a fever as high as 100 degrees. You have to take medication three times a day.
(5) Express your appreciation and tell your teacher that you plan to go back to school tomorrow.

Teacher:
(1) Acknowledge that it is you.

(2) Ask the student how he/she's feeling.
(3) Express sympathy. Ask if the student has a cold.

(4) Tell your student that there is supposed to be an exam tomorrow, but he/she does not have to take it (tomorrow).
(5) Tell the student not to worry and to rest well.

六課

【会話 - Formal style】

<The telephone rings at the Smith's residence.>

まり：もしもし、スミスさんの　お宅ですか。

ケンの母：はい、そうです。

まり：まりですが、ケンさん　いらっしゃいますか。

ケンの母：あのう、ケンは　病気で　寝ていますが ...

まり：もう　一週間も　学校を　休んでいますが、大丈夫ですか。

ケンの母：あ、ケンが　来ましたから、ちょっと　待って　下さいね。

<Ken comes to the telephone.>

ケン：もしもし、まりさん、かわりました。

まり：どう　しましたか。具合が　悪いんですか。

ケン：風邪を　ひきました。先週は　熱が　三十九度も　あって、夜
　　　寝ることが　出来ませんでした。お腹も　変で、あまり
　　　食べることが　出来ませんでした。毎日　三度も　薬を
　　　飲まなければ　なりませんでした。明日　日本語の　試験が
　　　あるはずですが、学校へは　行かないつもりです。

まり：気の毒に。

ケン：頭が　痛くて、漢字も　単語も　覚えることが　出来ません。

まり：あまり　心配しなくても　いいです。仕方が　ないですよ。
　　　よく　休んで　下さい。じゃ、お大事に。

<The telephone rings at the Smith's residence.>

まり：もしもし、スミスさんの　お宅ですか。

ケンの母：はい、そうです。

まり：まりですが、ケンさん　いらっしゃいますか。

ケンの母：あのう、ケンは　病気で　寝てるけど...

まり：もう　一週間も　学校を　休んで　ますが、大丈夫ですか。

ケンの母：あ、ケンが　来たから、ちょっと　待ってね。

<Ken comes to the telephone.>

ケン：もしもし、まりさん、かわったよ。

まり：どう　したの？　具合が　悪いの？

ケン：風邪を　ひいたんだ。先週は　熱が　三十九度も　あって、夜　寝ることが　出来なかったよ。お腹も　変で、あんまり　食べることが　出来なかったんだ。毎日　三度も　薬を　飲まなきゃ　いけなかったよ。明日　日本語の　試験が　あるはずだけど、学校へは　行かないつもりなんだ。

まり：気の毒に。

ケン：頭が　痛くて、漢字も　単語も　覚えることが　出来ないんだ。

まり：あまり　心配しなくても　いいわ。仕方が　ないわよ。よく　休んでね。じゃ、お大事に。

Let's review the previous vocabulary!

A. めいし　Nouns

1. スミスさん	Mr./Ms. Smith	9. 毎日〔まいにち〕	every day
2. びょうき	sickness, illness	10. くすり	medicine
3. 学校	school	11. あした	tomorrow
4. 先週〔せんしゅう〕	last week	12. 日本語〔にほんご〕	Japanese language
5. ねつ	fever	13. しけん	exam
6. よる	night	14. あたま	head
7. こと	thing [intangible]	15. かんじ	Chinese characters
8. おなか	stomach		

B. どうし　Verbs

16. ねて　います〔G2 ねる／ねます／ねない〕　　　　　is sleeping
17. やすんで　います〔G1 やすむ／やすみます／やすまない〕　is absent
18. 来ました〔IR 来る／来て／来ない〕　　　　came
19. まって　下さい〔G1 まつ／まちます／またない〕　please wait
20. あって〔G1 ある／あります／ない〕　　　have, there is
21. のまなければ　なりませんでした　　　　had to drink, take (medicine)
　　〔G1 のむ／のみます／のんで〕
22. ある〔G1 あります／あって／ない〕　　　have, there is
23. 行かない〔G1 行く／行きます／行って〕　　do not go
24. しんぱいしなくても　いいです　　　　no need to worry
　　〔IR しんぱいする／します／して〕

C. -い けいようし　I Adjectives

25. いたくて〔いたい〕　　　　　painful, sore

D. -な けいようし　NA Adjectives

26. 大丈夫〔だいじょうぶ〕　　　all right

E. ふくし　Adverbs

27. もう + Affirmative	already	29. ちょっと	a little
28. あまり	(not) very	30. よく	well

F. Expressions

31. はい、そうです。　　　Yes, that's right.
32. どう　しましたか。　　What happened?
33. お大事〔だいじ〕に。　　Please take care.

【会話】

Formal style: まり：今日　学校を　休んでいましたが、いかがですか。

ケン：お腹が　痛くて、何も　食べることが　出来ませんでした。

まり：お気の毒に。

Informal style: まり：今日　学校を　休んでたけど、どう？

ケン：お腹が　痛くて、何も　食べることが　出来なかった。

まり：気の毒に。

【文型】

Noun ＋が　出来ます。	be able to do something
Verb (Dictionary form) ＋こと＋が　出来ます。	be able to do ～
Sentence 1 ＋けど、　　　　Sentence 2。	Although/Though S1, S 2.
けれど、	
けれども、	[Formal]

【単語】

1. 具合が　悪いです

〔ぐあいが　わるいです〕

condition is bad, feel sick

2. 風邪を　ひきました

[G1 かぜをひく]

caught a cold

3. (お)気の毒に。

〔(お)きのどくに〕

I am sorry.

[Sympathy - formal expression]

lit., It's poison to your spirit.

4. ストレスが いっぱいです
is very stressed
ストレスが おおいです。is very stressed
ストレスが ありません。have no stress

5. 問題〔もんだい〕
もんだい
problem

6. 変〔へん〕
へん
[な Adjective]
strange, weird, unusual

7. 弾きます
ひ
[G1 ひく]
to play (a string instrument)

8. 〜が 出来ます
[G2 できる]
be able to do 〜

9. Sentence 1 ＋けど、 Sentence 2。
けれど、
Although/Though S1, S2.

【＊オプショナル単語】
たんご

1. ＊ほねを おりました   ＊ (I) fractured a bone.

2. ＊ねんざ（を）しました   ＊ (I) sprained (something).

3. ＊インフルエンザに かかりました   ＊ have/had the flu

4. ＊食中毒〔しょくちゅうどく〕   ＊ food poisoning
どく

5. ＊水〔みず〕ぼうそう   ＊ chicken pox

6. ＊せきが でる   ＊ to cough

7. ＊ふきます   ＊ to play (a wind instrument)

8. ＊たたきます   ＊ to play (a percussion instrument)

【漢字】

1. 手　　　hand　　　て　　　右手 right hand, 左手 left hand, 苦手 is weak at

☆　　　上手〔じょうず〕skillful, 下手〔へた〕unskillful

 →  → 手

2. 耳　　　ear　　　みみ　　　右耳 right ear, 左耳 left ear, 小さい　耳 small ears

 → 耳

【文法】

A. Something ＋が　出来ます。	can do, be able to do (something)

1. 母は　少し　日本語が　出来ます。　　　My mom can speak Japanese a little.

2. 父は　全然　料理が　出来ません。　　　My father cannot cook at all.

3. 「ピアノが　出来ますか。」　　　"Can you play the piano?"

　「いいえ、出来ません。」　　　" No, I can't."

B. Verb Dictionary form ＋ ことが　出来ます。

This form is used to express one's ability to do something. It is used more frequently in writing than in speaking. It is also used in more formal speech.

---

1. 手が　痛くて、書くことが　出来ません。　　　My hands hurt, and I cannot write.

2. 漢字を　いくつ　読むことが　出来ますか。　　　How many Chinese characters can you read?

3. 「料理することが　出来ますか。」　　　"Are you able to cook?"

　「はい、出来ますが、あまり　上手ではありません。」

　　　"Yes, I can, but I'm not very good at it."

六課

4.「フランス語を 話すことが 出来ますか。」 "Can you speak French?"

　「いいえ、全然 話すことが 出来ません。」 "No, I can't speak at all."

5.「ピアノを 弾くことが 出来ますか。」 "Can you play the piano?"

　「少し 出来ますが、まだ 下手です。」 "I can play a little, but I'm still unskillful at it."

C. Sentence 1 ＋ けど／けれど、Sentence 2。　　　　　　Although/Though S1, S2.
けど／けれど is a sentence-connecting particle used like the sentence connector が, both in usage and meaning. けど is less formal than けれど and けれども.

---

1. 先週 病気でしたけど、今は 元気です。 Though I was sick last week, I'm fine now.
2. 勉強しましたけど、成績は 悪かったです。 Although I studied, my grade was bad.

【 ● ぶんかノート】

Centigrade and Fahrenheit

The Japanese follow the metric system. In measuring temperature, therefore, the Centigrade (せっし), rather than Fahrenheit (かっし) scale, is used. Normal body temperature, which is 98.6 degrees in Fahrenheit, is 37 degrees in Centigrade.

Centigrade ℃ = (Fahrenheit ℉ - 32) X 5 / 9

Centigrade ℃	Fahrenheit ℉
20	68.0
25	77.0
28	82.4
30	86.0
32	89.6
33	91.4
34	93.2
35	95.0
36	96.8
37	98.6

【👤👤アクティビティー】

A. ペアワーク

Ask your partner how he/she is. Your partner answers as indicated. Take turns.

Ex. I am a little tired.

質問：「どうですか。 or いかがですか。」
しつもん

答え：「ちょっと　つかれて　います。」
こた

1. I am fine.
2. I am a little sick.
3. I am very sleepy.
4. I am very tired.
5. I am stressed.
6. I have a little problem.
7. I am very busy.

B. ペアワーク

Your partner does not look well. You ask him/her what is the matter. Your partner answers accordingly. You express sympathy. Take turns.

Ex. headache

You ：「どう　しましたか。」

Partner：「あたまが　いたいんです。」

You ：「お気の毒に。」
き　どく

1. stomachache

2. sore throat

3. high fever

4. caught a cold

181

| 5. toothache | 6. voice is funny | 7. left foot is sore | 8. headache |

C. クラスワーク

Ask your classmates in Japanese if they can do the following things. Circulate around the room and ask your classmates these questions until you find a person who can answer affirmatively. Write the name of the person in the blank space.

質問：「泳ぐことが　出来ますか。」

答え：「はい、出来ます。」or「いいえ、出来ません。」

しつもん	なまえ
1. おもちを　つくることが　出来ますか。	
2. 日本りょうりを　つくることが　出来ますか。	
3. ひだり手で　書くことが　出来ますか。	
4. ギターを　ひくことが　出来ますか。	
5. 日本の　うたを　うたうことが　出来ますか。	
6. 車を　うんてんすることが　出来ますか。	
7. 中ごくごを　はなすことが　出来ますか。	
8. はやく　はしることが　出来ますか。	

【会話】

ケン：もしもし、山本さんの　お宅ですか。

まり：はい、そうです。

ケン：ケンですが、まりさん　いらっしゃいますか。

まり：私ですが . . .

【文型】

Omitting particles in conversations.	
Sentence + が . . .	[Softens the statement.]

【単語】

1. もしもし

Hello.

Used in telephone
conversations.

2. お宅
〔おたく〕

(someone's) house, residence

A polite equivalent of うち.

3. 留守です
〔るすです〕

is not at home

4. 話し中です
〔はなしちゅうです〕

line is busy

[lit., It is in the middle of talk.]

5. 電話を　かけます

[G2 でんわを　かける]

to make a phone call

6. いらっしゃいます

[G1 いらっしゃる]

exist, be (for animate)

A polite equivalent of います.
Irregular MASU form.

7. まちがえました

[G2 まちがえる]

made a mistake

8. かわりました

[G1 かわる]

It's me.

[lit., We've changed over.]

9. 残念ですが ...
〔ざんねんですが〕
Sorry, but . . .
[Used to decline invitations.
lit., It's disappointing, but...]

10. Sentence + が ...   [Softens the statement.]

11. 何度も〔なんども〕 many times

【＊オプショナル単語】

1. ＊伝言を　お願いします。   ＊ May I leave a message?
2. ＊ファックスを　おくる   ＊ to send a fax
3. ＊イーメール or 電子メール   ＊ e-mail
4. ＊メッセージ   ＊ message
5. ＊けいたい(電話)   ＊ cellular phone
6. ＊こちらは　〜です。   ＊ This is 〜 [Identifying self on telephone]
7. ＊留守番電話〔るすばんでんわ〕   ＊ telephone answering machine/voice mail

【漢字】

1. 門 gate   モン   学校〔がっこう〕の　門 school gate
                                   家の門 house gate

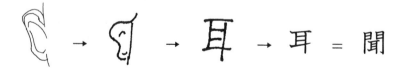

2. 聞 listen, hear   き（く）   聞きます listen
                            ブン   新聞 newspaper

A. Omitting particles in conversations.

It is quite common for Japanese to skip particles such as を, が, は and へ in informal conversations. The particles に, で, から, まで, と, etc. are not dropped as easily.

1.「私　ゆみですが、こうじさん　いますか。」   "I am Yumi. Is Kooji there?"

2.「コーヒー、飲みますか。」   "Do you drink coffee?"

3.「日本語、上手ですねえ。」   "You are so skillful in Japanese!"

B. Sentence + が ...

Japanese people tend to avoid directness in their speech. They often end sentences with が or けど and leave the sentences incomplete. The listener compensates by empathizing with the speaker and mentally completes the sentence in his/her own mind. Often the unmentioned portion of the sentence suggests a request or something the speaker does not want to express directly. The listener must respond accordingly. が or けど does not literally mean "but" in this case, but merely softens the directness of the sentence.

1.「山本ですが ... 」   "I am Yamamoto. [Expecting words from the listener.]"

2.「先生、分からないんですが ... 」   "Teacher, I don't understand. (Can you help me?)"

【 ● ぶんかノート】

1. 公衆電話（こうしゅうでんわ）Public phones

Since the debut of the cell phone, or mobile phone in Japan, traditional public phones are far less common than before. Public phones can still be found at airports, hotels, stations and some department stores in Japan. Public phones are either a bright lime green color or gray. The green phones are generally for domestic (within Japan) phone calls and gray phones are used for either domestic or international calls. Though both will take coins, it is best to buy a telephone card (テレホンカード) which can be purchased at vending machines, convenience stores, most hotels and some businesses. In hotels, do not confuse telephone cards with TV cards. TV cards (which look almost identical to telephone cards) are also sold in vending machines in order to view "pay per view" television programs.

2. 携帯電話（ケータイでんわ）Cell phones, also known as mobile phones.

In recent years, the ケータイ, derived from the word *keitaidenwa*, has become an essential part of the lives of Japanese. Almost everyone, with the exception of the most elderly, carry cell phones. While they still function as a communication tool, they also provide many Japanese with entertainment and information, function as daily organizers, serve as passes for public transportation and is even a source of e-cash! The ケータイ culture is an interesting recent phenomenon that reflects the lifestyle and social values of the Japanese.

【アクティビティー】

A. ペアワーク

You call your friend and invite him/her to an event. Carry on a telephone conversation. Your friend may either accept or decline your invitation. Switch roles.

Ex. There is a basketball game at the gym on Saturday from 6 p.m.

　　You ：「もしもし、(Partner's last name)さんの　お宅^{たく}ですか。」

　Friend ：「はい、そうです。」

　　You ：「(Own name) ですが、〜さんは　いらっしゃいますか。」

　Friend ：「はい、私ですが...」

　　You ：「土曜日の　午後六時^{ごごじ}から　体育館^{たいいくかん}で　バスケットの　試合^{しあい}が

　　　　　ありますが、いっしょに　行きませんか。」

　Friend ：「残念^{ざんねん}ですけど...　」

School dance Friday, 8:00 p.m. School gym	Concert Saturday, 7:30 p.m. Concert hall	Movie 8:20 p.m. Movie theater	Play （げき） 6:30 p.m. University

B. 二人か三人で

Carry on a telephone conversation in the following situations. Use your own names.

けんじの母　　山本けんじ

1. 三人で

You are in Japan now and call your Japanese friend 山本けんじ at home. His mother answers and calls けんじ for you. You then talk to けんじ.

2. 二人で

You try to call けんじ at home, but by mistake you call someone else's house. The person who answers the phone tells you that you have the wrong number. You admit you made a mistake and apologize.

3. 二人で

You call Yamamoto's house in Japan. Kenji's mother answers the phone and tells you Kenji is not at home and will be back around 6 p.m. You tell her you will call again around that time.

4. 二人で

You call your friend. Your friend complains and asks why you did not call him/her last night. You explain that you called many times, but the line was always busy.

5. 二人で

Your friend was absent from school today and you call him/her. You ask why he/she was absent. Your friend gives you a reason.

【会話】

Formal style:　まり：明日　学校へ　行きますか。

　　　　　　　　ケン：風邪で　まだ　熱が　高いから、試験が

　　　　　　　　　　　あるはずですが、学校へは　行かないつもりですよ。

Informal style:　まり：明日　学校へ　行く？

　　　　　　　　　ケン：風邪で　まだ　熱が　高いから、試験が

　　　　　　　　　　　　あるはずだけど、学校へは　行かないつもりだよ。

【文型】

Verb (Dictionary form) ＋つもりです。	I plan/intend to do 〜.
Verb (NAI form) ＋つもりです。	I do not plan/intend to 〜.
Verb (Dictionary form) ＋はずです。	is expected to do 〜, I expect 〜
Verb (NAI form) ＋はずです。	is not expected to do 〜, I do not expect 〜

【単語】

1. (行く／行かない) つもりです
　　plan to go, do not plan to go

2. (行く／行かない) はずです
　　I expect that he/she will/will not go.
　　He/she is expected to/not to go.

Not used to ask about a superior's intentions or plans.

六課　　　　　　　　188

3. （クラスを）取る
　　[G1 とります]
　　to take (a class)

4. （うんてんめんきょを）取る
　　[G1 とります]
　　to get (a driver's license)

5. 覚える
　　[G2 おぼえます]
　　to memorize

6. 仕方〔しかた〕が ありません。
or 仕方〔しかた〕が ないです。
It cannot be helped.

7. もちろん
of course

8. (reason) で
because of (reason)

【漢字】

1. 女　female　　おんな　　女の 人〔おんなの ひと〕 woman, lady
　　　　　　　　　　　　　　 女の 子〔おんなの こ〕 girl
　　　　　　　　　　　　　　 女の 学生〔おんなの がくせい〕 female student

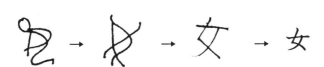

woman

六課

2. 好 like　　　　す（き）　　大好〔だいす〕き like very much

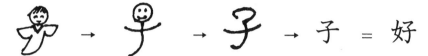

woman

child

Everyone likes girls (female children).

【文法】

A. Verb Dictionary form ＋つもりです。　　plan to do ～, intend to do ～

Verb NAI form ＋つもりです。　　　　　do not plan to ～, do not intend to ～

This construction is used to express an intent or plan to perform some action in the future. The dictionary form precedes the extender つもりです. This construction is generally not used when asking superiors of their intentions. The subject of a つもり sentence is generally first person. The second and the third person are used only in questions. The negation occurs before the extender つもり, not after. i. e., たべないつもりです. The past tense is formed after つもり, i.e., つもりでした.

---

1. 来年　日本へ　行くつもりです。　　　　Next year, I plan to go to Japan.

2. 今日　三時ごろ　帰るつもりです。　　　Today, I plan to return home at about 3 o'clock.

3. 今晩　十二時まで　寝ないつもりです。　Tonight, I don't plan to go to bed until 12 o'clock.

4. 図書館へは　行かないつもりです。　　　I don't plan to go to the library.

5. 昨日　買い物に　行くつもりでしたが、行きませんでした。

　　　　　　　　　　　　　　　　　　　I was planning to go shopping, but I didn't go.

6. クッキーを　食べないつもりでしたが、昨日 パーティーで　食べました。

　　　　　　　　　　　　　　　　　　　I was not planning to eat cookies, but I ate some at the party.

B. Verb Dictionary form / NAI form ＋はずです。　　　　to expect, is/is not expected to do

The supposition pattern is used when the speaker expects that a certain action or event will occur. The negation occurs with the verb (NAI form) and not at the end of the extender. The subject of a はず sentence is generally a third person. If the subject is the first person, then the sentence implies that someone else has an expectation that the speaker will do something.

---

1. 明日 試験が あるはずです。　　　　Tomorrow, there is supposed to be an exam.

2. 明日 試験は ないはずです。　　　　Tomorrow, there is not supposed to be an exam.

3. 東京には 午後一時ごろに 着くはずです。

It is expected to arrive in Tokyo at about 1 pm.

4. 友子さんは 明日の パーティーには 来ないはずですよ。

Tomoko is not expected to come to tomorrow's party.

C. (Reason-noun) で　　　　because of (reason)

1. 山本さんは 病気で 三日 学校を 休んで います。

Yamamoto is absent from school for three days because of illness.

2. 父は 仕事で 東京へ 行きました。　　My father went to Tokyo for work.

【 ● ぶんかノート】

Tookookyohi 登校拒否

Recently, Japanese schools are being faced with an absentee problem among some of their junior high and high school students who deliberately decide not to go to school for long periods of time. This phenomenon, called "*tookookyohi*," is sometimes translated as "school allergy." Victims of bullying (another mounting social problem in schools), called *ijime* いじめ, prefer to miss school than to face the cruelties inflicted on them by their schoolmates.

【アクティビティー】

A. ペアワーク

You ask what your partner plans to do at the following times. Your partner answers using つもりです.

Ex. この クラスの あとで
質問：「この クラスの あとで 何を するつもりですか。」
答え：「この クラスの あとで お昼御飯を 食べるつもりです。」

1. 学校の あとで	
2. こんばん うちで	
3. この しゅうまつ	
4. ふゆやすみに	

B. ペアワーク

You ask your partner if he/she plans to do the following things in the future using つもりです.

Ex. 来年　日本語を　取りますか。

質問：「来年　日本語を　取るつもりですか。」

答え：「はい、もちろん　取るつもりです。」

1. やすみに　日本へ　行きますか。	
2. やすみに　アルバイトを　しますか。	
3. やすみに　うんてんめんきょを　とりますか。	
4. やすみに　日本ごを　べんきょうしますか。	
5. 大学へ　行きますか。	

C. ペアワーク

You tell your partner about a problem. Your partner tells you what he/she thinks.

You：「病気で　学校へ　行くことが　出来ません。」

Partner：「仕方が　ありませんね。心配しなくても　いいですよ。」

1. 今日は　お金を　わすれて、ランチを かうことが　出来ません。	
2. ぐあいが　わるくて、私は　食べることが 出来ません。	
3. 私は　かんじを　おぼえることが 出来ません。	
4. あした　しけんが　ありますが、ねつが あって、べんきょうすることが　出来ません。	
5. なつやすみに　日本へ　行くつもりですが、 まだ　日本語が　下手です。	
6. かぜで　ゆうべは　ぜんぜん　ねることが 出来ませんでした。	

D. ペアワーク

You have a schedule like the one below. Your friend asks you when each event is. You are not quite sure, but you answer based on the information you have.

Ex. math exam

質問：数学の　試験は　いつですか。

答え：あさって　あるはずです。

スケジュール

Baseball game - Tomorrow

Math exam - The day after tomorrow

Keiko's birthday party - This weekend

Social studies paper - Next week

Wednesday concert - 15th of next month

E. クラスワーク

In the spaces below, list what students are expected to do and are not expected to do.

	何を　するはずですか。	何を　しては　いけない　はずですか。
日本語の　クラスで		
としょかんで		
うちで		

193

六課

【会話】

Formal style:　まり：病気は　まだ　悪いんですか。

　　　　　　　　ケン：はい、昨日　病院へ　行って、薬を　もらいましたよ。

　　　　　　　　　　　一日に　三度も　飲まなければ　いけません。

　　　　　　　　まり：お気の毒に。

Informal style:　まり：病気は　まだ　悪いの？

　　　　　　　　ケン：うん、昨日　病院へ　行って、薬を　もらったよ。

　　　　　　　　　　　一日に　三度も　飲まなきゃ　いけないんだ。

　　　　　　　　まり：気の毒に。

【文型】

Counter も	as many/long/high as ～
一日に　三度	three times per day

* Past tense review:
い Adjectives	あつかったです。	was hot
	あつくなかったです。 or あつくありませんでした。	was not hot
な Adjectives	しずかでした。	was quiet
	しずかではありませんでした。	was not quiet

【単語】

1. 一日に　三度〔ど〕

　　three times per day

2. counter も

　　as many/long as ～

3. どのぐらい

　　about how long/far/often?

	4. degree(s), time(s) 〜ど	5. minute(s) 〜分（間）	6. hour(s) 〜時間	7. day(s) 〜日（間）
一	いちど	いっぷん（かん）	いちじかん	いちにち
二	にど	にふん（かん）	にじかん	ふつか（かん）
三	さんど	さんぷん（かん）	さんじかん	みっか（かん）
四	よんど	よんふん（かん）	よじかん	よっか（かん）
五	ごど	ごふん（かん）	ごじかん	いつか（かん）
六	ろくど	ろっぷん（かん）	ろくじかん	むいか（かん）
七	ななど	ななふん（かん）	ななじかん	なのか（かん）
八	はちど	はっぷん（かん）	はちじかん	ようか（かん）
九	きゅうど	きゅうふん（かん）	くじかん	ここのか（かん）
十	じゅうど	じ(ゅ)っぷん（かん）	じゅうじかん	とおか（かん）
？	なんど	なんぷん（かん）	なんじかん	なんにち（かん）

	8. week(s) 〜週間	9. month(s) 〜か月	10. year(s) 〜年（間）
一	いっしゅうかん	いっかげつ	いちねん（かん）
二	にしゅうかん	にかげつ	にねん（かん）
三	さんしゅうかん	さんかげつ	さんねん（かん）
四	よんしゅうかん	よんかげつ	よねん（かん）
五	ごしゅうかん	ごかげつ	ごねん（かん）
六	ろくしゅうかん	ろっかげつ	ろくねん（かん）
七	ななしゅうかん	ななかげつ	ななねん（かん）
八	はっしゅうかん	はっかげつ	はちねん（かん）
九	きゅうしゅうかん	きゅうかげつ	きゅうねん（かん）
十	じ(ゅ)っしゅうかん	じ(ゅ)っかげつ	じゅうねん（かん）
？	なんしゅうかん	なんかげつ	なんねん（かん）

六課

【漢字<ruby>かんじ</ruby>】

1. 田　　rice field　　た　　田中〔たなか〕さん, 中田〔なかた〕さん,
　　　　　　　　　　　　　　　　　田口〔たぐち〕さん

　　　　　　　　　　　　だ　　　金田〔かねだ〕さん, 山田〔やまだ〕さん,
　　　　　　　　　　　　　　　　　上田〔うえだ〕さん

2. 男　　male　　　　おとこ　男の　人 man, 男の　子 boy,
　　　　　　　　　　　　　　　男の　学生 male student

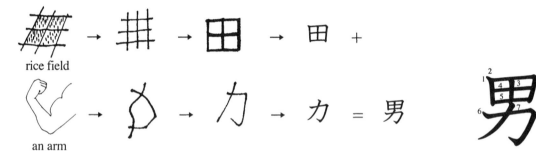

rice field

an arm

The source of strength in a ricefield is the male.

【文法<ruby>ぶんぽう</ruby>】

A. Counter も	as many/long/high as 〜

1. 学校を　三日<ruby>やす</ruby>も　休みました。　　　I was absent from school for as many as three days.
2. 熱<ruby>ねつ</ruby>が　三十九度<ruby>ど</ruby>も　ありました。　　　I had a fever as high as 39 degrees.

B. 一日に　三度<ruby>ど</ruby>	three times per day

1. 一日に　四度<ruby>ど</ruby>も　薬<ruby>くすり</ruby>を　飲<ruby>の</ruby>まなければ　なりませんでした。

　　　　　　　　　　　　I had to take medicine as often as four times per day.

2. 日本語の　クラスは　一週間に　何日　ありますか。

How many days per week do you have your Japanese class?

3. 一週間に　四日　あります。　　　I have it four days a week.

4. 一日に　何時間ぐらい　勉強しますか。　How many hours a day do you study?

【 ● ぶんかノート】

The School Year in Japan

The school year in Japan begins in April and ends in March. Summer vacations are about a month long. Summer vacation starts around the 20th of July, and school begins again at the beginning of September. Because it is not the end of the school year, students receive homework over their summer vacations. Winter break begins in late December and finishes around the 10th of January. It is usually about two weeks long. Spring vacation is the break that separates one school year from the next. Most schools' spring vacations are about three weeks long, beginning around the 20th of March and ending on the 10th of April. The total number of hours students spend in the classroom adds up to 1050 per year, which is far more than the amount of time American students spend in classes. The average high school class is 50 minutes long. Until several years ago, classes were held Monday through Saturday, with Saturday being a half day. Recently, however, schools are shortening their school week. Some have five-day weeks throughout the school year. Other schools alternate five- and six-day school weeks.

【アクティビティー】

A. ペアワーク

Interview your partner using the following questions.

質問：一日に　どのぐらい　うちで　勉強しますか。

答え：（だいたい）　一日に　二時間ぐらい　うちで　勉強します。

1. 一日に　どのぐらい　テレビを　見ますか。	
2. 一日に　どのぐらい　うちで　べんきょうしますか。	
3. 一日に　どのぐらい　でんわで　はなしますか。	
4. 一日に　何じかんぐらい　ねますか。	
5. 一しゅうかんに　何どぐらい　ハンバーガーを　食べますか。	
6. 一しゅうかんに　何どぐらい　うんどう(exercise)を　しますか。	
7. 一か月に　何どぐらい　えいがを　見ますか。	

六課

B. ペアワーク

Ask your partner about the Japanese school schedule. Your partner heard from a Japanese friend that the school year in Japan is different from America's. You partner should answer the questions based on the information he/she has.

質問：日本の　学校では　一週間に　何日　学校が　ありますか。

答え：日本の　学校では　一週間に　五日　学校が　あるはずです。

1. 日本の　学校は　何月に　はじまりますか。	
2. 日本の　学校は　一しゅうかんに　何日（なんにち） 　ありますか。	
3. 日本の　学校の　なつやすみは　何か月ぐらいですか。 　いつから　いつまでですか。	
4. 日本の　学校の　ふゆやすみは　どのぐらいですか。 　いつから　いつまでですか。	

C. ペアワーク

Your friend has been absent from school. Call your friend and ask the reason for his/her absence. Your friend should give one of the following reasons. Switch roles.

　　Ex. 風邪を　ひきました。熱が　高いです。

　You: もしもし、～さんの　お宅ですか。

Friend: はい、そうです。

　You: (Own name) ですが、～さん　いらっしゃいますか。

Friend: はい、私です。

　You: 二日も　学校を　休んでいますが、どう　しましたか。

Friend: かぜを　ひいて、熱が　高いんです。

　You: お気の毒に。

1. 食べることが　出来ません。おなかが　いたいんです。
2. はなすことが　出来ません。のどが　いたいんです。
3. ねることが　出来ません。ねつが　たかいんです。

Ask your partner these questions in Japanese.
Your partner should answer in Japanese.

1. Is it all right if I make a mistake?

2. What do you usually order at a Japanese restaurant?

3. Do I have to make reservations at (restaurant name)?

4. How big a tip (what percentage) do I have to leave at a restaurant?

5. Do I have to leave a tip in Japan, too?

6. Who (in your family) pays the bill at restaurants?

7. I will treat you to lunch today.

8. Please lend me $5. I will return it tomorrow.

9. What color is your wallet? Where do you keep it?

10. To which foreign country do you want to travel?

11. What time do you have to return home on weekends?

12. Who looks smart in this class?

13. [Telephone] Hello, is this the Tanaka residence?

14. [Telephone] Hello, is this the (partner's last name) residence? Is (partner's first name) there?

15. How many *kanji* have you memorized already?

六課

16. Can you play the piano?

17. Do you have a driver's license? When did you get it? or, When are you going to get it?

18. Do you have a cold now?

19. Is school stressful?

20. What kind of problems do American high school students have?

21. Were you absent from school yesterday?

22. How long do you talk to your friends on the telephone every day?

23. How long do you usually watch TV each day?

24. How many months is your summer vacation?

25. How many times a month do you go to the movies?

26. How many years have you been studying the Japanese language?

27. I have a headache because of a cold.

28. When are we supposed to have the next exam?

29. Would you like to go to the basketball game tonight?

30. What are you planning to do this weekend?

By the end of this lesson, you will be able to communicate the information below in the given situations.

【 ‖ - 7 タスク 1 】

An American student and a Japanese student discuss the winter holidays.

American Student:

(1) Ask your friend if he/she has ever been to church.

(2) Ask if he/she has ever seen a real Christmas tree.

(3) Ask if he/she has ever had eggnog (エッグノッグ).

(4) Answer. Ask if he/she has ever sent Christmas cards.

(5) Answer. Ask what Japanese people usually send.

(6) Answer based on your own experience. Comment.

(7) Answer based on your own experience.

(8) Answer based on your own experience. Comment.

Japanese Student:

(1) Answer based on your own experience.

(2) Answer based on your own experience. Comment.

(3) Answer no, but you want to taste it. Ask if it is delicious.

(4) Answer no, because Japanese people usually don't send Christmas cards. Ask if your partner writes many Christmas cards.

(5) Reply that Japanese people usually send New Year's cards. Ask your friend if he/she has ever received a New Year's card.

(6) Ask your friend if he/she has ever eaten *mochi*.

(7) Ask if he/she has ever worn a real Japanese *kimono*.

(8) Ask if he/she has ever gone to a Japanese shrine.

【 ‖ - 7 タスク 2 】

The American student is planning to have a Christmas party at his/her house and invites the Japanese student.

American student:

(1) Invite your friend to a Christmas party at your house. Tell him/her what day it will be.

(2) Give a time.

(3) Answer "yes" to bringing friends, but "no" to bringing beer.

(4) Thank your friend.

Japanese student:

(1) Thank your partner. Ask what time the party will start and end.

(2) Ask if you can bring two friends. Also ask if you can bring beer.

(3) Thank the American. Tell him/her who you will bring. Offer to wash the dishes and clean up after the party.

(4) Tell the American you will see him/her later.

七課

まり：外は　寒さむそうですねえ。

ケン：明日あしたは　たぶん　雪ゆきが　ふるでしょう。

まり：う～ん、いい　におい！　きれいですねえ！

ケン：クリスマスツリーを　見たことが　ありませんか。

まり：ええ、ありません。本当のは　はじめてです。

ケン：お正月の　前まえは　日本人は　いつも　どんな　事ことを　して　いますか。

まり：掃除そうじや　買かい物ものや　料理りょうりを　して、本当に　忙いそがしいんです。

　　　私は　いつも　母の　仕事しごとを　手伝つだいますが、今年は　出来ません。

ケン：日本人は　クリスマスカードを　送おくりますか。

まり：いいえ。でも、年賀状がじょうは　書きますよ。

ケン：ところで、まりさんは　教会きょうかいへ　行ったことが　ありますか。

まり：いいえ、ありません。日本では　キリスト教きょうの　人だけ　教会きょうかいへ

　　　行きます。クリスマスに　教会きょうかいへ　行って　みたいですね。

　　　連つれて　行って　下さい。ケンさんは　クリスマスの　歌うたを

　　　日本語で　歌うたったことが　ありますか。

ケン：いいえ、ありません。教おしえて　下さいよ。ぼくが　ギターを

　　　弾ひきますから。ギターを　持もって　来ますね。

まり：♪♪♪　きよし　この　夜よる　星ほしは　ひかり　すくいの　み子は

／ケン　　　　み母の　むねに　ねむりたもう　夢ゆめ　やすく　　♪♪♪

まり：外は　寒そうねえ。

ケン：明日は　たぶん　雪が　ふるだろう。

まり：う～ん、いい　におい！　きれいねえ！

ケン：クリスマスツリーを　見たこと　ないの。

まり：うん、ないわ。本当のは　はじめて。

ケン：お正月の　前は　日本人は　いつも　どんな　事　してるの。

まり：掃除や　買い物や　料理を　して、本当に　忙しいの。

　　　私　いつも　母の　仕事を　手伝うけど、今年は　出来ないわ。

ケン：日本人は　クリスマスカードを　送るの？

まり：ううん。でも、年賀状は　書くわよ。

ケン：ところで、まりは　教会へ　行ったことが　ある？

まり：ううん、ないわ。日本じゃ　キリスト教の　人だけ　教会へ　行くの。

　　　クリスマスに　教会へ　行って　みたいな。連れて　行って。

　　　ケンは　クリスマスの　歌を　日本語で　歌ったことが　ある？

ケン：ううん、ない。教えてよ。ぼくが　ギターを　弾くから。

　　　ギターを　持って　来るね。

まり：♪♪♪　きよし　この　夜　星は　ひかり　すくいの　み子は

／ケン　　　　み母の　むねに　ねむりたもう　夢　やすく　　　♪♪♪

A. めいし Nouns
1. 外　outside
2. あした　tomorrow
3. 本当〔ほんとう〕の　the real one
4. 日本人　Japanese person
5. 何　what?
6. かいもの　shopping
7. 私　I
8. 母　(my) mother
9. しごと　work
10. 今年〔ことし〕　this year
11. 日本　Japan
12. 人　person
13. うた　song
14. 日本語〔にほんご〕　Japanese language
15. ぼく　I [used by males]
16. ギター　guitar

B. どうし Verbs
17. 見た〔G2 見る／見ます／見ない〕　saw
18. ありません〔G1 ある／あって／ない〕　there is not
19. して　います〔IR する／します／して／しない〕　is doing
20. 書きます [G1 書く／書いて／書かない]　write
21. 出来ません〔G2 出来る／出来て／出来ない〕　cannot do
22. 行った〔G1 行く／行きます／行って／行かない〕　went
23. 行って　みたい〔G1 行く／行きます／行かない〕　want to try to go
24. うたった〔G1 うたう／うたいます／うたって／うたわない〕　sang
25. ない [G1 ある／あります／あって]　there is not
26. おしえて　下さい〔G2 おしえる／おしえます／おしえない〕　Please teach.
27. ひきましょう〔G1 ひく／ひいて／ひかない〕　I shall play [musical instrument].

C. -い けいようし I Adjectives
28. さむそう〔さむい〕　looks cold
29. いい　good
30. いそがしい　busy

D. -な けいようし NA Adjectives
31. きれい　pretty

E. ふくし Adverbs
32. 本当〔ほんとう〕に　really, truly
33. いつも　always

F. Others
34. でも、　However,
35. ところで　By the way
36. 〜だけ　only 〜

G. ぶんぽう Grammar
37. 〜の　まえに　before 〜
38. どんな　こと　what kind of things?
39. Dictionary form ＋ことが　出来ません。　cannot do 〜
40. TE form ＋下さい。　Please do 〜.

七課

【会話】

Formal style:　ケン：まりさんは　教会へ　行ったことが　ありますか。

　　　　　　　まり：いいえ、まだ　ないんです。

Informal style:　ケン：まりさんは　教会へ　行ったことが　ある？

　　　　　　　まり：ううん、まだ　ないの。

【文型】

| Verb (TA form) ＋ことが　あります | have done 〜 [Experience] |
| Verb (TA form) ＋ことが　ありません
　or　ことが　ない（ん）です | have never done 〜 [Experience] |

【単語】

1. クリスマス

Christmas

2. クリスマスツリー

Christmas tree

3. クリスマスカード

Christmas card

4. キリストきょう

Christianity

キリスト is Christ and
きょう means teaching.

5. （お）正月
〔（お）しょうがつ〕

New Year

[lit., the first proper month.]

6. （お）餅
〔（お）もち〕

pounded rice cakes

7. 着物
〔きもの〕

traditional Japanese wear

きます to wear ＋ もの things

8. 年賀状
〔ねんがじょう〕

New Year's card

9.お年玉
〔おとしだま〕

money received mainly
by children from adults
at New Year's
とし means "year" and たま
means "coins."

10.教会
〔きょうかい〕

church
(Christian)

11.神社
〔じんじゃ〕

shrine
(Shinto)

12.（お）寺
〔（お）てら〕

temple
(Buddhist)

13.花火（を　します）
〔はなび（を　します）〕

(to do) fireworks
はな is flowers and ひ is fire.

14.送る
[G1 おくります／おくって]

to send, mail

15.初めて〔はじめて〕
[Noun]

(for the) first time

【*オプショナル単語】

1.＊クリスマスイブ　　　　　　　　＊ Christmas Eve

2.＊クリスマスケーキ　　　　　　　＊ Christmas cake [a Japanese creation]

3.＊クリスマスプレゼント　　　　　＊ Christmas present

4.＊サンタクロース　　　　　　　　＊ Santa Claus

5.＊晦日〔みそか〕　　　　　　　　＊ December 30th

6.＊大晦日〔おおみそか〕　　　　　＊ New Year's Eve (December 31st)

7.＊かざります [G1]　　　　　　　 ＊ to decorate

8.＊つつみます [G1]　　　　　　　 ＊ to wrap

1. 言　say　　い（う）　もう　一度　言って　下さい。 Please say it again.

言 → 言 → 言 = 言

words coming out from the mouth

2. 語　language　ゴ

日本語〔にほんご〕Japanese language

英語〔えいご〕English

外国語〔がいこくご〕 foreign language

中国語〔ちゅうごくご〕Chinese language

何語〔なにご〕 What language?

語学〔ごがく〕 language study; linguistics

言 → 言 → 言 → 言 +

words coming out from the mouth

吾 → 吾 → 吾 → 吾 = 語

five parts (two eyes, two ears, one nose) and mouth

People speak languages using their mouths and the five other parts of their head.

【文法】

> A. Verb TA form
> The verb TA form has two main functions. It may be used to express a plain perfect verb form (past tense, plain equivalent of -ました), or it may be used preceding an extender as a past form.

1. **Group 1 verbs**

Group 1 verbs are identified by the verb stem, which is the verb form that remains after dropping -ます. If there are more than two *hiragana* characters remaining in the verb stem after dropping the ます and the final sound of the verb stem is an -i ending sound, the verb can usually be categorized as a Group 1 verb. To obtain the TA form, change the TE or DE sound of the verb TE form to the TA or DA sound. See the chart below for examples.

[⬚ -i ます]

	MASU form	Meaning	TE form	TA form
	-i			
[み]	のみます	to drink	のんで	のんだ
	よみます	to read	よんで	よんだ
	やすみます	to rest, be absent	やすんで	やすんだ
[に]	しにます	to die	しんで	しんだ
[び]	あそびます	to play	あそんで	あそんだ
[い]	あいます	to meet	あって	あった
[ち]	かちます	to win	かって	かった
[り]	わかります	to understand	わかって	わかった
	かえります	to return (place)	かえって	かえった
	がんばります	to do one's best	がんばって	がんばった
	はしります	to run	はしって	はしった
[き]	ききます	to listen, hear	きいて	きいた
	かきます	to write	かいて	かいた
	いきます	to go	いって＊	いった＊
	あるきます	to walk	あるいて	あるいた
[ぎ]	およぎます	to swim	およいで	およいだ
[し]	はなします	to talk	はなして	はなした

＊ irregular TE and TA form.

Do you remeber the TE form song?

TE Form Song (For the group 1 and irregular verbs)

Oh, み, に, び

Oh, み, に, び

み, に, び to んで！

Oh, い, ち, り

Oh, い, ち, り

い, ち, り to って！

き to いて

ぎ to いで

し to して

And きて, して

Oh, み, に, び

Oh, み, に, び！

Now we know our TE forms!   ＊ Sing to the tune of <u>Oh, Christmas Tree.</u>

2. Group 2 verbs

Group 2 verbs can be identified by a verb stem (verb without ます) that ends in an "-e sounding" *hiragana* or a verb stem that contains only one *hiragana*. See examples below. A few special verbs do exist. They must simply be learned as special verbs. Group 2 verb's TA forms are created simply by adding た after removing the -ます.

	MASU form	Meaning	TE form	TA form
[□ -e ます]	たべます	to eat	たべて	たべた
	まけます	to lose (e.g., game)	まけて	まけた
[One *hiragana*]	みます	to see, watch	みて	みた
	います	to be (animate)	いて	いた
	ねます	to sleep	ねて	ねた
[Special verbs]	おきます	to get up	おきて	おきた
	かります	to borrow	かりて	かりた
	おります	to get off	おりて	おりた
	できます	to be able to do	できて	できた

3. Group 3 Irregular verbs

Only きます, します and a noun + します verbs belong to this group. To obtain the TA form, change the TE sound of the verb TE form to the TA sound.

MASU form	Meaning	TE form	TA form
きます	to come	きて	きた
します	to do	して	した
べんきょう(を)します	to study	べんきょう(を)して	べんきょう(を)した
りょこう(を)します	to travel	りょこう(を)して	りょこう(を)した
かいもの(を)します	to shop	かいもの(を)して	かいもの(を)した
しょくじ(を)します	to have a meal	しょくじ(を)して	しょくじ(を)した
れんしゅう(を)します	to practice	れんしゅう(を)して	れんしゅう(を)した
うんてん(を)します	to drive	うんてん(を)して	うんてん(を)した

七課

B. Verb TA form＋ことが　あります。　　　　　　　have done ~ [Experience]

ありません／ない（ん）です。　　have never done ~ [Experience]

The verb TA ことが　あります pattern is often called the "experiential pattern." Literally, it means "to have done the act of ...." It is usually expressed in English as "ever done (something)" or "never done (something)." Negation occurs at the end of the extender. The extender never appears in the perfect (past) form, since it is already preceded by the past verb form of TA. In this usage, the time expressed cannot be too close to the present. Example:「きのう　おすしを 食べたことが　あります。」 "I have eaten *sushi* yesterday." is unacceptable.

1. この　本を　読んだことが　あります。　　　I have read this book.

2. 私は　まだ　日本へ　行ったことが　ありません。 I have not gone to Japan yet.

3.「にぎりずしを　食べたことが　ありますか。」　"Have you ever eaten *nigirizushi*?"

「いいえ、まだ　ないんです。」　　　　　"No, not yet."

【  ぶんかノート】

1. *Nengajoo* 年賀状

Japanese New Year's cards are postcards. Although some *nengajoo* can be purchased at stores, many Japanese like to purchase them from the post office, as these come with lottery numbers printed on the front. Around January 15, numbers are drawn, and people win prizes such as TVs, cameras, bicycles, collector's stamp sets, etc. Japanese may also design their own *nengajoo*, often with the zodiac animal of the New Year.

(Front)　　　　　　　Japanese New Year's Card　　　　　(Back)

2. Chinese Zodiac

Every New Year, Japanese wish farewell to an animal representing the old year and greet a new animal from the Chinese Zodiac. There are 12 animals in the Chinese zodiac cycle. Persons born in the year of these animals are said to possess some of the characteristics of these animals.

	子	Rat ねずみ	1924, 1936, 1948, 1960, 1972, 1984, 1996, 2008	Possess great charm. Concerned about details. Penny pinchers. Generous only with those they truly love.
	丑 (牛)	Ox うし	1925, 1937, 1949, 1961, 1973, 1985, 1997, 2009	Patient and quiet. Often successful, mentally alert, eloquent speakers, eccentric and stubborn.
	寅 (虎)	Tiger とら	1926, 1938, 1950, 1962, 1974, 1986, 1998, 2010	Sensitive, short-tempered, great thinkers, suspicious of others.
	卯 (兎)	Rabbit うさぎ	1927, 1939, 1951, 1963, 1975, 1987, 1999, 2011	Smooth talkers, talented, ambitious, successful, reserved.
	辰 (竜龍)	Dragon たつ	1928, 1940, 1952, 1964, 1976, 1988, 2000, 2012	Healthy, energetic, excitable, short-tempered, stubborn, honest, sensitive, brave, eccentric.
	巳 (蛇)	Serpent へび	1929, 1941, 1953, 1965, 1977, 1989, 2001, 2013	Quiet, wise, lucky with finances, stingy, sympathetic, passionate, good-looking.
	午 (馬)	Horse うま	1930, 1942, 1954, 1966, 1978, 1990, 2002, 2014	Popular, cheerful, talkative, wise, talented and skillful with money, enjoy entertainment such as music and theater.
	未 (羊)	Sheep ひつじ	1931, 1943, 1955, 1967, 1979, 1991, 2003, 2015	Pleasant, artistic, passionate, religious, timid, helpful.
	申 (猿)	Monkey さる	1932, 1944, 1956, 1968, 1980, 1992, 2004, 2016	Clever, skillful, inventive, possess common sense, decisive, thirst for knowledge and keen memories.
	酉 (鶏)	Rooster にわとり	1933, 1945, 1957, 1969, 1981, 1993, 2005, 2017	Deep thinkers, hard workers, busy, not shy, tend to undertake more than they can accomplish.
	戌 (犬)	Dog いぬ	1934, 1946, 1958, 1970, 1982, 1994, 2006, 2018	Strong sense of duty, loyal, honest, are good friends, can be selfish, stubborn.
	亥 (猪)	Boar いのしし	1935, 1947, 1959, 1971, 1983, 1995, 2007, 2019	Chivalrous, gallant, determined, short-tempered, affectionate, kind to loved ones.

According to legend, when Buddha was on his deathbed, he summoned all the animals in the kingdom. Only 12 animals came, and in gratitude, Buddha named a year after each of them in the order of their arrival. It is said that the clever mouse was the first to arrive because he caught a ride on the ox, then jumped off the head of the ox just before arriving at Buddha's side.

七課

3. Christmas in Japan

Because Japan is not a Christian nation, Christmas is not celebrated as it is in the West. Christmas is not a holiday in Japan. Recently, however, Japan has adopted some aspects of a secularized Christmas. Stores, taking the opportunity to increase sales, have lighted displays of trees, winter scenes, fairies, and Santa Claus. A few homes will decorate Christmas trees, but they are often fake and very small. One will probably not find mounds of gifts under the tree, either. An interesting practice among the Japanese, however, is the eating of Christmas cake on Christmas Day. Hoards of young wives will cram bakeries to purchase small white cakes decorated festively with Christmas themes to serve to their families on Christmas Day.

4. The New Year in Japan

New Year (お正月) is the most celebrated holiday in Japan. Most businesses close for several days, and students and workers enjoy the few days of rest that come at the beginning of the new year. It is a time for families to gather and celebrate with special foods and spirits. The preparations for January 1, though, really begin several days, or even weeks, before. The end of the year is filled with end-of-the-year parties, housecleaning, paying off of bills, writing New Year's cards, pounding *mochi*, preparing the special New Year's food called おせちりょうり and decorating the house with special New Year's decorations, such as the かどまつ.

On New Year's Eve and during the next few days, Japanese visit shrines to thank the gods for the previous year and to pray for another good year. Many will dress in their best kimonos for this occasion. On New Year's Eve, many families will enjoy としこしそば, a hot buckwheat noodle soup which, when eaten, is said to bring long life and help bridge one's path from one year to the next because of the length of the noodles. One New Year's morning, almost all Japanese will partake of おぞうに, a broth that contains *mochi*, vegetables and various types of shellfish, fish, or meats. The preparation of *ozoni* varies by regions in Japan.

Within the first few days of the year, people will read the many New Year's cards they have received and heads of households will visit relatives, neighbors, and others to extend their New Year's greetings. Traditionally Japanese children enjoyed flying kites, playing with tops, or playing はねつき, a game similar to badminton. Recently, however, they engage in daily activities such as watching TV, playing games, etc. Adults may participate in a poem competition, called *hyakuninisshu*, write poems, or write a meaningful message for the New Year in calligraphy. Others will enjoy song competitions on television, such as the こうはくうたがっせん.

The New Year is truly a festive time in Japan.

おせちりょうり

New Years food

おぞうに

mochi soup

かどまつ

New Year's entrance decoration

【 👥 アクティビティー】

A. ペアワーク

Ask your partner if he/she has ever done the following things using 〜たことが　あります.
Your partner should answer based on the facts. Switch roles.

Ex. 日本へ　行きましたか。

質問：日本へ　行ったことが　ありますか。
　しつもん

答え：はい、あります。 or いいえ、ありません／ないです。
　こた

1. おすしを　食べましたか。	
2. おさけを　のみましたか。	
3. 車を　うんてんしましたか。	
4. たばこを　すいましたか。	
5. カラオケを　うたいましたか。	
6. アルバイトを　しましたか。	
7. 日本の　きものを　きましたか。	
8. ピアノを　ならいましたか。	

B. ペアワーク

Ask your partner if he/she has ever done the following things using 〜たことが　あります. Your partner should answer. Switch roles.

1. きょうかいへ　行きました。	
2. じんじゃへ　行きました。	
3. おもちを　食べました。	
4. 日本から　ねんがじょうを　もらいました。	
5. お年だまを　もらいました。	
6. クリスマスケーキを　食べました。	
7. 大きい　はなびを　見ました。	

七課

C. ペアワークかグループワーク

Copy the verbs below onto small cards. To start the game, stack cards face down. Flip one card at a time and say the TA form. If you produce the correct form, the card is yours. Continue until you make a mistake. Your partner now has a chance to give the correct answer. If he/she does, the card is his, and he continues the game. If both players are unable to give the correct answer, the card is returned to the stack. The game continues until all the cards in the stack are gone. The person with more cards wins. See the following page for answers.

のみます	うたいます	見ます
おきます	ねます	かちます
やすみます	はなします	書きます
すみます	来ます	かえります
あいます	よみます	食べます
行きます	（めがねを）かけます	うんてんをします
（ふくを）きます	アルバイトをします	聞きます
かります	ならいます	はしります
もらいます	かぶります	りょこうをします

[こたえ]

のんだ [のみます]	うたった [うたいます]	見た [見ます]
おきた [おきます]	ねた [ねます]	かった [かちます]
やすんだ [やすみます]	はなした [はなします]	書いた [書きます]
すんだ [すみます]	来た [来ます]	かえった [かえります]
あった [あいます]	よんだ [よみます]	食べた [食べます]
行った [行きます]	（めがねを）かけた [かけます]	うんてんをした [うんてんをします]
（ふくを）きた [きます]	アルバイト（を）した [アルバイト（を） します]	聞いた [聞きます]
かりた [かります]	ならった [ならいます]	はしった [はしります]
もらった [もらいます]	かぶった [かぶります]	りょこうをした [りょこうをします]

七課

【会話】

Formal style:　　　ケン：明日の　天気は　どうでしょうか。

まり：たぶん　雪でしょう。

ケン：寒いでしょうね。

Informal style:　　　ケン：明日の　天気は　どうかな。

まり：たぶん　雪でしょう。

ケン：寒いだろうね。

【文型】

明日	+でしょう。↓ It is probably tomorrow.	+でしょう。↑ It is tomorrow, isn't it?
明日じゃない or 明日ではない	+でしょう。↓ It is probably not tomorrow.	+でしょう。↑ It is not tomorrow, is it?
さむい	+でしょう。↓ It is/will probably be cold.	+でしょう。↑ It is cold, isn't it?
さむくない	+でしょう。↓ It is/will probably not be cold.	+でしょう。↑ It is not cold, is it?
さむかった	+でしょう。↓ It was probably cold.	+でしょう。↑ It was cold, wasn't it?
さむくなかった	+でしょう。↓ It was probably not cold.	+でしょう。↑ It was not cold, was it?
雨が ふる	+でしょう。↓ It will probably rain.	+でしょう。↑ It will rain, won't it?
雨が ふらない	+でしょう。↓ It will probably not rain.	+でしょう。↑ It will not rain, will it?
雨が ふった	+でしょう。↓ It probably rained.	+でしょう。↑ It rained, didn't it?
雨が ふらなかった	+でしょう。↓ It probably did not rain.	+でしょう。↑ It did not rain, did it?

【単語】

1.（お）天気
〔（お）てんき〕
weather

2. 雨
〔あめ〕
rain

3. 雪
〔ゆき〕
snow

4. 降る
[G1 ふります／ふって]
(rain, snow) to fall

5. 曇り〔くもり〕

[noun]

cloudy (weather)

6. 晴れ〔はれ〕

[noun]

clear (weather)

7. 風〔かぜ〕

[noun]

wind

8. 温度〔おんど〕

temperature (general)

〜ど counter for degree(s)

9. 〜でしょう ↘

probably 〜

10. 〜でしょう ↗

Isn't it 〜?

An invitation for the listener to agree with the speaker.

11. たぶん

probably

【*オプショナル単語〔たんご〕】

1. *雲〔くも〕	* cloud [noun]
2. *曇〔くも〕る　[G1 くもります]	* to become cloudy
3. *晴〔は〕れる　[G2 はれます]	* to clear up
4. *吹〔ふ〕く　[G1 ふきます]	* to blow
5. *台風〔たいふう〕	* typhoon
6. *地震〔じしん〕	* earthquake
7. *津波〔つなみ〕	* tsunami
8. *ハリケーン	* hurricane
9. *天気予報〔てんきよほう〕	* weather forecast
10. *気温〔きおん〕	* temperature (atmospheric)
11. *マイナス	* minus
12. *後〔のち〕	* later [Ex.あめ　のち　はれ Rain, later clear]

七課

【漢字】

1. 寺　temple　　　てら　　寺に　行く go to the temple

寺田〔てらだ〕さん

寺山〔てらやま〕さん

寺本〔てらもと〕さん

でら　　山寺〔やまでら〕 temple in a mountain

ジ　　本願寺〔ほんがんじ〕 *Honganji* temple

measurement (one-tenth)

At the temple, the monks measure plots of farm land to grow their crops.

2. 時　time, o'clock　　とき　　時々〔ときどき〕sometimes

ジ　　何時〔なんじ〕What time?

一時間〔いちじかん〕one hour

measurement (one-tenth)

The temple bells ring out the time of the day.

七課　　　　　220

【文法】

> A. Verb NAKATTA form
>
> The verb NAKATTA form is the plain negative past form equivalent of the polite ませんでした form. It may be used at the end of informal sentences or may precede extenders. For all verbs, drop the final い, then replace by -なかった.

1. **Group 1 verbs**

[☐ -i ます]

	MASU form	Meaning	DIC. form	NAI form	TA form	NAKATTA form
			nonpast	neg. nonpast	past	neg. past
	-i		-u	-a	(TE form)	-a
[み]	のみます	to drink	のむ	のまない	のんだ	のまなかった
	よみます	to read	よむ	よまない	よんだ	よまなかった
[に]	しにます	to die	しぬ	しなない	しんだ	しななかった
[び]	あそびます	to play	あそぶ	あそばない	あそんだ	あそばなかった
[い]	あいます	to meet	あう	あわない	あった	あわなかった
[ち]	かちます	to win	かつ	かたない	かった	かたなかった
[り]	わかります	to understand	わかる	わからない	わかった	わからなかった
	かえります	to return (place)	かえる	かえらない	かえった	かえらなかった
	あります	to exist (inanimate)	ある	ない＊	あった	なかった＊
[き]	ききます	to listen, hear	きく	きかない	きいた	きかなかった
	かきます	to write	かく	かかない	かいた	かかなかった
	いきます	to go	いく	いかない	いった＊	いかなかった
[ぎ]	およぎます	to swim	およぐ	およがない	およいだ	およがなかった
[し]	はなします	to talk	はなす	はなさない	はなした	はなさなかった

＊ Special forms.

2. **Group 2 verbs**

	MASU form	Meaning	DIC. form	NAI form	TA form	NAKATTA form
			nonpast	neg. nonpast	past	neg. past
[☐ -e ます]	たべます	to eat	たべる	たべない	たべた	たべなかった
[One *hiragana*]	みます	to see, watch	みる	みない	みた	みなかった
	います	to be (animate)	いる	いない	いた	いなかった
	ねます	to sleep	ねる	ねない	ねた	ねなかった
[Special verbs]	おきます	to get up	おきる	おきない	おきた	おきなかった
	かります	to borrow	かりる	かりない	かりた	かりなかった
	おります	to get off	おりる	おりない	おりた	おりなかった
	できます	to be able to do	できる	できない	できた	できなかった

221

七課

3. **Group 3 Irregular verbs**

MASU form	Mean -ing	DIC. form nonpast	NAI form neg. nonpast	TA form past	NAKATTA form neg. past
きます	to come	くる	こない	きた	こなかった
します	to do	する	しない	した	しなかった
うんてん(を)します	to drive	うんてん(を)する	うんてん(を)しない	うんてん(を)した	うんてん(を)しなかった

B. Noun / Noun じゃない or ではない
　　Verb Dictionary form / NAI form / TA form / NAKATTA form
　　I Adjective (-い) / (-くない) / (-かった) / (-くなかった)
　　NA Adjective / NA Adjective じゃない or ではない

　　＋でしょう。↘ probably ～
　　でしょう？↗ Isn't it ～?

When でしょう appears at the end of the sentence and is uttered with a falling intonation, the sentence takes on the meaning of "probably." If でしょう is uttered in a rising intonation, however, it is an invitation for the listener to agree with the speaker, much like ね when it is used at the end of sentences.

1. 明日は　多分　くもりでしょう。↘　　It will probably be cloudy tomorrow.

2. 明日は　くもりじゃないでしょう。↘　　It will probably not be cloudy tomorrow.

3. 明日は　たぶん　雨が　ふるでしょう。↘　　It will probably rain tomorrow.

4. 明日は　雨が　ふらないでしょう。↘　　It will probably not rain tomorrow.

5. 雪が　たくさん　ふったでしょう。↘　　It probably snowed a lot.

6. 昨日　雪が　ふらなかったでしょう。↘　　It probably did not snow yesterday.

7. 日本の　冬は　たぶん　さむいでしょう。↘　　Japanese winters are probably cold.

8. 建物の　中は　さむくないでしょう。↘　　It is probably not cold inside the building.

9. お天気は　わるかったでしょう。↘　　The weather was probably bad.

10. 風は　強くなかったでしょう。↘　　The wind was probably not strong.

11. 雪の　京都は　たぶん　きれいでしょう。↘　　Snow-covered Kyoto is probably pretty.

12. この　音楽を　知って　いるでしょう？↗　　You know this music, don't you?

13. さしみは　食べないでしょう？↗　　You don't eat raw fish, do you?

14. もう　この　本を　読んだでしょう？↗　　You've already read this book, haven't you?

15. この　事を　お母さんに　話さなかったでしょうね？↗

You didn't talk to your mother about this matter, did you?

【 ● ぶんかノート】

1.(O)mochi （お）もち

Mochi is a popular food in Japan. On New Year's morning, most families enjoy bowls of おぞうに for breakfast. The *mochi* for the おぞうに is made several days before January 1. Traditionally, families gather for もちつき, the pounding of *mochi* using special sticky rice（もちごめ）in mortars called うす. Huge mallets（きね）are used to soften and pound the rice into a smooth, glutinous ball, which is then removed from the うす and set out to cool or to be divided into little balls that are then are shaped into edible sizes. Recently, however, many families choose instead to make もち with a *mochi*-making machine or order *mochi* from confectioneries. It is considered good luck to eat もち at the New Year, because its sticky consistency symbolizes family unity, its often round shape suggests fulfillment and continuity, and the word もち is part of the verb もちます, which means to have, or possess, which suggests prosperity.

もちつき *Mochi* pounding

2. *Otoshidama* お年玉

Otoshidama is a monetary gift that adults often give to children at the New Year. Just as Western children look forward to receiving Christmas gifts, Japanese children enjoy receiving their little packets of money at the New Year. As children get older, the amount of money they receive increases. Little children may receive the equivalent of a few dollars in each packet, while teens may receive totals of several hundred dollars, depending on the generosity of their adult friends and family. Some working adults may even give おとしだま to elderly relatives who no longer have incomes. All おとしだま are presented in attractive little envelopes, as shown below.

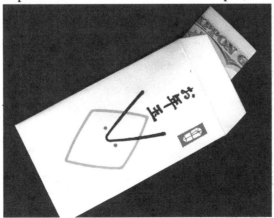

おとしだま New Year monetary gift

七課

【 アクティビティー】

A. ペアワーク

Your partner has the following map with weather information on it. You ask your partner for
the information and fill in the blanks on the chart on the next page.

／　のち
　　　later

｜　時々
　〔ときどき〕
　　　sometimes

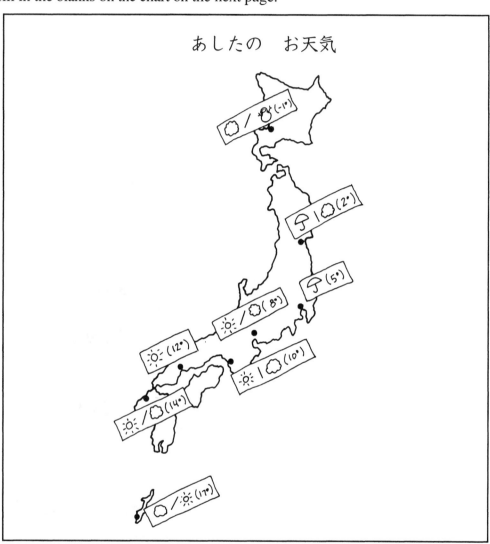

あしたの　お天気

Ex. Tokyo

質問１：「明日の　東京の　お天気は　どうですか。」

答え１：「東京は　雨でしょう。↘」

質問２：「明日の　東京の　温度は　どのぐらいですか。」

答え２：「五度ぐらいでしょう。↘」

質問３：「明日　東京は　寒いでしょうか。」

答え３：「ええ、寒いでしょう。↘」

Place	Weather	Temperature	Cold or not
Ex. 東京〔とうきょう〕	あめ	5℃	さむい
1. 沖縄〔おきなわ〕			
2. 北海道〔ほっかいどう〕			
3. 広島〔ひろしま〕			
4. 福岡〔ふくおか〕			
5. 大阪〔おおさか〕			
6. 名古屋〔なごや〕			
7. 仙台〔せんだい〕			

B. ペアワーク

Ask your partner if he/she plans to do the following things for the holidays. Write a check mark for はい or いいえ according to your partner's answer.

質問：クリスマスに　教会へ　行くつもりですか。

答え：ええ、たぶん　行くでしょう。↘

　　　　　or　いいえ、たぶん　行かないでしょう。↘

しつもん	はい	いいえ
1. クリスマスに　きょうかいへ　行くつもりですか。		
2. お正月〔しょうがつ〕に　じんじゃに　行くつもりですか。		
3. クリスマスカードを　ともだちに　おくるつもりですか。		
4. 本とうの　クリスマスツリーを　かうつもりですか。		
5. おおみそか (New Year's Eve) に　はなびを　するつもりですか。		
6. お正月〔しょうがつ〕に　おもちを　食べるつもりですか。		
7. お正月〔しょうがつ〕に　フットボールの　しあいを　見るつもりですか。		

七課

【会話】

Formal style: まり：クリスマスの　前に　何を　しなければ　いけませんか。

ケン：部屋を　そうじしなければ　いけませんよ。

Informal style: まり：クリスマスの　前に　何を　しなきゃ　いけない？

ケン：部屋を　そうじしなきゃ　いけないよ。

【単語】

1. そうじ(を)する
[Ir.] to clean up

2. せんたく(を)する
[Ir.] to do laundry

3. りょうり(を)する
[Ir.] to cook

4. (さらを)　あらう
[G1 あらいます]
to wash (dishes)

5. 手伝う
[G1 てつだいます]
to help

6. (ごみを)　出す
[G1 だします]
to take out (the garbage)

【*オプショナル単語】

1. *家事〔かじ〕　　　　　　* housework, chores

2. *庭仕事〔にわしごと〕　　* yard work

3. *ごちそう　　　　　　　　* a big meal, feast

【漢字】

1. 間　between, among, interval　あいだ　学校〔がっこう〕と　家〔いえ〕の　間に　ある。

It's between school and my house.

カン　時間〔じかん〕 time

一時間〔いちじかん〕 one hour

 +

 = 間

The sun emerges through the gate and takes an interval to set.

2. 分　minute　わ(かる)　分かりません。 I do not understand.

フン　二分〔にふん〕 two minutes

プン　六分〔ろっぷん〕 six minutes

ブン　半分〔はんぶん〕 a half

eight

 分

a sword

A sword will divide a stick into eight parts in a minute.

【 ぶんかノート】

1. How Often?

An expression similar to English "how often" does not exist in Japanese. One needs to be more specific, and frame the question by providing a space of time, then attach the question word such as 「どのぐらい」. For example, 「一しゅうかんに　どのぐらい...」(In one week, about how much ...).

2. Japanese Religions

Japan's two major religions are Shintoism and Buddhism. Shinto is the native Japanese religion, whereas Buddhism arrived in Japan in 532 A.D. from India via China and Korea. Both religions co-exist in Japan. Most Japanese practice both Shinto and Buddhist customs and beliefs. For example, at the New Year, it is common for Japanese to go to the Buddhist temple just before midnight to listen to the ringing of the 除夜の鐘 [じょやのかね]. The huge temple bell is rung 108 times. It is said that man has 108 sins, and each ring rids us of one of them. On New Year's Day, and a few days following, the same Japanese may go to the Shinto shrine for the first shrine visit of the year. This visit is called 初詣 [はつもうで]. Japanese pray for a good year, and often will buy fortunes to see what the New Year has in store for them. Another example illustrating the coexistence of both Shinto and Buddhism in most Japanese lives is the practice of getting married at a Shinto shrine, but having one's funeral at a Buddhist temple. Christianity exists in Japan, but less than one percent of the population claim to be Christians.

じょやのかね

The temple bell is rung 108 times on the New Year.

はつもうで

The first shrine visit on New Year's Day

【👤👤アクティビティー】

A. ペアワーク

Ask your partner who does the following work at his/her home and how many times in a week the family member does it. Write your partner's answers. Take turns.

Ex. 家を　掃除します。
　　質問１：「だれが　家を　掃除しますか。」
　　答え１：「（たいてい）　母が　します。」
　　質問２：「一週間に　何度ぐらい　家を　掃除しますか。」
　　答え２：「一週間に　一度ぐらい　家を　掃除します。」

うちの　しごと	だれ？	一しゅうかんに　なんど？
1. うちを　そうじします。		
2. あなたの　へやを　そうじします。		
3. スーパーで　かいものを　します。		
4. せんたくを　します。		
5. おさらを　あらいます。		
6. ごみを　外に　出します。		
7. 車を　あらいます。		
8. にわを　そうじします。		

七課

B. ペアワーク

Ask your partner what chores he/she has to do at home.

質問：「あなたは　うちで　何を　しなければ　なりませんか。」

```
┌─────────────────────────────────────────────────────────────┐
│                                                             │
│                                                             │
│                                                             │
│                                                             │
└─────────────────────────────────────────────────────────────┘
```

C. ペアワーク

Ask your partner what chores he/she does NOT have to do at home.

質問：「あなたは　うちで　何を　しなくても　いいですか。」

```
┌─────────────────────────────────────────────────────────────┐
│                                                             │
│                                                             │
│                                                             │
│                                                             │
└─────────────────────────────────────────────────────────────┘
```

D. ペアワーク

Ask your partner what he/she has to do before Christmas.

質問：「クリスマスの　前に　何を　しなければ　なりませんか
　　　　／いけませんか。」

```
┌─────────────────────────────────────────────────────────────┐
│                                                             │
│                                                             │
│                                                             │
│                                                             │
└─────────────────────────────────────────────────────────────┘
```

E. ペアワーク

What preparations do the Japanese have to make before New Year's Day? List them.

質問：「日本人は　お正月の　前に　何を　しなければ　なりませんか
　　　　／いけませんか。」

```
┌─────────────────────────────────────────────────────────────┐
│                                                             │
│                                                             │
│                                                             │
│                                                             │
└─────────────────────────────────────────────────────────────┘
```

【会話】

Formal style:
まり：パーティーに 友達を 連れて 行っても いいですか。

ケン：はい、かまいません。ぜひ 連れて 来て 下さい。

Informal style:
まり：パーティーに 友達を 連れて 行っても いい？

ケン：うん、いいよ。ぜったい 連れて 来て。

【文型】

	to take	to bring	to take/bring home
Thing を	持って 行きます	持って 来ます	持って 帰ります
Person/Animal を	連れて 行きます	連れて 来ます	連れて 帰ります

【単語】

1. 明けまして おめでとう （ございます）

New Year's greeting

あけまして means "(New Year) opens" and おめでとう （ございます）
means "Congratulations." It is used from January 1 through the first few
weeks of January. Not used before New Year's Day.

2. におい

smell, fragrance

3. ぜひ [Adverb]

by all means, definitely

においが いい／わるい です smells good/bad

4. 持って 行きます

[G1 持って 行く]

to take (things)

5. 持って 来ます

[Ir. 持って 来る]

to bring (things)

6. 持って 帰ります

[G1 持って 帰る]

to take/bring (things) back home

7. 連れて 行きます

[G1 連れて 行く]

to take (animate)

8. 連れて 来ます

[Ir. 連れて 来る]

to bring (animate)

9. 連れて 帰ります

[G1 連れて 帰る]

to take/bring (animate) back home

【漢字】

1. 正　correct　　　ただ（しい）　正しいです is correct

　　　　　　　　　ショウ　　　お正月〔しょうがつ〕 the New Year

　　　　　　　　　正田〔しょうだ〕さん

正 is also used to tally numbers in groups of five.

1　　2　　3　　4　　5

一　丁　下　正　正

2. 家　house　　　　　　いえ　　　　　大きい　家 a big house

カ　　　　　　家族 family

the roof of a house

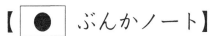

pig

A pig in house.

= 家

3. 々　[pluralizer]　　　時々〔ときどき〕 sometimes

木々〔きぎ〕 trees

山々〔やまやま〕 mountains

日々〔ひび〕 days

人々〔ひとびと〕 people

家々〔いえいえ〕 houses

【 ● ぶんかノート】

Kimono 着物

The word *kimono* literally means "thing to wear" (きるもの). Before the arrival of Western clothes, *kimono* was all the Japanese wore. Now, Japanese wear *kimono* only on special occasions. The most common occasions for one to wear a *kimono* are New Year's Day, on Coming-of-Age Day for 20-year-olds, weddings, and funerals. There are many varieties of *kimonos*. The type of *kimono* one wears depends on the occasion or purpose, age, and sex of the individual wearing it.

Wedding *kimono*

七課

【👩👩アクティビティー】

A. ペアワーク

You partner is planning a class party. You ask if you can bring the following to the party. Your partner answers. Check はい or いいえ according to your partner's answer.

You: 「〜を　持って／連れて　来ても　いいですか。」

Yes Answer: 「はい、（ぜひ）　持って／連れて　来て　下さい。」

No Answer: 「いいえ、（ぜったい）　持って／連れて　来ないで　下さい。」

	はい	いいえ
1. おすし		
2. かみの　おさら		
3. ともだち		
4. ピザ		
5. ビール		
6. きょうだい		
7. （ビデオの　なまえ）		

B. クラスワーク

Find a person among your classmates who does and does not do the following things on Christmas Eve. Circulate among your classmates and ask them these questions. Write their names in the appropriate spaces below.

Ex. Open presents on Christmas Eve?

「クリスマスイブに　プレゼントを　開けますか。」

しつもん	YES Person's Name	NO Person's Name
1. クリスマスイブに　プレゼントを　あけますか。		
2. クリスマスイブに　きょうかいへ　行きますか。		
3. クリスマスイブに　ごちそうを　食べますか。		
4. クリスマスイブに　アルコールを　のみますか。		
5. クリスマスイブに　クリスマスキャロルを　うたいますか。		
6. クリスマスイブに　家を　そうじしますか。		
7. クリスマスイブに　はやく　ねますか。		

C. ペアワーク

Plan your class party in Japanese. Fill in the information below. Decide who will bring the items listed.

何人？：

かみざら, フォーク, おはし, スプーン, ナプキン, コップ：

おも(main)な　食べ物：

飲み物：

デザート：

その　ほか (Others):

質問しよう！ 答えよう！
しつもん　　　こた

Ask your partner these questions in Japanese.
Your partner should answer in Japanese.

1. How is the weather today?

2. What is the temperature now?

3. How will the weather be tomorrow?

4. Have you ever gone to Japan before?

5. What smells do you like? What smells do you dislike?

6. What do you do to help at home?

7. Do you clean your room?

8. How many times a month do you clean your room?

9. Who does your laundry?

10. What can you cook?

11. At your house, who washes the dishes after dinner?

12. How many Christmas cards do you send to your friends?

13. Have you ever received New Year's cards from Japan?

14. Do you go to church? When do you go?

15. Have you ever gone to a shrine or temple?

16. Can you sing a Japanese song?

17. Is it raining (or snowing) now?

18. Is the wind strong now?

19. Can you play the guitar?

20. Have you ever had (done) fireworks at your house?

21. Does your family buy a real Christmas tree every year?

22. What do you do on New Year's Eve?

23. What do you do on New Year's Day?

24. Do you receive money on Christmas or New Year's Day?

25. Have you ever eaten *mochi*?

26. Can you make *mochi*?

27. May I bring my friend to this class tomorrow?

28. What are you planning to bring to our class party?

29. Please take me to the volleyball game this Saturday.

30. What do you have to do before Christmas?

七課

1. きよし この夜
(Silent Night)

* きよし この 夜 星は 光り
すくいの み子は み母の むねに
ねむりたもう 夢 やすく

* くりかえし repeat

2. ジングルベル

(Jingle Bells)

* 雪_{ゆき}を　けって　そりは　すすむ

　のはら　こえて　もりを　こえて

　うまの　すずは　なりわたるよ

はやしに　こだまして　たからかに　　（ヘイ）

　ジングル・ベル　ジングル・ベル

　　　鈴_{すず}は　なる

　　そりは　すすむよ

　　はやての　ように

　ジングル・ベル　ジングル・ベル

　　　そりは　ゆく

雪_{ゆき}けり　すすむ　その　たのしさよ

　　＊くりかえし repeat

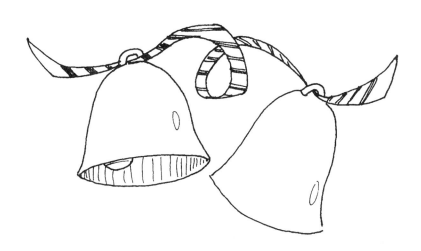

239

七課

3. サンタが 町_{まち}に やって 来る
(Santa Claus is Coming to Town)

さあ あなたから メリー・クリスマス
私から メリー・クリスマス
サンタクロース・イズ・カミング・トウ・タウン
ネ 聞こえて 来るでしょ
鈴_{すず}の 音_ねが すぐ そこに
サンタクロース・イズ・カミング・トウ・タウン

＊待_まちきれないで おやすみした子に
きっと すばらしい プレゼント 持_もって

さあ あなたから メリー・クリスマス
私から メリー・クリスマス
サンタクロース・イズ・カミング・トウ・タウン

♪♪♪

さあ あなたから メリー・クリスマス
私から メリー・クリスマス
サンタクロース・イズ・カミング・トウ・タウン

ネ 聞こえて 来るでしょ
鈴_{すず}の 音_ねが すぐ そこに
サンタクロース・イズ・カミング・トウ・タウン
クリスマスイブを 指_{ゆび}おり かぞえた
おさない 思_{おも}い出も こよい なつかし

さあ あなたから メリー・クリスマス
私から メリー・クリスマス
サンタクロース・イズ・カミング・トウ・タウン
　＊くりかえし

4. お正月

(New Year)

東くめ 作詞
滝廉太郎 作曲

♩ = 112

1. もう　い　く　つ　ね　る　と　　お　しょう　が　つ
2. もう　い　く　つ　ね　る　と　　お　しょう　が　つ

おしょうがつには　たこあげて　こまを　まわして　あそびましょう
おしょうがつには　まりついて　おいばねついて　あそびましょう

は　　や　くーこ　い　こ　い　お　しょう　が　つ
は　　や　くーこ　い　こ　い　お　しょう　が　つ

七課

FUN CORNER 7: ねんがじょう NEW YEAR'S CARD

Let's make a *Nengajo*!

Things you need: 4X6 white unlined index card, black pen, colored pens or pencils. Neatly write a New Year's message, the appropriate New Year's date, and your name with a black pen as shown below. Draw a design for the New Year in the blank space.

賀正

二〇〇〇年一月一日

なまえ

あけましておめでとう

二〇〇〇年 元旦

なまえ

賀正（がしょう）〔がしょう〕， 謹賀新年（きんがしんねん）〔きんがしんねん〕

Happy New Year, ２０００年〔にせんねん〕

元旦（がんたん）〔がんたん〕First day of the year, 一月一日〔いちがつついたち〕January 1

謹賀新年

二〇〇〇年 元旦

なまえ

あけましておめでとう

２０００年１月１日

な ま え

[The numbers preceding each sentence indicate the lesson in which the underlined constructions were introduced.]

Sentence Patterns

2課

2-1 ベンさんは 今（いま） <u>走（はし）って います</u>。　Ben is running now.

2-1 姉（あね）は <u>結婚（けっこん）して います</u>。　My older sister is married.

2-2 猫（ねこ）が <u>車（くるま）の 上（うえ）に</u> います。　The cat is on the car.

2-2 犬（いぬ）が <u>ドアの ところに</u> います。　The dog is where the door is.

2-3 赤（あか）ちゃんは <u>まだ</u> 一才（さい）です。　The baby is still a year old.

2-3 兄（あに）は <u>もう</u> サンフランシスコに 住（す）んで いません。

My older brother is not living in SF any more.

2-3 Verb Dictionary form

2-4 母（はは）は 歌（うた）を <u>歌（うた）うの／こと</u>が 好きです。　My mother likes to sing.

2-4 日本語（にほんご）を <u>勉強（べんきょう）するの／こと</u>は 楽（たの）しいです。　Studying Japanese is fun.

3課

3-1 父（ちち）は 青（あお）い シャツを <u>着（き）ています</u>。　My father is wearing a blue shirt.

3-1 あの 生徒（せいと）は 黒（くろ）いズボンを <u>はいて います</u>。　That student is wearing black pants.

3-1 姉（あね）は 白（しろ）いネックレス <u>して います</u>。　My older sister is wearing a white necklace.

3-1 弟（おとうと）は いつも ぼうしを <u>かぶって います</u>。　My younger brother always wears a hat.

3-1 母（はは）は めがねを <u>かけて います</u>。　My mother is wearing glasses.

3-2 この学校（がっこう）では Tシャツを <u>着（き）ても いいです</u>。　You may wear T-shirts at this school.

3-2 プレゼントは <u>高（たか）くても かまいません</u>。　I don't mind if the present is expensive.

3-2 パーティーは 一時（じ）<u>でも いいです</u>。　I don't mind if the party is at 1 o'clock.

3-2 教室（きょうしつ）で <u>食（た）べては いけません</u>。　You may not eat in the classroom.

3-2 ショートパンツは <u>短（みじか）くては いけません</u>。　Shorts should not be (too) short.

3-2 この 本（ほん）では <u>だめです</u>。　This book will not do.

3-3 図書館（としょかん）へ 本（ほん）を <u>借（か）りに</u> 来（き）ました。　I came to the library to borrow a book.

3-3 旅行（りょこう）<u>に 行（い）きます</u>。　I will go on a trip.

243

3-4 「昨日は　海に　行きませんでしたか。」   "Yesterday, didn't you go to the beach?"

   「はい、行きませんでした。」   "No, I didn't go."

3-4 ピアスを　一つだけ　しても　いいです。   You may wear only one pierced earring.

3-4 結婚したいんです。   I really want to get married.

4課

4-1 Verb NAI form

4-1 Informal conversation

4-1 「行く？」　　「うん、行く。」   "Are you going? "　"Yes, I will go."

4-1 「今　お昼　食べる？」   "Are you going to eat lunch now?"

   「ううん、今　食べない。」   "No, I am not eating now."

4-2 宿題を　忘れないで　下さい。   Please don't forget (your) homework.

4-2 今日　おそく　起きました。   I got up late today.

4-2 漢字を　もっと　きれいに　書いて　下さい。   Please write the *kanji* more neatly.

5課

5-1 ぼくは　ピザと　コーラに　します。   I will have pizza and a coke.

5-1 わあ、おいしそうですねえ。   Wow, that looks delicious, doesn't it!

5-1 あの　学生は　とても　頭が　よさそうですね。

    That student over there looks very smart, doesn't he?

5-1 あの　人は　テニスが　上手そうですねえ。   That person looks skillful at tennis!

5-1 今日　雨が　ふりそうですねえ。   It looks like it will rain today.

5-1 私の　朝ご飯は　毎日　パンに　コーヒーです。

    Every day my breakfast is bread and coffee.

5-2 今　授業に　行かなければ　なりません。   I have to go to class now.

5-2 お昼ご飯を　食べなくても　いいです。   I don't have to eat lunch.

5-3 おすしを　食べて　みましょう。   Let's try eating *sushi*.

5-3 この　くつを　はいて　みて　ください。   Please try wearing these shoes.

八課   244

6課

6-1 母は 少し 日本語が 出来ます。　　　My mom can speak a little Japanese.

6-1 手が いたくて、書くことが 出来ません。　　My hands hurt, and I cannot write.

6-2 「私 ゆみですが、こうじさん いますか。」　　"I am Yumi. Is Koji there?"

6-2 「山田ですが... 」　　"I am Yamada." [Expecting a response from the listener.]

6-3 来年 日本へ 行くつもりです。　　Next year, I plan to go to Japan.

6-3 今晩 十二時まで 寝ないつもりです。　Tonight, I don't plan to go to bed until 12 o'clock.

6-3 明日 試験が あるはずです。　　Tomorrow, there is supposed to be an exam.

6-3 明日 試験は ないはずです。　　Tomorrow, there is not supposed to be an exam.

6-3 父は 仕事で 東京へ 行きました。　My father went to Tokyo for work.

6-4 学校を 三日も 休みました。　　I was absent from school for as many as three days.

6-4 一日に 何時間ぐらい 勉強しますか。　How many hours a day do you study?

7課

7-1 Verb TA form

7-1 この 本を 読んだことが あります。　　I have read this book.

7-1 まだ 日本へ 行ったことが ありません。　I have not gone to Japan yet.

7-2 Verb NAKATTA form

7-2 明日は たぶん くもりでしょう。　　It will probably be cloudy tomorrow.

7-2 昨日は 雪が ふらなかったでしょう。　　It probably did not snow yesterday.

7-2 お天気は わるかったでしょう。　　The weather was probably bad.

7-2 この 音楽を 知って いるでしょう？　You know this music, don't you?

7-4 友達を パーティーに 連れて 行っても いいですか。

May I bring my friends to your party?

7-4 ぜひ 友達を 連れて 来て 下さい。　　By all means, please bring your friends.

7-4 ケーキを クラスに 持って 来ても いいですか。　　May I bring cake to class?

7-4 おばあさんの うちに プレゼントを 持って 行きました。

I took a present to my grandmother's house.

八課

By the end of this lesson, you will be able to communicate the information below in the given situations.

【11-9 タスク1】

A salesperson and a young Japanese customer are at a department store.

Salesperson:

(1) Welcome the customer and ask if he/she needs help.

(2) Ask what kind of hats he/she wants.

(3) Mention that the prices range from $4.99 to $125.50.

(4) Tell the customer that you have them in various designs, sizes, and colors.

(5) Give the price of the hat, the tax, and the total price. (Use one sentence.)

(6) Answer yes, he/she can. Ask to see the customer's I.D.

(7) Answer that you do not have a box, and that you only have bags.

Japanese Customer:

(1) Answer yes, and request to see some caps.

(2) Answer that you want a good one.

(3) Say that you don't mind if the hat is a little expensive.

(4) Say that you want a certain hat (use two adjectives to describe the one you select).

(5) Ask if you may pay with a traveler's check.

(6) Show your I.D. Ask the salesperson if he/she can put it in a box because it's a souvenir gift.

(7) Say that you do not mind a bag.

【11-9 タスク2】

A salesperson and a young Japanese customer are at a department store.

Salesperson:

(1) You know that the customer is a tourist. Ask what he/she thinks of your state/city.

(2) Ask if Japanese students and American students are the same.

(3) Ask which he/she likes more, Japan or America. Ask why.

(4) Ask the customer where in the state/city he/she wants to go to the most.

(5) Thank the customer and ask him/her to come again.

Japanese Customer:

(1) Give your opinion of the state/city. (Use two adjectives.)

(2) Answer yes, American students and Japanese students both study hard.

(3) Answer that Japan is not as dangerous as America. However, you prefer America because it is more free than Japan.

(4) Say which place in the state/city you want to see the most. Explain why.

< Ken is working part time at a souvenir T-shirt shop. A Japanese customer enters the shop.>

ケン：いらっしゃいませ。何を　さしあげましょうか。

日本人：Tシャツを　見せて　下さい。

ケン：どんな　デザインが　いいですか。
　　　この猫や　犬の　デザインは　いかがですか。

日本人：猫の　デザインの方が　犬のより　可愛いですねえ。

ケン：鼠のは　いかがですか。猫と　犬と　鼠の　デザインの　中では
　　　どれが　一番　お好きですか。

日本人：そうですねえ...　この　中では　鼠のが　一番　いいですね。

ケン：鼠の　デザインのは　白と　青だけです。白と　青とでは
　　　どちらが　お好きですか。

日本人：白は　青ほど　好きでは　ありません。青の　Mサイズを　下さい。
　　　アメリカの　Mサイズは　日本の　Mサイズと　同じですか。

ケン：さあ...　　<Ken shows a medium T-shirt to the Japanese customer.>
　　　くらべて　みて　下さい。

日本人：違いますね。アメリカの　サイズの方が　もっと　大きいですね。
　　　じゃ、Sサイズを　下さい。お土産ですから、箱に　入れて
　　　下さい。

ケン：すみません。袋だけですが...　でも、これは　セールですから、
　　　お値段は　安いです。

日本人：トラベラーズチェックで　払っても　いいですか。

ケン：はい、かまいませんが、パスポートを　見せて　下さい。税金が
　　　かかりますから、二十八ドル五十セントです。おつりは
　　　二十一ドル五十セントです。有難うございました。また、どうぞ。

Let's review previous vocabulary!

A. めいし　Nouns
1.	Ｔシャツ	T-shirt	10.	白〔しろ〕	white
2.	Ｔシャツや	T-shirt store	11.	あお	blue
3.	アルバイト	part-time job	12.	アメリカ	America
4.	ねこ	cat	13.	Ｍサイズ	medium size
5.	シャツ	shirt	14.	Ｓサイズ	small size
6.	犬〔いぬ〕	dog	15.	これ	this
7.	ねずみ	mouse	16.	二十八ドル	$ 28
8.	どれ？	which one?	17.	五十セント	50 cents
9.	いろ	color	18.	二十一ドル	$ 21

B. どうし　Verbs
19. 見せて　下さい〔G2 見せる／見せます〕　　　please show me
20. あります〔G1 ある〕　　　　　　　　　　　　there is
21. はらっても　いいですか〔G1 はらう〕　　　　May I pay? Is it all right if I pay?
22. かまいません　　　　　　　　　　　　　　　do not matter

C. -い けいようし　I Adjectives
23.	かわいい	cute	25.	安い〔やすい〕	cheap
24.	大きい	big			

C. -な けいようし　NA Adjectives
26.	好き	like	27.	好きではありません	do not like

D. Others
28.	どんな	what kind of?	31.	～だけ	only ～
29.	犬〔いぬ〕＋の	dog's	32.	でも、	However, But
30.	じゃ、	Then,			

E. Expressions
33. いらっしゃいませ。　　　Welcome.
34. そうですねえ...　　　　　Let me see . . . [let me think about this a little]
35. すみません　　　　　　　Sorry, Excuse me.

F. ぶんぽう　Grammar
36. ～は　いかがですか。　　　　　　　　　How about ～? [Polite]
37. ～を　下さい。　　　　　　　　　　　　Please give me ～.
38. Verb Te form ＋て　みて　下さい。　　　Please try doing ～.
39. Sentence 1 ＋から、Sentence 2。　　　　S1, so S2.

【会話】

Formal style： ケン：猫の　デザインと　犬の　デザインとでは　どちらが

お好きですか。

客：犬の　デザインの方が　猫の　デザインより　好きです。

【文型】

Noun 1 と　Noun 2 (と) で (or と or で)は　どちら (or どっち)(の方) が　〜ですか。
Which is more 〜, Noun 1 or Noun 2?
Noun 1 の方が　Noun 2 より　（もっと）　〜です。or Noun 2 より　　Noun 1 の方が　　（もっと）　〜です。 Noun 1 is more 〜 than Noun 2.

【単語】

1. A と B で
between A and B

2. どっち
which (one of two)?
[Informal]

3. どちら
which (one of two)?
Polite expression of どっち.

4. こちら, そちら, あちら
this one, that one,
that one over there
Polite eqiv. of これ, それ, あれ.

5. (〜の) 方〔ほう〕
alternative
♡のほうが　好きです。
I prefer ♡.

6. 〜より
more than 〜
Bは　Aより　たかいです。
B is more expensive than A.

7. もっと
more
もっと　たかいです。
It is more expensive.

8. ずっと
by far
ずっと　たかいです。
It is far more expensive.

九課

9. 両方〔りょうほう〕

both

りょうほう　好きです。

I like both.

10. どちら(or どっち)も + Neg.

neither, not either ～

どちら(or どっち)も　好きではありません。[Polite expression of 好きですか。]

I do not like either.

11. お好きですか。

Do you like it?

12. Superior に＋さしあげます

[G2 さしあげる]

to give (to a superior)

[Humble form of あげます]

13. 何を　さしあげましょうか。

May I help you?

[lit., What shall I give you?]

【＊オプショナル単語】
1. ＊ てんいん　　　　　　　　＊ store clerk
2. ＊ （お）きゃく（さま）　＊ customer, guest [お and さま added for politeness.]

【漢字】

1. 白　white　　しろ　　白い　シャツ a white shirt

白木屋〔しろきや〕 *Shirokiya* department store

ハク　　白人〔はくじん〕 Caucasian

⊙　→　⊟　→　白　＝　白

sun's rays pointing up

九課

2. 百　hundred　ヒャク　百人〔ひゃくにん〕 100 people

ビャク　三百〔さんびゃく〕 300

ピャク　六百〔ろっぴゃく〕 600

八百〔はっぴゃく〕 800

pointing hand

sun's rays pointing up

One white coin is a ¥100.

【文法】

A. Noun 1 と　Noun 2(と)では (or と or で)　どちら(or どっち)(の方) が
　～ですか。

　　Which is more ～, Noun 1 or Noun 2?

When asking a question that solicits a comparison between two nouns, this pattern is used. Both alternatives (nouns) are listed before the question is asked. The interrogative (question word) used in comparing two nouns is どちら or どっち. どちら is slightly more formal than どっち. Note that some portions of this pattern are optional. The particle が follows the interrogative word.

1.「こちらと　そちらと　どちら (の方) が　お好きですか。」

　　"Which do you like better, this or that?"

2.「Lサイズと　Mサイズでは　どちらが　いいですか。」

　　"Which is better, the large size or the medium size?"

3.「日本の　夏と　アラスカの　夏と　どっちの方が　暑いですか。」

　　"Which is hotter, Japan's summers or Alaska's summers?"

B. Noun 1 の方が (or は)　Noun 2 より　(もっと)　～です。or

Noun 2 より　Noun 1 の方が　(もっと)　～です。

　　Noun 1 is more ～ than Noun 2.

This construction is used when two nouns are compared. The noun followed by は or のほうが is the subject, and the noun that is comparatively less (い adjective/な adjective) than the subject is followed by より. The use of もっと is optional.

1.「犬と　猫と　どちら　(の方)　が　好きですか。」

"Which do you like better, dogs or cats?"

　　「犬の　方が　好きです。」　　　　　　　　"I like dogs better."

2.私は　犬の　方が　猫より　好きです。　　I like dogs more than cats.

3.赤い　シャツより　青い　シャツの　方が　いいです。

The blue shirt is better than the red shirt.

4.日本語の　方が　ずっと　むずかしいです。　Japanese is far more difficult.

【 ● 文化ノート】

1. おみやげ　*Omiyage*

Japan is a gift-giving culture. For various social reasons, the practice of gift-giving is one of the many ways Japanese maintain relationships. One highly visible practice seen even as Japanese go beyond their own country is that of purchasing おみやげ. Traditionally, travelers receive monetary gifts (おせんべつ) upon embarking on a trip. In return, the traveler shops for and purchases souvenirs for all those who have given them these gifts of money. おみやげ are gifts that are made in or representative of the area to which the traveler is visiting. It is common for Japanese travelers to carry lists of names of persons for whom おみやげ must be purchased. Purchasing of おみやげ can become quite a burden, financial and otherwise, to travelers. This explains the reason for the extravagant spending of Japanese as they frantically shop when they travel abroad. It also explains the existence of so many gift and souvenir shops throughout Japan, especially at famous tourist attractions. Gifts may range from anything such as designer leather goods, perfumes, liquor, food items, and T-shirts to little keychains and trinkets. Generally, one shops for items that match the amount of the parting gift one receives.

2. A Japanese Proverb　「はなより　だんご」
　「はなより　だんご」means "*Dango* (sweet rice balls) rather than flowers." The similar Western expression is "The belly is not filled with fair words."

九課

【アクティビティー】

A. ペアワーク

Using the cues below, ask your partner comparative questions. Take turns asking and answering questions.

Ex. 日本, アメリカ (広_{ひろ}い)

質問_{しつもん}:「日本と　アメリカとで　どちら (or どっち) の方_{ほう}が
　　　　　広_{ひろ}いですか。」

答_{こた}え:「アメリカの　方_{ほう}が　日本より　もっと　広_{ひろ}いです。」

1. おにいさん, おとうとさん (せが　たかい)

2. (あたまが　いい)

3. (たかい)

¥8000　　¥3000

4. 化学_かの　先生, 日本語の　先生 (やさしい)

5. (ふとって　います)

6. (おもしろい)

7. (かみが　ながい)

18　　　　16

8. (年を　とって　います)

65　　70

九課　　　　　256

B. ペアワーク

Interview each other using the cues below. Answer based on facts. Write your partner's response.

Ex. 犬,猫 (好き)

質問：「犬と　猫とで　どちら (or どっち)　(の方)　が　好きですか。」

答え：「犬の　方が　猫より　もっと　好きです。」or

　　　「両方　好きです。」or

　　　「どちら (or どっち) も　好きではありません。」

1. チョコレートアイスクリーム, 　バニラアイスクリーム (好き)	
2. コーラ, ソーダ (好き)	
3. さかな, とりにく (好き)	
4. やきゅう, フットボール (好き)	
5. ヴァイオリン, ギター (やさしい)	
6. すう学, えい語 (むずかしい)	
7. お父さん, お母さん (きびしい)	
8. (Think of your own.)	

C. ペアワーク

You are a customer. Your partner is a store clerk. Carry on a conversation in Japanese. Take turns.

Ex. とけい (You don't mind if it is expensive, but want a good watch.)

店員 (clerk)　：「いらっしゃいませ。何を　さしあげましょうか。」

客 (customer)　：「すみません。とけいを　見せて　下さい。」

店員 (clerk)　：「どんな　とけいが　お好きですか。」

客 (customer)　：「そうですねえ ...　高くても　いいです。いい　とけいが

　　　　　　　　ほしいです。」

| 1. シャツ (white M size) | 2. バッグ (big black) | 3. くつ (famous brand) |

九課

【会話】

Formal style: ケン：犬の　デザインと　猫の　デザインと
どちら（の方）が　お好きですか。
客：猫の　デザインは　犬の　デザインほど
好きではありません。

【文型】

Noun 1 は　Noun 2 ほど　Negative predicate.	Noun 1 is not as 〜 as Noun 2.

【単語】

1.〜ほど＋ Neg.

(not) as 〜 as

ねこは　いぬほど　良くないです。

Cats are not as good as dogs.

2.(お)ねだん

price

[お for politeness]

3.デザイン

design

4.セール(中)

on sale

(at a markdown)

5.いろいろ

various [な Adj.]

いろいろな　いろ various colors
いろいろ　あります。There is a variety.

6.ほか

other

ほかの　いろ other colors
ほかに　何か？ Anything else?

7.ありがとうございました。

Thank you very much.

[Used after one has received something, or after a deed has been done.]

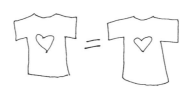

8. くらべる

[G2 くらべます／くらべて]

to compare

N1と　N2を　くらべます。

(I) compare N1 and N2.

N1を　N2と　くらべます。

(I) compare N1 to N2.

9. 同じ〔おなじ〕

same

N1と　N2は　おなじです。

N1 and N2 are the same.

N1は　N2と　おなじです。

N1 is the same as N2.

おなじ　いろ

same color

10. ちがう

[G1 ちがいます]

is different, is wrong

N1と　N2は　ちがいます。

N1 and N2 are different.

N1は　N2と　ちがいます。

N1 is different from N2.

ちがう　いろ

different color, wrong color

【漢字】

1. 千　　1,000　　　　セン　　二千〔にせん〕2,000

八千〔はっせん〕8,000

ゼン　　三千〔さんぜん〕3,000

an army of soliders is marching

2. 万　　10,000　　　　マン　　一万〔いちまん〕10,000

十万〔じゅうまん〕100,000

百万〔ひゃくまん〕one million

Manji symbol (a religion from India)

A. Noun 1 は   Noun 2 ほど   Negative Predicate。

This construction is used to compare two nouns in a negative ending sentence, i. e., "not as ... as."
The noun followed by は is the one that is comparatively less (い adjective / な adjective).
ほど follows the noun that is comparatively more (い adjective / な adjective). The predicate must
<u>always</u> appear in the negative form.

1. 私<u>は</u>　兄や　姉<u>ほど</u>　頭が　良くないです。

   I am not as smart as my older brother and older sister.

2. アメリカ<u>は</u>　カナダ<u>ほど</u>　広くありません。

    America is not as spacious as Canada.

3. 白いの<u>は</u>　黒いの<u>ほど</u>　好きではありません。

   I don't like the white one as much as the black one.

4. アメリカのＣＤ<u>は</u>　日本のＣＤ<u>ほど</u>　高くありません。

   America's CDs are not as expensive as Japan's CDs.

B. お〜

  A prefix that expresses politeness. Do not attach お to words unless you have previously heard
or seen them used with お.

1. 「<u>お</u>好きですか。」   "Do you like it?"

2. 「今日　シャツは　<u>お</u>安いですよ。」 "Shirts are cheap today."

3. 「すみません。これは　<u>お</u>いくらですか。」 "Excuse me, how much is this?"

 「五百円です。」   "It is ￥500."

【 ● 文化ノート】

日本のサイズと　アメリカのサイズ

Clothing Sizes

 Clothing sizes in Japan and America differ slightly. For T-shirts, American sizes are generally one
size larger than Japanese sizes. In Japan, shoes are sized by metric measurement. While in Japan,
it is best to try on clothing for fit.

【アクティビティー】

A. ペアワーク

Using the cues below, ask your partner questions. Your partner should answer your questions using ほど. Take turns.

Ex. 中国,アメリカ (大きい)

質問：「中国と　アメリカとで　どちら（or どっち）（の方）が
　　　　　大きいですか。」

答え：「アメリカは　中国ほど　大きくないです。」

1. 中国,アメリカ (大きい)

2. あき,ふゆ (さむい)

3. 日本語,スペイン語 (むずかしい)

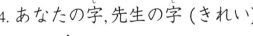 Buenos dias.

4. あなたの字,先生の字 (きれい)

5. ひこうき,じどう車 (あぶない)

6. 月曜日,金曜日 (いそがしい)

月曜日　　金曜日

7. ごきぶり,ねずみ (おおい)

8. すもうとり,あなた (ふとっています)

 YOU

261

九課

B. ペアワーク

Ask your partner questions using the cues below. Your partner should answer using より and ほど.
Take turns.

Example: Two subjects （好き）

質問：「日本語と　数学とで　どちら（or どっち）（の方）が

　　　　　好きですか。」

答え１：「（日本語）の方が　（数学）より　好きです。」

答え２：「（数学）は　（日本語）ほど　好きではありません。」

1. Two sports （上手）	
2. Two subjects （せいせきが　いい）	
3. お父さん, お母さん （きびしい）	
4. Two movies （好き）	
5. Two singers （好き）	
6. Two TV programs （おもしろい）	
7. Two friends （せが　たかい）	
8. 土曜日, 日曜日 （いそがしい）	

C. ペアワーク

Find out things in common and things not in common between you and your partner while carrying on a conversation in Japanese.

「あなたと　私は　どこが　同じでしょうか。」

「あなたと　私は　どこが　ちがうでしょうか。」

おなじこと	
ちがうこと	

D. ペアワーク

Role play the following conversation between a store clerk and a customer. You may replace the words in the ☐ with other words.

店員：いらっしゃいませ。何を　さしあげましょうか。

客：くつを　見せて下さい。

店員：どんな　くつが　お好きですか。

客：白い　くつが　ほしいんですが...

店員：このくつは　いかがですか。

客：ほかのを　見せて　下さい。

店員：では、こちらは　いかがでしょうか。

客：ああ、いいですね。じゃ、これを　下さい。おいくらですか。

店員：セール中ですから、お値段は　お安いです。50ドルです。

　　　ありがとうございました。

【会話】

Formal style: ケン：犬と　猫と　鼠の　デザインの　中で　どれが　一番
お好きですか。

客：この中で　犬のが　一番　好きです。

【文型】

N1と　N2と　N3 (と) で　どれ/何/どこ/だれ/いつ etc. が　一番　〜ですか。

〜 (の中) で　〜が　一番　〜です。

【単語】

1. どれ

which one (of three or more)?

どれが　好きですか。

Which one do you like?

2. (〜の中) で

among 〜

この　シャツの　中で

Among these shirts,

3. この中で

among these

4. 一番〔いちばん〕

the most

♡が　一ばん　好きです。

I like ♡ the most.

5. 世界〔せかい〕

world

6. 国〔くに〕

country, nation

7. 州〔しゅう〕

state

8. 市〔し〕

city

9. 島〔しま〕

island

10. さあ . . .

Well . . . [Used when one does not know or is unsure of the answer.]

九課

264

【漢字】

1. 方　　person (polite)　　かた　　　あの方　that person (polite)

　　　　alternative　　　　　ホウ　　　この　方が　好きです。I like this better?

　　　　　　　　　　　　　　　　　両方〔りょうほう〕both

〇 → ヽ → ヽ ＋

head

卍 → Ｘ → 万 → 万 ＝ 方

Manji symbol (a religion from India)

The head of 10,000 people determines the direction.

2. 玉　　ball, coin　　　　　たま　　　玉田〔たまだ〕さん

　　　　　　　　　　　　　　　　　玉川〔たまかわ〕さん

　　　　　　　　　　　　　　　　　玉城〔たましろ〕さん

　　　　　　　　　　　　だま　　　お年玉〔としだま〕New Year's money gift to children

　　　　　　　　　　　　　　　　　十円玉〔じゅうえんだま〕￥10 coin

　　　　　　　　　　　　　　　　　目玉〔めだま〕eyeball

jewel

3. 国　　country　　　　　　くに、ぐに　　どこの　国？　Which country?

　　　　　　　　　　　　　　　　　国本〔くにもと〕さん

　　　　　　　　　　　　コク、ゴク　　外国〔がいこく〕foreign country

　　　　　　　　　　　　　　　　　韓国〔かんこく〕Korea

　　　　　　　　　　　　　　　　　中国〔ちゅうごく〕China

九課

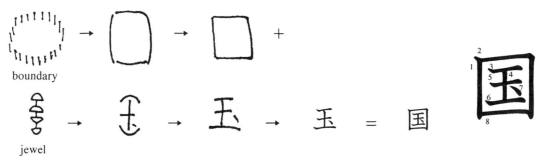

boundary

jewel

国 = 国

Jewels within boundaries symbolize a country.

【文法】

A.	Noun 1 と　　Noun 2 と　　Noun 3 （と）	で	どれ 何 だれ どこ いつ etc.	が	一番(いちばん)〜ですか。
	Category				
	Place				
	この中／その中／あの中				

When comparing three or more objects, the objects are listed before the question. Other than listing the individual choices, a category may be named, from which a choice would have to be named in the answer. The question word is most often どれ, but may also be なに, だれ, どこ, etc., depending on the question. The particle following the interrogative (question) word is が. いちばん must precede the い adjective or な adjective.

1. 「赤と　白と　黒で　どの色が　一番　好きですか。」

   "Which color do you like best, red, white, or black?"

2. 「魚と　豚肉と　チキンで　どれが　一番　いいですか。」

   "Which is best, fish, pork, or chicken?"

   「私は　魚に　します。」　　"I will have fish."

3. 「日本語と　中国語と　ドイツ語で　どれが　一番　難しいですか。」

   "Which is most difficult, Japanese, Chinese, or German?"

   「さあ...　日本語でしょう。」　"Hmm ... probably Japanese."

4. 「この　クラスで　だれが　一番　背が　高いですか。」

   "In this class, who is the tallest?"

   「マイクさんです。」　　"Mike is."

B. ～（の 中〔なか〕）で ～が 一番〔ばん〕 (い adjective / な adjective / Verb)。

This construction is used when three or more nouns are being compared. It singles out one noun as the one that is most (い adjective / な adjective / Verb) among at least three items. The particle で follows a category or group of items from which one is being singled out as the superlative.
一番〔いちばん〕 is the required superlative that precedes the い adjective, な adjective or verb.

1. この 中で これが 一番〔ばん〕 好きです。　　Among these, I like this best.

2. 「友達〔ともだち〕の 中で だれが 一番〔ばん〕 字〔じ〕が きれいですか。」

"Among your friends, who has the best writing?"

「ジーナさんです。」　　"Gina does."

3. 「先生の 中で だれが 一番〔ばん〕 きびしいですか。」

"Among the teachers, who is the strictest?"

「体育〔たいいく〕の 先生です。」　　"My P.E. teacher is."

【 ● 文化〔ぶんか〕ノート】

Specialty Shops

Tokyo abounds with specialty shops. Certain areas of Tokyo are known for their collections of shops where special goods can be purchased. Perhaps the best known is *Akihabara*, which boasts dozens of stores featuring electrical and electronic goods and parts. Prices are generally good, and the variety is amazing. One can also expect to bargain at most of the stores here. It is not uncommon to spend a whole day here shopping for a stereo, CD player, or TV. Other areas in Tokyo known for special items are *Kanda* for books, *Tsukiji* for fish and seafood, and *Okachimachi* and *Ueno* for wholesale food items. *Shinjuku* is also known for its many camera shops. There are other interesting places known for their specialties. One that has become popular recently is *Kappabashi*, which is lined with shops that sell the plastic food samples found in windows of restaurants throughout Japan.

Electronic goods stores at *Akihabara*

Plastic *sushi* samples at a *Kappabashi* shop

九課

【🄰🄰アクティビティー】

A. ペアワーク - Tic-Tac-Toe

Directions:

1. You and your partner take turns doing the following: Each partner takes an O or X card below. Choose a square and tell your partner the number of that square.

2. When your partner hears the number you give, he/she will read the item in that square. Do not read the word in parenthesis. If you tell your partner "number 5," for example, your partner reads the item in square 5. If your partner says "Number 2," you read question 2.

3. Listen to your partner's answer. The correct answer appears in parenthesis in your box .

4. Let's say that you are "O" and your partner is "X." If you answer correctly, both you and your partner must mark an O in the numbered space on the Tic-Tac-Toe game sheet. If you answer question 5 correctly, for example, both players must mark an O in space # 5. If your partner gives a correct answer, tell him/her that the answer is correct, and then both of you must mark an X in the correct square. For example, if your partner answers question 2 correctly, both of you must put an X in space # 2.

5. If you don't answer correctly, it is your partner's turn to give a number. You may ask for the same number again later if you missed it the first time and if that square is still unmarked. If your partner gives an incorrect answer (one that is not in parenthesis after the question), tell your partner that the answer is wrong, but do NOT give the answer. Your partner may ask the same question again later in the game. If an answer is wrong, no mark is put on the game sheet, and it is the other person's turn again to try to answer a question.

Who wins?

1. The first person to get three in a row (horizontally, vertically, or diagonally), OR

2. The first person to answer five questions correctly, OR

3. When all the squares have been filled, the person with the most marks (five marks), OR

4. When both are not able to answer any more questions, the person with the most marks wins.

ゲーム 1 : What is the antonym (opposite)?

[O person]

1. あつい （さむい）	2. はやい （おそい）	3. くろい （白い）
4. 大きい （小さい）	5. ながい （みじかい）	6. うるさい （しずか）
7. やさしい （むずかしい）	8. ちかい （とおい）	9. あたらしい （ふるい）

1. ひろい （せまい）	2. 年を とって います （わかい）	3. ふとって います （やせて います）
4. あつい （さむい）	5. おもしろい （つまらない）	6. いい （わるい）
7. 好き （きらい）	8. たかい （やすい）	9. おいしい （まずい）

ゲーム２：Give the correct answer.

[O person]

1. アメリカで　どの しゅうは　一番 小さいですか。 （ロードアイランド） なかむら	2. せかいで　どの国が 一番　大きいですか。 （ロシア） かさま	3. せかいで　どの　山が 一番　たかいですか。 （エベレスト） こにし
4. アメリカで　どの 川が　一番 ながいですか。 （ミシシッピー）	5. 日本と　中国と かん国とで　どの　国が アメリカに　一番 ちかいですか。 （日本）	6. はると　なつと ふゆとで　いつが　一番 さむいですか。 （ふゆ）
7. せかいで　どの どうぶつが　一番 はやいですか。 （チーター） さいき	8. ほっかいどうと 本しゅうと　九しゅうで どこが　一番　みなみに ありますか。 （九しゅう）いいい	9. アメリカで　どの しゅうが　一番　にしに ありますか。 （ハワイ） いがわ

九課

1. アメリカで どの しゅうが 一番 大きいですか。 (アラスカ) *いりえ*	2. せかいで どの しまが 一番 大きいですか。 (グリーンランド)	3. はると なつと ふゆとで いつが 一番 あついですか。 (なつ)
4. せかいで どの 川が 一番 ながいですか。 [2つ] (アマゾンとナイル)	5. せかいで どのうみが 一番 大きいですか。 (たいへいよう Pacific Ocean)	6. アメリカで どの たてものが 一番 たかいですか。 (シアーズタワー)
7. ひこうきと 車と しんかんせんとで 何が 一番 はやいですか。 (ひこうき)	8. せかいで どの どうぶつが 一番 大きいですか。 (くじら whale)	9. 日本と 中国と アメリカとで どこが 一番 小さいですか。 (日本)

ゲーム3 : Answer using はい or いいえ.

1. ひこうきの 方が 車より はやいです。 (はい)	2. きょうか書の 方が ノートより やすいです。 (いいえ)	3. 日本人は アメリカ人より だいたい せが たかいです。 (いいえ)
4. アメリカは 日本ほど ひろくないです。 (いいえ) *はまさき*	5. いぬは ぶたほど あたまが よくないです。 (いいえ)	6. ぶたより ねずみの 方が 大きいです。 (いいえ)
7. あきは ふゆほど さむくないです。 (はい)	8. はるやすみは ふゆやすみより みじかいです。 (はい)	9. ホノルルしの 方が ニューヨークしより 人が おおいです。 (いいえ)

1. 日本の　学校の きそくは アメリカの　学校の きそくより　じゆうです。 （いいえ）	2. 私は すもうとりほど 大きくないです。 （はい）	3. アラスカは ハワイほど あつくないです。 （はい） よしはう
4. スペイン語は 日本語ほど むずかしくないです。 （はい）	5. スーパーの　ものは デパートの　ものほど たかくないです。 （はい）	6. だいたい　子どもより おばあさんの　方が しずかです。 （はい）
7. レストランの　方が カフェテリアより やすいです。 （いいえ）	8. 私より すもうとりの　方が ふとっています。 （はい）	9. 学校は 家より せまいです。 （いいえ）　みのだ

九課

【会話】

Formal style:　客：おいくらですか。

ケン：税金が　かかりますから、全部で　三十ドル五十セント
　　　です。

客：トラベラーズチェックで　払っても　いいですか。

ケン：はい、どうぞ。

【単語】

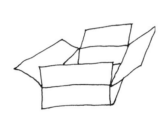

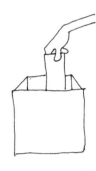

1.（お）みやげ

souvenir gift

2. はこ

box

3. ふくろ

paper bag

4. (container) に　入れる
[G2 いれます]

to put in ～

5. 税金
〔ぜいきん〕

tax

6. おつり

change (from a larger
unit of money)

7. トラベラーズ
チェック

traveler's check

8. クレジット
カード

credit card

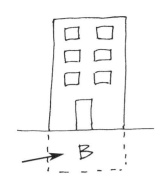

9. 地下
〔ちか〕

basement

10. かかる
[G1 かかります]

to require (tax), to take (time)

11. 売って います
[G1 うる／うります]

are selling

12. また どうぞ。

Please come again.

13. FLOOR

？F	なん<u>が</u>い？
10 F	じ(ゅ)っかい
9 F	きゅうかい
8 F	はっかい
7 F	ななかい
6 F	ろっかい
5 F	ごかい
4 F	よんかい
3 F	さん<u>が</u>い
2 F	にかい
1 F	いっかい
B 1 F	ちかいっかい

【＊オプショナル単語】

1. ＊ レシート   ＊ receipt
2. ＊ しょうひぜい   ＊ sales tax
3. ＊ 現金 〔げんきん〕 or キャッシュ   ＊ cash
4. ＊ 小切手 〔こぎって〕   ＊ a check

九課

【漢字】

1. 安　cheap　　やす（い）　安い　本〔やすい　ほん〕a cheap book

安田〔やすだ〕さん

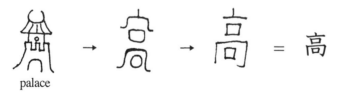

house → → +

woman → → 女 ＝ 安

安

A woman in a house feels peaceful and secure. A woman who stays at home does not earn money, so the household's income is cheap (low).

2. 高　expensive,　　たか（い）　高い　家〔たかい　いえ〕an expensive house

high

高田〔たかた／たかだ〕さん

高山〔たかやま〕さん

高木〔たかき／たかぎ〕さん

コウ　高校〔こうこう〕high school

高校生〔こうこうせい〕high school student

palace → 高 → 高 ＝ 高

高

【 🔴 文化ノート】

1. トラベラーズチェック Traveler's Checks

Although the practice of using traveler's checks is gradually increasing among Japanese who travel abroad, it is still more common to see Japanese using cash. Recently, more Japanese people have started to use credit cards. Using checks is not as common in Japan as in the United States. Traditionally, Japanese have not used signatures as a form of identification. Personal seals (はんこ) were used to verify and approve important transactions.

はんこ Personal Seal

2. 日本のデパート Japanese Department Stores

Japanese department stores provide a much broader range of goods and services to their customers than their American counterparts. Japanese department stores are known to carry quality items, including many designer goods. In addition to clothing, housewares, gift items and stationery items, large Japanese department stores also house numerous restaurants and basement floor vendors that sell groceries and food items similar to supermarkets. Many department stores also accommodate art galleries, playgrounds for children on their rooftops, and even nurseries for mothers to rest with their children. Ticket outlets sell tickets for concerts and special performances in town. Pet shops and garden shops can also be found in some department stores. During the summer, "beer gardens", or outdoor bars crop up on the rooftops of some department stores. The number of clerks and other employees far outnumber those at American department stores. They are trained to serve their customers with utmost politeness. They are dressed in neat uniforms. Department stores also often hire elevator and escalator girls to greet and assist customers as they get on and off. At each floor, elevator girls announce the main departments located on the floor and press appropriate buttons in the elevators as customers request the floors they want to visit. At the register, Japanese usually pay in cash, though the use of credit cards is gradually increasing. Purchased items are carefully wrapped in the department store's special gift paper. Huge bargain sales take place about twice a year, and it is common for women to mob the bargain counters, sometimes with bickering among them. All department stores close one day a week. Different department stores close on different days of the week.

Elevator girl at a Japanese department store

【👧👧アクティビティー】

A. クラスワーク

Ask your partner where in the Japanese department store each item on your shopping list is sold.

Ex. T-shirt

客：すみません。Tシャツは 何階で
売って いますか。
店員：Tシャツですか。Tシャツは
〜がいで 売って います。

Aさんの お買い物

1. おべんとう	
2. バッグ	
3. 女の人の ズボン	
4. 男の人の ズボン	
5. ペン	

Bさんの お買い物

1. 女の人の シャツ	
2. さかな	
3. くつ	
4. おはし	
5. CD	

おくじょう (rooftop)	
8 F	
7 F	
6 F	
5 F	
4 F	
3 F	
2 F	
1 F	
B 1 F	
B 2 F	

B. クラスワーク

Let's find a classmate who fits the following description. Write the person's name after the description.

質問：「あなたは　コカコーラより　ペプシの　方が　好きですか。」

1. ペプシの　方が　コカコーラより　好きです。	
2. マクドナルドの　ハンバーガーは　バーガーキングの　ハンバーガーほど　好きではありません。	
3. いぬの　方が　ねこより　好きです。	
4. 中国りょうりは　日本りょうりほど　好きではありません。	
5. 食べものの　中で　ピザが　一ばん　好きです。	
6. パスポートを　もって　います。	
7. ハンバーガーを　うったことが　あります。	
8. レストランで　アルバイトを　しても　いいです。	
9. Ｓサイズの　シャツを　きることが　出来ます。	
10. Ｔシャツの　みせで　はたらいたことが　あります。	

C. クラスワーク

Half of the class are clerks. The other half are customers. The store clerks prepare the items and put prices on them. The clerks greet the customers. Each customer has a certain budget and chooses items very carefully. The clerk calculates the tax and total price, gives the correct change, and hands the customer the purchased items. Be realistic in your prices and purchases.

九課

Find the answers from books, by talking to friends, or by using the Internet.

1. What kinds of things can you typically find on the top floors of major department stores in Japan?

2. What kind of things can you typically find in the basement of major department stores in Japan?

3. Department stores in Japan are often much more comprehensive in their offerings than American stores. For instance, they may have entire stationery stores within them that sell hundreds of different types of pens and pencils. Would you want your local department store to be more comprehensive, so you could do all your shopping in one place?

4. Elevators in major Japanese department stores are operated by women in uniform. All day long they ride up and down in the elevators, pushing buttons for customers and announcing floors. What do you think about this custom?

5. The Japanese custom of removing your shoes before entering a house has carried over to clothing stores, where you are often expected to remove your shoes before you enter a dressing room. Should Americans adopt this practice? Why or why not?

FUKUWARAI (lit., "happy laugh") is a beloved Japanese children's game similar to Pin the Tail on the Donkey. A large outline of a woman's face (see the following page) is pinned to a wall. The woman's face represents the face of OTAFUKU, easily identified in Japanese culture for her full round cheeks, a face wider at the bottom than at the top, a flat nose, curved, laughing eyes, and a small mouth. *Otafuku* is an expression of a homely, but delightful, charming and good natured woman. Children who play FUKUWARAI are blindfolded and handed parts of the face one by one. The object of the game is to place each of the facial parts in their correct positions. It is a game that truly draws "happy laughs" from everyone involved.

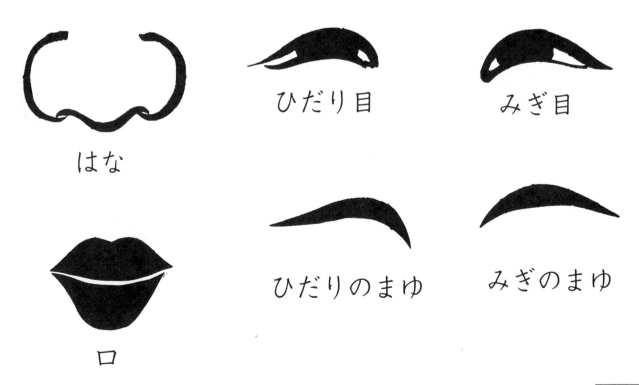

はな

ひだり目

みぎ目

口

ひだりのまゆ

みぎのまゆ

九課

福 笑

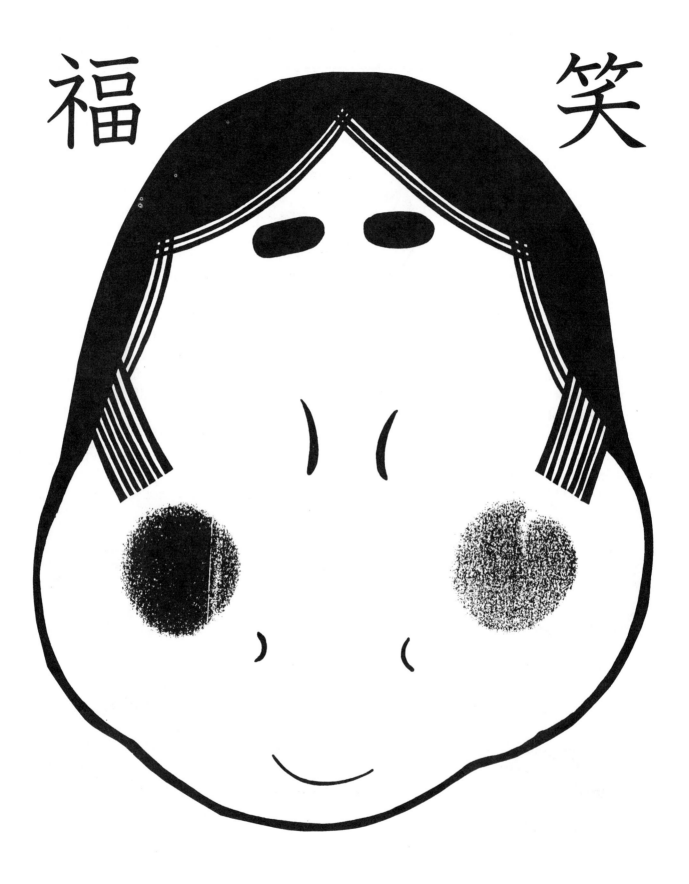

By the end of this lesson, you will be able to communicate the information below in the given situations.

【II-10 タスク1】

An American student invites a Japanese student to go see a school basketball game ON THE PHONE.

American Student:

(1) Call your friend's house and ask if your Japanese friend is there.

(2) Invite your friend to go to (for the purpose of) see a basketball game.

(3) Inform your friend when the game is, as well as what time it starts and finishes.

(4) Tell your friend which two schools are playing. Mention that the game is at your school gymnasium.

(5) Offer to drive. Tell your friend that you will go pick him/her up at a certain time.

Japanese Student:

(1) Since you are the one who answered the phone, acknowledge that it is you.

(2) Comment that it sounds fun. Say yes, you want to go. Ask when the game is, as well as from what time it starts to what time it finishes.

(3) Ask which schools are playing.

(4) Ask where you should meet.

(5) Thank your friend. Mention that you have to be home by 9 p. m.

【II-10 タスク2】

AT THE GAME.

Since the Japanese student does not know much about basketball, the American student patiently explains what is happening.

Japanese Student:

(1) Ask what the score is.

(2) Ask your friend which team he/she is cheering for.

(3) Ask your friend who the player with the No. 5 uniform is.

(4) Ask which team is stronger.

(5) Your school team wins. Comment that the game was very interesting.

American Student:

(1) Report what the score is now.

(2) Identify which team you are cheering for.

(3) Identify that player by name. Mention that this player is the best player on the team.

(4) Reply that there are many good players on (a certain) team, so that team will probably win. Mention that there is only one minute left, and that you are very excited.

(5) You are very happy.

十課

【会話 - Formal style】

<Tシャツの　お店で>

まり：ケンさん、こんにちは。二階に　来ましたから、寄って　みました。

ケン：こんにちは。今晩　バスケットの　試合が　ありますが、見に　行きませんか。大事な　試合ですから、応援に　行きましょうよ。

まり：始まる　時間や　場所は？

ケン：試合の　時間は　午後七時で、場所は　学校の　体育館です。

六時半ごろに　車で　迎えに　行きますよ。

まり：ありがとう。じゃ、その　頃に　家の　外で　待って　いますね。

夜は　十一時までに　帰らなければ　いけませんけど。

<体育館で>

まり：どっちが　強いですか。

ケン：もちろん　ぼく達の　チームですよ。あの　五番の

ユニフォームの　選手は　ぼくの　友達ですよ。

まり：あの　背が　高い　選手ですか。足が　速そうですね。

今、スコアーは？

ケン：５５対５４で　負けて　います。あと　一点。あと　三分だけですよ。

ぼく達は　ぜったい　勝てますよ。ドキドキしますね。

<試合の　終りに>

ケン：やったあ！　勝った、勝った！　すごい！　ばんざ～い！

まり：良かったですねえ。

＜Ｔシャツの　お店で＞

まり：ケンさん、こんにちは。二階に　来たから、寄って　みたんだけど。

ケン：こんにちは。今晩　バスケットの　試合が　あるけど、見に

　　　行かない。大事な　試合だから、応援に　行こうよ。

まり：始まる　時間や　場所は？

ケン：試合の　時間は　午後七時で、場所は　学校の　体育館だよ。

　　　六時半ごろに　車で　迎えに　行くよ。

まり：ありがとう。じゃ、その　頃に　家の　外で　待ってるね。

　　　夜は　十一時までに　帰らなきゃ　いけないんだけど。

＜体育館で＞

まり：どっちが　強い？

ケン：もちろん　ぼく達の　チームだよ。あの　五番の　ユニフォームの

　　　選手は　ぼくの　友達だよ。

まり：あの　背が　高い　選手？　足が　速そうね。今、スコアーは？

ケン：５５対５４で　負けてる。あと　一点。あと　三分だけだよ。

　　　ぼく達　ぜったい　勝てるよ。ドキドキするね。

＜試合の　終りに＞

ケン：やったあ！　勝った、勝った！　すごい！　ばんざ〜い！

まり：良かったわねえ。

十課

Let's review previous vocabulary!

A. めいし Nouns

1. バスケット	basketball	12. 外	outside
2. しあい	sports game	13. よる	night
3. Tシャツ	T-shirt	14. 十一時	11 o'clock
4. （お）みせ	store	15. どっち	which (one of two)?
5. 二階〔にかい〕	second floor	16. ぼくたち	we [used by males]
6. 今晩〔こんばん〕	tonight	17. チーム	team
7. ごご七時	7 p. m.	18. ぼく	I [used by males]
8. 学校	school	19. 友達〔ともだち〕	friend
9. 六時半ごろ	about 6:30	20. あし	foot, leg
10. 車	car	21. 今	now
11. 家	house	22. 三分〔さんぷん〕	three minutes

B. どうし Verbs

23. 来ました〔IR くる〕	came
24. あります〔G1 ある〕	there is
25. 見に〔G2 みる〕	to see [purpose]
26. 行きませんか〔G1 いく〕	won't you go? [Invitation]
27. 行きましょう〔G1 いく〕	let's go
28. 待って います〔G1 まつ〕	is waiting
29. 帰らなければ なりません〔G1 かえる〕	have to go back
30. まけて います〔G2 まける〕	is losing
31. かちます〔G1 かつ〕	win

C. -い けいようし I Adjectives

32. つよい	strong	34. あしが はやそう〔はやい〕	looks fast
33. せが 高い	tall	35. すごい	terrific

D. -な けいようし NA Adjectives

36. 大事〔だいじ〕	important

E. ふくし Adverbs

37. もちろん	of course
38. ぜったい	absolutely

F. Expressions

39. こんにちは。	Hello.	41. じゃ、	Then, [Informal]
40. ありがとう。	Thank you.	42. 良かったですねえ。	How nice! [past event]

G. ぶんぽう Grammar

43. Sentence 1 + から、 Sentence 2。	S1, so S2.
44. Verb Te form + みました。	tried doing ~
45. Sentence 1 [Noun] + で、 Sentence 2。	S1 and S2.
46. ～だけ	only ~

１０課ー１：THE GAME WILL START AT 6:30.

【会話】

Formal style:　　ケン：今日　バスケットの　試合に　行きませんか。

　　　　　　　　まり：試合は　何時に　始まりますか。

　　　　　　　　ケン：六時半です。

Informal style:　ケン：今日　バスケットの　試合に　行かない？

　　　　　　　　まり：試合は　何時に　始まる？

　　　　　　　　ケン：六時半だよ。

【文型】

しあいが　はじまります。	The game will start. [Intransitive Verb]
しあいを　はじめます。	(Someone) will start the game. [Transitive Verb]
＊しあいは　たいいくかんで　あります。	There is a game at the gym.

＊ Previously introduced.

【単語】

1. 時間〔じかん〕

time

2. 場所〔ばしょ〕

location, place

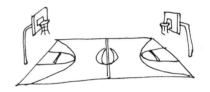

3. 体育館〔たいいくかん〕

gym

たいいく　P.E.

4. 運動場
〔うんどうじょう〕

athletic field

うんどう　sports

うんどうぐつ　sports shoes

うんどう（を）する　to exercise

No.1	いちばん	No.6	ろくばん
No.2	にばん	No.7	ななばん
No.3	さんばん	No.8	はちばん
No.4	よんばん	No.9	きゅうばん
No.5	ごばん	No.10	じゅうばん

5. No. ～

十課

6. ユニフォーム

(sports) uniform

7. 選手
〔せんしゅ〕

(sports) player

8. 試合に　出る
[G2 でます]

to participate in a (sports) game
しあいをする to have a game

9. 応援（を）する
[IR おうえん（を）します]

to cheer

10. ～が　始まる
[G1 はじまります]

(something) begins, starts
* (something)を　はじめる
(someone) will start, begin (something)

11. ～が　終わる
[G1 おわります]

(something) finishes, ends
* (something)を　おわる
(someone) will finish (something)

【*オプショナル単語】
1. *陸上 [りくじょう]　　　　　　 * track
2. *チヤーリーダー　　　　　　　 * cheerleader
3. *プロ　　　　　　　　　　　　 * professional
4. *アマ（チア）　　　　　　　　 * amateur
5. *スタジアム　　　　　　　　　 * stadium
6. *ドーム　　　　　　　　　　　 * dorm
7. *きょうぎじょう　　　　　　　 * track field
8. *トーナメント　　　　　　　　 * tournament

1. 牛　cow　　うし　　　　　牛が　いる。 There are cows.

　　　　　　　ギュウ　　　　牛肉〔ぎゅうにく〕beef

　　　　　　　　　　　　　　牛乳〔ぎゅうにゅう〕milk (cow)

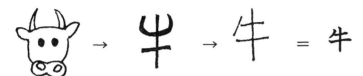

Face of a cow.

2. 半　half　　ハン　　　　　半分〔はんぶん〕a half

　　　　　　　　　　　　　　五時半〔ごじはん〕5:30

divide into half

Divide the cow into half and share.

* 3. 手　hand　　て　　　　　大きい　手 big hands

　　　　　　　シュ　　　　　バスケット選手 basketball player

　　　　　　　☆　　　　　　上手（じょうず）skillful

　　　　　　　　　　　　　　下手（へた）unskillful

* Previously introduced.

【文法】

A. Intransitive and Transitive Verbs

In Japanese, certain verbs have two separate, but similar-sounding forms, one of which is intransitive and one of which is transitive. An intransitive verb does not take a direct object. A transitive verb takes a direct object, which is always marked by the particle を.

a. Intransitive verb: (something)が or は　始まる [begin]

　　試合が or は　五時に　始まります。　　　　The game will start at 5 o'clock.

b. Transitive verb: Subject は (something) を　始める [begin]

　　私は　五時に　宿題を　始めました。　　　I started my homework at 5 o'clock.

---

1. 日本語の　授業は　何時に　始まりますか。　　What time will Japanese class begin?

2. バスケットの　試合は　何時に　始まりますか。

　　　　　　　　　　　　　　　　　　　　What time will the basketball game begin?

3. 映画は　何時に　始まりますか。　　　What time will the movie start?

4. ビデオを　今　始めて　下さい。　　　Please start the video now.

5. 先生は　ちょっと　おそく　授業を　始めました。

　　　　　　　　　　　　　　　　　　The teacher started class a little late.

B. Noun Modifier

In Japanese, the most important principle of word order is that the modifier precedes the word being modified. When a verb modifies a noun, the plain form such as a dictionary form, NAI form, TA form, NAKATTA form precedes the noun. This usage is quite common in the Japanese language.

Verb (Plain form) ＋ Noun	はじまる　じかん	starting time
* い adjective ＋ Noun	はやい　じかん	early time
* な adjective ＋ な ＋ Noun	だいじな　じかん	important time
* Noun ＋ の ＋ Noun	あさの　じかん	morning time

---

1. 試合の　始まる　時間は　何時ですか。　　What time does the game start?

2. 映画の　終わる　時間は　いつですか。　　When does the movie end?

3. 今日の　試合は　とても　大事な　試合です。　Today's game is a very important game.

4. 今日の　試合は　おもしろい　試合でした。　Today's game was a very interesting game.

C. Sentence 1 + が、 Sentence 2。

が, much like "but" in English, combines two sentences. The が, however, is not as contrastive in meaning as the English "but." It is sometimes used to combine two sentences for stylistic reasons, even if those two sentences do not represent contrasting ideas. It may be used simply as a transition word to connect two sentences.

1. 今日　試合が　ありますが、行きませんか。

    There is a game today. Wouldn't you like to go?

2. 私の　数学の　先生は　山田先生ですが、いい　先生ですよ。

    My math teacher is Mr. Yamada. He is a good teacher.

【 ● 文化ノート】

1. バスケットボール　Basketball

Although basketball is gaining some following in Japan, it still does not rank among the favorite sports of the Japanese people. The most popular leisure sports in Japan are baseball, soccer, tennis, swimming, golf, and fishing. Baseball, *sumo*, soccer, and volleyball are the top spectator sports. Professional sports include baseball, *sumo*, soccer, boxing, tennis, and golf. Baseball, *sumo*, and soccer are by far the most popular professional sports. Baseball draws about 20 million spectators annually, while about 800,000 spectators view *sumo* at its six annual tournaments. Millions more watch on TV. Sports and sports-related activities are extremely popular in Japan. Participation in sports at secondary schools and universities is heavy, and many large companies encourage and support sports activities for their employees.

2. おうえんだん　Cheering Squad

Although the Japanese *oendan* (cheering squad) orginated with the introduction of Western sports, it is very different from American cheerleading as it has traditionally been all male and its moves and cheers are masculine, stylized poses adopted from *kabuki* (Japanese theatre) and *sumo*. They dress in their traditional black uniforms and use flags and streamers, much like drill teams in the U. S. Recently, U. S. style cheerleading has become popular with girls performing cheers at their schools.

おうえんだん
Cheering Squad

十課

【🧑👩アクティビティー】

A. ペアワーク

Invite your friend to a game. Before beginning this exercise, fill in the blanks below with appropriate information. Your friend (partner) will ask you the 10 questions listed below. Based on the information you wrote, answer your partner's questions.

[Your game information]

＿＿＿＿サッカー＿＿＿＿の　試合

チーム：＿＿赤＿＿と＿＿青＿＿＿＿

試合の場所：＿学校＿＿＿＿

試合の日　：＿日曜日＿＿＿＿

始まる時間：＿一時＿＿＿＿

終わる時間：＿二時＿＿＿＿

会う場所　：＿門＿＿＿＿

会う時間　：＿十二時＿＿＿＿

[質問]

1. 何の　しあいが　ありますか。	
2. どこのチームと　どこのチームが　しあいを　しますか。	
3. しあいは　どこで　ありますか。	
4. しあいは　いつ　ありますか。	
5. しあいは　何時に　はじまりますか。	
6. しあいは　何時ごろに　おわりますか。	
7. どこで　あいましょうか。	
8. 何時に　あいましょうか。	
9. どちらの　チームを　おうえんしますか。	
10. どちらの　チームが　かつでしょうか。	

B. ペアワーク

Ask your friend about an athletic game he/she played recently. If your partner does not participate in competitive sports, he/she may pretend to do so for the purpose of this exercise.

1. 何の　しあいを　しましたか。	
2. いつ　しあいを　しましたか。	
3. どこで　しあいを　しましたか。	
4. どの　学校と　しあいを　しましたか。	
5. しあいに　かちましたか。まけましたか。	
6. しあいに　出ましたか。	
7. あなたの　ユニフォームは　何ばんでしたか。	
8. チームの　ユニフォームは　何いろですか。	
9. しあいは　何時に　はじまりましたか。	
10. しあいは　何時に　おわりましたか。	

C. ペアワーク

Ask your partner for what purpose he/she goes to the following places. Take turns.

Ex. 日本
質問〔しつもん〕：「日本へ　何を　しに　行きますか。」
答え〔こたえ〕　　：「日本へ　えい語を　おしえに　行きます。」

1. としょかん		5. たいいくかん	
2. カフェテリア		6. こうえん	
3. ともだちの　家		7. うみ	
4. スーパー		8. ショッピングセンター	

D. ペアワーク

Interview your partner about exercising. Take turns.

1. よく　うんどうを　しますか。	
2. どんな　うんどうを　しますか。	
3. 一しゅう間に　どのぐらい　うんどうを　しますか。	

十課

１０課ー２: SHALL I PICK YOU UP?

【会話】

Formal style: ケン：何時に 迎えに 行きましょうか。

まり：六時ごろ 迎えに 来て 下さい。どうも すみません。

Informal style: ケン：何時に 迎えに 行こうか。

まり：六時ごろ 迎えに 来て。すみません。

【文型】

Person を　　むかえに Thing を　　とりに	行く 来る 帰る	go, come, return to pick up (someone)
		go, come, return to pick up (something)
＊ Person を　　つれて ＊ Thing を　　持って		take, bring, take/bring home (someone)
		take, bring, take/bring home (something)

＊ Previously introduced.

【単語】

1. (Personを) 迎えに 行く
   go to pick up (person)

2. (Personを) 迎えに 来る
   come to pick up (person)

3. (Personを) 迎えに 帰る
   return to pick up (person)

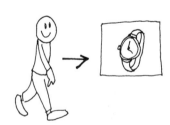

4. (Thingを)取りに 行く
   go to pick up (thing)

5. (Thingを)取りに 来る
   come to pick up (thing)

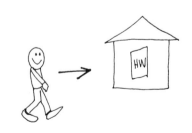

6. (Thingを)取りに 帰る
   return to pick up (thing)

十課

294

7. (Place に) 寄る

[G1 よります／よって]

stop by, drop by (at a place)

8. (time) までに

by (a certain time)

七時までに　かえらなければ　なりません。

I have to go home by 7 o'clock.

9. その頃〔ころ〕

around that time

┌─────────────────────────────┐
【*オプショナル単語】
1. *とちゅうで　　　　　* on the way
2. *帰りに〔かえりに〕　* on the way home
└─────────────────────────────┘

10. それは　いい　かんがえです。
     That's a good idea.

【漢字】

1. 友　　friend　　　　とも　　　友達〔ともだち〕friend

友子〔ともこ〕さん

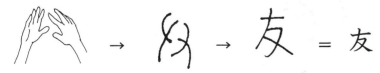

two people's hands

Two peoples' hands join together in friendship.

十課

2. 帰　　return　　かえ（る）　　家へ　帰る〔いえへ　かえる〕 return home

a road

→ リ → リ　＋

→ → 帚 ＝ 帰

a hand on broom

Go down the road, return home and put your hand on the broom.

【 ● 文化ノート】
（ぶん　か）

Timeliness

Japanese are very prompt people. If the agreed meeting time is 10 a.m., it is very likely that a Japanese would be at the meeting place well ahead of time. It is considered very rude and inconsiderate to be late. If one is delayed, a simple apology is much more appropriate than a detailed excuse. One of the reasons one cannot get away with being late, especially in Tokyo, is the transportation system, which runs on a very precise schedule. It is said that one is able to set one's watch by the arrival and departure of trains in Tokyo.

Trains run on a very precise schedule in Japan.

「すみません。
おそく
なりました。」

十課　　　　296

【アクティビティー】

A. ペアワーク

Interview your partner. Take turns.

1. たいてい　学校に　何時に　つきますか。	
2. あさ　学校へ　何で　来ますか。	
3. あさ　だれが　あなたを　学校へ　つれて　来ますか。	
4. 学校へ　おべんとうを　もって　来ますか。	
5. 学校へ　ＣＤプレーヤーを　もって　来ますか。	
6. たいてい　何時に　家へ　帰りますか。	
7. 家へ　何で　帰りますか。	
8. だれが　学校へ　むかえに　来ますか。	
9. 毎日　しゅくだいを　ぜんぶ　家へ　もって　帰りますか。	

B. ペアワーク

You want to go to a basketball game at another school, but you don't know anything about the place, etc. Ask your friend the following questions. Your friend answers. Take turns.

1. しあいの　はじまる　時間は、いつですか。	
2. しあいの　ばしょは、どこですか。	
3. その　ばしょを　しりませんから、つれて　行って　下さい。	
4. 何時に　学校を　出ますか。	
5. お金が　いりますか。	
6. しょうめいしょを　もって　行かなければ　なりませんか。	
7. ばんごはんを　かいに　ファーストフードの　みせに　よっても　いいですか。	

C. ペアワーク

You call your friend and make plans to go out together on Saturday evening. You are driving. Your friend answers accordingly. Take turns.

1. 車で むかえに 行きましょうか。	
2. どこで あいましょうか。	
3. 私の 友だちも つれて 行っても いいですか。	
4. 私の 車で 家へ 帰りましょうか。	
5. 家へ 何時に 帰りたいですか。	
6. 何時までに 家へ 帰らなければ なりませんか。	

D. ペアワーク

You are a student and your partner is a teacher. Ask permission from your teacher to do the following. The teacher answers. Take turns.

1. ロッカーに しゅくだいを わすれました。 とりに 行っても いいですか。	
2. あした 日本の 友だちを この クラスに つれて 来ても いいですか。	
3. May I bring (YOUR CHOICE) to class tomorrow?	

10課－3: CAN YOU WIN?

【会話】

Formal style:　　　まり：今日の　試合は　勝てますか。

　　　　　　　　　ケン：さあ ... 分かりません。

Informal style:　　まり：今日の　試合は　勝てる？

　　　　　　　　　ケン：さあ ... 分からない。

【文型】

Verb Potential Form

Group 1	のみます	→	のめます		can drink
Group 2	たべます	→	たべられます		can eat
Irregular Verb	きます	→	こられます or これます		can come
	します	→	出来ます		can do

【単語】

1. ゆうしょう（を）する
　　[IR します／して]
　to win a championship

2. うそです（よ）。
It is a lie (you know).

うそでしょう？
Are you kidding?; Are you serious?

3. じょうだんです（よ）。
It is a joke (you know).
I'm just kidding.

【*オプショナル単語】

1. *けっしょうせん	* a championship game
2. *シュートする	* to shoot [basketball]
3. *ドリブルする	* to dribble [basketball]
4. *ファウルする	* to foul
5. *てんを　いれる	* to make a point
6. *しんじられません。	* I can't believe it. It's unbelievable.

十課

【漢字】

1. 待　wait　　　　ま（つ）　待って　下さい。 Please wait.

You have to wait at the intersection by the temple.

2. 持　have, hold　　も（つ）　持って　います。 I have it.

At the temple, you hold your hands together.

【文法】

A. Verb Potential Form

The potential verb form is used frequently in speaking or in less formal writing situations to express one's capability or possibility of doing a certain action. When one uses a potential form, the verb becomes intransitive. Therefore, when a transitive sentence is converted to its potential form, the noun which originally functioned as the direct object loses that function, and the を becomes が or は. More recent trends show a movement of retaining the を, though が is more widely accepted.

　　Example: おさしみを　食べます。 →　おさしみが　食べられます。

All other particles are not affected.

　　Example: 学校に　行けません。

　　　The verb potential form conjugates as a group 2 verb.

　　Example: 食べられます　can eat, 食べられません cannot eat,

　　　　　　食べられました could eat, 食べられませんでした could not eat, etc.

＊ Verb Dictionary form＋ことが　出来ます is also used to express one's ability to do something. It is used more frequently in writing than in speaking. It is also used in more formal speech.

＊ Previously introduced.

1. **Group 1 verbs**:

Group 1 verbs are identified by the verb stem, which is the verb form that remains after dropping -ます. If there are more than two *hiragana* characters remaining in the verb stem after dropping the ます and the final sound of the verb stem is an -i ending sound, the verb can usually be categorized as a Group 1 verb. To obtain the potential form, change the final -i sound of the verb stem to the corresponding -e sound, then add ます or る. See the chart below for examples.

[□ -i ます]

	NAI FORM	MASU FORM	DIC. FORM	POTENTIAL	TA FORM
み verbs mi	のまない nomanai	のみます　drink nomimasu	のむ nomu	のめる nomeru	のんだ nonda
に verbs ni	しなない shinanai	しにます　die shinimasu	しぬ shinu	しねる shineru	しんだ shinda
び verbs bi	あそばない asobanai	あそびます　play asobimasu	あそぶ asobu	あそべる asoberu	あそんだ asonda
い verbs i	かわない kawanai	かいます　buy kaimasu	かう kau	かえる kaeru	かった katta
ち verbs chi	またない matanai	まちます　wait machimasu	まつ matsu	まてる materu	まった matta
り verbs ri	つくらない tsukuranai	つくります　make tsukurimasu	つくる tsukuru	つくれる tsukureru	つくった tsukutta
き verbs ki	かかない kakanai	かきます　write kakimasu	かく kaku	かける kakeru	かいた kaita
ぎ verbs gi	およがない oyoganai	およぎます　swim oyogimasu	およぐ oyogu	およげる oyogeru	およいだ oyoida
し verbs shi	はなさない hanasanai	はなします　speak hanashimasu	はなす hannasu	はなせる hanaseru	はなした hanashita

2. **Group 2 verbs**: [-IRU, -ERU Verbs]

Group 2 verbs can be identified by a verb stem (verb without ます) that ends in an "-e sounding" *hiragana* or a verb stem that contains only one *hiragana*. See examples below. A few special verbs do exist. They must simply be learned as special verbs. Group 2 verb potential forms are created simply by replacing ます by られます. Younger Japanese tend to use -れます instead of the -られます ending.

	NAI FORM	MASU FORM	DIC. FORM	POTENTIAL	TA FORM
[□ -e ます]	たべない	たべます　to eat	たべる	たべられる	たべた
[One *hiragana*]	ねない	ねます　to sleep	ねる	ねられる	ねた
	でない	でます　to leave, go out	でる	でられる	でた
	みない	みます　to see, watch	みる	みられる	みた
	きない	きます　to wear	きる	きられる	きた
[Special verbs]	おきない	おきます　to get up	おきる	おきられる	おきた
	かりない	かります　to borrow	かりる	かりられる	かりた
	おりない	おります　to get off	おりる	おりられる	おりた
	できない	できます　to be able to do	できる	☆できる	できた

十課

Compare:

みえる, "can be seen, is visible" cannot be used interchangeably with みられる "can look at."

きこえる, "can be heard; audible" cannot be used interchangeably with きける "can listen to."

3. **Group 3 Irregular verbs**:

Only きます, します and noun + します verbs belong to this group.

	NAI FORM	MASU FORM	DIC. FORM	POTENTIAL	TA FORM
きます	こない	きます to come	くる	こられる	きた
します	しない	します to do	する	できる	した

1. 「この 土曜日に 家へ <u>来られますか</u>。」　"Can you come to my house this Saturday?"

　　「はい、もちろん <u>行けます</u>よ。」　　　　　　"Yes, of course I can."

2. 七時に 予約<u>出来ました</u>。　　　　　　　I was able to make a reservation for 7 o'clock.

3. 父は 中国語が <u>話せます</u>が、私は <u>話せません</u>。

　　　　　　　　　　　　　　　My father can speak Chinese, but I cannot.

4. 母は おさしみが <u>食べられません</u>。　　My mother cannot eat raw fish.

【 ● 文化ノート】

うそです。

　うそ is translated as "lie", however, it does not carry as serious or as negative a connotation as its English equivalent. 「うそでしょう。」 is used lightly among young friends, much as English speakers would use, "Are you kidding?" or "Are you serious?" In casual conversations, young people may even use it to replace 「そうですか。」.

【🧑👩アクティビティー】

A. ペアワーク

Interview your partner. After your partner answers, respond with そうですか, or 本当(とう)ですか, or うそでしょう。 Take turns.

1. サーフィンが　出来ますか。	
2. スキーが　出来ますか。	
3. スペイン語が　はなせますか。	
4. 十マイル　はしれますか。	
5. 車の　うんてんが　出来ますか。	
6. りょうりが　出来ますか。	
7. ダンスが　出来ますか。	
8. ギターが　ひけますか。	

B. ペアワーク

Circulate and find a person in class who can do the following things.

Ex. 質問(しつもん)：「車の　運転(うんてん)が　出来ますか。」

　　答(こた)え：「はい、出来ます。」or「いいえ、出来ません。」

1. いぬの　かんじが　書けますか。	
2. 中国語が　はなせますか。	
3. さしみが　食べられますか。	
4. 日本語の　うたが　うたえますか。	
5. およげますか。	
6. 日本りょうりが　つくれますか。	
7. はやく　はしれますか。	
8. ピアノが　おしえられますか。	
9. ヴァイオリンが　ひけますか。	

十課

【会話】

Formal style:

まり：スコアは　どうでしたか。

ケン：５５対５４で　勝ちましたよ。

まり：それは　良かったですねえ。

Informal style:

まり：スコアは　どうだった？

ケン：５５対５４で　勝ったよ。

まり：それは　良かったわねえ。

【文型】

私は　チームに　かって　ほしいです。　　　I want the team to win.

【単語】

1. スコア

score

2. ５５たい２

55 to 2

Aチームたい　Bチーム

A team vs. B team

3.		Points
	1	いってん
	2	にてん
	3	さんてん
	4	よんてん
	5	ごてん
	6	ろくてん
	7	ななてん
	8	はってん
	9	きゅうてん
	10	じ(ゅ)ってん
	?	なんてん

4. あと～

~ more

あと　いってん

one more point

5. ドキドキします

is excited, is nervous

ドキドキ represents the sound of a heartbeat.

十課

6. やったあ！
We did it!

[Used when a person accomplished
a goal after hard work.] やる is
an informal equiv. of する.

7. ばんざい！
Hurray!

[Used for happy occasions.]
It originally represented a cheer of "10,000
years" (まんさい) to the Emperor.

8. かった！かった！
(We) won! (We) won!

When one talks to oneself,
the plain form is used.

【＊オプショナル単語】

| 1. ＊まんてん | ＊ perfect score |
| 2. ＊けっか | ＊ result |

【漢字】

1. 米   rice   こめ   米を 買〔か〕う buy rice

米屋 rice store

○ → 米 → 米 = 米

rice grains

米

2. 番   number   バン   一番〔いちばん〕 No. 1

♀ → ♀ → ♀ +

a drop

○ → 米 → 米 → 米 +

田

= 番

番

rice field

A drop of rain on rice makes it "number" one!

305   十課

3. 事　matter　　　こと　　　　　どんな事？ What kind of things?

　　　　　　　　　　　ごと　　　　　仕事〔しごと〕job

　　　　　　　　　　　ジ　　　　　　食事〔しょくじ〕meal

　　　　　　　　　　　　　　　　　　大事〔だいじ〕important

　　　　　　　　　　　　　　　　　　事務所〔じむしょ〕office

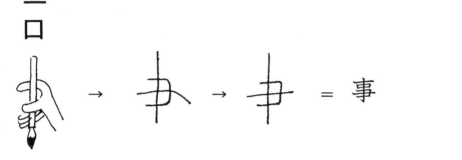

I handle the matter with one mouth and a brush in my hand.

【文法】

A. Person 1 は + (Person 2 + に) + Verb [TE form] + ほしいです。

　　　Person 1 wants Person 2 (not higher in status than Person 1) to do 〜.

When the subject wants another person (Person 2) to do something, the Person 2 is marked by
に. This construction is not used if the Person 2 has a higher status than the subject. The
subject is usually the first person (I) in declarative sentences and the second person (you) in
interrogative sentences.

Compare:

＊ a. 私は　かちたいです。　　　　　　　　I want to win.

　　b. 私は　あなたに　かって　ほしいです。 I want you to win.

＊ Previously introduced.

1. 私は　チームに　かって　ほしいです。　　　　　　I want the team to win.

2. 私は　あなたに　日本語を　教えて　ほしいです。

　　　　　　　　　　　　　　　　　　　　　　　　　I want you to teach me Japanese.

3. あなたは　だれに　来て　ほしいですか。　　　　　Who do you want to come?

【 ● 文化ノート】

1. Loan Words in Sports

Because many of the popular sports in Japan are of Western origin, the majority of the sports terminology used in Japan are borrowed words. Even names of sports, i.e. バスケットボール, テニス, ゴルフ, フットボール, スキー, スケート, バレーボール, サッカー, etc. are loan words. Can you think of more? Terms in baseball, the favorite sport of Japanese, are frequently loan words such as ストライク (strike), アウト (out), バッター (batter), ホームベース (home base), キャッチャー (catcher), etc. There are even some words that appear to be English, but were actually created in Japan, e.g., ナイター (nighter), which is a game played at night.

2. A Japanese Proverb: 「まけるが　かち」

This proverb means "Defeat is a win." An equivalent English proverb is, "Losers gainers."

【 アクティビティー】

A. ペアワーク

Your partner is planning to have a birthday party. Ask your partner the following questions. Your partner should answer based on the fact. Take turns.

1. あなたの　たんじょうパーティーには　だれに　来て　ほしいですか。	
2. たんじょうパーティーには　何人　来て　ほしいですか。	
3. ともだちに　どんな　プレゼントを　持って来て　ほしいですか。	

十課

B. ペアワーク

Ask your partner about a recent (athletic) game.

1. 何の　しあいを　見ましたか。	
2. その　しあいは　いつでしたか。	
3. その　しあいは　どこで　ありましたか。	
4. どの　学校の　チームと　どの　学校の　チームの　しあいでしたか。	
5. どちらの　学校が　かちましたか。	
6. その　しあいの　スコアは　何でしたか。	
7. どちらの　チームを　おうえんしましたか。	

C. ペアワーク

Role play the following conversation using appropriate expressions and gestures.

A: あっ、スコアは　５５たい５４です。

B: あと　三分だけですよ。

A: 私たちの　チームは　かてますか。

B: もちろん、ぜったい　かちますよ。

A: ドキドキしますね。

B: あと　一分！

A: あっ、シュートが　入(はい)った！

A & B: やったあ！　かった、かった！　ばんざい！

Ask your partner these questions in Japanese.
Your partner should answer in Japanese.

1. Which is more difficult, Chinese or Japanese?

2. Among the foreign languages, what language is the easiest?

3. Among beef, pork, chicken and fish, which do you like the best?

4. Are you taller than me?

5. Which country in the world do you want to travel to the most?

6. [You are a store clerk at a T-shirt shop.] Welcome. May I help you?

7. Which do you prefer, a white shirt or a blue shirt?

8. What T-shirt design do you like to wear?

9. What size T-shirt do you wear?

10. How is this school different from other schools?

11. Who do you want to come to your birthday party?

12. Please compare your country and Japan.

13. What city do you want to live in?

14. What is the sales tax in this state?

15. What kind of famous souvenirs are there in this state?

16. In a Japanese department store, on what floor is food sold (do they sell food)?

17. Do you usually put gifts in a box?

18. What sports can you play?

19. What is the color of our school team uniform?

20. Do you often go to cheer on our school's sports teams?

21. Is our school basketball team strong this year?

22. Has our school basketball team ever won the state championship?

23. What time do the basketball games usually start?

24. Where will our basketball team play the next game?

25. Who brought you to school this morning?

26. Who will come to pick you up today?

27. What time do you have to be (= go) home by on weekends?

28. May I go to my locker to pick up my homework now?

29. Do you get nervous before exams?

30. Can you speak any other language?

By the end of this lesson, you will be able to communicate the information below in the given situations.

【11-11 タスク1】

An American student and Japanese student discuss and compare folk tales.

Japanese Student :

(1) Ask if there are many folk tales in America.

(2) Ask which one he/she likes best of all the American folk tales.

(3) Provide names of a few.

American Student :

(1) Answer yes, there are. Name some of the American folk tales you know.

(2) Identify which one is your favorite. Explain why. Ask about famous Japanese folk tales.

(3) Acknowledge the ones you know.

【11-11 タスク2】

The two students discuss the Japanese folk tale, "Mouse Wedding."

(1) Mention that you heard that he/she read the Japanese folk tale, "Mouse Wedding."

(2) You have forgotten this story. Ask why the Father Mouse did not like Chuukichi at the beginning.

(3) Ask why the Father Mouse went to meet the Sun first (はじめに).

(4) Ask why the Wall was stronger than the Wind.

(5) Respond why the Mouse was the greatest of all.

(1) Acknowledge that yes, you read it in your Japanese language class. Comment that you thought it was very interesting.

(2) Explain why.

(3) Explain why.

(4) Explain why. Explain that the Mouse was the greatest. Ask why.

十一課

十一課

十一課

【日本昔話：ねずみのよめいり】

昔々　ある　くらの　中に、お金持ちの　鼠の　お父さんと　お母さんと
娘が　住んで　いました。チュウ子は　若くて　美しい　娘でした。

　　ある日、貧乏な　チュウ吉が　チュウ子の　家に　来て、言いました。

チュウ吉：「お父さん、私は　チュウ子さんと　結婚したいんです。

　　　　　　　チュウ子さんを　私に　下さい。」

お父さん：「えっ、とんでもない。娘は　世界で　一番

　　　　　　　偉い　人と　結婚するんですよ。」

チュウ吉：「お父さん、ぼく、一生懸命　働きます。だから、お願いします。」

お父さん：「だめ　だめ。帰って　下さい。」

　　次の日、お父さんは　お日様の　所へ　出かけました。

お父さん：「お日様、お日様、こんにちは。私の　娘を　もらって　下さい。

　　　　　　　お日様は　世界で　一番　偉い　方です。お日様が

　　　　　　　いらっしゃいますから、この　世界は　明るいんです。」

お日さま：「いや、世界で　一番　偉いのは、雲さんですよ。」

お父さん：「えっ、なぜですか。」

お日さま：「雲さんは　私を　かくして　しまいます。

　　　　　　　だから、雲さんの方が　私より

　　　　　　　ずっと　偉いんですよ。」

お父さん：「なるほど。では、雲さんに　お願いしましょう。」

　　お父さんは　雲さんの　所へ　行きました。
お父さん：「雲さん、雲さん、こんにちは。私の　娘を　もらって　下さい。
　　　　　雲さんは　世界で　一番　偉い　方です。」 
　　　雲：「いや、世界で　一番　偉いのは、風さんですよ。」
お父さん：「えっ、なぜですか。」
　　　雲：「風さんは　私を　吹き飛ばして　しまいます。だから、
　　　　　風さんの方が　私より　ずっと　偉いんですよ。」
お父さん：「なるほど。では、風さんに　お願いしましょう。」

　　お父さんは、風さんの　所へ　行きました。
お父さん：「風さん、風さん、こんにちは。　私の　娘を　もらって
　　　　　下さい。風さんは　世界で　一番　偉い　方です。」
　　　風：「いや、世界で　一番　偉いのは、壁さんですよ。」
お父さん：「えっ、なぜですか。」 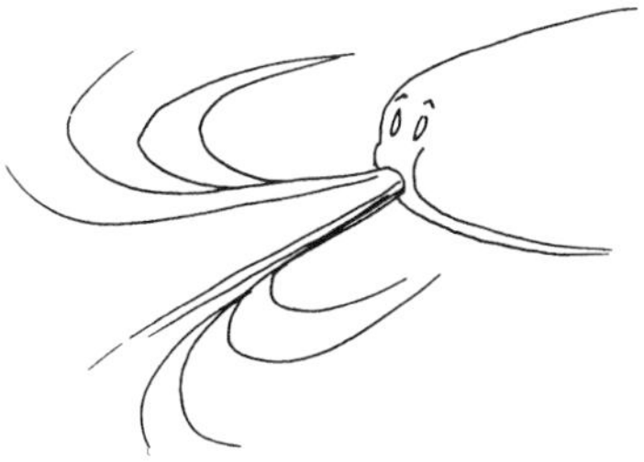
　　　風：「壁さんは　私の　力では　動きません。
　　　　　だから、壁さんの方が　私より　ずっと
　　　　　偉いんですよ。」
お父さん：「なるほど。では、壁さんに　お願いしましょう。」

十一課

お父さんは、壁さんの 所へ 行きました。

お父さん：「壁さん、壁さん、こんにちは。私の 娘を もらって 下さい。

壁さんは 世界で 一番 偉い 方です。」

壁：「いや、世界で 一番 偉いのは、

鼠さんですよ。」

お父さん：「えーっ、なぜですか。なぜですか。」

壁：「鼠さんは ガリガリ 私に 穴を 開けて しまいます。

だから、鼠さんの方が 私より ずっと 偉いんですよ。」

お父さん：「なるほど。」

お父さんと お母さんは チュウ吉が 世界で 一番 偉いと
思いました。そして、チュウ吉は チュウ子と とうとう 結婚することが
出来ましたとさ。

　　　　　　　　　　　　　　　　　　　　おしまい。

Let's review previous vocabulary!

A. めいし Nouns
1. ねずみ	mouse	8. せかい	world
2. 中	inside	9. 人	person
3. お父さん	father	10. ぼく	I [used by males]
4. お母さん	mother	11. つぎ	next
5. 日〔ひ〕	day	12. ところ	place
6. 家〔いえ〕	house	13. (えらい)の	(great) one
7. 私	I	14. なぜ	why?

B. どうし Verbs
15. すんで いました〔G1 すむ〕	was living
16. 来て〔IR くる〕	come
17. 言いました〔G1 いう〕	said
18. 〜と けっこんしたいんです〔IR けっこんする〕	want to marry 〜
19. 〜を ください。	Please give me 〜.
20. はたらきます〔G1 はたらく〕	work
21. 帰って 下さい〔G1 かえる〕	please return
22. 出かけました〔G2 でかける〕	left
23. もらって 下さい〔G1 もらう〕	please accept
24. いらっしゃいます〔G1 いらっしゃる〕	exist [polite]
25. 〜に おねがいしましょう〔IR おねがいする〕	let's ask 〜 (a favor)
26. あけて〔G2 あける〕	open
27. けっこんすることが 出来ました〔IR けっこんする〕	could marry

C. -い けいようし I Adjectives
28. わかくて [わかい]	young	29. うつくしい	beautiful

D. -な けいようし NA Adjectives
30. だめ	no good

E. ふくし Adverbs
31. 一番〔いちばん〕	the most	32. ずっと	by far

F. Expressions
33. Plain form ＋ んです。	[offers an explanation to a listener]
34. おねがいします。	Please. I ask you a favor.
35. こんにちは。	Hello.
36. では、	And then, [Formal]
37. Sentence (reason)＋ から。	It is because (reason).

１１課－1 : WHO IS GREATER, THE SUN OR THE CLOUD?

【会話】

Formal style: まり：お日様と　雲さんと　どちらの方が　偉いですか。

　　　　　　　　 ケン：お日様の方が　雲さんより　偉いですよ。

Informal style: まり：お日様と　雲さんと　どちらの方が　偉いの？

　　　　　　　　　 ケン：お日様の方が　雲さんより　偉いよ。

【単語】

1. 昔話〔むかしばなし〕

folk tale

2. ナレーター

narrator

3. お日様〔おひさま〕

sun [polite]

4. 雲
〔くも〕

cloud

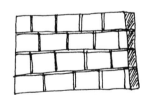

5. かべ

wall

6. (お)金持ち
〔(お)かねもち〕

rich person

7. びんぼう

poor [なAdj.]

8. 明〔あか〕るい
is bright [いAdj.]

9. 暗〔くら〕い
is dark   [いAdj.]

10. えらい
is great   [いAdj.]

えらい is used to describe people.

【＊オプショナル単語】

1. ＊嫁入り〔よめいり〕   ＊ wedding [A classical Japanese word. よめ is "bride," いり is a derived form of いります "to enter." Entering into a family as a bride was the equivalent of a marriage, or a wedding.

2. ＊チュウ吉〔チュウきち〕   ＊ Chuukichi [name of the male mouse in the story]

3. ＊チュウ子   ＊ Chuuko [name of the female mouse in the story]

4. ＊紙芝居〔かみしばい〕   ＊ paper play [Japanese traditional storytelling using pictures.]

【漢字】

1. 雨   rain   あめ   雨が ふって います。 It is raining.

 → 雨 → 雨 = 雨   雨

From clouds up above falls the rain.

2. 電   electricity   デン   電話 telephone
電気 electricity
電車 electric train

 → 雨 → 雨 = 雨

多多 → 幼 → 甲 = 電

Rain and thunder, flying a kite, Ben Franklin discovers electricity.

Guess the meaning of the following *kanji*.

a. 雪　　　　　b. 雷　　　　　c. 雲

（　ゆき　）　　（かみなり）　　（　くも　）

【 ● 文化ノート】

日本の昔話　　Japanese Folk Tales

As in all cultures, the Japanese enjoy a rich collection of legends and folk tales. Researchers of these literary genres find that Japan's folk tales possess amazingly universal themes. As one would expect, many of the folk tales share storylines similar to tales of India, China, and other parts of eastern Asia. Some Japanese tales, however, even share themes and motifs similar to those in Europe, particularly Greece, the southern Eurasian continent, and also the northern polar areas. Certain tales also resemble those told in the South Pacific. Although there are many beloved folk tales, perhaps the favorite among Japanese and best known among foreigners is the story of ももたろう, or Peach Boy, which is about a boy born from a peach who grows up to be the hero of his village because of his bravery in overcoming the evil ogres of Ogre Island.

【アクティビティー】

A. ペアワーク

List as many Japanese folk tales as you can think of:

B. ペアワーク

Each of the following is a scene from a popular Japanese folk tale. Ask your partner which story each comes from. Folk tale titles are listed below.

質問：「この　むかしばなしは　何の　おはなしですか。」

（ ももたろう ）

（うらしまたろう）

（はなさかじいさん

（ねずみのよめいり）

（かぐやひめ）

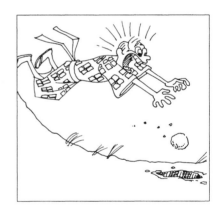

（おむすびころりん）

Choices:

ア. おむすびころりん　　イ. 浦島太郎　　ウ. かぐや姫

エ. 花咲かじいさん　　オ. ねずみのよめいり　　カ. 桃太郎

十一課

C. ペアワーク

The characters in the folk tale "Mouse Wedding" are illustrated below. Identify them all by asking your partner for their names and write them down.

ナレーター	父	母	チュウ吉	チュウ子
1.	2.	3.	4.	5.
日	雲	風	壁	
6.	7.	8.	9.	

D. ペアワーク

Ask your partner comparison questions using the cues accompanying the pictures. Take turns.

Ex. お父さん ＆ チュウ吉, お金持ち

質問：「お父さんと　チュウ吉と　どちらの方が　お金持ちですか。」

答え：「お父さんの方が　チュウ吉より　お金持ちです。」

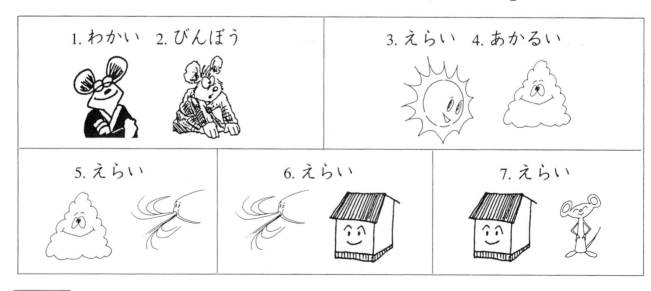

1. わかい　2. びんぼう

3. えらい　4. あかるい

5. えらい

6. えらい

7. えらい

【会話】

Formal style:　ケン：宿題を　全部　して　しまいました。

まり：それは　良かったですねえ。

Informal style:　ケン：宿題を　全部　して　しまった。

まり：それは　良かったわねえ。〔良かったねえ by male〕

【文型】

Verb TE form + しまいます	do 〜 completely [regret, criticism]
Sentence 1。だから or ですから、 sentence 2。	Sentence 1. Therefore, sentence 2.

【単語】

1. (thing を) かくす
[G1 かくします]
to hide (thing)
[Transitive verb]

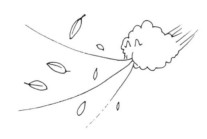

2. ふきとばす
[G1 ふきとばします]
to blow away
ふく to blow +とばす to fly

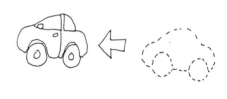

3. (thing が) 動く
[G1 うごきます]
(thing) moves
[Intransitive verb]

4. ガリガリ
chew away; gnaw
[onomatopoetic]

5. あな（を　あける）
(to open) a hole

6. 力〔ちから〕
power, strength, ability
ちからが　つよい has strong power

325

十一課

7. Verb (TE) ＋ しまいます

do ～ completely　[regret]

食べて　しまいました。I ate (it) up.

8. だから、

Therefore,

[Informal]

9. ですから、

Therefore,

[Formal]

【＊オプショナル単語】

1. ＊蔵〔くら〕　＊ storehouse, warehouse

[A classical Japanese word. *Samurai* and wealthy business families used to have くら in their backyards and kept money and treasures in it.]

【漢字】

1. 天　　heaven　　テン　　天ぷら *tenpura*, 天どん *tenpura donburi*

sky

a big man

↗ → 大 → 大 ＝ 天

The Big Man in the sky waits in heaven.

2. 気　　spirit　　キ　　天気〔てんき〕weather, 病気 illness,

合気道 *aikido*, お気の毒に。 I am sorry. [sympathy]

↗ → 气 → 气 ＋

yelling man

↗ → 米 → メ ＝ 気

rice

In order to get a good rice harvest, a person calls the spirits.

【文法】

A. Verb TE form ＋ しまいます

The verb TE plus extender しまいます has two interpretations:

1. It expresses the completion of an action. Sometimes the completion of the action may have been unexpected.
   Ex. しゅくだいを　して　しまいました。　I completely finished my homework.

2. It implies the speaker's regret about what has been done or a negative reaction to a completed action or event.
   Ex. しゅくだいを　車に　わすれて　しまいました。
   I forgot my homework in the car (by mistake).

1. 弟は　私の　ケーキも　食べて　しまいました。
   My younger brother ate up all of my cake, too.

2. 疲れて　いましたから、ゆうべは　早く　寝て　しまいました。
   I was tired, so I ended up going to bed early.

3. この　本を　全部　読んで　しまいました。　I read this whole book.

B. Sentence 1。ですから、sentence 2。　　Sentence 1. Therefore, sentence 2. [Formal]

　Sentence 1。だから、sentence 2。　　Sentence 1. Therefore, sentence 2. [Informal]

　＊Sentence 1 ＋ から、sentence 2。　　Sentence 1, so sentence 2.

1. 昨日は　病気でした。ですから、宿題が　出来ませんでした。
   I was sick yesterday. Therefore, I could not do my homework.

2. 母は　仕事で　東京へ　行きました。だから、私が　料理を　しなければ
   なりません。　　My mother went to Tokyo on business. Therefore, I have to cook.

【 ● 　文化ノート】

Onomatopoetic Sounds of Animals

The names チュー子 and チューきち are derived from the Japanese onomatopoetic cries of mice. While English speakers perceive the cry of mice as "squeak, squeak," the Japanese perceive it as チューチュー. Other Japanese animal cries are the dog's, which is ワンワン, the pig's, which is ブーブー, the rooster's, which is コケコッコー, the frog's, which is ケロケロ, and the cow's, which is モーモー. Each culture perceives the sounds of animal cries differently. Are your sound perceptions of these cries closer to the English or Japanese sounds?

チューチュー

327

十一課

【   アクティビティー】

A. ペアワーク

Match the pictures with the onomatopoetic words from below.

1. （ ザーザー ）

2. （ ピューピュー ）

3. （ フワフワ ）

4. （ ギラギラ ）　　　　　5. （ ガリガリ ）　　　　　6. （ ドキドキ ）

ガリガリ， ドキドキ， フワフワ， ギラギラ， ザーザー， ピューピュー

B. ペアワーク

You say the following. Your partner comments on it using one of the expressions from the box below. Take turns.

Ex. You:　　「宿題を　全部　<u>して　しまいました</u>。」
しゅくだい　ぜんぶ

　　Partner:「それは　良かったですねえ。」

Choices:　¹「それは　良かったですねえ。」
²「ざんねんでしたねえ。」　　³「大変でしたね。」へん

1. 本を　ぜんぶ　よんで　しまいました。	3
2. いぬが　私の　ひるごはんを　食べて　しまいました。	2
3. かんじも　たん語も　ぜんぶ　おぼえて　しまいました。	1
4. えい語の　レポートを　書いて　しまいました。	3
5. いぬが　私の　さいふを　かくして　しまいました。	3
6. バッグを　なくして　しまいました。	2
7. ポケットに　あなを　あけて　しまいました。	2

C. ペアワーク

Pairs of characters from the Mouse Wedding are given below. Ask your partner who is greater of the two characters. After your partner answers, ask why. Your partner should answer based on the story. Take turns.

質問１：「～と　～と　どちらの方が　偉いですか。」

答え１：「～の方が　～より　偉いです。」

質問２：「なぜですか。」

答え２：「(Reason)。だから、～の方が　～より　偉いです。」

1.

2.

3.

4.

D. グループゲーム：うでずもう

Arm wrestle with each member of a group of students in your class. Decide who is strongest. One student from your group reports the results to the class.

「～さんが　一番　力が　強いです。」

If time allows, continue by having winners of each group challenge one another until the strongest student in your class can be determined.

十一課

【会話】

Formal style:　　まり：チュウ子の　お父さんは　何と　言いましたか。

　　　　　　　　ケン：お父さんは　「だめ　だめ。」と　言いましたよ。

Informal style:　まり：チュウ子の　お父さんは　何と　言ったの？

　　　　　　　　ケン：お父さんは　「だめ　だめ。」と　言ったよ。

【文型】

マイクさんは　「おはよう。」と　言いました。　　Mike said, "Good morning."

【単語】

1. 娘〔むすめ〕

(own) daughter, young lady

むすめさん (someone else's) daughter, young lady [polite]

2. 息子〔むすこ〕

(one's own) son

むすこさん (someone else's) son

3. 一生懸命〔いっしょうけんめい〕

with one's utmost effort

いっしょうけんめい　べんきょうして　います。

He is studying with his utmost effort.

4. とんでもない(です)。

How ridiculous!
That's impossible!

5. なるほど。

Indeed! I see!

6. 「　　　」と 言いました。　　　7. えっ　　　　　8. いや（っ）

(Someone) said, "　."　　　　　　　Huh?　　　　　　No

と is a quotation particle.　　　　　　　　　　Stronger negation than いいえ.
Used in speaking only.

【*オプショナル単語】

1. *主人〔しゅじん〕　　* (own) husband; master [lit. "main person"]
2. *ご主人〔しゅじん〕　* (someone else's) husband
3. *家内〔かない〕　　　* (own) wife [lit. "inside the house"]
4. *奥〔おく〕さん　　　* (someone else's) wife, a middle aged lady [lit. "inner, far back"]

【漢字】

1. 会　　meet　　あ（う）　　会いましょう。Let's meet.
　　　　　　　　　カイ　　　　会社〔かいしゃ〕company
　　　　　　　　　　　　　　　社会〔しゃかい〕social studies; society
　　　　　　　　　　　　　　　教会〔きょうかい〕church

roof

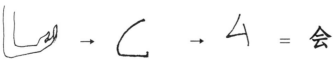

Under the roof, two people meeting extend their arms to each other.

2. 話　talk　はな（す）　　　話して　下さい。　Please speak.

　　　　　はなし　　　　　　お話〔はなし〕　story

　　　　　ばなし　　　　　　昔話〔むかしばなし〕folk tale

　　　　　ワ　　　　　　　　電話〔でんわ〕telephone

　　　　　　　　　　　　　会話〔かいわ〕conversation

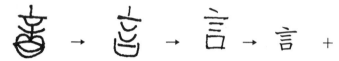

words coming out from mouth

千　(a thousand)　＋

口　(mouth)　　　　　　　　　　　　　　＝　話

Saying a thousand words is a good talk.

【文法】

A.「　　　　　　　　　　」と　言いました。

　　と is a particle used to mark a quotation. It follows the quotation. In Japanese, the marks 「　」 are the equivalent of English quotation marks "　".

---

1. デレックさんは　「こんにちは。」と　言いました。　　Derek said, "Hello."

2. 父は　「今日は　遅く　帰るよ。」と　言いました。

　　　　　　　　　　　　　　　Dad said, "I will be home late today."

3. 友達は　「映画に　行かない。」と　言いました。

　　　　　　　　　　　　　　　My friend said, "I won't go to a movie."

4. 山田さんは　「五時に　会いましょう。」と　言いました。

　　　　　　　　　　　　　　　Mr. Yamada said, "Let's meet at 5 o'clock."

【 ● 文化ノート】

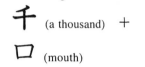

かみしばい

Although seen rarely in Japan these days, a popular treat for young Japanese children is an opportunity to listen to stories through かみしばい, or paper shows. Told on street corners, the かみしばい man calls the neighborhood children with his wooden clappers. As the children gather, he prepares for his show and opens his box of candies. Children who purchase the sweets sit in the front row. A series of brightly colored pictures are slid through a wooden frame as the かみしばい man recites his stories to his intent audience.

かみしばい
paper shows

【 アクティビティー】

A. ペアワーク

Ask your partner what he/she wants to do over the weekend. Then report to the class what he/she told you.

質問：この　週末は　どんな　ことを　したいですか。

レポート：〜さんは　「　　　　　　　　　」と　言いました。

B. ペアワーク

You have a Japanese guest today. Interview him/her by asking the following questions. Your guest answers. Assume that your guest has at least two children.

1. おなまえは？	
2. どこに　すんで　いらっしゃいますか。	
3. おしごとは　何ですか。	
4. お子さんが　いらっしゃいますか。	
5. お子さんは　むす子さんですか。むすめさんですか。	
6. （むす子さん）の　おなまえは　何ですか。 何さいですか。何年生ですか。	
7. （むす子さん）は　どんな　事が　上手ですか。	
8. （むす子さん）は　いっしょうけんめい べんきょうして　いますか。	

十一課

C. ペアワーク

Ask your partner the following questions. Your partner should respond with answers from the "Mouse Wedding" story.

Ex. What did Chuukichi say to Chuuko's father?

質問：チュウ吉さんは　チュウ子さんの　お父さんに　何と

言いましたか。

答え：「チュウ子さんを　下さい。」と　言いました。

1. お父さんは　チュウきちに　何と　言いましたか。	
2. お母さんは　チュウきちに　何と　言いましたか。	
3. お父さんは　お日さまに　何と　言いましたか。	
4. お日さまは　お父さんに　何と　言いましたか。	
5. くもさんは　お父さんに　何と　言いましたか。	
6. かぜさんは　お父さんに　何と　言いましたか。	
7. かべさんは　お父さんに　何と　言いましたか。	

D. ペアワーク

Ask your partner who in the story said the following things. Take turns.

質問：だれが　「　　　　」と　言いましたか。

1. 「ぼく、いっしょうけんめい　はたらきます。」	チュウ吉
2. 「えっ、とんでもない。」	父
3. 「だめ　だめ、帰って　下さい。」	父
4. 「せかいで　一番　えらいのは　くもさんですよ。」	日
5. 「なるほど。では、くもさんに　おねがいしましょう。」	父
6. 「かぜさんの方が　私より　もっと　えらいです。」	雲
7. 「せかいで　一番　えらいのは　ねずみさんですよ。」	壁

【会話】

Formal style:
まり：この　お話を　どう　思いますか。

ケン：おもしろいと　思います。

Informal style:
まり：この　お話　どう　思う？

ケン：おもしろいと　思うよ。

【文型】

Plain form ＋と　思います。	I think that ～.

【単語】

1. 昔々〔むかしむかし〕

long, long ago

2. ある（ところに）

(at) a certain (place)

ある日 one day

3. とうとう

finally, at last [after much effort]

4. おしまい

the end

5. 思います

[G1 おもう]

to think

6. (Noun/な Adj.)だ

[Plain form of a copula です]

好きだ。I like (you).

7. (Noun/な Adj.)だった

[Plain form of a copula でした]

好きだった。I liked (her).

十一課

【＊オプショナル単語】

1. ＊ Sentence ＋ とさ。　　　　　＊ and so it is. [Used at the end of folk tales.]
2. ＊ 年〔とし〕とった人　　　　　＊ an elderly person

【漢字】

1. 売　sell　　　う（る）　　　売って いますか。Are they selling?

samurai

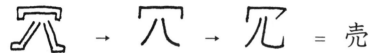

two legs with a stand

　　　　A poor *samurai* standing at a counter selling his goods.

2. 読　read　　　よ（む）　　　本を　読む read a book

言　＋　売　＝　読

to say　　　　to sell　　　　to read

　　　　In order to do a good sales talk, one must read.

【文法】

A. Indirect quotation (Plain form) ＋ と 思います。　　　think that ～

　　　　　　　　　　　　　　　言いました。　　　said that ～

　　　　　　　　　　　　　　　答えました。　　　answered that ～

　　　　　　　　　　　　　　　聞きました。　　　heard that ～ ; asked that ～

The subject of the sentence, that is, the person who thinks, says, answers, etc. is usually marked by the particle は. The subject of the quote, if different from the subject of the sentence, is followed by が.

	Formal form:	Plain form:	
Verb	行きます	行く	go, will go
	行きません	行かない	do not go, will not go
	行きました	行った	went
	行きませんでした	行かなかった	did not go
い Adj.	やすいです	やすい	is cheap
	やすくないです	やすくない	is not cheap
	やすかったです	やすかった	was cheap
	やすくなかったです	やすくなかった	was not cheap
な Adj.	好きです	好き(だ)	like
	好きじゃ(or では)ありません	好きじゃ(or では)ない	do not like
	好きでした	好き(だった)	liked
	好きじゃ(or では)ありませんでした	好きじゃ(or では)なかった	did not like
Noun	学生です	学生(だ)	is a student
	学生じゃ(or では)ありません	学生じゃ(or では)ない	is not a student
	学生でした	学生(だった)	was a student
	学生じゃ(or では)ありませんでした	学生じゃ(or では)なかった	was not a student

1. 明日 日本語の 試験が あると 思います。 I think there is a Japanese exam tomorrow.

2. 母は 今 四十五才だと 思います。 I think my mother is 45 years old now.

3. この 話は おもしろいと 思います。 I think this story is interesting.

4. 父は 前 ピアノが 上手だったと 聞きました。

I heard that my father was good at the piano before.

5. 私は パーティーへ 行かないと 言いました。 I said that I will not go to the party.

6. エミさんは お母さんが 来なかったと 答えました。

Emi answered that her mother didn't come.

【  文化ノート】

Marriages in Japan

Until several years ago, there was considerable pressure for Japanese to get married in their 20's. These days, however, alternate lifestyles have become more acceptable, relieving some of the pressure on young women and men. To this day, there are two types of marriages, arranged (おみあい) and love (れんあい) marriages. The traditional arranged marriage is a practice that still lives on. A prospective bride and groom are formally introduced to one another by a go-between. Each prospective partner and their families are involved in perusing each other's family background prior to the arranged meeting. It is acceptable to refuse to meet the partner at this first stage, but it becomes more difficult after the face-to-face meeting has taken place. Recently, love marriages have become more common. Problems can arise, though, if families do not approve of one's choice of a marriage partner. It is common for family relationships to be (at least temporarily) broken if either partners' family does not approve.

十一課

【アクティビティー】

A. ペアワーク

Read the information provided by エミ and ケン below. Then, A asks B the questions listed after A. B answers based on the information given below. B asks A the questions listed after B. A answers based on the information given below.

Ex. A: 「ケンさんは　パーティーに　行くと　言いましたか。」

    B: 「いいえ、ケンさんは　パーティーに　行かないと　言いました。」

A.

質問	答え
1. エミさんは　きのうの　しゅくだいを　したと　言いましたか。	(はい)
2. エミさんは　すう学の　しけんが　良かったと　言いましたか。	はい
3. エミさんは　まえ　ピアノが　上手だったと　言いましたか。	(はい)
4. エミさんは　今　十五才だと　言いましたか。	(はい)
5. エミさんは　いい　子どもだったと　言いましたか。	はい

B.

質問	答え
1. ケンさんは　パーティーに　行くと　言いましたか。	いいえ
2. ケンさんは　日本語の　せいせきが　良かったと　言いましたか。	いいえ
3. ケンさんは　おもちが　好きだと　言いましたか。	いいえ
4. ケンさんは　十五才だと　言いましたか。	いいえ
5. ケンさんは　いい　子どもだったと　言いましたか。	いいえ

「パーティーに行きます。」
「きのうのしゅくだいをしました。」
「日本語のせいせきはいいです。」
「すう学のしけんは良かったです。」
「おもちが好きです。」
「まえピアノが上手でした。」
「私は今十五才です。」
「私はいい子どもでした。」

「パーティーに行きません。」
「きのうのしゅくだいをしませんでした。」
「日本語のせいせきは良くないです。」
「すう学のしけんは良くなかったです。」
「おもちが好きじゃありません。」
「まえピアノが上手じゃありませんでした。」
「私は今十五才ではありません。」
「私はいい子どもではありませんでした。」

エミ

ケン

B. ペアワーク

Based on the picture below, ask your partner what he/she thinks each person is about to do. Take turns.

Ex. 質問：「ゆきさんは　これから　何を　すると　思いますか。」

答え：「ゆきさんは　これから　泳ぐと　思います。」

さかなを　つります to fish

Now ask your partner what he/she thinks each person did. Take turns.

Ex. 質問：「ゆきさんは　何を　したと　思いますか。」

答え：「ゆきさんは　泳いだと　思います。」

ひやけを　します to get sunburned

　　　十一課

C. ペアワーク

Ask your partner's opinions about a teacher both of you know. Write down your partner's response.

Ex. Do you think that your Japanese teacher can run fast?

質問：「〜先生は　走るのが　速いと　思いますか。」

答え：「そうですねえ...　〜先生は　走るのが　速くないと　思います。」

1.〜先生は　毎日　うんどうを　すると　思いますか。	
2.〜先生は　おすしが　好きだと　思いますか。	
3.〜先生は　きびしいと　思いますか。	
4.〜先生は　スキーが　出来ると　思いますか。	
5.〜先生は　たくさん　しゅくだいを　出すと　思いますか。	
6.〜先生の　しけんは　やさしいと　思いますか。	
7.〜先生は　お金持ちだと　思いますか。	
8.〜先生は　うたが　上手だと　思いますか。	
9.〜先生は　いい　先生だと　思いますか。	

By the end of this lesson, you will be able to communicate the information below in the given situations.

【Ⅱ-12 タスク1】

A group of American students performed the play "Mouse Wedding" in their Japanese language class. A Japanese student asks one of them about it.

Japanese Student:

(1) You heard that your friend's class put on a play in Japanese class. Ask if it is true.

(2) Answer that it is. Ask who played the Sun, the Cloud, the Wind, and the Wall.

(3) Ask which role your partner played (if it's not one of the above).

(4) Ask which role he/she didn't want to play.

(5) Tell which character you like best and why.

American Student:

(1) Say yes, you did perform "Mouse Wedding." Ask your partner if it is a famous story.

(2) Identify who played which part.

(3) Identify which role you played. Tell which role you actually wanted to play. (choose one other than the one you actually played). Explain why.

(4) Answer which role you would not have wanted to play (other than the one you actually played). Explain why.

【Ⅱ-12 タスク2】

A group of American students performed the play "Mouse Wedding" in their Japanese language class. A Japanese student asks one of them about it.

Japanese Student:

(1) Ask if he/she enjoyed the play or not.

(2) Ask why.

(3) Ask if he/she wants to do a play again next year.

(4) Ask which group he/she thought was the best.

(5) Answer. Explain why.

American Student:

(1) Give your opinion. Tell your partner whether it was difficult or not.

(2) Explain.

(3) Give your opinion. Explain why.

(4) Give your opinion. Explain why. Ask if your partner likes doing plays.

(5) Comment.

【会話】

Formal style:	まり：あなたは　何に　なりたいですか。
	ケン：ぼくは　お日様に　なりたいです。
Informal style:	まり：あなたは　何に　なりたい？
	ケン：ぼくは　お日様に　なりたい。

【文型】

Noun に　なります　　　　　become ～

【単語】

1. げきを　します　[IR する]

give/put on a (stage) play

2. ～に　なります　[G1 なる]

become ～

【＊オプショナル単語】

1. ＊小道具〔こどうぐ〕　　　　　＊ props

【文法】

A. Noun に　なります　　　　to become ～

1. 「何に　なりたいですか。」　　　"What do you want to be?"

「医者に　なりたいです。」　　　"I want to be a doctor."

2. 私は　十五才に　なりました。　　"I have turned 15 years old."

【👤👤アクティビティー】

A. クラスワーク

Re-read the "Mouse Wedding." List the characters you will need to put on the play. First, list the most essential characters. Then list other characters you may wish to add.

[Essential characters]

[Additional characters]

B. クラスワーク

You will put on the play "Mouse Wedding." Divide the class into several groups of seven to nine persons each. Have a mixture of male and female students. Decide who will play each part and write the names of the students and their roles.

質問：「だれが　～に　なりますか。」

答え：「私は　～に　なりたいです。」

[Group members]   [Character]

十二課

Ask your partner these questions in Japanese.
Your partner should answer in Japanese.

1. Was *Chuukichi* rich?

2. What Japanese folk tales do you know?

3. Is this classroom bright or dark now?

4. Who do you think is the greatest person in the world?

5. Is the sun out today?

6. Are there lots of clouds today?

7. What color are the walls of your house?

8. Do you always complete your homework?

9. In the "Mouse Wedding" story, who said that he wants to marry Chuuko?

10. What did Chuuko's father say to Chuukichi?

11. Who was the greatest of all?

12. Why was the Cloud stronger than the Sun?

13. Who was stronger, the Cloud or the Wind? Why?

14. Was the Wall stronger than the Wind? Why?

15. Why was the Mouse stronger than the Wall?

16. How many children did the mouse father and mother have?

17. Was Chuuko their son or daughter?

18. Do you think your group play was good?

19. What (character) did you become in the play?

20. Who do you think was the best actor/actress (most skillful) in your group?

21. Do you think this is a good school?

22. Do you think that you are studying with your utmost effort?

23. Do you think that the school library is quiet?

うらない

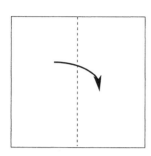

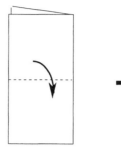

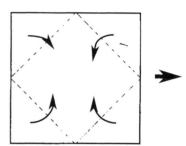

1. Fold a square piece of paper in half both horizontally and vertically.

2. Open up to the original square.

3. Fold each corner to the center along the creases.

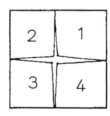

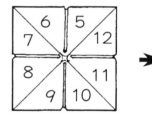

4. Fold each corner again toward the center so each corner meets at the center.

5. Write the numbers 1 - 4 on each square.

6. Turn around and number each triangle 5 - 12. Write a fortune on the reverse side of each triangle numbered 5 - 12.

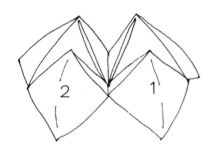

7. Open up the folded toy as shown in the illustration. Place thumbs and forefingers under each pocket and open and close.

8. With a partner, take turns choosing numbers while the toy is being held in an open or closed position. Read each other's fortunes and enjoy!

By the end of this lesson, you will be able to communicate the information below in the given situations.

【 II-13 タスク1 】

A Japanese tourist stops an American on the street and asks for directions. Use the maps on pages 364-365 for reference.

Japanese Tourist:

You are at the starting point.

(1) You have never been in this city before. Politely get the American person's attention and say that you want to go to the zoo.
Ask if there is one nearby.
Ask the American where it is.

(2) Repeat the directions you heard to make sure you understood. Ask how long it will take from where you are (time).

(3) Thank the American.

American Person:

(1) Answer yes, it's nearby.

Give directions according to the map on pages 378-379.

(2) Answer that it takes about 15 minutes on foot.

(3) Respond.

【 II-13 タスク2 】

The Japanese tourist is back at the same starting point.
Use the maps on pages 378-379 for reference.

Japanese Tourist:

(1) You want to visit a shrine.

(2) Ask the American where it is.

(3) Ask how far it is from here (distance).
(4) You ask which is faster, going by bus or on foot.
(5) Ask where the bus stop is.

(6) Thank the American.

American Person:

(1) Inform the tourist that the shrine is a little far.

(2) Give directions according to the map on pages 378-379.
(3) Say that it is about two kilometers.
(4) Reply that it is probably faster to go by bus because the streets are not crowded now.
(5) Tell the tourist to go straight ahead on this street. The bus stop is next to the post office. Instruct him/her to ride Bus #2.

(6) Respond.

十三課

【会話 - Formal style】

＜道で＞

日本人：あのう... ちょっと、伺いますが、この　辺に　動物園が

　　　　ありますか。

　ケン：ああ、動物園ですか。ここから、近いですよ。この通りを

　　　　まっすぐ　行って、二番目の　交差点で　右に　まがって　下さい。

日本人：あの　白くて　高い　建物の　所ですか。

　ケン：そうです。そうです。あの　角を　右に　まがって　下さい。

　　　　それから、次の　交差点を　左に　まがると、動物園の　入口が

　　　　見えます。

日本人：分かりました。　有難うございました。

　ケン：どう　いたしまして。

日本人：それから、後で　郵便局へ　行きたいんですが、ここから

　　　　歩いて　どのぐらい　かかりますか。

　ケン：歩いて　二十分ぐらいでしょう。

日本人：そうですか。バスで　行くのと　歩いて　行くのと　どちらの方が

　　　　速いですか。

　ケン：そうですねえ... 今　道が　混んでいますから、たぶん

　　　　歩く方が　速いでしょう。

日本人：どうも　有難うございました。

　ケン：どう　いたしまして。

十三課　　　　　　350

Let's review previous vocabulary!

A. めいし　Nouns

1. みち	street, road	7. つぎ	next
2. ここ	here	8. 左〔ひだり〕	left side
3. 右〔みぎ〕	right side	9. 二十分くらい	about 20 minutes
4. 建物〔たてもの〕	building	10. 今	now
5. 所〔ところ〕	place	11. 私	I
6. かど	corner		

B. どうし　Verbs

12. あります〔G1 ある〕 — there is
13. 行って〔G1 行く〕 — go
14. まがって　下さい〔G1 まがる〕 — please turn
15. 〜が　見えます〔G2 見える〕 — 〜 can be seen
16. 分かりました〔G1 分かる〕 — I understand.
17. 行きたいんです〔G1 行く〕 — want to go
18. あるいて〔G1 あるく〕 — walk
19. 行くの〔G1 行く〕 — going [Noun form]
20. あるいて　行くの〔あるいて行きます〕 — go on foot [Noun form]
21. 見〔G2 みます／みる〕 — see, watch [Stem form]

C. -い けいようし　I Adjectives

22. 近い〔ちかい〕 — near
23. 白くて〔しろくて〕 — is white [TE form]
24. 高い〔たかい〕 — tall, high
25. はやい — fast

D. じょし　Particles

26. (Place)に　(thing)が　あります — There is (thing) at (place).
　　あそこに　としょかんが　あります。 — There is a library over there.
27. 〜から — from 〜
　　うちから　ちかいです。 — It is near my house.

351

28. (place) を   through, along (place)

    かどを　みぎに　まがります。   I will turn right at the corner.

29. (Place) で + Action verb   do 〜 at (place)

    としょかんで　べんきょうします。   I study at the library.

30. (Direction) に／へ + Direction verb   go 〜 to (direction)

    学校に／へ　行きます。   I will go to school.

31. Sentence 1 + が、 Sentence 2。   Sentence 1。 Sentence 2。 [が is a sentence connector.]

    としょかんへ　行きたいんですが、としょかんは　どこですか。

                 I want to go to the library. Where is the library?

32. (Mode of) transportation で + Direction verb   go by (mode of) transportation

    バスで　行きます。   I will go by bus.

33. Sentence 1 (reason) +から、 Sentence 2。   Sentence 1 (reason), so sentence 2。

    学校は　うちから　ちかいから、あるいて　行きます。

                 School is close to my house, so I walk there.

E.   Others

34. それから、   And then,

35. あとで   later

36. たぶん   probably

F.   ぶんぽう　Grammar

37. Sentence (plain form) + でしょう。   It is probably 〜.

    バスは　おそいでしょう。   The bus is probably slow.

38. Noun 1 と　Noun 2 と　どちらの方が　〜ですか。   Which is more 〜 , Noun 1 or Noun 2?

    バスと　電車と　どちらの方が　はやいですか。   Which is faster, the bus or the electric train?

39. Noun 1 の方が　Noun 2 より　〜です。   Noun 1 is more 〜 than Noun 2.

    電車の方が　バスより　はやいです。   The electric train is faster than the bus.

G.   Expressions

40. そうです。そうです。   Yes, it is. Yes, it is.

41. ありがとう　ございました。   Thank you very much.

42. どう　いたしまして。   You are welcome.

43. そうですか。   Is that so?

44. そうですねえ . . .   Let me see . . . Well . . .

【会話】

Formal style:　日本人：あのう... ちょっと　伺^{うかが}いますが、この　辺^{へん}に

動物園^{どうぶつえん}が　ありますか。

ケン：ああ、動物園^{どうぶつえん}ですね。動物園^{どうぶつえん}は　近^{ちか}いですよ。

【単語^{たん}】

1. あのう... ちょっと　伺^{うかが}いますが...

[G1 うかがう]

Excuse me . . . I have a question . . .

うかがう is a polite equiv. of 聞きます

2.（この）辺^{へん}

〔（この）へん〕

(this) area

3. バス停^{てい}

〔バスてい〕

bus stop

4. 動物園^{どうぶつえん}

〔どうぶつえん〕

zoo

どうぶつ animals

5. 郵便局^{ゆうびんきょく}

〔ゆうびんきょく〕

post office

ゆうびん postage

ゆうびんばこ mailbox

6. 美術館^{びじゅつかん}

〔びじゅつかん〕

art museum

びじゅつ fine arts

7. 公衆電話^{こうしゅう}

〔こうしゅうでんわ〕

public phone

こうしゅう public

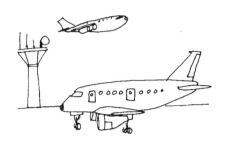

8. 空港
〔くうこう〕
airport

9. 駅
〔えき〕
train station

10. コンビニ

convenience store

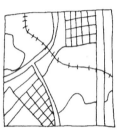

11. 駐車場
〔ちゅうしゃじょう〕
parking lot
IR ちゅうしゃする to park

12. 地図
〔ちず〕
map

13. 町
〔まち〕
town

14. ああ

Oh!

【*オプショナル単語】

1. *村〔むら〕   * village

2. *中華料理〔ちゅうかりょうり〕   * Chinese food

3. *八百屋〔やおや〕   * greengrocer [vegetable store]

4. *タクシー乗り場〔のりば〕   * taxi station

5. *ガソリンスタンド   * gas station

6. *交番〔こうばん〕   * police box

7. *ビル   * building [tall, Western style]

【漢字】

1. 右　right　　みぎ　　右手〔みぎて〕right hand, 右目〔みぎめ〕right eye,

　　右耳〔みぎみみ〕right ear, 右田〔みぎた〕さん

right hand → ㄨ → ナ +

thing → 口 → 口 = 右

People carry things in their right hands.

2. 左　left　　ひだり　　左手〔ひだりて〕left hand, 左目〔ひだりめ〕left eye,

　　左耳〔ひだりみみ〕left ear

left hand → メ → ナ +

ruler → 丁 → 工 = 左

A person holds his ruler with his left hand.

【 ● 文化ノート】

Asking for Directions

　Japanese are usually very helpful when foreigners stop them for directions. In residential or rural areas, it is even common for Japanese to walk you to your destination if it is within a reasonable distance. Police boxes (こうばん) are located conveniently throughout cities and villages and are good places to ask for directions. In certain cities such as Tokyo, knowing the address of a place is not necessarily helpful, as the numbering system of addresses is not always systematic. Therefore, it is best to stop at the police box and ask for assistance there. Typically, the police box will have a very detailed and extensive map of the vicinity. The officers who are stationed at police boxes generally get around the area on bicycles.

こうばん police box

十三課

【👩👩アクティビティー】

A. ペアワーク

Ask your partner whether the locations of the following places are in your present vicinity. Answer based on fact.

質問：「あのう... ちょっと 伺いますが、この 辺に
　　　 〜が ありますか。」

答え：「はい、あります。」or

　　　 「いいえ、ありません。」or

　　　 「さあ... 知りません。」

Places you want to locate:	Places your partner wants to locate:
1. こうえん	1. どうぶつえん
2. びじゅつかん	2. と書かん
3. えいがかん	3. くうこう
4. 大学	4. 小学校
5. 中学校	5. ゆうびんきょく
6. びょういん	6. じんじゃ
7. お寺	7. デパート
8. きょう会	8. こうしゅう電話
9. えき	9. ちゅう車じょう
10. ぎん行	10. きっさてん
11. くすりや	11. コンビニ
12. スーパー	12. バスてい

B. ペアワーク

You want to do the following things. Your partner suggests where you can go. Take turns.

Ex. I want to buy milk.

質問：「ミルクを　買いたいんですが。」

答え：「じゃ、スーパーへ　行きましょう。」

Things you want to do
1. 中国りょうりを食べたいです。
2. おいしいコーヒーをのみたいです。
3. 日本にこの手がみを 　　おくりたいです。
4. 日本の友だちがごぜん九時に 　　つきます。むかえに行きたいです。
5. 母に電話をしたいです。
6. ゆうめいなえを見たいです。
7. バスにのりたいです。
8. 車をちゅう車したいです。

Things your partner wants to do
1. このまちのちずをかいたいです。
2. 電車にのりたいです。
3. シャツをかいたいです。
4. 本を読みたいです。
5. あたまがいたいです。 　　くすりがほしいです。
6. ちょっとうんどうしたいです。
7. いいえいがを見たいです。
8. お金を出したいです。

C. ３人から５人のグループワーク：サイモンゲーム

Play Simon Says using direction words. Your partner should point to the correct location in relation to himself/herself at the appropriate time.

Words to use:

十三課

１３課－２か: TURN RIGHT AT THE NEXT CORNER.

【会話】

Formal style:　ケン：この道を　まっすぐ　行って、次の　交差点で
　　　　　　　　　　右に　曲がると、動物園は　そこに　あります。

　　　　　　　　日本人：どうも　有難うございました。

【文型ぶんけい】

> Verb (Dictionary form) + と、～　　　　　　when, if
>
> 右に　まがると、動物園が　あります。　If you turn right, the zoo will be there.

【単語たん】

1. 通りとお
〔とおり〕
street, avenue

2. 交差点こうさてん
〔こうさてん〕
intersection

3. 入口
〔いりぐち〕
entrance

4. 出口
〔でぐち〕
exit

5. 橋はし
〔はし〕
bridge

6. 向こうむ
〔むこう〕
other side, beyond

7. まっすぐ

straight

8. ～を　渡るわた
〔G1 わたります〕
to cross, go over ～

十三課　　　　　358

9. 二番目
〔にばんめ〕
second (in order)

10. 〜側
〔〜がわ〕
〜 side
右がわ right side, 左がわ left side

11. すると、

Thereupon

【漢字】

1. 入　put in　い（れる）　入れて　下さい。Please put it in.

　　enter　はい（る）　入って　下さい。Please enter.

　　　　い り　　入口〔いりぐち〕entrance

A person enters.

2. 物　thing　も の　食べ物〔たべもの〕food, 飲み物 drink, 建物 building,

着物 kimono (things to wear), 買い物 shopping,

読み物〔よみもの〕things to read

　　　ブツ　　動物 animal, 動物園 zoo

Streamer

Cattle follow streamers, which lead them to find things.

359

A. Sentence 1 + と、 Sentence 2。 　　　　When/If/Whenever S1, S2.

The conditional ("if") conjunction と follows a plain verb, noun, いadjective, or なadjective, either affirmative or negative. Affirmative nouns and なadjectives are followed by だ before と. It is often used to describe scientific principles or mathematical facts, static locations, or explainable natural occurrences. Sentence 2 is a logical or predictable follow-up of the preceding part of the sentence. Sentence 2 is not usually a sentence which expresses a command, request, suggestion, invitation, or volition. The final tense of Sentence 2 determines the tense of the entire sentence.

Verb	食べる		eat, will eat
	食べない		do not eat, will not eat
いAdjective	たかい		is expensive
	たかくない	+ と	is not expensive
なAdjective	好きだ		like
	好きじゃない or 好きではない		do not like
Noun	学生だ		is a student
	学生じゃない or 学生ではない		is not a student

かど　　　　　　　ま　　　　　　こうしゅう
1. その角を　右に　曲がると、公衆電話が　ありますよ。

　　　If you turn right at that corner, there is a public phone.

はし　　　　　わた　　　　　えいがかん
2. その橋を　渡ると、映画館は　すぐ　そこですよ。

　　　If you cross that bridge, the movie theater is right there.

し
3. 日本語が　上手だと、いろいろな　仕事が　出来ます。

　　　If you are good at Japanese, you can do various jobs.

もの　　　　　　　　　　　　　　　　か
4. 物は　高いと、だれも　買いません。

　　　If things are expensive, nobody buys them.

ぶんか
【 ● 文化ノート】

の　　どうぶつえん
上野動物園 Ueno Zoo

The most famous and popular zoo in Japan is undoubtedly Ueno Zoo, located in Tokyo. It is the largest zoo in Tokyo, with more than 7,000 mammals, reptiles, amphibians, birds, and other animals. There is also a children's zoo and an aquarium. Ueno Zoo's most popular attraction is its pandas. The zoo is adjacent to Ueno Park, known for its huge *Shinobazu* Pond. The pond is a favorite boating area and is home to many water birds. In the middle of the pond is a small island called *Bentenjima*, where a temple dedicated to *Benten*, the Goddess of Fortune, stands.

In the same area are numerous museums, art galleries, and other shrines and temples. During the spring, Ueno Park is a popular gathering place for cherry blossom viewing parties.

Panda at Ueno Zoo

【アクティビティー】

A. クラスワーク

Randomly number the following sets of directions from 1-5. Read the directions to your partner in the order in which you marked them. Your partner will listen to your instructions, then draw in the correct route (from beginning to end) on the maps below. Take turns. Check your maps carefully to see that you have communicated accurately.

(　)	この　とおりを　まっすぐ　行って、つぎの　こうさてんで　左に　まがって　下さい。
(　)	この　とおりを　まっすぐ　行って、つぎの　こうさてんで　右に　まがって　下さい。
(　)	この　とおりを　まっすぐ　行って、二番目の　こうさてんで　右に　まがって　下さい。
(Ex.)	この　とおりを　まっすぐ　行って、二番目の　こうさてんで　右に　まがって　下さい。
(　)	この　とおりを　まっすぐ　行って、二番目の　こうさてんで　左に　まがって　下さい。
(　)	この　とおりを　まっすぐ　行って、二番目の　こうさてんを　わたって　もっと　まっすぐ　行って　下さい。

十三課

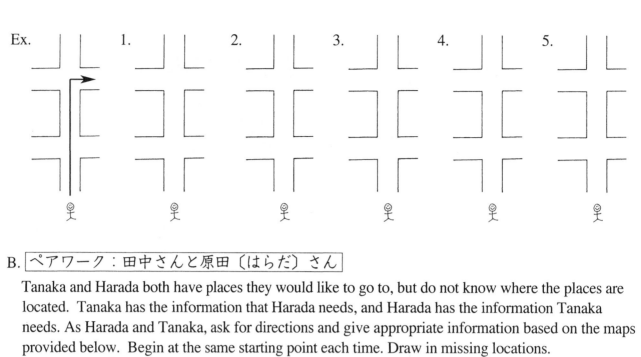

Ex.　　　1.　　　　2.　　　　3.　　　　4.　　　　5.

B. ペアワーク：田中さんと原田〔はらだ〕さん

Tanaka and Harada both have places they would like to go to, but do not know where the places are located. Tanaka has the information that Harada needs, and Harada has the information Tanaka needs. As Harada and Tanaka, ask for directions and give appropriate information based on the maps provided below. Begin at the same starting point each time. Draw in missing locations.

Ex. すし屋

田中：「あのう ... ちょっと　伺いますが、この　辺に　すし屋が
　　　　ありますか。」

原田：「すし屋ですか。この　道を　まっすぐ　行って、二番目の
　　　　交差点で　右に　まがると、右側に　あります。
　　　　すし屋は　かど／交差点から　三番目の　お店ですよ。」

田中：「右側の　三番目の　お店ですね。どうも　有難うございました。」

原田：「どう　いたしまして。」

[田中さんの地図]

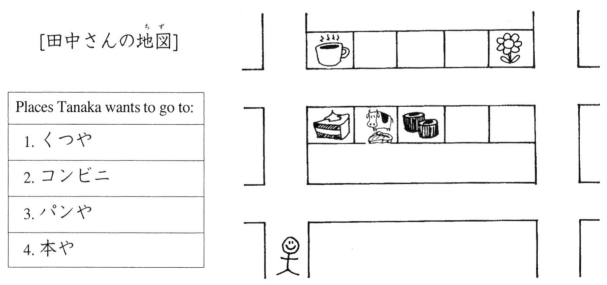

Places Tanaka wants to go to:
1. くつや
2. コンビニ
3. パンや
4. 本や

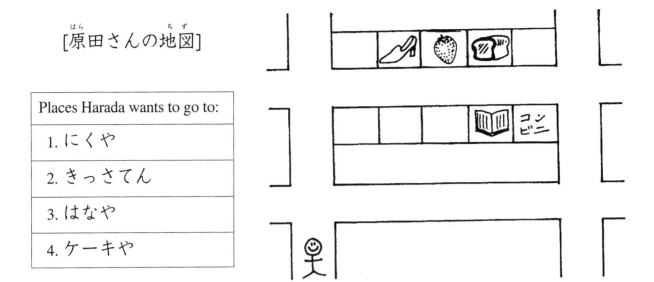

[原田さんの地図]

Places Harada wants to go to:
1. にくや
2. きっさてん
3. はなや
4. ケーキや

十三課

C. ペアワーク：コミュニケーションゲーム

Both partners have the same basic map. Each partner's map, however, is missing the five places listed above his/her map. Ask your partner for directions to the five places, since his/her map shows the places you are looking for. Your partner will give you directions from the starting point. Draw in the entire route from beginning to end. Compare your answers each time. Take turns. Begin at the same starting point each time. The starting point is marked by two people encircled by a ◯.

Places you want to go to.

1. こうえん　　2. すしや　　3. 大学　　4. えいがかん　　5. ホテル

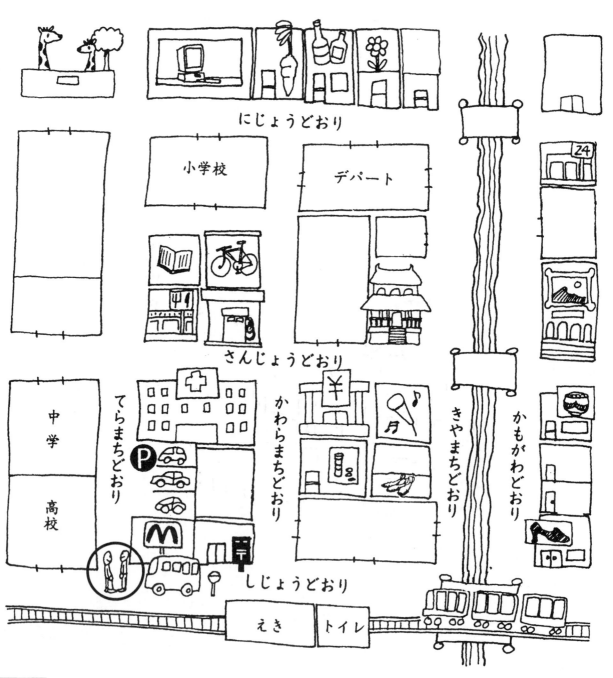

Ex. びょういん
質問：「あのう... ちょっと 伺いますが、病院は どこですか。」
答え：「病院ですね。寺町通りを まっすぐ 行って、次の 交差点を
　　　　右に 曲がると、右側に 病院の 入口が あります。」

Places your partner wants to go to.
1. 中学　　2. はなや　　3. くすりや　　4. 本屋　　5. ラーメン屋

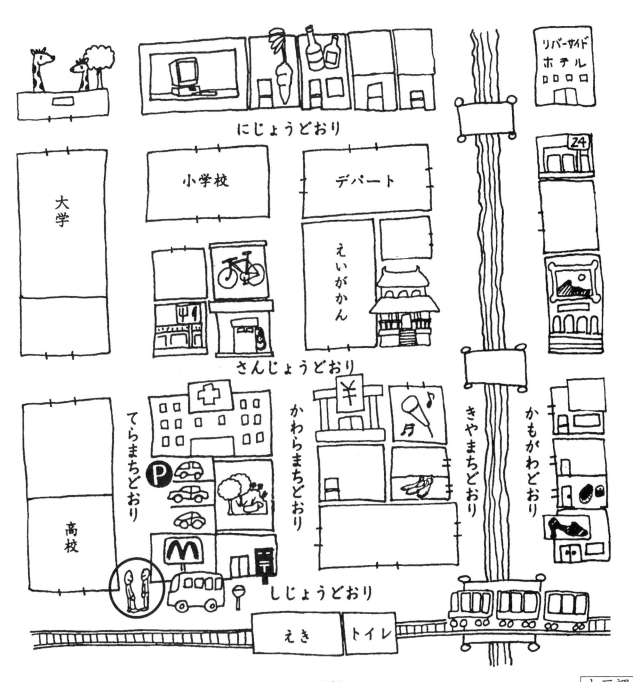

十三課

１３課－３：WHICH IS FASTER, TO GO BY BUS OR TO WALK?

【会話】

Formal style:　日本人：郵便局は　バスで　行くのと　歩いて　行くのと
　　　　　　　　　　　どちらの方が　速いですか。
　　　　　　　　ケン：バスで　行く方が　速いでしょう。

【単語】

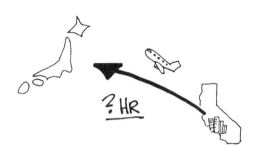

1.～から　～まで
どのぐらい　かかりますか。
or どのぐらい　ですか。

How long does it take from ～ to ～?　[Time]

2.～から　～まで
どのぐらい　ありますか。
or どのぐらい　ですか。

How far is it from ～ to ～?　[Distance]

【*オプショナル単語】

1.＊マイル	＊ mile(s)
2.＊キロ	＊ kilometer(s)
3.＊メートル	＊ meter(s)
4.＊センチ（メートル）	＊ centimeter(s)
5.＊ミリ（メートル）	＊ millimeter(s)

【漢字】

1. 名 name   な   名前 name

             メイ   有名〔ゆうめい〕famous

In the darkness of the evening, you have to confess and tell your name.

2. 前 front, before   まえ   名前〔なまえ〕name

                           家の　前〔いえの　まえ〕front of the house

                           前田〔まえだ〕さん、前川〔まえかわ〕さん

              ゼン   午前〔ごぜん〕a.m.

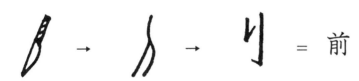

Before cooking, you must cut off the horns of the animal.

【 ● 文化ノート】

1. Metric System

As in other countries of the world, the metric system is used in Japan.

1 マイル (mile) = 1.6 キロ (kilometers)   1 キロ (kilometer) = 0.62マイル (mile)

1 ヤード (yard) = 91.4 センチ (centimeters)   1 メートル (meter) = 3.28 フィート (feet)

1 フィート (foot) = 30.5 センチ (centimeters)   1 センチ (centimeter) = 0.39 インチ (inch)

1 インチ (inch) = 2.54 センチ (centimeters)   1 ミリ (millimeter) = 0.04 インチ (inch)

2. 郵便局　Post Offices

The postal system in Japan is very efficient. Post offices can be found in most cities and towns, and mailboxes are available in convenient areas. Mailboxes (ゆうびんばこ) in Japan are orange, and are identifiable by the symbol 〒, which looks much like the *katakana* テ. In addition to postal services, such as the mailing of letters and packages and the selling of stamps, mail delivery, etc., Japan's postal system offers additional services. Customers may open savings accounts, transfer money by telephone or telegram, and pay utility bills and government bills at post offices in Japan.

ゆうびんばこ

Mailbox

【アクティビティー】

A. ペアワーク

Ask your partner how far it is from his/her house to the following places. Answer based on facts. Take turns.

Ex. 家から　学校まで

質問１：「家から　学校まで　どのぐらい　ありますか。」

答え１：「１５マイルぐらいでしょう。」

質問２：「家から　学校まで　どのぐらい　かかりますか。」

答え２：「車で　３０分ぐらい　かかります。」

Places	Distance	Time and mode of transportation
Ex. 家から　学校まで	１５マイルぐらい	車で　３０分ぐらい
1. 家から　スーパーまで		
2. 家から　ガソリンスタンドまで		
3. 家から　えいがかんまで		
4. 家から　ぎん行まで		
5. 家から　こうえんまで		

【会話】

Formal style:　ケン：今　道が　混んでいますから、歩く方が　速いでしょう。

　　　　　　　日本人：どうも　有難うございました。

【文型】

Verb 1 (Dic. form)＋のと　　Verb 2 (Dic. form)＋のと　　どちら／どっち(の方)が　〜ですか。

　　　　　Which is more 〜, to do verb 1 or to do verb 2?

Verb 1 (Dict. form)＋方が　　Verb 2 (Dict. form)＋（の）より　〜です。

　　　　　To do verb 1 is more than to do verb 2.

Verb 1 (Dic. form)＋のは　　Verb 2 (Dic. form)＋ほど　　Negative predicate。

　　　　　To do verb 1 is not 〜 as much as to do verb 2.

【単語】

1. こんで　います
　　[G1 こむ]
　　is crowded

2. すいて　います
　　[G1 すく]
　is not crowded, is empty

【＊オプショナル単語】

1. ＊ラッシュアワー　　　　　＊ rush hour

2. ＊フリーウェイ　　　　　　＊ freeway

3. ＊ハイウェイ　　　　　　　＊ highway

【漢字】

1. 戸　door　　　と　　　　　　　戸を　閉めて　下さい。 Please close the door.

戸田〔とだ〕さん

戸口〔とぐち〕さん

戸川〔とがわ〕さん

ど　　　　木戸〔きど〕さん

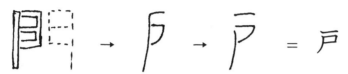

Here's a door. Lift the latch on top.

2. 所　place　　ところ　　　　しずかな　所 a quiet place

どころ　　　　田所〔たどころ〕さん

ショ　　　　　住所〔じゅうしょ〕 address

事務所〔じむしょ〕 office

戸 +

door　　ax

Axe marks on the door indicate the place.

3. 近　near　　　ちか（い）　　　近い　所〔ちかい　ところ〕 a nearby place

川近〔かわちか〕さん

斤 +

ax

go back and forth

Going back and forth with an axe to a nearby place.

ラッシュアワー　Rush Hour

Morning and evening rush hours are horrendous in Japanese cities, particularly in the Tokyo area. Whenever one encounters ラッシュアワー in the train or subway systems or on the streets and highways, one learns to be patient. Rush hours in the cities are generally from 7 to 9 a.m. and from 5 to 7 p.m. Traffic jams also commonly occur on Saturdays, Sundays, and holidays. Large traffic signs are strategically placed on major highways leading to major cities to let motorists know where and how long (in kilometers) traffic jams are. Commuters turn on their television sets in the morning not only to get information about the news, time, and weather, but also to learn about traffic conditions on the different routes heading into the cities.

Rush hour at a Tokyo train station.

【文法】

A. Verb (Dic. form) ＋のと　Verb (Dic. form) ＋のと　どちら／どっち(の方)が　～ですか。

This pattern is used to compare two actions. The two actions expressed in their dictionary forms are both followed by the nominalizer の. The interrogative (question) word is どちら or どっち, which is always followed by the particle が.

---

1. 「外で　食べる<u>のと</u>　家で　食べる<u>のと</u>　どっちの方が　好きですか。」

"Which is better, eating out or eating at home?"

2. 「バスで　行く<u>のと</u>　タクシーで　行く<u>のと</u>　どちらの方が
速いですか。」

"Which is faster, going by bus or going by taxi?"

「そうですねえ...　タクシーの方が　速いでしょう。」

"Let's see . . . The taxi is probably faster."

B. Verb (Dict. form)＋のは　Verb (Dict. form)＋（の）より　〜です。

Verb (Dict. form)＋（の）より　Verb (Dict. form)＋のは　〜です。

Verb (Dict. form)＋方が　Verb (Dict. form)＋（の）より　〜です。

Verb (Dict. form)＋（の）より　Verb (Dict. form)＋方が　〜です。

When comparing two actions, the actions are expressed in verb dictionary forms. The subject is marked by のは or ほうが. The alternative that is less (いadjective / なadjective) is followed by (の)より.

1. 映画を　見るのは　ビデオを　見るより　好きです。

      I like watching movies more than watching videos.

2. はしで　食べるのは　フォークで　食べるより　難しいです。

      It is more difficult to eat with chopsticks than to eat with a fork.

3. バスで　行く方が　歩くより　速いですよ。

      It is faster to go by bus than to walk.

4. 買い物に　行くより　家に　いる方が　いいです。

      It is better to stay at home than to go shopping.

C. Verb (Dic. form)＋のは　Verb (Dic. form)＋ほど　Negative predicate。

Two actions may also be compared negatively. Verbs must be placed in their verb dictionary forms. The alternative followed by のは is the action which is not (いadjective / なadjective). The predicate must appear in its negative form.

    Often, this pattern is also used with the subject clause "as you think" or "as someone says." This clause is placed in the dictionary form and precedes ほど.

1. 日本語を　話すのは　聞く　ほど　難しく　ありません。

      Speaking Japanese is not as difficult as hearing (understanding) it.

2. バスで　学校へ　行くのは　車で　行くほど　速くありません。

      Going to school by bus is not as fast as going by car.

3. 数学は　あなたが　言う　ほど　やさしく　ないです。

      Math is not as easy as you say.

4. 漢字を　おぼえるのは　先生が　思う　ほど　やさしく　ありません。

      Memorizing *kanji* is not as easy as the teacher thinks.

【アクティビティー】

A. ペアワーク

Using the cues below, ask your partner which means of transportation is faster. Assume that school is the starting point. Answer based on fact. Take turns.

Ex. えいがかん, あるいて 行く, バスで 行く

質問：「すみません、映画館へ 行きたいんですが、歩いて 行くのと
　　　　バスで 行くのと どちらの方が 速いですか。」

答え：「バスで 行く方が 歩いて 行くより 速いです。」

1. びょういん, あるいて 行く, タクシーで 行く	
2. ショッピングセンター, あるいて 行く, バスで 行く	
3. くうこう, バスで 行く, タクシーで 行く	
4. こうえん, じてん車で 行く, あるいて 行く	
5. コンビニ, あるいて 行く, バスで 行く	

B. ペアワーク

Ask your partner which he/she likes more. Your partner answers using ～ほど. Take turns.

Ex. スポーツを　見る or スポーツを　する

質問：「スポーツを　見るのと　するのと　どちらの方が　好きですか。」
答え：「スポーツを　するのは　スポーツを　見るほど
　　　　好きではありません。」

1. かい物に　行く or 家で　テレビを　見る	
2. 本を　読む or テレビゲームで　あそぶ	
3. およぐ or バスケットを　する	
4. えいがかんで　えいがを　見る or 　　家で　ビデオを　見る	
5. 家で　食べる or レストランで　食べる	

C. ペアワーク

Interview your partner. Answer based on the facts. Take turns.

1. 何時に　家を　出ますか。	
2. 学校へ　何で　来ますか。	
3. あなたは　学校へ　車を　うんてんして　来ますか。 　　(If not) だれが　車を　うんてんしますか。	
4. あさ、みちは　こんで　いますか。	
5. 家から　学校まで　どのぐらい　ありますか。	
6. 家から　学校まで　どのぐらい　かかりますか。	
7. あさ、何時に　学校に　つきますか。	
8. こうつうの　もんだいの　一番の　げんいん(reason)は 　　何だと　おもいますか。	

Find the answers from books, by talking to friends, or by using the Internet.

1. Name the types of mass transportation (public transportation) available in your area. How much do they cost? Are they very safe and reliable?

2. What types of mass transportation are available in Japan? How much do they cost? Are they safe and reliable?

3. In Japan, it is very rare to see cars that are more than five or so years old. Can you find out why?

4. Name some makes and models of common Japanese cars in the U.S. See if you can find out what their names are in Japan. (The model names are often different in Japan.)

5. Why do the Japanese drive on the left side of the street?

6. What percentage of Japanese own a car? What percentage of Americans? If the numbers are quite different, try to figure out why.

7. What percentage of Americans use mass transportation regularly? What percentage of Japanese? If the numbers are quite different, try to figure out why.

8. What kinds of cars are popular among young Japanese? How much does one of those cars cost there? How much does one of those cars cost in America?

9. How much does it cost for a gallon of gas where you live? How about in another city or town in a different setting in another state? (For example, if you live in an urban area, try to find out gas prices in a rural area.) How much does it cost for a gallon of gas in Japan? (Remember, gas is sold by the liter in Japan, so you will have to convert.)

日本の　乗^のり物

Transportation in Japan

バス

Bus

電車

Electric train

タクシー

Taxi

自転車^{じ てん}

bicycle

By the end of this lesson, you will be able to communicate the information below in the given situations.

【Ⅱ-14 タスク1】

An American student and a Japanese student are cooking together in the kitchen. The American student has never cooked *sukiyaki* before, so the Japanese student teaches him/her how to make it.

American Student:

(1) Ask your friend if he/she knows how to make *sukiyaki*.

(2) Thank your friend. Ask what is needed for *sukiyaki*.

(3) Ask how to cut the beef, shredded *konnyaku*, and vegetables.

(4) Announce that you are finished cutting everything. Ask what to do next.

(5) Say that the pot has become hot, so you will put oil in it.

(6) You taste the sauce. Say that it's a little too sweet.

(7) You taste it again, and announce that it has become tasty.

Japanese Student:

(1) Answer yes. Offer to teach him/her how to make it.

(2) Tell your friend that you need beef, shredded *konnyaku*, various vegetables, sugar, and soy sauce.

(3) Instruct your friend to slice the beef thin, cut the shredded *konnyaku* in half, and the vegetables into small pieces (use one sentence).

(4) Tell your friend to please heat the pot.

(5) Instruct him/her to put the beef in first, then the sugar and soy sauce.

(6) Suggest putting in more soy sauce to make it saltier.

(7) Respond.

【Ⅱ-14 タスク2】

An American student and a Japanese student cooked *sukiyaki* together.

American Student:

(1) Announce that the *sukiyaki* is ready.

(2) You say, "How unpleasant!"

(3) You try it, and find that it is good. Tell your friend that you made a strawberry cake for dessert, and offer him/her some.

(4) Tell your friend that you want to become a cook (*ryorinin*) in the future because you like cooking.

Japanese Student:

(1) Tell your friend to dip the *sukiyaki* into raw egg.

(2) Insist that it will taste good.

(3) Comment that the strawberries are a little sour, but the cake is good.

(4) Say that it is a good idea. Offer to clean up the kitchen.

十四課

【 会話 - Formal style】

<ケンの　家の　台所で>

ケン：すき焼きの　作り方を　教えて　下さい。どんな　物を　入れますか。

まり：そうですねえ... 牛肉や　糸こんにゃくや　野菜などを　入れます。

ケン：ぼくが　切りましょうか。

まり：じゃ、牛肉は　うすく　切って、糸こんにやくは　半分に　切って

　　　下さい。そして、野菜は　よく　洗って、小さく　切って　下さいね。

　　　まず、始めに　おなべを　熱く　して、油を　入れます。

　　　それから、牛肉を　入れて、砂糖と　醬油を　入れます。

ケン：どのくらい　入れますか。このくらいですか。

　　　<Ken adds *shoyu* and sugar. Mari tastes it.> 味は　どうですか。

まり：ちょっと　甘すぎますね。もう　少し　醬油を　入れて、からく

　　　しましょう。お酒も　少し　入れましょう。おいしく　なりますよ。

<テーブルで>

まり：出来ましたよ。おいしそうですねえ。生卵に　つけて、食べましょう。

ケン：えっ、気持ちが　悪い。でも、食べて　みましょう。いただきます。

　　　おいしい！

まり：はい、どうぞ。デザートの　果物です。

ケン：この　苺は　ちょっと　すっぱいけど、おいしいですね。

　　　お腹が　いっぱいに　なりましたよ。ごちそうさま。ぼくが　全部

　　　かたづけますよ。

【会話 - Informal style】

<ケンの　家の　台所で>

ケン：すき焼きの　作り方を　教えて。どんな　物を　入れるの？

まり：そうねえ…　牛肉や　糸こんにゃくや　野菜などを　入れるの。

ケン：ぼくが　切ろうか。

まり：じゃ、牛肉は　うすく　切って、糸こんにゃくは　半分に　切って。

　　　そして、野菜は　よく　洗って、小さく　切ってね。

　　　まず、始めに　おなべを　熱く　して、油を　入れるの。

　　　それから、牛肉を　入れて、砂糖と　醤油を　入れるの。

ケン：どのくらい　入れる？　このくらい？

　　　<Ken adds *shoyu* and sugar. Mari tastes it.>　味は　どう？

まり：ちょっと　甘すぎるわね。もう　少し　醤油を　入れて、からく

　　　しましょう。お酒も　少し　入れましょう。おいしく　なるわよ。

<テーブルで>

まり：出来たわよ。おいしそうねえ。生卵に　つけて、食べましょう。

ケン：えっ、気持ちが　悪い。でも、食べて　みよう。いただきます。

　　　おいしい！

まり：はい、どうぞ。デザートの　果物。

ケン：この　苺は　ちょっと　すっぱいけど、おいしいね。お腹が

　　　いっぱいに　なったよ。ごちそうさま。ぼくが　全部　かたづけるよ。

十四課

Let's review previous vocabulary!

A. めいし　Nouns
1. 家　　　house
2. 物〔もの〕　thing [tangible]
3. ぼく　　I [used by males]
4. テーブル　table

5. おなか　　stomach
6. いっぱい　full
7. ぜんぶ　　everything

B. どうし　Verbs
8. 作り〔G1 つくる〕　make (stem form)
9. おしえて　下さい〔G2 おしえる〕　please teach me
10. 入れます〔G2 いれる〕　put in
11. あらって〔G1 あらう〕　wash
12. なります〔G1 なる〕　become
13. 食べましょう〔G2 たべる〕　let's eat
14. 食べて　みましょう〔G2 たべる〕　let's try eating

C. -い けいようし　I Adjectives
15. あつく〔あつい〕　hot
16. おいしく〔おいしい〕　delicious

17. おいしそう〔おいしい〕　looks delicious

D. ふくし　Adverbs
18. よく　　often, well
19. 小さく　small [Adverb form]

20. ちょっと　a little
21. もう　少し〔すこし〕　a little more

E. Others
22. どんな～　what kind of ～
23. そして、　And
24. それから、　And then,
25. どのくらい？　About how much?

26. このくらい？　This much?
27. どうですか？　How is it?
28. でも、　However,

F. Expressions
29. そうですねえ . . .　Let me see . . .
30. じゃ、　Then, [Informal of では]
31. えっ、　What?
32. いただきます。　[Expression used before a meal]
33. はい、どうぞ。　Please go ahead (and eat)
34. ごちそうさま。　[Expression used after a meal]

G. ぶんぽう　Grammar
35. ～や～や～など　　～ and ～ and ～ etc.
36. Sentence 1 ＋けど、 Sentence 2。　S1, but S2.

１４課ー１: DO YOU KNOW HOW TO MAKE *SUKIYAKI*?

【会話】

Formal style:　　　ケン：すき焼きの　作り方を　知って　いますか。

まり：はい、知って　いますよ。

ケン：じゃ、教えて　下さい。

Informal style:　　ケン：すき焼きの　作り方　知ってる？

まり：ええ、知ってるわよ。

ケン：じゃ、教えて。

【文型】

| すきやきの　作り方〔つくりかた〕 | how to make *sukiyaki* |
| 車の　うんてんの　し方 | how to drive a car |

【単語】

1. 作り方
〔つくりかた〕
how to make

2. すき焼き
〔すきやき〕
sukiyaki

3. 牛肉
〔ぎゅうにく〕
beef

4. 豚肉
〔ぶたにく〕
pork

5. 鳥肉
〔とりにく〕
chicken (meat)

6. 卵
〔たまご〕
egg

7. 野菜
〔やさい〕
vegetable

8. 果物
〔くだもの〕
fruit

十四課

9. 苺
〔いちご〕
strawberry

10. 糸こんにゃく
〔いとこんにゃく〕
shredded *konnyaku*

grey or transparent tuber root gelatin

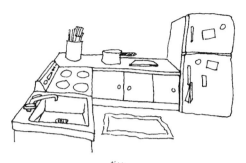

11. 台所
〔だいどころ〕
kitchen

【*オプショナル単語】

1. *材料〔ざいりょう〕	* ingredients
2. *カップ	* cup (measurement)
3. *大サジ〔おおサジ〕	* tablespoon
4. *小サジ〔こサジ〕	* teaspoon
5. *二分の一〔にぶんのいち〕	* 1/2

6. *やさいと　くだ物の　名前

トマト
tomato

じゃがいも
potato

にんじん
carrots

たまねぎ
round onion

きゅうり
cucumber

なす
eggplant

キャベツ
cabbage

レタス
lettuce

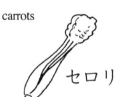
セロリ
celery

ビーマン
green pepper

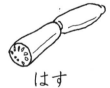
はす
lotus root

ねぎ
green
onion

ほうれんそう
spinach

まめ
peas; beans

だいこん
turnip

ごぼう
burdock

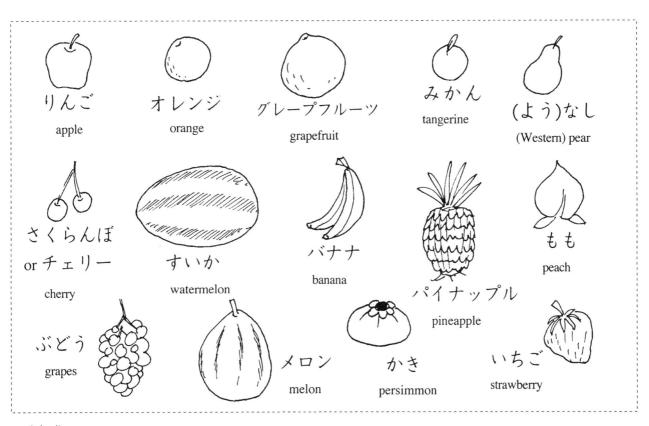

りんご apple	オレンジ orange	グレープフルーツ grapefruit	みかん tangerine	（よう）なし (Western) pear

さくらんぼ
or チェリー
cherry

すいか
watermelon

バナナ
banana

パイナップル
pineapple

もも
peach

ぶどう
grapes

メロン
melon

かき
persimmon

いちご
strawberry

【漢字】

1. 立   stand   た（つ）   立って 下さい。 Please stand.

  リツ   起立〔きりつ〕 Stand up.

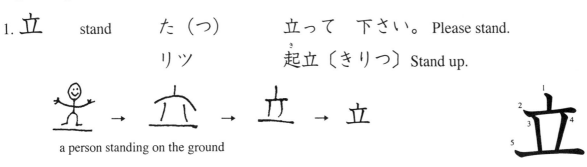

a person standing on the ground

2. 作   make   つく（る）   作って 下さい。 Please make.

  サク   作文 composition, 作田〔さくだ〕さん,
  作本〔さくもと〕さん

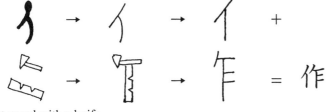

cut wood with a knife

A person who cuts wood makes two marks.

十四課

【文法】

> A. Something の　　Verb [Stem form] + 方〔かた〕
>
> When -kata is attached to a verb stem, it becomes a noun that is translated as "how to do (such and such)." Nouns preceding V-stem + 方 must be followed by の.

1. すき焼きの　作り方を　教えて　下さい。　　　　Please teach me how to make *sukiyaki*.

2. 「この　漢字の　書き方を　知って　いますか。」「いいえ、知りません。」

"Do you know how to write this character?"　　"No, I don't know."

3. 漢字の　辞書の　使い方を　習いたいです。I want to learn how to use the *kanji* dictionary.

4. 父から　自動車の　運転の　し方を　習いました。

I learned how to drive from my father.

【 ● 文化ノート】

すきやき　*Sukiyaki*

Along with *sushi* and *tenpura*, *sukiyaki* is probably one of the most readily identifiable "Japanese" dishes. Surprisingly, however, *sukiyaki* is a relatively modern dish that has been in existence for only about a century. It has just been in the last 100 years that Japanese began consuming beef. Although there are many theories as to how this dish came to be named "*sukiyaki*," the most widely accepted is that this dish was formerly cooked on the blades of plows, called 鋤 (すき). 焼き(やき) means to roast, grill, bake, or fry. Even today, *sukiyaki* tastes best when prepared in a thick, heavy pot. The method of preparing *sukiyaki* in the *Kansai* (West) and *Kanto* (East) regions of Japan differ slightly. In the *Kansai* area, many people will first cook the meat with the seasonings, then cook the vegetables in the same sauce. In the *Kanto* area, most persons cook the meat, vegetables, and other ingredients together.

すきやき

Sukiyaki

【😊😊アクティビティー】

A. ペアワーク

   Ask your partner if he/she knows how to do the following things, then check the YES or NO column. Take turns.

Ex. おすし<u>の　作り方</u>

   質問：「おすし<u>の　作り方</u>を　知って　いますか。」

   答え：「はい、知って　います。」or 「いいえ、知りません。」

しつもん	YES	NO
1. ギターの　ひき方		
2. 車の　うんてんの　し方		
3. おはしの　つかい方		
4. りょうりの　し方		
5. すきやきの　つくり方		
6. 日本の　き物の　き方		
7. サーフィンの　し方		
8. かんじの　じ書の　つかい方		
9. せんたくの　し方		

B. ペアワーク

   You want to make the following dishes. Ask your partner what you need to make them. Your partner gives the ingredients. Take turns.

Ex. ハムサンド

   質問：「ハムサンドを　作りたいんですが、何が　いりますか。」

   答え：「ハムと　パンと　レタスが　いります。」

十四課

Your menu	Partner's menu
1. たまごサンド	1. やさいサラダ
2. スパゲッティ	2. ハンバーガー
3. (Your choice)	3. (Partner's choice)

C. クラスのみんなでビンゴゲーム

Prepare a set of small cards before class using all the words below. Cut them small enough to fit in the blocks on the Bingo card below. Randomly fill in your Bingo card with them. One person who is the caller, picks a card from his/her stack of cards and reads it aloud to the class. Continue the game until someone wins with five in a row (horizontal, vertical, or diagonal). Continue practicing using any version of Bingo.

すきやき	ぎゅうにく	いちご	いとこんにゃく	だいどころ
しゃぶしゃぶ	ぶたにく	りんご apple	にんじん carrot	おさら
やきにく	とりにく	みかん tangerine	いも potato	コップ
どんぶり	たまご	メロン	たまねぎ onion	ナイフ
うどん	かい shellfish	なし (Western) pear	レタス	フォーク
すし	やさい	バナナ	トマト	スプーン
ラーメン	くだもの	すいか watermelon	きゅうり cucumber	はし

14課－2: PLEASE HEAT THE POT.

【会話】

Formal style:
ケン：初めに　何を　しますか。

まり：まず　おなべを　熱く　して　下さい。

Informal style:
ケン：初めに　何を　するの？

まり：まず　おなべを　熱く　して。

【文型】

あつく　　＋します。	(I) will make (it) hot. [I will heat it.]
きれい＋に＋します。	(I) will make (it) clean. [I will clean it.]
＊小さく　きって　下さい。	Please cut them small.
半分に　きって　下さい。	Please cut them in half.

＊ Previously introduced.

【単語】

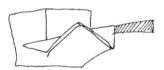

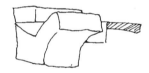

1. なべ
pot, pan

2. 油〔あぶら〕
oil

3. うすく
thin
Adverbial form of うすい

4. あつく
thick
Adverbial form of あつい

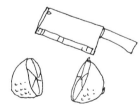

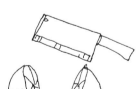

5. 半分に
〔はんぶんに〕
(in) half
半分 a half [noun]

6. 切る
〔G1きります〕
to cut; slice

7. 熱く　します
〔あつく〕
to make hot; to heat

8. きれいに　します
to make clean; to clean

9. まず

First of all

10. 初めに
〔はじめに〕

at the beginning

11. 次に
〔つぎに〕

next [adverb]

12. 終わりに
〔おわりに〕

at the end

【＊オプショナル単語】

1. ＊フライパン	＊ frying pan
2. ＊まぜます [G2]	＊ to mix [transitive]
3. ＊おきます [G1]	＊ to put; to place
4. ＊まきます [G1]	＊ to roll
5. ＊おします [G1]	＊ to push; to press
6. ＊ふっとうします [IR]	＊ to boil
7. ＊その　あとで	＊ after that
8. ＊その　間 [あいだ]	＊ meanwhile

【漢字】

1. 肉　meat　にく

肉を　食べる〔にくを　たべる〕eat meat

牛肉〔ぎゅうにく〕beef

豚肉〔ぶたにく〕pork

鳥肉〔とりにく〕chicken

焼き肉〔やきにく〕*yakiniku*

筋肉〔きんにく〕muscle

tender meat

十四課　　　　　390

2. 魚　fish　さかな

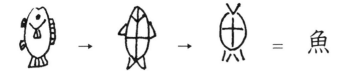 = 魚

【文法】

A. い Adjective　（ー く）　　　する

　　な Adjective / Noun ＋ に　　する

The verb "します" functions in this pattern as "to decide on a certain thing" or to make something (different from its present condition). The rules for this construction are exactly the same as those for the "なります" pattern. That is, い Adjectives take the ー く form while な Adjectives are followed by に before the verb they modify. Often, this pattern includes or suggests a direct object.

---

1. この　ピザを　少し　熱く　して　下さい。　　Please heat up this pizza.

2. 次の　試験を　やさしく　して　下さい。　　Please make the next exam easy.

3. ここを　きれいに　して　下さい。　　Please make this place clean. (Please clean up this place.)

4. 静かに　して　下さい。　　　　　　Please be quiet.

5. すきやきに　しましょう。　　　　　Let's have (decide on) *sukiyaki*.

B. (Review) Adverbial Usage of Adjectives

In Japanese, some adverbs are derived from adjectives.

☞ Remember: Adverbs describe verbs, adjectives, and other adverbs. Adjectives describe nouns.

a. い Adjective (- い)		→	い Adjective (- く) Adverb	
はやい	is fast, is early	→	はやく	fast, quickly, early
おそい	is slow, is late	→	おそく	slowly, late
いい	is good	→	よく＊	well
うるさい	noisy	→	うるさく	noisily
b. な Adjective		→	な Adjective ＋ に Adverb	
しずか	is quiet	→	しずかに	quietly
じゆう	is free, is liberal	→	じゆうに	freely
きれい	is pretty, is clean	→	きれいに	neatly
きゅう	is urgent, is sudden	→	きゅうに	suddenly

＊ irregular form

十四課

1. 牛肉を　薄く　切って　下さい。　　　Please cut the beef thin.

2. 糸こんにゃくを　半分に　切って　下さい。　Please cut the shredded *konnyaku* in half.

3. 野菜を　小さく　切って　下さい。　　Please cut the vegetables small (in small pieces).

4. 今日　早く　お昼を　食べたいです。　I want to eat lunch early today.

5. もっと　静かに　食べて　下さい。　　Please eat more quietly.

【 ● 文化ノート】

Cooking Terminology

Using the correct Japanese verbs in cooking can be confusing. Because the cooking styles of Western foods and Japanese foods were traditionally so different, the verb usage is also quite different. For example, in traditional Japanese cooking, roasting, baking, and toasting were not common. Because there were no words to express these actions, the verb closest to this type of cooking, namely the verb used for grilling, burning, or frying, やく, was used to describe these actions. On the other hand, Western cooking does not involve very much boiling. The Japanese vocabulary, however, allows for many different verbs to indicate boiling, depending on what one boils. For example, when one boils water, the verb わかす is used. For rice, the verb たく is used. For eggs, the verb ゆでる is used. Other verbs that translate into "boil" are ゆがく and にる. Be very careful to select the correct verb when discussing Japanese cooking!

【  アクティビティー】

A. ペアワーク

You are a cooking teacher. Your partner is a student. You give step-by-step cooking instructions. Your student confirms each step and acts out each step. Take turns.

Ex. 先生：まず　野菜を　小さく　切って　下さい。

　　生徒：はい、野菜を　小さく　切ります。　[Then act this out.]

　　先生：次に　牛肉を　薄く　切って　下さい。

　　生徒：はい、牛肉を　薄く　切ります。　[Then act this out.]

1. まず、手を あらって 下さい。
2. はじめに、やさいを あらって 下さい。
3. つぎに、やさいを 小さく きって 下さい。
4. それから、牛肉を うすく きって 下さい。
5. それから、こんにゃくを 半分に きって 下さい。
6. つぎに、おなべを あつく して 下さい。
7. つぎに、おなべに あぶらを 入れて 下さい。
8. それから、牛肉を おなべに 入れて 下さい。

B. ペアワーク

You and your friend are unhappy about the conditions of certain things at your school. You point out something you don't like, and your friend makes a request based on that point.

Ex. あなた：この 部屋(へや)は 寒(さむ)いです。

友達(だち)：はい、寒(さむ)いですねえ。この 部屋(へや)を 温(あたた)かく して 下さい。

1. 日本語の しけんは ながいです。	
2. 日本語の しけんは むずかしいです。	
3. この きょうしつは きたないです。	
4. この きょうしつは くらいです。	
5. 学校の きそくは きびしいです。	
6. カフェテリアの 食べ物は 高いです。	
7. カフェテリアの 食べ物は まずいです。	
8. カフェテリアの サービスは おそいです。	

十四課

【会話】

Formal style:　　　まり：ちょっと　お酒を　入れましょう。

　　　　　　　　　ケン：ええ、おいしく　なりましたね。

Informal style:　　まり：ちょっと　お酒を　入れましょう。

　　　　　　　　　ケン：うん、おいしく　なったね。

【文型】

おいしく　なりました。	It has become delicious.
しずかに　なりました。	It has become quiet.
＊いしゃに　なりたいです。	I want to become a doctor.

＊　Previously introduced.

【単語】

1.砂糖〔さとう〕
sugar

2.塩〔しお〕
salt

3.胡椒〔こしょう〕
pepper

4.酢〔す〕
vinegar

5.甘い
〔あまい〕
is sweet

6.塩辛い
〔しおからい〕
is salty

7.辛い
〔からい〕
is salty, is spicy

8.酸っぱい
〔すっぱい〕
is sour

9. (お)酒
〔(お)さけ〕
rice wine; liquor in general

10. 味
〔あじ〕
taste, flavor

11. 将来
〔しょうらい〕
future

12. 大人
〔おとな〕
adult

13. すみません、おそく なりました。
I'm sorry to be (= become) late.

【＊オプショナル単語】

1. ＊苦い〔にがい〕 　　　　　　＊ is bitter
2. ＊調味料〔ちょうみりょう〕 　＊ seasonings
3. ＊マヨネーズ 　　　　　　　　＊ mayonnaise
4. ＊ケチャップ 　　　　　　　　＊ ketchup
5. ＊ドレッシング 　　　　　　　＊ dressing
6. ＊わさび 　　　　　　　　　　＊ wasabi [Japanese horseradish used for sushi]
7. ＊ソース 　　　　　　　　　　＊ sauce

【漢字】

1. 多　are many　　　おお（い）　　人が 多いです。 There are many people.
　　　　　　　　　　　タ　　　　　　　多分〔たぶん〕 probably

タ ＋ タ ＝ 多

early evening　　early evening　　many

Two evenings are too many.

2. 少　　are few　　　　すく（ない）　人が　少ないです。There are few people.

すこ（し）　　少し　食べました。I ate a little.

ゞ → 少 = 少

Separating small things.

Small amounts, when separated, are few.

【文法】

A.　いAdjective　（ー く）　　　　なる

なAdjective / Noun ＋ に　　　なる

The verb "なります" may be modified by なadjectives, nouns or いadjectives. When modified by a なadjective or noun, the particle に follows the noun or なadjective. When modified by an いadjective, the adjective takes its adverbial form (- く form). Never use the - く form and に together.

---

1. 暑く　なりましたねえ。　　　　　　　It's gotten hot, hasn't it?

2. 背が　高く　なりましたねえ。　　　　You've grown tall, haven't you?

3. おそく　なって、すみません。　　　　I'm sorry to be late.

4. 私は　将来　医者に　なりたいです。　I want to become a doctor in the future.

5. 早く　大人に　なりたいです。　　　　I want to become an adult soon.

6. おすしが　好きに　なりました。　　　I have come to like *sushi*.

7. 図書館は　静かに　なりましたねえ。　The library has become quiet, hasn't it?

【　●　文化ノート】

調味料　Seasonings

Japanese seasonings are simple and limited. Almost all traditional Japanese dishes can be prepared using soy sauce, sugar, vinegar, さけ, *mirin* (heavily sweetened さけ), salt, and みそ (soy bean paste). The only other seasonings one may use for additional flavor are しちみとうがらし (similar to cayenne pepper), わさび (horseradish) and からし (Japanese mustard). Sesame seeds (ごま) are often also used as garnish.

【🧑‍🦰😊アクティビティー】

A. ペアワーク

You tell your partner what seasoning to put in a certain dish and ask about the flavor. Your partner describes how the flavor has changed. Take turns.

Ex. さとう

　　You:　「砂糖を　入れて　下さい。味は　どうですか。」

　　Partner:　「甘く　なりました。」

1. （お）しお	
2. （お）す	
3. こしょう	
4. （お）さとう	
5. （お）さけ	

B. ペアワーク

You are in Japan. Greet a Japanese person during the following seasons. Take turns.

Ex. It has become warm in the spring.

　　あなた：「おはようございます。」

　　日本人：「おはようございます。」

　　あなた：「暖かく　なりましたねえ。」

　　日本人：「そうですねえ。春に　なりましたねえ。」

1. It has become hot in the summer.	
2. It has become cool in the fall.	
3. It has become cold in the winter.	
4. It has become warm in the spring.	
5. It rains a lot during the rainy season (つゆ).	

十四課

C. ペアワーク

Tell your friend about something that has happened to you, as listed immediately below. Your partner should respond appropriately with one of the comments listed at the bottom. Take turns.

Ex. あなた：「成績が　良く　なりました。」
　　友達：「それは　良かったですねえ。」

1. せいせきが　わるく　なりました。
2. この　土曜日に　十六さいに　なります。
3. 私たちの　チームは　つよく　なりました。
4. おじいさんが　びょう気に　なりました。
5. 〜が　上手に　なりました。
6. 私の　いぬが　お父さんに　なりました。
7. 私は　〜さんが　好きに　なりました。
8. 私たちの　チームが　一番に　なりました。

それは　いいですねえ。
それは　良かったですねえ。
それは　ざんねんですねえ。
それは　ざんねんでしたねえ。
本とうですか。
お気のどくに。

D. ペアワーク

Ask your partner whether he/she wants to become any of the following in the future. Your partner should answer based on fact. Check はい or いいえ, and ask for the reason. Take turns.

Ex. 医者

質問１：「将来　医者に　なりたいですか。」

答え１：「はい、医者に　なりたいです。」or

　　　　「いいえ、医者に　なりたくないです。」

質問２：「なぜですか。」

答え２：「私は　血(blood)が　こわいんです。」

	はい	いいえ	なぜ？
1. べんごし (lawyer)			
2. 先生			
3. ゆうびんやさん (mailman)			
4. カウンセラー			
5. パイロット (pilot)			
6. コックさん (cook)			
7. だいとうりょう (President of a country)			

【会話】

Formal style: まり：ちょっと　甘すぎますね。

ケン：じゃ、ちょっと　醤油を　入れましょう。

Informal style: まり：ちょっと　甘すぎるわね。

ケン：じゃ、ちょっと　醤油を　入れよう。

【文型】

食べ　＋すぎます。	(I) eat too much.
たか　＋すぎます。	It's too expensive.
よ　　＋すぎます。	It's too good.
しずか＋すぎます。	It's too quiet.

【単語】

1. デザート

dessert

2. 生卵
〔なまたまご〕

raw egg

3. 気持ちが　悪い
〔きもちが　わるい〕

unpleasant; uncomfortable

4. 気持ちが　いい
〔きもちが　いい〕

pleasant, comfortable

5. 食べすぎます

eat too much

6. 高すぎます
〔たかすぎます〕

is too expensive

7. 静かすぎます
〔しずかすぎます〕

is too quiet

8. 〜が　出来ました

〜 is ready, 〜 is done

9. (Object)を (thing)に　つける
[G2 つけます]

to dip (object) in (thing)

10. (Object)を　片付ける
[G2 かたづけます]

to clean up, put away

【*オプショナル単語】
1. *アイスクリーム   * ice cream
2. *シャーベット   * sherbet
3. *パイ   * pie
4. *クッキー   * cookie
5. *饅頭〔まんじゅう〕   * Japanese buns filled with sweetened red beans

【漢字】

1. 古　old　　　　ふる（い）　　古い　車〔ふるい　くるま〕old car

古川〔ふるかわ〕さん

古本〔ふるもと〕さん

古田〔ふるた〕さん

十　＋　口　＝　古
10   mouth   is old
If you tell a story 10 times, it becomes old.

2. 新　new　　　あたら（しい）　新しい　本〔あたらしい　ほん〕a new book
シン　　　　　新聞〔しんぶん〕newspaper
新幹線〔しんかんせん〕bullet train

401

十四課

立 ＋ 木 ＋ 斤 ＝ 新
to stand   tree   ax   is new

Stand on a tree and cut it with an axe. It is new.

3. *生　be born　　う（まれる）　　日本で　生まれました。I was born in Japan.

　　　　　　　　　なま　　　　　生卵〔なまたまご〕 raw egg

　　　　　　　　　　　　　　　　生野菜〔なまやさい〕 fresh vegetable

　　　　　　　　　セイ　　　　　先生〔せんせい〕 teacher

　　　　　　　　　　　　　　　　学生〔がくせい〕 student

【文法】

A. Verb (Stem form)／い Adjective (Stem form)／ な Adjective ＋すぎます

When the verb すぎます (to exceed) is attached to a verb stem, it is expressed in English as "to do (such and such) in excess." When attached to an adjective without its final -i or to a な Adjective, it is translated as "too . . . " The extender "-sugimasu" may be conjugated in any tense.
---

1. 食べすぎました。　　　　　　　　　　　　I ate too much.

2. 父は　お酒を　飲みすぎます。　　　　　My father drinks too much *sake*.

3. 漢字の　宿題は　多すぎます。　　　　　There is too much *kanji* homework.

4. あの　学生は　うるさすぎます。　　　　That student is too noisy.

5. この　犬は　頭が　良すぎます。　　　　This dog is too smart.

6. あの　人は　テニスが　下手すぎます。　That person is too unskillful at tennis.

7. ここは　静かすぎると　思います。　　　I think this place is too quiet.

8. 勉強しすぎないで　下さい。　　　　　　Please do not study too hard.

【 ● 文化ノート】

デザート　Desserts

Recently, Japanese have acquired a taste for Western sweets and enjoy ice cream, cakes, and pastries as much as Americans do. Most of these sweets, however, are consumed as treats, and not necessarily as desserts. Traditionally, Japanese did not include dessert as part of the meal. The closest one got to dessert was an occasional piece or two of seasonal fresh fruit. Sweets such as *manju, mochi,* or *senbei* were considered snacks, or foods to accompany tea.

【😠😊アクティビティー】

A. ペアワーク

Your friend visits your room and complains about everything! You are a good friend, and try to satisfy him/her by doing something about it.

Ex.　友達：「この　部屋は　暑すぎますね。」

　　　あなた：「そうですか。　じゃ、部屋を　涼しく　しましょう。」

1. この　へやは　くらすぎます。	
2. この　へやは　きたなすぎます。	
3. おんがくが　うるさすぎます。	
4. この　テープは　ながすぎます。	
5. この　肉は　あつすぎます。	
6. この　いすは　高すぎます。	

B. ペアワーク

Your friend loves to do the following things. You warn your friend not to do these things in excess.

Ex.　友達：「私は　食べるのが　大好きです。」

　　　あなた：「でも、食べすぎないで　下さいよ。」

1. 私は　コーラを　のむのが　大好きです。	
2. 私は　本を　読むのが　大好きです。	
3. 私は　サーフィンを　するのが　大好きです。	
4. 私は　テレビを　見るのが　大好きです。	
5. 私は　テレビゲームで　あそぶのが　大好きです。	
6. (Your choice)	

十四課

C. ペアワーク

Interview your partner. Take turns.

1.家で たいてい だれが りょうりを しますか。	
2.ばんごはんの あとで、だれが 台所〔だいどころ〕を かたづけますか。	
3.あなたは 時々 かたづけるのを 手つだいますか。	
4.時々 おさらを あらいますか。	
5.家ぞくに ばんごばんを 作ったことが ありますか。	
6.今、すきやきの 作り方を しって いますか。	
7.すきやきを 生たまごに つけて 食べたことが ありますか。	
8.どんな デザートが 好きですか。	

D. ペアワーク

Role play, using appropriate facial expressions and gestures.

A:　「すきやきが 出来ましたよ。」

B:　「おいしそうですねえ。」

A:　「この 生卵〔たまご〕を つけて 食べて下さい。」

B:　「えっ、気持ちが 悪〔わる〕いですねえ。」

A/B:「いただきます。」

A/B:「う〜ん、おいしいですねえ！」

Ask your partner these questions in Japanese.
Your partner should answer in Japanese.
The underlined words may be substituted with other appropriate words.

1. Excuse me, may I ask a question? Is there (an art museum) in this area?

2. I want to go to (the university). Where is the bus stop?

3. Where is (the hospital)? Please show (=teach) it to me on the map.

4. How far is it from your house to school?

5. How do you come to school?

6. What time do you leave home in the morning?

7. What time do you arrive at school in the morning?

8. How long does it take from (your) home to school in the morning?

9. Are the streets crowded every morning?

10. Who will come to pick you up today?

11. Which do you like more, playing sports or watching sports?

12. I want to go to (the convenience store).

   Which is faster, going by bus or going on foot (by walking)?

13. On what color traffic light are you allowed to cross the intersection?

14. Do you know how to drive a car? Who taught (or will teach) you?

405

15. Can you cook *sukiyaki*?

16. What do I need to make *sukiyaki*?

17. How do you slice (= cut) beef for *sukiyaki*?

18. How do you cut shredded *konnyaku* for *sukiyaki*?

19. After you heat the pot, what do you put in it?

20. What seasonings (ちょうみりょう) do you put in *sukiyaki*?

21. Do you like vegetables? What vegetables don't you like?

22. What seasoning (ちょうみりょう) makes food spicy?

23. Among fruits, what do you like the most?

24. Do you like sweet food more than salty food?

25. Do you like spicy food?

26. Who cleans up the kitchen after dinner at your house?

27. Who washes the dishes at your house?

28. Do you think that you study too hard?

29. What do you want to become in the future?

30. Do you think that Japanese is too difficult?

FUN CORNER 11: すきやき *SUKIYAKI*

Sukiyaki Recipe

Sukiyaki is a favorite beef dish of the Japanese. Since the consumption of meat only began at the very start of the 1900's, it is a relatively new Japanese dish. It is a dish usually eaten at home, but is generally reserved for special occasions.

Ingredients:

1 lb.	thinly sliced beef (tenderloin or boneless sirloin)
1	round onion, sliced into wedges
4 - 6	medium dried *shiitake* mushrooms, previously soaked and softened
1/2 lb.	Chinese cabbage, sliced into 1 1/2 inch widths
1 bunch	green onions, sliced into 2" lengths
10 oz.	*itokonnyaku,* chopped slightly
1 block	*tofu*, cubed
	raw eggs (1 per person)
	oil

Broth (*Warishita*):

2/3 C.	*dashi* stock (instant *dashi* mix and water combination)
1/4 C.	*shoyu*
1/3 C.	*mirin*
2 T.	sugar
1 T.	*sake* (rice wine)

Optional ingredients:

shungiku (chrysanthemum leaves)

sliced bamboo shoots

spinach leaves

carrot slices

fresh mushrooms

Serves 4 - 6 people.

すきやきの　作り方

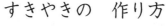

1. Heat a large, fairly shallow heavy pot. Grease. Ideally, the *sukiyaki* is cooked in a pot on a hot plate or small gas stove on the dining table.

2. Cook a portion of the meat slightly.

3. Push beef to the side. Add portions of the vegetables and other ingredients.

4. Add a portion of the *warishita* to cover ingredients halfway and let boil.

5. As the *sukiyaki* cooks, remove from the pot and self serve. Crack eggs, scramble in small individual serving bowls. Dip hot, cooked beef, vegetables, *tofu*, etc. into raw scrambled egg. Eat with hot rice. Continue cooking *sukiyaki* by replenishing the pot with ingredients, including the broth.

My child made *sukiyaki* at home.

_____
Parent's signature.

By the end of this lesson, you will be able to communicate the information below in the given situations.

【Ⅱ-15 タスク1】

A Japanese student wants to find out about an American student's family and asks many questions.

Japanese Student:

(1) Ask your friend if he/she is an only child.

(2) Respond. Talk about your family members' hobbies. Ask about your partner's family's hobbies.

(3) Ask how old his/her mother (or father) is.

(4) Ask if that person wears glasses.

(5) Ask your friend who he/she talks to if he/she has a problem.

American Student:

(1) Answer based on your own family. Describe who is in your family. Ask about your partner's family.

(2) Answer accordingly.

(3) Answer accordingly.

(4) Answer accordingly.

(5) Answer based on your own experience.

【Ⅱ-15 タスク2】

Since Mother's Day is almost here, the Japanese student is curious to find out about the American student's relationship with his/her mother.

Japanese Student:

(1) Ask your partner what kind of things your partner's mother does for him/her.

(2) Ask what kind of things your partner does for his/her mother.

(3) Respond. Tell your partner that you appreciate your mother.

(4) Respond.

American Student:

(1) Answer based on your own experience.

(2) Answer based on your own experience. Ask your partner similar questions about his/her mother.

(3) Reply that you do, too. Tell your partner what your plans are for Mother's Day. Ask your partner what he/she will do.

411

十五課

【 お話 】

　私の　母は　四十三才で、本屋に　勤めて　います。
五年前　父と　離婚しました。私は　一人っ子です。母は
背が　低くて、ちょっと　太って　います。眼鏡を　かけて
いて、いつも　金の　ネックレスを　して　います。

　母の　趣味は　旅行を　することです。ひまな　時には　泳いだり、
犬と　散歩を　したり、絵を　かいたり　して　います。いつも　ニコニコ
笑って　いますから、家の　中が　明るいです。しかし、私が　たまに
何か　悪い　ことを　したら、おこります。

　私は　よく　母に　宿題を　手伝って　もらいます。母は　私の
質問に　よく　答えて　くれます。掃除も　洗濯も　して　くれます。
問題が　あったら、いつも　助けて　くれます。

　先月の　十四日に　ピアノの　コンクールが　あって、私は　一生懸命
練習しましたが、三位でした。悲しくて、自分の　部屋で　泣いて
しまいました。その　時、母は　そばに　座って、暗い　部屋の　中に
ずっと　一緒に　いて　くれました。

　私は　母に　何も　して　あげませんが、母は　いつも　私に
いろいろな　ことを　して　くれます。私は　心の　中で　いつも
感謝して　いますが、母に　感謝の　言葉を　言ったことが　ありません。
　お母さん、有難う。私は　お母さんが　大好きです。

お母さん、ありがとう。

いつも 私に いろいろな
ことを して くれて、かんしゃ
して います。 お母さんは
世界で 一番 すばらしい
お母さんです。

　　　　　　　　エミ

413

Let's review previous vocabulary!

A. めいし　Nouns

1.	母の日	Mother's Day	14. 中	inside
2.	私	I	15. しゅくだい	homework
3.	四十三才〔さい〕	43 years old	16. しつもん	question
4.	本屋〔ほんや〕	bookstore	17. もんだい	problem
5.	五年	five years	18. 先月	last month
6.	父	(one's own) father	19. 十四日	14th (of the month)
7.	めがね	eyeglasses	20. ピアノ	piano
8.	ネックレス	necklace	21. 部屋〔へや〕	room
9.	しゅみ	hobby	22. そば	nearby
10.	こと	thing [intangible]	23. 何も + Neg.	(not) anything
11.	犬〔いぬ〕	dog	24. 心〔こころ〕	heart
12.	え	painting, picture	25. せかい	world
13.	家	house		

B. どうし　Verbs

26. ～に　つとめて　います〔G2つとめる〕　is employed at ～
27. 太って　います〔G1ふとる〕　is fat
28. かけて　いて〔G2かける〕　is wearing (glasses), (and)
29. Accessory ＋を　して　います〔IRする〕　is wearing (accessory)
30. りょこうをする〔IR りょこうをします〕　travel
31. およいだり〔G1およぐ〕　swim [TARI form]
32. したら〔IRする〕　if (I) do,
33. 手つだって〔G1てつだう〕　help (and)
34. もらいます〔G1もらう〕　receive
35. こたえて〔G2こたえる〕　answer (and)
36. くれます〔G2くれる〕　give (me)
37. そうじを　して〔IRそうじを　する〕　clean (and)
38. せんたくを　して〔IRせんたくを　する〕　do laundry, (and)
39. あったら〔G1ある〕　if (I) have [TARA form]
40. あって〔G1ある〕　there is/was, (and)
41. れんしゅう（を）しました〔IRれんしゅう（を）する〕　practiced

42. すわって〔G1 すわる〕   sit
43. いて〔G2 いる〕   be, exist
44. あげません〔G2 あげる〕   do not give
45. 言ったことが ありません〔G2 いう〕   have never said

C. -い けいようし　I Adjectives

46. せが ひくくて[ひくい]　short [height]
47. あかるい　bright
48. わるい　bad
49. かなしくて　sad
50. くらい　dark
51. すばらしい　wonderful

D. -な けいようし　NA Adjectives

52. いろいろ　various
53. 大好き　like very much

E. ふくし　Adverbs

54. ちょっと　a little
55. いつも　always
56. よく　often
57. いっしょうけんめい　with utmost effort
58. いっしょに　together
59. 一番　the most

F. ぶんぽう　Grammar

60. Dictionary form ＋ こと　verb nominalization
61. 〜たことが ありません　have never done 〜

G. Expressions

62. お母さん、ありがとう。　Mom, thank you.

１５課ー１：MY MOTHER'S HOBBY IS PAINTING.

【会話】

Formal style:
　　まり：お母さんの　趣味は　何ですか。

　　ケン：母の　趣味は　絵を　かくことですよ。

Informal style:
　　まり：お母さんの　趣味は　何？

　　ケン：母の　趣味は　絵を　かくことだよ。

【文型】

＊ Verb (Dictionary form) ＋ こと／の	Verb nominalization
＊ Verbs "to wear"　（シャツを）着ます，（くつ，パンツを）はきます，（めがねを）かけます，（ぼうしを）かぶります，（ネックレスを）します	

　　＊ Previously introduced.

【単語】

1. 散歩(を)する
[IRさんぽ(を)します]
to take a walk

2. 絵を　描く
[G1かきます]
to draw, paint a picture

3. ニコニコ

smilingly

4. 笑う
[G1わらいます]
to smile, laugh

5. 泣く
[G1なきます]
to cry

6. 怒る
[G1おこります]
to become angry
おこっています is angry

7. 叱る
[G1しかります]
to scold

8. 離婚(を)する
[IRりこん(を)します]
to divorce
りこん(を)しています is divorced

9. 金
〔きん〕
gold

10. 銀
〔ぎん〕
silver

11. ずっと
throughout, all the time

12. たまに
occasionally,
once in a while

【*オプショナル単語】

1.* 別居〔べっきょ〕（を）します　　　　to be separated; to live separately

【漢字】

1. 才　　～ years old　　サイ　　　　十六才〔じゅうろくさい〕16 old

才 → 才

Obaasan, how old are you?

2. 心　　heart, mind　　こころ　　　　心が　きれいです。good-hearted person

シン　　　　心配しないで　下さい。Please don't worry.

ᗐ → 心 → 心 → 心

heart

3. 思　　think　　　　おも（う）　　いいと　思います。I think it is good.

田　＋　心　＝　思

rice field　　　heart　　　to think

Japanese people think about the rice field from the heart.

417

十五課

【文法】

＊ A. Verb (Dictionary form) ＋の／こと

By attaching の (matter) or こと to a verb in its dictionary form, one creates a nominal (noun) usage of a verb.

---

1. 私は 泳ぐのが 好きです。   I like swimming.

2. 日本語を 話すのは 難しいですが、楽しいです。

Speaking Japanese is difficult, but it is fun.

3. 母の 趣味は 絵を かくことです。   My mother's hobby is drawing pictures.

4. 私の 趣味は 食べることです。   My hobby is eating.

＊ B. Japanese verbs of wearing

The Japanese verb "to wear" varies according to where or how one wears the clothing or accessory. If one wears something above the waist on one's entire body, one uses the verb きます. The verb はきます is used when one wears something below the waist, します is used when one wears accessories. かぶります is used when things are worn on or draped over the head. The verb かけます is used for wearing glasses.

きます	will wear (above the waist, or on the entire body)
はきます	will wear (below the waist)
します	will wear (accessories)
かぶります	will wear (on or draped over the head)
かけます	will wear (glasses)

＊ Previously introduced.

1. 姉は 赤と 白の 帽子を かぶって います。

My older sister is wearing a red and white hat.

2. 黒い ドレスを 着て、紫の 靴を はいて います。

She is wearing a black dress and purple shoes.

3. 母は いつも 金の ネックレスを して います。

My mother always wears a gold necklace.

4. 私は 眼鏡を かけて います。   I am wearing glasses./ I wear glasses.

【 ● 文化ノート】
ぶん か

Japanese Mothers and Families

Just as the American family has seen dramatic change over the past century, the structure and dynamics of the Japanese family have also changed. Traditionally, Japanese families included at least three generations living together in one household. Today, nuclear families are much more common, though in a few instances, a return to three-generation homes has occurred simply because the high cost of living demands it. Traditionally, mothers always stayed at home to tend for the needs of the family, which included looking out for the needs of her husband and children, caring for in-laws, housework, cooking, daily shopping, and managing the budget. Today, with smaller families to care for, more mothers work outside the home, most as part-timers. Although still not very common, more and more husbands are willing to shoulder some of the responsibilities of taking care of the household chores and the family.

【アクティビティー】

A. ペアワーク

This drawing represents the family of one of your imaginary friends. Fill your friend's name in the [   ] after 名前, then fill in the hobbies of each of your friend's family members in the （ ） by that family member's picture. Choose the hobbies from the list in the box below. Ask your partner what the hobbies of his/her friend's family members are, then write in the answers on the second picture.

私の　友達の　家族
だち　　　ぞく

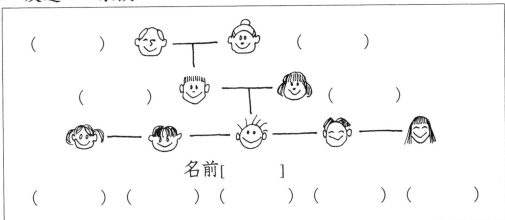

Selection of hobbies:

1. えを　かく	4. およぐ	7. バスケットを　する
2. しゃしんを　とる	5. ねる	8. ピアノを　ひく
3. さんぽを　する	6. 食べる	9. (your choice)

十五課

質問1：友達の　名前は　何ですか。

質問2：〜さんの　おじいさんの　趣味は　何ですか。

パートナーの　友達の　家族

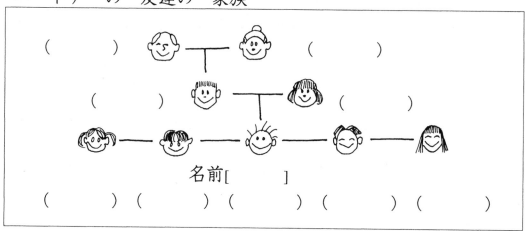

名前[　　　　]

B. ペアワーク

Interview each other. You may talk about your father, or another family member, instead of your mother.

1. お母さんの　しゅみは　何ですか。	
2. お母さんは　せが　高いですか。ひくいですか。	
3. お母さんは　めがねを　かけて　いますか。	
4. お母さんは　いつも　ネックレスを　して　いますか。	
5. お母さんは　犬が　好きですか。	
6. お母さんは　よく　テレビを　見ますか。	
7. お母さんは　時々　おこりますか。	
8. お母さんは　時々　あなたを　しかりますか。	
9. お母さんは　いい　お母さんだと　思いますか。	

C. クラスワーク

What is everybody wearing today?

1. The teacher will distribute pieces of paper with a different number on each.

2. Write your name next to the number on the paper you receive.

3. The teacher collects all the papers and re-distributes them to the students, making sure that students do not receive their original papers back.

4. Write about the student whose name appears at the top of your paper by describing what he/she is wearing from head to toe. Sign your name at the bottom of the paper.

5. The teacher collects the papers. The teacher will read only the numbers and descriptions to the class.

6. You and your classmates will guess which student is being described by writing down one of your classmates' names beside the correct number on the chart below.

7. After all the descriptions have been read, one student will volunteer to read out the correct answers. Check your answers.

1.		6.		11.		16.		21.	
2.		7.		12.		17.		22.	
3.		8.		13.		18.		23.	
4.		9.		14.		19.		24.	
5.		10.		15.		20.		25.	

十五課

【会話】

Formal style:　　まり：ひまな　時　何を　しますか。

　　　　　　　　ケン：テレビを　見たり、音楽を　聞いたり　します。

Informal style:　まり：ひまな　時　何を　するの？

　　　　　　　　ケン：テレビを　見たり、音楽を　聞いたり　するよ。

【文型】

~たり　~たり　します

およいだり　はしったり　します。　　　　We do such things as swimming and running.

あつかったり　さむかったり　します。　　It is sometimes hot and sometimes cold.

はれだったり　くもりだったり　します。　It is sometimes sunny and sometimes cloudy.

【単語】

1. ひま
[なAdj.]
is free (time)
ひまな　時
when (someone) is free

2. その　時
[その　とき]
at that time

3. コンクール

competition [music]
コンクールに　出ます
participate in a competition

4. Rank	
1	いちい
2	にい
3	さんい
4	よんい
5	ごい
6	ろくい
7	なない
8	はちい
9	きゅうい
10	じゅうい
？	なんい

5. 一人っ子
〔ひとりっこ〕
only child

6. 双子
〔ふたご〕
twin(s)

7. 五年前
〔ごねんまえ〕
five years ago

8. Sentence 1。 しかし、 Sentence 2。   Sentence 1.   However, sentence 2.
[Formal expression of でも]

【*オプショナル単語】

1. *賞〔しょう〕   * award; prize
2. *性格〔せいかく〕   * personality

【漢字】

1. 休   rest, absent   やす（む）   学校を　休んで　います is absent from school

    お休み holiday, day off

 → イ ＋ 木 ＝ 休   休

a person   a tree   to rest

A person rests by a tree.

2. 買   buy   か（う）   買いたいです。 I want to buy it.

    買い物〔かいもの〕 shopping

 ＋

net

 → 貝 ＝ 買

shell

You must collect shells (used for currency) in a net in order to buy anything.

十五課

【文法】

A. 〜たり　〜たり　します/です

This sentence construction lists two or more verbs, い adjectives, な adjectives or nouns in their -た forms, to which a り is attached. The two interpretations of this construction are "do such things as 〜 and/or 〜," or "sometimes 〜 and sometimes 〜." The たり forms are generally followed by forms of the verbs します, including the potential できます form, or forms of です. です endings are used more commonly used with い adjectives, な adjectives, and noun たり forms. The tense of the します or です ending determines the tense of the entire sentence. Although the listing of two actions or states is most common, more may be listed. Occasionally, only one たり form is used in a sentence. In such cases, the sentence can only be interpreted as "do such things as . . ."

---

1. 休みには　映画に　行ったり　コンサートに　行ったり　します。

I go to movies and concerts on my days off.

2. 物は　高かったり　安かったり　します。

Things are sometimes expensive and sometimes cheap.

3. 生徒は　上手だったり　下手だったり　します。

Some students are skillful and some students are unskillful.

4. 日本語の　先生は　日本人だったり　アメリカ人だったり　します。

Teachers of Japanese are sometimes Japanese and sometimes American.

5. 冬休みには　スキーをしたり　スケートをしたり　出来ます。

People can do such things as skiing and skating during the winter vacation.

6. 私の　成績は　良かったり　悪かったり　です。

My grades are sometimes good and sometimes bad.

7. ビールを　飲んだり　しては　いけません。

You should not do such things as drinking beer.

【 ● 文化ノート】

Japanese Women and Leisure

Favorite pastimes of Japanese women are shopping, meeting their friends over meals, taking short trips, participating in health clubs, swim clubs, or going to beauty clinics. Most enjoy crafts, sports, and cultural events. Mothers often called きょういくママ devote their waking hours trying to advance their children educationally and socially by shuttling them to and from classes and catering to their every need. Recently, more housewives are finding time to do volunteer work in their communities as well.

【アクティビティー】

A. ペアワーク

Ask your partner what he/she does during the following times or at the following places. Answer based on fact. Name several activities. Take turns.

Ex. しゅうまつ

質問：「週末は　たいてい　どんな　ことを　しますか。」

答え：「週末は　たいてい　映画を　見たり、友達と　会ったり　します。」

1. 学校の　休み時間に	
2. 学校の　あとで	
3. ばん　家で	
4. ひまな　時に	
5. なつ休みに	
6. と書かんで	
7. ショッピングモールで	
8. 友だちの　家で	

B. ペアワーク

Ask your partner how his/her family members spend the weekend. Name several activities. Take turns.

Ex. お父さん

質問：「お父さんは　週末は　たいてい　何を　しますか。」

答え：「父は　週末　たいてい　ゴルフに　行ったり、テレビを　見たり　します。」

お父さん	
お母さん	
(other family member)	
(other family member)	
あなた	

C. ペアワーク

Interview each other. Write down your partner's responses.

1. 一人っ子ですか。	
2. おんがくの　コンクールに　出たことが　ありますか。	
3. しょう(award)を　もらったことが　ありますか。	
4. 学校の　やきゅうチームは、今　何いですか。	
5. やきゅうの　チームを　おうえんしに　行きますか。	
6. ないたことが　ありますか。いつでしたか。	
7. 今　どんな事を　よく　れんしゅうしていますか。	
8. あなたの　せいかく(personality)は　あかるいと　思いますか。くらいと　思いますか。	
9. あなたは　時々　おこりますか。	
10. 今　どんな　もんだいが　ありますか。	

15課－3：I WANT TO BECOME A DOCTOR.

【会話】

Formal style:　まり：大人に　なったら、どんな　仕事を　したいですか。

　　　　　　　　ケン：そうですねえ... 医者に　なりたいです。

Informal style：　まり：大人に　なったら、どんな　仕事を　したい？

　　　　　　　　ケン：そうだねえ... 医者に　なりたいな。

【文型】

日本へ　行ったら、	If/When (I) go to Japan,
天気が　良かったら、	If/When the weather is good,
好きだったら、	If/When (you) like it,
あしただったら、	If/When (it) is tomorrow,

【単語】

1. 自分	2. 何か	3. 助ける
〔じぶん〕	〔なにか〕	[G2 たすけます／たすけて]
oneself	something	to rescue, help

【＊オプショナル単語】

1.＊相談〔そうだん〕（を）します [IR]　　　to consult

427

十五課

1. 早　early　　　　はや（い）　　　早い　is early

(time)　　　　　　　　　　　　　早見〔はやみ〕さん

　　　　　　　　　　　　　　　　早川〔はやかわ〕さん

　　　日　＋　十　＝　早

　　　sun　　　10　　　　is early

On Sundays, 10 o'clock is early.

☞　速〔はや〕い　　is fast (speed)

2. 自　oneself　　ジ　　　　　自分〔じぶん〕の車 one's own car

　　　　　　　　　　　　　　　自動車〔じどうしゃ〕car

　　　　　　　　　　　　　　　自転車〔じてんしゃ〕bicycle

　　　　　　　　　　　　　　　自由〔じゆう〕is free

　　　　　＋　目　＝　自

　　point　　　eye　　　oneself

The eye is the window of one's soul.

【文法】

A. Verb (TA form)＋ら、

　　　いAdjective（ーかった）＋ら、

　　　なAdjective / Noun ＋だった＋ら、

1. This conditional is formed by taking the plain past (TA forms) of verbs, い and な adjectives and nouns, adding a ら at the end of the first clause, then attaching a resulting clause to form one complex sentence.

2. It is used to mean "after doing ..., then ...," "when doing ..., then ..." or "if doing ..., then ..." The second clause generally expresses a wish, volition, suggestion, invitation, opinion, request, or emotion.

---

1. 日本へ　行ったら、いろいろな　物を　見たいです。

When (if) I go to Japan, I want to see various things.

2. 先生に　聞いたら、すぐ　わかりました。

When (if) I asked my teacher, I understood it right away.

3. お金を　借りたら、返さなければ　なりません。

When (if) you borrow money, you must return it, you know.

4. 休みが　もっと　長かったら、嬉しいです。　　If the vacation is longer, I will be happy.

5. 服が　安かったら、たくさん　買いたいです。

If the dresses are cheap, I want to buy a lot of them.

6. 貧乏だったら、結婚したくないです。　　If he is poor, I don't want to marry him.

7. 日本語が　上手だったら、仕事が　あります。　If I am good at Japanese, I will have a job.

【 ● 文化ノート】

Mother's Day and Father's Day

Traditionally, neither of these celebrations existed in Japan. Through Western influence and encouragement by commercial enterprises, however, both these days are now observed by some families in Japan. As in America, Mother's Day is celebrated more than Father's Day. Mother's Day is observed on the second Sunday of May and Father's Day on the third Sunday of June. The traditional Mother's Day gift in Japan is a bouquet of red carnations. These flowers become very expensive around Mother's Day, and it is nearly impossible for young children to afford them. Most mothers, however, are just as pleased to receive handmade gifts from their youngsters. Fathers may receive ties or other appropriate gifts on Father's Day.

十五課

【🙎‍♀️🙎‍♀️アクティビティー】

A. ペアワーク

Ask your partner what he/she would want to do in the following situations. Take turns.

Ex. ひまな　時間が　あったら、

質問：「今　ひまな　時間が　あったら、何を　したいですか。」

1.今、千ドル　あったら、	
2.あした　学校が　なかったら、	
3.日本へ　行けたら、	
4.自分の　車が　あったら、	
5.大学生に　なったら、	
6.大人に　なったら、	

B. ペアワーク

Ask your partner who he/she would talk to in the following situations. Take turns.

Ex. If you had a disagreement with your friend, who would you talk to?

質問：「友達と　けんかを　したら、だれに　話しますか。」

答え：「友達と　けんかを　したら、ほかの　友達に　話します。」

1.友だちが　何か　わるい事を　したら、	
2.もんだいが　あったら、	
3.せいせきが　わるかったら、	
4.こうつう事こを　見たら、	
5.しゅくだいが　分からなかったら、	
6.しけんの　せいせきが　Fだったら、	
7.お金が　なかったら、	

C. ペアワーク

The first chart represents what you and your family members received last year on either your birthdays or at Christmas. Write the names of your family members in the brackets. Then, write what gifts each family member gave and received in the parentheses from the other family members. The gifts may be made up. Ask your partner what gifts he/she and his/her family members gave and received. Fill in the blanks on the second chart below.

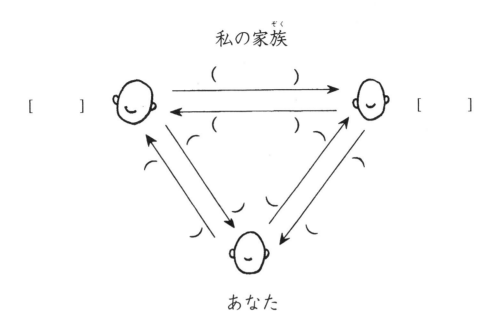

私の家族

あなた

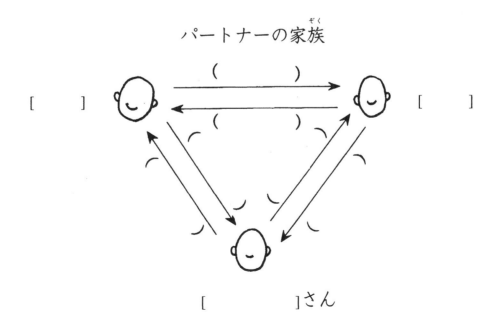

パートナーの家族

十五課

15課－4：MY MOTHER COOKS FOR ME.

【会話】

Formal style:　　まり：お母さんに　どんな　ことを　して　あげますか。
　　　　　　　　ケン：ぼくは　何も　して　あげません。

Informal style:　まり：お母さんに　どんな　ことを　して　あげるの？
　　　　　　　　ケン：ぼくは　何も　して　あげない。

【文型】

＊ Giver は　Receiver (equal) に　Something を　あげます。
＊ Giver は　Receiver (superior) に　Something を　さしあげます。
＊ Giver は　Receiver (inferior) に　Something を　やります。
＊ Giver は　Receiver (me) に　Something を　くれます。
＊ Receiver は　Giver に／から　Something を　もらいます。
Giver は　Receiver (equal) に　　Verb (TE form)　あげます。
Giver は　Receiver (Inferior) に　Verb (TE form)　やります。
Giver は　Receiver (me) に　　　Verb (TE form)　くれます。
Receiver は　Giver に　　　　　Verb (TE form)　もらいます。

＊ Previously introduced.

【単語】

1. 感謝（を）する
[IR かんしゃ（を）します]
　to appreciate, thank
かんしゃ appreciation [noun]
Someone に　かんしゃをしています。
I am grateful to (someone).

2. 愛して　います
[G1 あいします]
　to be in love
あい love, affection [noun]

3. 言葉
〔ことば〕
words, language

【＊オプショナル単語】

1.＊家事〔かじ〕	＊ chores, housework
2.＊庭仕事〔にわしごと〕	＊ yard work

【漢字】

1. 犬　　dog　　　いぬ　　　白い　犬〔しろい　いぬ〕 a white dog

大　＋　◊　＝　犬
big　　　tail　　　dog

A big dog wagging his tail.

2. 太　　is fat　　　ふと（る）　　太って　います。is fat

大　＋　◊　＝　太
big　　additional　　is fat

A big person with his belly button showing is fat.

3. 屋　　store　　　や　　　本屋〔ほんや〕bookstore

パン屋 bakery

白木屋〔しろきや〕*Shirokiya* department store

部屋〔へや〕room

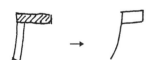

a roof and *noren* (shop curtain)

 (one)

 ＋

土 (ground)　　　　　＝　屋

Inside an open door, a shopkeeper sells his merchandise with one arm as he stands on the earthen ground.

【文法】

[＊Review]

A. Verbs of giving

Giver は　Receiver (equal) に　Something を　あげます。

Giver は　Receiver (superior) に　Something を　さしあげます。

Giver は　Receiver (inferior) に　Something を　やります。

Giver は　Receiver (me) に　Something を　くれます。

Giver (Outsider) は　Receiver (my family member) に　Something を　くれます。

B. Verb of receiving

Receiver は　Giver に／から　Something を　もらいます。

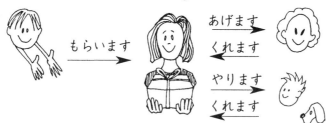

1. 友達は　私に　風船を　くれました。　　My friend gave me some balloons.

2. 私は　友達に　お金を　もらいました。　　I received some money from my friend.

3. これを　あなたに　あげます。　　I will give this to you.

4. 母は　毎日　犬に　食物を　やります。　　My mother gives food to the dog every day.

C.　Giver　＋は　Receiver (equal)　＋に　Verb (TE form)＋あげます。

　　Giver　＋は　Receiver (Inferior)　＋に　Verb (TE form)＋やります。

　　Giver　＋は　Receiver (me)　＋に／を　Verb (TE form)＋くれます。

　　Receiver　＋は　Giver　＋に　Verb (TE form)＋もらいます。

The system of verbs of giving and receiving is more complex in Japanese than in English. It is a reflection of Japanese society, which is structured hierarchically. Verbs differ depending on the relative status of the giver and receiver. "あげます," "やります," and "くれます" are all translated "to give." "あげます," however, is used when the giver gives to another person who is of equal status. "やります" is used to express "giving to someone or something lower in status." "くれます" is generally used when the receiver is the speaker. "もらいます" is used when the subject is the receiver. When these verbs are attached to the verb in its TE form, the same general rules apply except that one is now giving or receiving a favor instead of a gift. When the verbs of giving are used after the verb TE, the favor is being done on the initiative of the giver. When "もらいます" is used in this construction, it is implied that the receiver of the favor initiated the favor (i.e., made a request), and as a result, receives the favor.

1. 私は　母に　晩御飯を　作って　あげました。　I made dinner for my mother.

2. 妹に　本を　読んで　やりました。　I read a book to my younger sister.

3. 父は　私を　学校に　連れて　行って　くれます。　My father takes me to school.

4. 友達は　私を　助けて　くれました。　My friend helped me (as a favor.)

5. 父は　私を　迎えに　来て　くれました。　My father came to pick me up (as a favor.)

6. 僕は　友達に　お金を　貸して　もらいました。

I had my friend lend me some money (as a favor.)

7. 私は　姉に　宿題を　手伝って　もらいました。

I asked my older sister to help me with my homework.

【 ● 文化ノート】

1. Family Time

Until a few years ago, Japanese families rarely spent very much time together, as fathers remained at work until late at night and worked at least six days a week. Recently, more fathers are spending time with their wives and families. Traditionally, the times families spend time together are the first week of the New Year, during Golden Week (the end of April to the beginning of May), and *O-bon* (mid-August). Most employees also receive about three one-week vacations per year. Many company workers, however, did not to take full advantage of these vacations, as it was thought that this would show that one was not devoted to one's job. In recent years, however, more and more men are taking all of their vacation time. Because so many people have the same few holidays off, travel, whether on planes, trains, or by car, is hectic. Common destinations on holidays are visits home to one's place of birth in the countryside, to hot springs and other tourist attractions, the ocean side during the summer and ski resorts during the winter. Recently, travel abroad has also become common. Shorter outings may be taken to the department stores, amusement parks, museums, and restaurants. A favorite family outing site is Tokyo Disneyland, located in Chiba Prefecture east of Tokyo. It is modelled after Disneyland in California, except that it is one and a half times larger. More than 10 million people visit Tokyo Disneyland each year.

2. A Japanese Proverb　「山より　高く、海より　深い　母の　愛」

ふかい means "deep." This proverb means "Mother's love is higher than the mountains and deeper than the ocean."

十五課

【アクティビティー】

A. ペアワーク

Interview each other. Write your partner's response. For questions 1 to 8, if you do these things for your family, use 〜て　あげます. If someone else does these things for you, use 〜て　くれます.

1. 家で　だれが　りょうりを　しますか。	
2. 家で　だれが　家を　そうじしますか。	
3. 家で　だれが　せんたくを　しますか。	
4. 家で　だれが　おさらを　あらいますか。	
5. 家で　だれが　ごみを　外に　出しますか。	
6. 家で　だれが　食べ物の　買い物を　しますか。	
7. 家で　だれが　にわし事を　しますか。	
8. 家で　だれが　車を　あらいますか。	
9. 家で　あなたの　し事は　何ですか。	
10. 家で　りょうしんを　手つだうのが　好きですか。	

B. ペアワーク

Ask your partner what favors he/she asks of the following people. Write your partner's responses. Take turns.

Ex. お母さん

質問：「あなたは　お母さんに　何を　して　もらいますか。」
答え：「私は　母に　お昼御飯を　作って　もらいます。」

1. お父さん	
2. お母さん	
3. きょうだい	
4. 友だち	
5. 先生	

十五課　　　　　　　　436

C. ペアワーク

Ask your partner what he/she does as a favor for the following people. Write your partner's response. Take turns.

Ex. お母さん

質問(しつもん):「あなたは　お母さんに　何を　して　あげますか。」

答え(こた):「私は　母に　時々　お皿(さら)を　洗(あら)って　あげます。」

1. お父さん	
2. お母さん	
3. おじいさんと　おばあさん	
4. きょうだい	
5. 友だち	
6. ペット	

D. ペアワーク

Interview each other. Write your partner's response.

1. お母さんは　時々　あなたを　しかりますか。	
2. お母さんと　時々　けんかを　しますか。	
3. お母さんを　手つだって　あげたことが　ありますか。	
4. お母さんが　大好きですか。	
5. お母さんに　「ありがとう」と　言ったことが　ありますか。	

437

十五課

E. ペアワーク

Ask your partner if he/she is planning to do the following things on Mother's Day. Write your partner's response. Take turns.

Ex. 花を　買う

質問：「母の日に　お母さんに　花を　買って　あげるつもりですか。」

答え：「はい、花を　買って　あげるつもりです。」 or

「いいえ、花を　買って　あげないつもりです。」

1. かんしゃの　カードを　書く	
2. あさごはんを　作る	
3. レストランへ　つれて　行く	
4. プレゼントを　買う	
5. 何も　しない	

Ask your partner these questions in Japanese.
Your partner should answer in Japanese.
You may substitute "mother" with "father" or another family member.

1. How old is your mother?

2. Where does your mother work?

3. Is your mother tall or short?

4. Does your mother wear glasses?

5. What kind of accessories (アクセサリー) does your mother wear all the time?

6. What is your mother's hobby?

7. What kind of things does your mother do for you [as a favor]?

8. What kind of things do you do for your mother [as a favor]?

9. What kind of things do you ask your mother to do for you?

10. When does your mother scold you?

11. Have you ever thanked your mother?

12. What are you going to do for your mother on Mother's Day?

13. Do you think that your mother is a wonderful mother?

14. Are you an only child?　If not, how many siblings do you have?

15. Are your parents divorced?

16. When do you get angry?

17. What do you do during your free time?

18. When you have a problem, with whom do you talk?

19. When you do something wrong (bad), with whom do you talk?

20. If you had $1,000, what would you want to do with it?

21. How many years ago have you been coming to this school?

22. Have you ever participated in a music competition? If so, what rank (place) were you?

23. Do you think that your personality (せいかく) is bright or dark?

24. Do you often cry?

25. Do you often smile?

26. Do you like to wear hats?

27. What color clothing do you like to wear?

28. When you become an adult, what kind of work do you want to do?

29. Do you have your own car?

    If not, what kind of car do you want? If so, what kind of car do you have?

30. What do you want to do during your summer vacation?

母の日にお母さんに感謝のカードをおくりましょう。

Actual size —

Things you need:

はさみ scissors

のり glue stick

あかペン red pen (for lips)

くろペン black pen (for message)

ちよがみ designed *origami* paper (for *kimono*)

くろのかみ black paper (for hair and eyes)

いろがみ colored paper (for ribbon and sash)

マニラフォールダー small index card (for face)

十五課

パターン

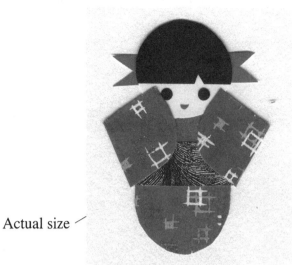

Actual size ╱

1. Trace and cut these on appropriate paper.

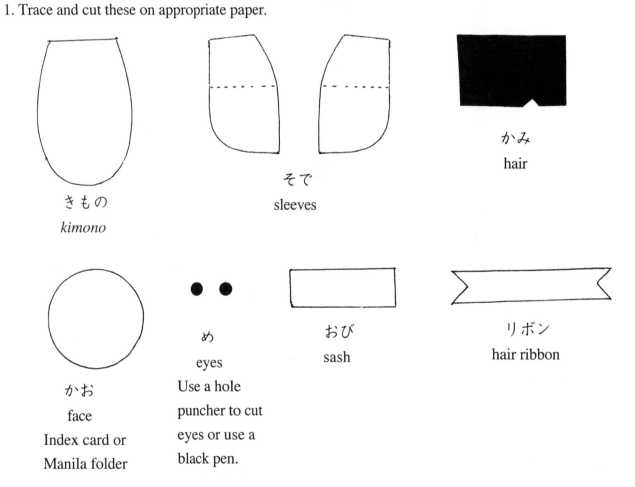

きもの

kimono

そで

sleeves

かみ

hair

かお

face

Index card or

Manila folder

め

eyes

Use a hole

puncher to cut

eyes or use a

black pen.

おび

sash

リボン

hair ribbon

2. Assemble and glue pieces on a piece of paper (Japanese *washi* prefered), frame if desired, then glue
   on the cover of another larger index-weight paper that has been folded in half.

3. Write your Mother's Day message inside the card.

十五課   442

おにんぎょうカード

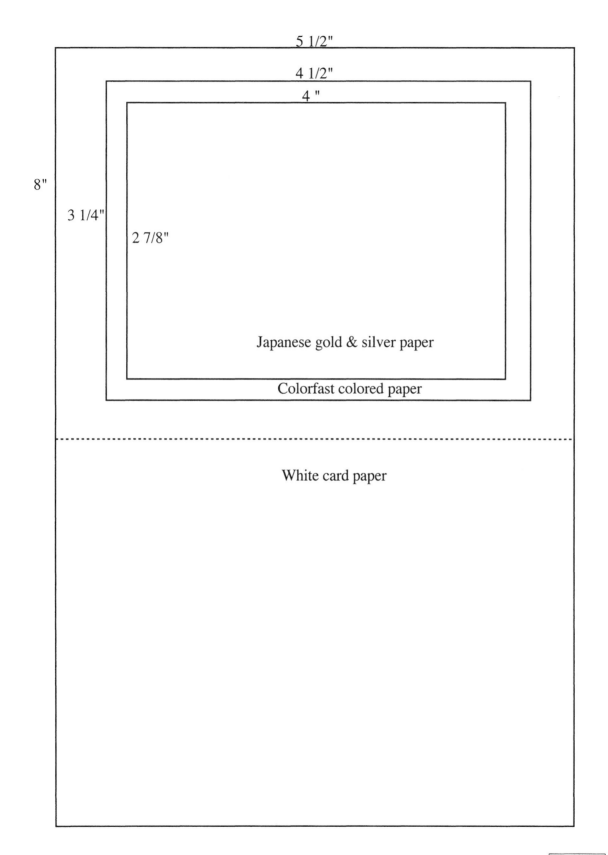

[The numbers preceding each word indicate the lesson in which the word or expression was introduced.]

I. Sentence Patterns

9課

9-1 犬(ねこ)と 猫(ねこ)と どちらの方(ほう)が 好きですか。 Which do you like better, dogs or cats?

9-1 私は 猫(ねこ)より 犬の方(ほう)が 好きです。 I like dogs more than cats.

9-2 アメリカは 中国ほど 広(ひろ)くありません。 America is not as spacious as China.

9-2 お好きですか。 Do you like it?

9-3 魚(さかな)と 豚肉(ぶたにく)と チキンで 何が 一番(ばん) いいですか。

Which is best, fish, pork, or chicken?

9-3 この クラスで だれが 一番(ばん) 背(せ)が 高(たか)いですか。

In this class, who is the tallest?

9-3 この 中で これが 一番(ばん) 好きです。 Among these, I like this best.

10課

10-1 しあいが はじまります。 The game will start. [Intransitive Verb]

10-1 しあいを はじめます。 (Someone) will start the game. [Transitive Verb]

10-1 試合(しあい)の 始(はじ)まる時間(かん)は 何時ですか。 What time does the game start? [lit., What time is

the game starting time?]

10-1 今日 試合(しあい)が ありますが、行きませんか。

There is a game today. Won't you go?

10-2 だれが あなたを 学校へ 迎(むか)えに 来ますか。

Who comes to pick you up at school?

10-2 宿題(しゅくだい)を 取(と)りに 行っても いいですか。 May I go to get my homework?

10-3 Verb Potential Form

10-3 父は 中国語が 話せますが、私は 話せません。

My father can speak Chinese, but I cannot.

10-3 母は さしみが 食べられません。 My mother cannot eat *sashimi*.

10-3 うるさくて、勉強(べんきょう) 出来ません。 It is noisy, so I cannot study.

10-4 私は チームに かって ほしいです。 I want the team to win.

11-2 この　本を　全部　読んでしまいました。　I read this entire book.

11-2 疲れていましたから、ゆうべは　早く　寝てしまいました。
I was tired, so I ended up going to bed early last night.

11-2 昨日は　病気でした。ですから、宿題が　出来ませんでした。
I was sick yesterday. Therefore, I could not do my homework.

11-2 母は　仕事で　東京へ　行きました。だから、私が　料理しなければ
なりません。　My mother went to Tokyo for work. Therefore, I have to cook.

11-3 デレックさんは　「こんにちは。」と　言いました。　Derek said, "Hello."

11-4 明日　日本語の　試験が　あると　思います。
I think there is a Japanese exam tomorrow.

11-4 母は　今　四十五才だと　思います。　I think my mother is 45 years old now.

11-4 父は　前　ピアノが　上手だったと　聞きました。
I heard that my father was good at the piano before.

12課

12-1 医者に　なりたいです。　I want to be a doctor.

13課

13-2 右に　まがると、動物園が　あります。
If you turn right, the zoo is (right) there.

13-3 家から　学校まで　どのぐらい　かかりますか。
How long does it take from home to school?

13-3 家から　学校まで　どのぐらい　ありますか。　How far is it from home to school?

13-3 バスで　行くのと　タクシーで　行くのと　どちらの方が　速いですか。
Which is faster, going by bus or going by taxi?

13-3 バスで　行く方が　歩くより　速いです。　It is faster to go by bus than to walk.

13-3 バスで　学校へ　行くのは　車で　行くほど　速くありません。
Going to school by bus is not as fast as going by car.

14課

14-1 すき焼きの　作り方を　教えて　下さい。　Please teach me how to make *sukiyaki*.

14-2 かみの　けを　短く　して　下さい。　Please make (cut) my hair short.

14-2 ここを　きれいに　して　下さい。　Please clean up this place.

14-2 牛肉を 薄く 切って 下さい。　　　Please slice the beef thin.

14-2 糸こんにゃくを 半分に 切って 下さい。Please cut the shredded *konnyaku* in half.

14-3 背が 高く なりましたねえ。　　　You've grown tall, haven't you!

14-3 私は 将来 医者に なりたいです。　I want to become a doctor in the future.

14-4 父は お酒を 飲みすぎます。　　　My father drinks too much *sake*.

14-4 この 犬は 頭が 良すぎます。　　This dog is too smart.

14-4 あの 人は テニスが 下手すぎます。That person is too unskillful at tennis.

14-4 勉強しすぎないで 下さい。　　　Please do not study too hard.

15課

15-2 休みには 映画に 行ったり コンサートに 行ったり します。

I do such things as go to the movies and concerts on my days off.

15-2 私の 成績は 良かったり 悪かったり します。

My grades are sometimes good and sometimes bad.

15-2 生徒は 上手だったり 下手だったり します。

Some students are skillful and some students are unskillful.

15-2 日本語の 先生は 日本人だったり アメリカ人だったり します。

Teachers of Japanese are sometimes Japanese and sometimes American.

15-3 日本へ 行ったら、いろいろな 物を 見たいです。

When (if) I go to Japan, I want to see various things.

15-3 休みが もっと 長かったら、嬉しいです。　If the vacation is longer, I will be happy.

15-3 日本語が 上手だったら、仕事が あります。

If I am good at Japanese, I will have a job.

15-4 私は 母に 晩御飯を 作って あげました。　I made dinner for my mother.

15-4 妹に 本を 読んで やりました。　I read a book to my younger sister.

15-4 父は 私を 学校に 連れて行って くれます。　My father takes me to school.

15-4 僕は 友達に お金を 貸して もらいました。

I had my friend lend me some money (as a favor.)

十六課　　　446

II. 動詞 Verbs, い Adjectives and な Adjectives

[The numbers preceding each word indicate the volume or lesson in which the word was introduced.]

A. Verbs

Group 1 Verbs

-む	-ぬ	-ぶ	-う	-つ
I　のむ	I しぬ	I あそぶ	I　　いう	I　　かつ
I　よむ			I　　あう（会）	I　　たつ
I　やすむ			I　　かう	I　　まつ
2-1　すむ			I　　うたう	2-1 もつ
3-2　かむ			I　　もらう	
13-4 こむ			2-1　ならう	
			2-4　ちがう	
			3-2　すう	
			5-2　はらう	
			7-3　あらう	
			7-3　てつだう	
			9-2　ちがう	
			11-2 (TE)しまう	
			11-4 おもう	
			13-1 うかがう	
			15-1 わらう	

-る		-く	-ぐ	-す
I おわる　　3-1　かぶる		I　　きく	I およぐ	I　　はなす
I わかる　　4-2　とまる（止）		I　　かく（書）		I　　だす
I しる　　　4-2　まがる		I　　行く		I　　かす
I ふとる　　4-3　のる		I　　あるく		4-2　スピードをだす
I とる　　　6-2　いらっしゃる		2-1　はたらく		5-3　かえす
I かえる　　6-2　かわる		3-1　はく		7-3　ゴミをだす
I ある　　　7-1　おくる（送）		4-3　つく		11-2 かくす
I がんばる 7-2　ふる		5-2　おく put, leave		11-2 ふきとばす
I はしる　　9-4　かかる		6-1　かぜを　ひく		15-4 あいす
I すわる　　9-4　うる		6-1　ピアノを　ひく		
I やる　　　10-1 はじまる		10-2 むかえに行く		
I つくる　　10-1 おわる		10-2 とりに行く		
10-2 むかえにかえる		11-2 うごく		
10-2 とりにかえる		13-4 すく		
10-2 よる（寄）		15-1 かく（描）		
12-1 なる		15-1 なく		
13-2 わたる				
14-2 きる（切）				
15-1 おこる（怒）				
15-1 しかる				

十六課

Group 2 Verbs

-E		One ひらがな	Special
I　はじめる	2-4　こたえる	I　みる	I　おきる
I　みえる	3-1　（めがねを）かける	I　ねる	3-3　かりる
I　きこえる	3-2　（ごみを）すてる	I　いる	4-3　おりる
I　たべる	3-3　きをつける	3-1　きる	6-1　できる
I　やせる	4-1　おしえる	4-3　でる	14-4　-すぎる
I　つかれる	4-3　でかける		
I　まける	6-2　（でんわを）かける		
I　みせる	6-2　まちがえる		
I　あける	6-3　おぼえる		
I　しめる	9-1　さしあげる		
I　わすれる	9-2　くらべる		
I　くれる	9-4　いれる		
I　あげる	14-4　つける		
2-1　うまれる	14-4　かたづける		
2-1　つとめる	15-3　たすける		

Group 3 Irregular Verbs

I　くる	I　する	5-1 thing に　する
10-2 むかえにくる	I　べんきょう（を）する	5-2　よやく（を）する
10-2 とりにくる	I　タイプ（を）する	5-2　ちゅうもん（を）する
	I　りょこう（を）する	5-3　ごちそう（を）する
	I　かいもの（を）する	7-3　そうじ（を）する
	I　しょくじ（を）する	7-3　せんたく（を）する
	I　でんわ（を）する	7-3　りょうり（を）する
	I　れんしゅう（を）する	10-1　うんどう（を）する
	2-1　アルバイト（を）する	10-1　おうえん（を）する
	2-1　けっこん（を）する	10-3　ゆうしょう（を）する
	2-1　ホームステイ（を）する	12-1　げきをする
	2-1　しょうかい（を）する	14-2　あつくする
	2-1　じこしょうかい（を）する	14-2　きれいにする
	2-4　しつもん（を）する	15-1　さんぽ（を）する
	3-1　アクセサリーを　する	15-1　りこん（を）する
	3-2　うんてん（を）する	15-4　かんしゃ（を）する
	4-2　しんぱい（を）する	
	4-3　シートベルトを　する	
	4-4　けんか（を）する	

Japanese 1 Verbs

[The numbers preceding each word indicate the lesson in which the word was introduced in *Adventures in Japanese 1*.]

1-4 はじめます	to begin, start	10-1 います	there is (animate)
1-4 おわります	to finish	10-1 あります	there is (inanimate)
2-1 わかります	to understand	11-2 あります	to have
2-1 しりません	do not know	12-1 しにます	to die
2-1 みえます	can see	12-2 やすみます	to rest, be absent
2-1 きこえます	can hear	12-2（くすりを）のみます	to take (medicine)
2-1 いいます	to say	12-2 つかれています	to be tired
4-1 はなします	to speak, talk	12-3 かちます	to win
4-2 たべます	to eat	12-3 まけます	to lose
4-2 のみます	to drink	12-4 がんばります	to do one's best
4-4 よみます	to read	12-5 あいます	to meet
4-4 ききます	to listen, hear, ask	12-5 れんしゅう（を）します	to practice
4-4 します	to do	12-5 はしります	to run
4-4 べんきょう（を）します	to study	13-2 すわります	to sit
4-5 みます	to see, watch, look	13-2 たちます	to stand
4-5 かきます	to write	13-2 だします	to turn in
4-5 タイプ（を）します	to type	13-2 みせます	to show
6-4 ふとっています	is fat	13-2 あけます	to open
6-4 やせています	is thin	13-2 しめます	to close
6-4 としを とっています	is old (age)	13-2 しずかにします	to be quiet
7-3 いきます	to go	13-2 いいます	to say
7-3 きます	to come	13-2 まちます	to wait
7-3 かえります	to return (place)	13-2 かいます	to buy
7-3 おきます	to get up, wake up	14-3 わすれます	to forget
7-3 ねます	to go to bed, sleep	14-3（～が）いります	to need ～
7-4 あるいて いきます	to go on foot	14-3 かします	to lend
7-4 あるいて きます	to come on foot	15-1 うたいます	to sing
7-4 あるいて かえります	to return on foot	15-2 くれます	to give (me)
7-5 スポーツを します	to play sports	15-2 もらいます	to receive, get
7-5 パーティー をします	to have a party	15-3 あげます	to give (to equal)
7-5 りょこう（を）します	to travel	15-3 やります	to give (to inferior)
7-5 かいもの（を）します	to shop	15-5 あそびます	to play (for fun)
7-5 しょくじ（を）します	to have a meal, dine	15-5 およぎます	to swim
7-5 でんわ（を）します	to make a phone call	15-5 ゲームをします	to play a game
		15-5 つくります	to make
		15-5（しゃしんを）とります	to take (a picture)

十六課

Japanese 2 Verbs

[The numbers preceding each word indicate the lesson in which the word was introduced.]

2-1	Place で うまれる	G2	to be born in (place)
2-1	Place に すんで いる	G1	to be living in (place)
2-1	Place に つとめて いる	G2	to be employed at (place)
2-1	Place で はたらく	G1	to work at (place)
2-1	Place で アルバイト（を）する	IR	to work part-time at (place)
2-1	Person と けっこん（を）する	IR	to marry (a person)
2-1	もって いる	G1	to have
2-1	しっている	G1	to know
2-1	しらない	G1	do not know
2-1	ならう	G1	to learn
2-1	ホームステイを する	IR	to do a homestay
2-3	しょうかい（を）する	IR	to introduce
2-3	じこしょうかい（を）する	IR	to introduce oneself
2-4	ちがう	G1	to differ, is wrong
2-4	しつもん（を）する	IR	to ask a question
2-4	こたえる	G2	to answer
3-1	きる	G2	to wear [above the waist]
3-1	はく	G1	to wear [below the waist]
3-1	する	IR	to wear [accessories]
3-1	かぶる	G1	to wear [on the head]
3-1	かける	G2	to wear [glasses]
3-2	いけません	G2	won't do, must not do
3-2	かまいません	G1	I do not mind if . . .
3-2	たばこを すう	G1	to smoke cigarettes
3-2	ガムを かむ	G1	to chew gum
3-2	ごみを すてる	G2	to litter, throw away garbage
3-2	うんてん（を）する	IR	to drive
3-2	Person に あう	G1	to meet (a person)
3-2	Person に 聞く	G1	to ask (a person)
3-3	かりる	G2	to borrow
3-3	きを つける	G2	to be careful
3-4	Thing が 見える	G2	(Thing) can be seen
3-4	Thing が 聞こえる	G2	(Thing) can be heard
4-1	おしえる	G2	to teach
4-2	とまる	G1	to stop

4-2	まがる	G1	to turn
4-2	スピードを　だす	G1	to speed
4-2	しんぱいを　する	IR	to worry
4-3	Thing に　のる	G1	to ride (thing); to get on
4-3	Thing から／を　おりる	G2	to get off, to get out (of something)
4-3	シートベルトを　する	IR	to wear a seatbelt
4-3	出かける	G2	to go out
4-3	Place を　出る	G2	to leave (a place)
4-3	Place に　つく	G1	to arrive (at a place)
4-4	けんか（を）する	IR	to fight
5-1	Thing に　する	IR	to decide on (something)
5-2	よやく（を）する	IR	to make a reservation
5-2	ちゅうもん（を）する	IR	to order
5-2	おきます	G1	to put, leave
5-2	はらいます	G1	to pay
5-3	ごちそう（を）する	IR	to treat someone
5-3	かえす	G1	to return (something)
6-1	かぜを　ひく	G1	to catch a cold
6-1	ひく	G1	to play (string instrument)
6-1	Thing が　出来る	G2	can do (something)
6-2	（でんわを）かける	G2	to make a phone call
6-2	いらっしゃいます［いらっしゃる］	G1	to exist [polite equiv. of います]
6-2	まちがえる	G2	to make a mistake
6-2	かわりました［かわる］	G1	It's me. [lit., We've changed over.]
6-3	クラス／うんてんめんきょを　とる	G1	to take (a class), get (a driver license)
6-3	おぼえる	G2	to memorize
7-1	おくる	G1	to send, mail
7-2	（あめ／ゆきが）ふる	G1	to (rain/snow) fall
7-3	そうじ（を）する	IR	to clean (house, room)
7-3	せんたく（を）する	IR	to do laundry
7-3	りょうり（を）する	IR	to cook
7-3	あらう	G1	to wash
7-3	てつだう	G1	to help
7-3	ごみを　だす	G1	to take out the garbage
9-1	Person に　さしあげます	G2	to give (to a superior)
9-2	くらべます	G2	to compare
9-2	ちがいます	G1	is different, is wrong
9-4	いれます	G2	to put in ～
9-4	かかります	G1	to require (tax), to take (time)

9-4	うります	G1	to sell
10-1	うんどう（を）します	IR	to exercise
10-1	（しあいに）出ます	G2	to play (a game)
10-1	おうえん（を）します	IR	to cheer
10-1	（～が）はじまります	G1	(something) begins, starts
10-1	（～が）おわります	G1	(something) finishes, ends
10-2	（Placeに）よります	G1	to stop by, drop by (a place)
10-2	（Personを）むかえに行きます	G1	to go to pick up (a person)
10-2	（Personを）むかえに来ます	IR	to come to pick up (a person)
10-2	（Personを）むかえにかえります	G1	to return to pick up (a person)
10-2	（Thingを）とりに行きます	G1	to go to pick up (something)
10-2	（Thingを）とりに来ます	IR	to come to pick up (something)
10-2	（Thingを）とりにかえります	G1	to return to pick up (something)
10-3	ゆうしょう（を）します	IR	to win a championship
10-4	ドキドキしています	IR	to be excited, be nervous
11-2	（Thing を）かくします	G1	to hide (something)
11-2	ふきとばします	G1	to blow away
11-2	（Thing が）うごきます	G1	(something) moves
11-2	Verb (TE) しまいます	G1	to do ～ completely
11-4	おもいます	G1	to think
12-1	げきをします	IR	to give (put on) a (stage) play
12-1	～に　なります	G1	to become ～
13-1	うかがいます	G1	to ask, inquire [polite equiv. of ききます]
13-2	～を　わたります	G1	to cross, go over ～
13-4	こんでいます	G1	to be crowded
13-4	すいています	G1	not to be crowded, is empty
14-2	きります	G1	to cut
14-2	あつくします	IR	to make hot, to heat
14-2	きれいにします	IR	to make clean, to clean
14-4	～すぎます	G2	to exceed, too ～
14-4	～が　出来ました	G2	～ is ready, ～ is done
14-4	（Objectを）（Thingに）つけます	G2	to dip (object) in (thing)
14-4	かたづけます	G2	to clean up, put away
15-1	さんぽ（を）します	IR	to take a walk
15-1	わらいます	G1	to smile, laugh
15-1	なきます	G1	to cry
15-1	おこります	G1	to get angry
15-1	しかります	G1	to scold
15-1	りこん（を）します	IR	to divorce
15-3	たすけます	G2	to rescue, help
15-4	かんしゃ（を）します	IR	to appreciate, thank
15-4	あいしています	G1	to love

B. い Adjectives

Japanese 1 い Adjectives

あつい	hot	うつくしい	beautiful
さむい	cold	ひろい	spacious, wide
ずずしい	cool	せまい	narrow, small (space)
いい	good	ちかい	near
たかい	tall, high	とおい	far
ひくい	short (height), low	むずかしい	difficult
よい	good	やさしい	easy
わるい	bad	たのしい	fun, enjoyable
大きい	big	おもしろい	interesting
小さい	small	つまらない	boring, uninteresting
ながい	long	ひどい	terrible
みじかい	short (length)	うれしい	happy
あかい	red	かなしい	sad
しろい	white	おおい	many
くろい	black	すくない	few, a little
あおい	blue	(〜が)ほしい	want (something)
きいろい	yellow	いたい	sore, painful
ちゃいろい	brown	ねむい	sleepy
わかい	young	つよい	strong
きびしい	strict	よわい	weak
やさしい	kind, nice	たかい	expensive; high
きたない	dirty	やすい	cheap
かわいい	cute	おいしい	delicious, tasty
うるさい	noisy	まずい	not tasty
はやい	early	すごい	terrific, terrible
おそい	late	すばらしい	wonderful
いそがしい	busy	つめたい	cold (to the touch)
あたらしい	new	あたたかい	warm
ふるい	old (not for person's age)		

Japanese 2 い Adjectives

2-4	ただしい	correct, right	14-3	あまい	sweet
4-3	あぶない	dangerous	14-3	しおからい	salty
4-3	こわい	scary	14-3	からい	salty, spicy
11-1	あかるい	bright	14-3	すっぱい	sour
11-1	くらい	dark	14-4	きもちがわるい	unpleasant, uncomfortable
11-1	えらい	great (for people)	14-4	きもちがいい	pleasant, comfortable
14-2	うすい	thin			
14-2	あつい（厚）	thick			

Conjugation of い Adjectives

Function	Formal form	Informal form	Meaning
nonpast	あついです	あつい	is hot
neg. nonpast	あつくないです or あつくありません	あつくない	is not hot
past	あつかったです	あつかった	was hot
neg. past	あつくなかったです or あつくありませんでした	あつくなかった	was not hot
pre-noun	あつい　おちゃ		hot tea
conjoining	あつくて、おいしいです。		It is hot and tasty.

Conjugation of irregular い adjective: いい

Function	Formal form	Informal form	Meaning
nonpast	いいです	いい	is good
neg. nonpast	よくないです or よくありません	よくない	is not good
past	よかったです	よかった	was good
neg. past	よくなかったです or よくありませんでした	よくなかった	was not good
pre-noun	いい　ひと		good person
conjoining	あたまが　よくて、せが　たかいです。		He is smart and tall.

C. な Adjectives

Japanese 1 な Adjectives

げんき	healthy, fine	苦手〔にがて〕	be weak in
だめ	no good	きれい	pretty, clean, neat
好き	like	しずか	quiet
大好き	like very much, love	じゃま	is a hindrance, nuisance,
きらい	dislike		is in my way
大きらい	dislike a lot, hate	ゆうめい	famous
上手	skillful, be good at	大変〔たいへん〕	hard
下手	unskillful, be poor at	大丈夫〔だいじょうぶ〕	all right
とくい	be strong in, can do well	大事〔だいじ〕	important

Japanese 2 な Adjectives

3-2	じゆう	free, liberal	9-2	いろいろ	various
4-3	あんぜん	safe	11-1	びんぼう	poor
6-1	へん	strange, weird, unusual	15-2	ひま	free (time)

Conjugation of な Adjectives

Function	Formal form	Informal form	Meaning
nonpast	すきです	すきだ	like
neg. nonpast	すきではありません or すきじゃありません	すきではない or すきじゃない	do not like
past	すきでした	すきだった	liked
neg. past	すきではありませんでした or すきじゃありませんでした	すきではなかった or すきじゃなかった	did not like
pre-noun	すきなひと		person I like
conjoining	すきで、まいにち　たべます。		I like it and eat it every day.

III. Adverbs, particles, sentence conjunctions, sentence interjectives, suffixes, expressions.

[The numbers preceding each word indicate the lesson in which the word or expression was introduced.]

A. Adverbs

2-3	まだ + Aff.	still
2-3	もう + Neg.	(not) any more
2-4	とくに	especially
3-2	ぜったい(に)	absolutely
3-4	本当〔ほんとう〕に	truly, really
4-2	はやく	fast, early
4-2	きゅうに	suddenly
4-2	けっして	never
5-2	だいたい	roughly
5-4	ほかに	besides
6-2	何度〔なんど〕も	many times
6-3	もちろん	of course
7-4	ぜひ	by all means
9-1	もっと	more
9-1	ずっと	by far
9-1	りょう方〔ほう〕	both
9-3	一番	the most
10-2	そのころ	around that time
11-2	ガリガリ	chew away, gnaw
11-3	いっしょうけんめい	with one's utmost effort
11-4	とうとう	finally, at last
13-2	まっすぐ	straight
14-2	うすく	thin
14-2	あつく	thick
14-2	はんぶんに	in half
14-2	まず	first of all
14-2	はじめに	at the beginning
14-2	つぎに	next
14-2	おわりに	at the end
15-1	ニコニコ	smilingly
15-1	ずっと	throughout, all the time
15-1	たまに	occasionally, once in a while
15-2	その とき	at that time

B. Particles

3-4	～だけ	only
4-2	を	along, through
5-1	～に～	～ and ～ (as a set)
6-1	S1+け(れ)ど、S2.	Although, Though S1, S2.
6-2	Sentence+が	[Softens the statement.]
6-3	～で	because of ～
6-4	に	per
6-4	も	as many/long as
9-1	AとBで	between A and B
9-1	～より	more than ～
9-2	～ほど + Neg.	(not) as ～ as
9-3	（～の中）で	among ～
10-2	(time) までに	by (a certain time)
11-3	「 」と	[Quotation particle]

C. Question Words

5-4	どちら？	which way? [Formal]
6-4	どのぐらい？	how much? how long?
9-1	どっち？	which (one of two)? [Informal]
9-1	どちら？	which [one of two)? [Formal]
9-3	どれ？	which one (of three or more)?

D. Sentence Interjectives

4-1	うん	Yes [Informal]
4-1	ううん	No [Informal]
5-1	う～ん	Yummm . . .
9-3	さあ	Well . . .
11-3	えっ	What?
11-3	いや（っ）	No [Stronger negation than いいえ.]
13-1	ああ	Oh!

E. Sentence conjunctions

3-3 ところで	By the way
11-2 だから	Therefore [Informal]
11-2 ですから	Therefore [Formal]
15-2 しかし	However [Formal equiv. of でも]

F. Dependent Nouns

2-3 ～について	about ～
2-3 ～ちゃん	used instead of ～さん for small, cute children or animals
10-4 あと～	～ more
11-4 ある～	a certain ～
13-2 ～がわ	～ side
14-1 ～かた	how to ～
15-2 ～まえ	～ ago

G. Copula

11-4 (Noun/なAdj.) だ	[Plain form of です」
11-4 (Noun/なAdj.) だった	[Plain form of でした」

H. Expressions

5-4 いらっしゃいませ。	Welcome.
5-4 どうぞ こちらへ。	This way, please.
5-4 ほかに 何か。	Anything else?
5-4 それだけです。	That is all.
5-4 すみません。	Excuse me.
6-1 ぐあいが わるいです。	I don't feel well.
6-1 ストレスが いっぱいです。	I am stressed.
6-1 （お）きのどくに。	I'm sorry. [Sympathy]
6-2 もしもし	Hello. [Telephone]
6-2 るすです。	No one is at home.
6-2 はなし中[ちゅう]です。	The line is busy.
6-3 しかたが ありません。	It can't be helped.
7-4 あけまして おめでとう ございます。	Happy New Year!
9-1 お好きですか。	Do you like it? [Polite expression of 好きですか]
9-1 何を さしあげましょうか。	May I help you? [lit., What shall I give you?]

十六課

9-2 ありがとうございました。	Thank you very much. [Used after a deed has been done]
9-4 また　どうぞ。	Please come again.
10-2 それは　いいかんがえです。	That's a good idea.
10-3 うそです（よ）。	It is a lie (you know).
10-3 うそでしょう？	Are you kidding? Are you serious?
10-3 じょうだんです（よ）。	It's a joke (you know). I'm just kidding.
10-4 やったあ！	We did it!
10-4 ばんざい！	Hurray!
10-4 かった！　かった！	(We) won! (We) won!
11-3 とんでもない（です）。	How ridiculous! That's impossible!
11-3 なるほど。	Indeed! I see!
13-1 あのう ... ちょっと　うかがいますが ...	Excuse me . . . I have a question.
13-3 どのぐらい　かかりますか。	How long does it take? [time]
13-3 どのぐらい　ありますか。	How far is it? [distance]
14-4 ～が　出来ました。	～ is ready. ～ is done.

VI. Counters

	∗	∗	∗	∗	∗	∗
1	いちだい	いちわ	いっぴき	いっぽん	いっぱい	いっさつ
2	にだい	にわ	にひき	にほん	にはい	にさつ
3	さんだい	さんわ	さんびき	さんぼん	さんばい	さんさつ
4	よんだい	よんわ	よんひき	よんほん	よんはい	よんさつ
5	ごだい	ごわ	ごひき	ごほん	ごはい	ごさつ
6	ろくだい	ろくわ	ろっぴき	ろっぽん	ろっぱい	ろくさつ
7	ななだい	ななわ	ななひき	ななほん	ななはい	ななさつ
8	はちだい	はちわ	はっぴき	はっぽん	はっぱい	はっさつ
9	きゅうだい	きゅうわ	きゅうひき	きゅうほん	きゅうはい	きゅうさつ
10	じゅうだい	じゅうわ	じゅっぴき	じゅっぽん	じゅっぱい	じゅっさつ
?	なんだい？	なんわ？	なんびき？	なんぼん？	なんばい？	なんさつ？

Days of the month ∗

1	ついたち	11	じゅういちにち	21	にじゅういちにち
2	ふつか	12	じゅうににち	22	にじゅうににち
3	みっか	13	じゅうさんにち	23	にじゅうさんにち
4	よっか	14	じゅうよっか	24	にじゅうよっか
5	いつか	15	じゅうごにち	25	にじゅうごにち
6	むいか	16	じゅうろくにち	26	にじゅうろくにち
7	なのか	17	じゅうしちにち	27	にじゅうしちにち
8	ようか	18	じゅうはちにち	28	にじゅうはちにち
9	ここのか	19	じゅうくにち	29	にじゅうくにち
10	とおか	20	はつか	30	さんじゅうにち
?	なんにち？			31	さんじゅういちにち

∗ Introduced in *Adventures in Japanese 1*.

十六課

[The numbers in the upper right corner indicate the lesson in which the counter was introduced.]

	5-2	5-3 %	9-4 Floor	*	*	*
1	いっこ	いっパーセント	いっかい	いちまい	ひとつ	ひとり
2	にこ	にパーセント	にかい	にまい	ふたつ	ふたり
3	さんこ	さんパーセント	さんがい	さんまい	みっつ	さんにん
4	よんこ	よんパーセント	よんかい	よんまい	よっつ	よにん
5	ごこ	ごパーセント	ごかい	ごまい	いつつ	ごにん
6	ろっこ	ろくパーセント	ろっかい	ろくまい	むっつ	ろくにん
7	ななこ	ななパーセント	ななかい	ななまい	ななつ	ななにん
8	はっこ	はっパーセント	はっかい	はちまい	やっつ	はちにん
9	きゅうこ	きゅうパーセント	きゅうかい	きゅうまい	ここのつ	きゅうにん
10	じ(ゅ)っこ	じ(ゅ)っパーセント	じ(ゅ)っかい	じゅうまい	とお	じゅうにん
?	なんこ?	なんパーセント?	なんがい?	なんまい?	いくつ?	なんにん?

	Age *	Month *	Grade *	Hour *	Minute *	Point(s) 10-4
1	いっさい	いちがつ	いちねんせい	いちじ	いっぷん	いってん
2	にさい	にがつ	にねんせい	にじ	にふん	にてん
3	さんさい	さんがつ	さんねんせい	さんじ	さんぷん	さんてん
4	よんさい	しがつ	よねんせい	よじ	よんふん	よんてん
5	ごさい	ごがつ		ごじ	ごふん	ごてん
6	ろくさい	ろくがつ		ろくじ	ろっぷん	ろくてん
7	ななさい	しちがつ		ななじ	ななふん	ななてん
8	はっさい	はちがつ		はちじ	はっぷん	はってん
9	きゅうさい	くがつ		くじ	きゅうふん	きゅうてん
10	じ(ゅ)っさい	じゅうがつ		じゅうじ	じ(ゅ)っぷん	じ(ゅ)ってん
11		じゅういちがつ		じゅういちじ		
12	20 はたち	じゅうにがつ		じゅうにじ		
?	なんさい?	なんがつ?	なんねんせい?	なんじ?	なんぷん?	なんてん?

* Introduced in *Adventures in Japanese 1*.

十六課　　　　　　　　460

[The hyphenated numbers indicate the lesson in which the counter was introduced.]

	degree(s), time(s) ～ど 6-4	No. of minute(s) ～分（間） 6-4	No. of hour(s) ～時間 6-4	No. of day(s) ～日（間） 6-4
1	いちど	いっぷん（かん）	いちじかん	いちにち（かん）
2	にど	にふん（かん）	にじかん	ふつか（かん）
3	さんど	さんぷん（かん）	さんじかん	みっか（かん）
4	よんど	よんふん（かん）	よじかん	よっか（かん）
5	ごど	ごふん（かん）	ごじかん	いつか（かん）
6	ろくど	ろっぷん（かん）	ろくじかん	むいか（かん）
7	ななど	ななふん（かん）	ななじかん	なのか（かん）
8	はちど	はっぷん（かん）	はちじかん	ようか（かん）
9	きゅうど	きゅうふん（かん）	くじかん	ここのか（かん）
10	じゅうど	じ（ゅ）っぷん（かん）	じゅうかん	とおか（かん）
?	なんど？	なんぷん（かん）？	なんじかん？	なんにち（かん）？

	No. of week(s) ～週間 6-4	No. of month(s) ～か月 6-4	No. of year(s) ～年（間） 6-4
1	いっしゅうかん	いっかげつ	いちねん（かん）
2	にしゅうかん	にかげつ	にねん（かん）
3	さんしゅうかん	さんかげつ	さんねん（かん）
4	よんしゅうかん	よんかげつ	よねん（かん）
5	ごしゅうかん	ごかげつ	ごねん（かん）
6	ろくしゅうかん	ろっかげつ	ろくねん（かん）
7	ななしゅうかん	ななかげつ	ななねん（かん）
8	はっしゅうかん	はっかげつ	はちねん（かん）
9	きゅうしゅうかん	きゅうかげつ	きゅうねん（かん）
10	じ（ゅ）っしゅうかん	じ（ゅ）っかげつ	じゅうねん（かん）
?	なんしゅうかん？	なんかげつ？	なんねん（かん）？

10-1　No. ～
　　　～ばん

10-4　Rank
　　　～い

十六課

かんじリスト

Hiragana is used for *KUN* (Japanese) readings and *Katakana* for *ON* (Chinese) readings.

1課 ☆ Special reading * Previously introduced.

1. 一 one
   - ひと 一つ〔ひとつ〕one (general object)
   - イチ 一月〔いちがつ〕January
   - ☆ 一日〔ついたち〕the first day of the month

2. 二 two
   - ふた 二つ〔ふたつ〕two (general objects)
   - ニ 二月〔にがつ〕February
   - ☆ 二日〔ふつか〕the second day of the month

3. 三 three
   - みっ 三つ〔みっつ〕three (general objects)
   - 三日〔みっか〕the third day of the month
   - サン 三月〔さんがつ〕March

4. 四 four
   - よ（っ）四つ〔よっつ〕four (general objects)
   - 四日〔よっか〕the fourth day of the month
   - よん 四本〔よんほん〕four (long objects)
   - シ 四月〔しがつ〕April

5. 五 five
   - いつ 五つ〔いつつ〕five (general objects)
   - 五日〔いつか〕the fifth day of the month
   - ゴ 五月〔ごがつ〕May

6. 六 six
   - むっ 六つ〔むっつ〕six (general objects)
   - ☆ 六日〔むいか〕the sixth day of the month
   - ロク 六月〔ろくがつ〕June

7. 七 seven
   - なな 七つ〔ななつ〕seven (general objects)
   - なの 七日〔なのか〕the seventh day of the month
   - シチ 七月〔しちがつ〕July

8. 八 eight
   - やっ 八つ〔やっつ〕eight (general objects)
   - よう 八日〔ようか〕the eighth day of the month
   - ハチ 八月〔はちがつ〕August

9.	九	nine	ここの	九つ〔ここのつ〕 nine (general objects)
				九日〔ここのか〕 the ninth of the month
			キュウ	九十〔きゅうじゅう〕 90
			ク	九月〔くがつ〕 September
10.	十	10	とお	十日〔とおか〕 the 10th day of the month
			ジュウ	十月〔じゅうがつ〕 October
11.	月	moon	ガツ	一月〔いちがつ〕 January
			ゲツ	月曜日〔げつようび〕 Monday
12.	日	sun, day	ひ	その日〔ひ〕 that day
			び	月曜日〔げつようび〕 Monday
			か	十四日〔じゅうよっか〕 the 14th of the month
			ニチ	日曜日〔にちようび〕 Sunday
13.	火	fire	カ	火曜日〔かようび〕 Tuesday
14.	水	water	みず	お水〔みず〕 water
			スイ	水曜日〔すいようび〕 Wednesday
15.	木	tree	き	おおきい木〔き〕 a big tree
			モク	木曜日〔もくようび〕 Thursday
16.	金	gold	かね	お金〔かね〕 money
			キン	金曜日〔きんようび〕 Friday
17.	土	soil	ド	土曜日〔どようび〕 Saturday

2課

18.	口	mouth	くち, ぐち	
19.	目	eye	め	
20.	人	person	ひと	あの人 that person
			ニン	三人〔さんにん〕 three people
			ジン	アメリカ人 American
			☆	一人〔ひとり〕 one (person)
				二人〔ふたり〕 two (persons)

漢字

21. **本** origin, book　　もと　　山本〔やまもと〕さん

中本〔なかもと〕さん

川本〔かわもと〕さん

木本〔きもと〕さん

ホン　　本を　よむ read a book

日本〔にほん or にっぽん〕Japan

ポン　　一本〔いっぽん〕one (long object)

ボン　　三本〔さんぼん〕three (long objects)

22. **今** now　　いま　　今、一時です。It's now 1 o'clock.

今田〔いまだ〕さん

コン　　今月〔こんげつ〕this month

今週〔こんしゅう〕this week

☆　　今日〔きょう〕today

今年〔ことし〕this year

23. **年** year　　とし　　今年〔ことし〕this year

毎年〔まいとし〕every year

ネン　　毎年〔まいねん〕every year

来年〔らいねん〕next year

去年〔きょねん〕last year

一年〔いちねん〕one year

四年生〔よねんせい〕fourth grader

二〇〇三年〔にせんさんねん〕the year 2003

24. **私** I, me　　わたくし　　私は　中本です。I am Nakamoto.

わたし

25. **曜** day of the week　　ヨウ　　日曜日〔にちようび〕Sunday

月曜日〔げつようび〕Monday

火曜日〔かようび〕Tuesday

漢字　　464

水曜日〔すいようび〕Wednesday

木曜日〔もくようび〕Thursday

金曜日〔きんようび〕Friday

土曜日〔どようび〕Saturday

何曜日〔なんようび〕What day of the week?

3課

26. 上　above　うえ　上田〔うえだ〕さん

目上〔めうえ〕の人 superiors

27. 下　under　した　木下〔きのした〕さん

くだ　食べて　下さい。 Please eat.

28. 大　big　おお　大きい　人 a big person

大下〔おおした〕さん

大月〔おおつき〕さん

タイ　大変〔たいへん〕hard, difficult, very

ダイ　大学〔だいがく〕college

大好き like very much

29. 小　small　ちい(さい)　小さい　人 a small person

ショウ　小学生 elementary school student

小学校 elementary school

30. 夕　early evening　ゆう　夕方 late afternoon, early evening

31. 何　what　なに　何人〔なにじん〕What nationality?

なん　何人〔なんにん〕How many people?

何月〔なんがつ〕What month?

何曜日〔なんようび〕What day of the week?

何日〔なんにち〕What day of the month?

32. 中　inside, middle　なか　中本〔なかもと〕さん

中口〔なかぐち〕さん

今中〔いまなか〕さん

漢字

		チュウ	中学〔ちゅうがく〕 junior high school
			中学生〔ちゅうがくせい〕 junior high school student
			中国〔ちゅうごく〕 China
			中国人〔ちゅうごくじん〕 Chinese citizen
33.	外　outside	そと	家の　外〔うちの　そと〕 outside the house
		ガイ	外国〔がいこく〕 foreign country
			外国人〔がいこくじん〕 foreigner
			外国語〔がいこくご〕 foreign language

4課

34.	行　go	い（く）	行きます go
		コウ	旅行〔りょこう〕します travel
			銀行〔ぎんこう〕 bank
35.	来　come	き（ます）	来て　下さい。Please come.
			よく　出来ました。 He/she/they did well.
		く（る）	来る come
		こ（ない）	来ないで　下さい。Please do not come.
		ライ	来年〔らいねん〕 next year
			来月〔らいげつ〕 next month
			来週〔らいしゅう〕 next week
36.	子　child	こ	子ども child
37.	車　vehicle	くるま	車に　のる ride in a car
		シャ	自動車 car
			自転車 bicycle
			電車 electric train
			外車〔がいしゃ〕 foreign car

38. 学	study	ガク	学生〔がくせい〕student
			小学生〔しょうがくせい〕
			elementary school student
			中学生〔ちゅうがくせい〕
			junior high school student
			大学〔だいがく〕college
		ガッ	学校〔がっこう〕school
39. 校	school	コウ	学校〔がっこう〕school
			中学校〔ちゅうがっこう〕junior high school
			小学校〔しょうがっこう〕elementary school
			高校〔こうこう〕high school
			高校生〔こうこうせい〕high school student
40. 見	look, see	み（る）	見ます look
41. 良	is good	よい	良くないです is not good
42. 食	eat	た（べる）	食べましょう。 Let's eat.
		ショク	食事を します to have a meal
			夕食〔ゆうしょく〕supper
			外食〔がいしょく〕eating out

5課

43. 川	river	かわ	川口〔かわぐち〕さん
		がわ	小川〔おがわ〕さん
44. 山	mountain	やま	山口〔やまぐち〕さん
			山本〔やまもと〕さん
			大山〔おおやま〕さん
			小山〔こやま〕さん
			中山〔なかやま〕さん
			山下〔やました〕さん
		サン	富士山〔ふじさん or ふじやま〕Mt. Fuji

45. 出　go out　　　　で（る）　出かけます leave

出て　下さい。Please go out.

よく　出来ました。 He/she/they did well.

出口〔でぐち〕exit

だ（す）　出して　下さい。Please turn it in.

スピードを　出す speed up

46. 先　first, previous　セン　　先生 teacher

先月〔せんげつ〕last month

先週 last week

47. 生　be born　　　う（まれる）生まれました was born

person　　セイ　　先生〔せんせい〕teacher

学生〔がくせい〕college student

生徒〔せいと〕 K-12 student

48. 父　father　　　ちち　　父 one's own father

とう　　お父さん someone else's father

49. 母　mother　　　はは　　母 one's own mother

かあ　　お母さん someone else's mother

50. 毎　every　　　マイ　　毎日 every day

毎月〔まいつき〕every month

毎年〔まいねん or まいとし〕every year

毎週 every week

毎食〔まいしょく〕every meal

51. 書　write　　　か（く）　書いて　下さい。Please write.

writing　　ショ　　教科書 textbook

辞書 dictionary

図書館 library

書道 calligraphy

52. 手 hand　　て　　右手 right hand
　　　　　　　　　　　左手 left hand
　　　　　　　　　　　苦手 is weak at
　　　　　　　　☆　　上手〔じょうず〕 skillful
　　　　　　　　　　　下手〔へた〕 unskillful

53. 耳 ear　　みみ　　右耳 right ear
　　　　　　　　　　　左耳 left ear
　　　　　　　　　　　小さい　耳 small ears

54. 門 gate　　モン　　学校〔がっこう〕の　門 school gate
　　　　　　　　　　　家の　門 gateway to a house

55. 聞 listen, hear　　き（く）　　聞きます listen
　　　　　　　　　　　ブン　　新聞 newspaper

56. 女 female　　おんな　　女の　人〔おんなの　ひと〕 woman, lady
　　　　　　　　　　　女の　子〔おんなの　こ〕 girl
　　　　　　　　　　　女の　学生〔おんなの　がくせい〕 female
　　　　　　　　　　　student

57. 好 like　　す（き）　　大好〔だいす〕き like very much

58. 田 rice field　　た　　田中〔たなか〕さん
　　　　　　　　　　　中田〔なかた〕さん
　　　　　　　　　　　田口〔たぐち〕さん
　　　　　　　　　　だ　　金田〔かねだ〕さん
　　　　　　　　　　　山田〔やまだ〕さん
　　　　　　　　　　　上田〔うえだ〕さん

59. 男 male　　おとこ　　男の人 man
　　　　　　　　　　　男の子 boy
　　　　　　　　　　　男の学生 male student

漢字

60. 言 say   い（う）   もう 一度 言って 下さい。Please say it again.

61. 語 language   ゴ   日本語 〔にほんご〕 Japanese language

    英語〔えいご〕 English language

    外国語〔がいこくご〕 foreign language

    中国語〔ちゅうごくご〕 Chinese language

    何語〔なにご〕 What language?

    語学 〔ごがく〕 language study

62. 寺 temple   てら   寺に 行く go to the temple

    寺田〔てらだ〕 さん

    寺山〔てらやま〕 さん

    寺本〔てらもと〕 さん

    でら   山寺〔やまでら〕 temple in a mountain

    ジ   本願寺〔ほんがんじ〕 Honganji temple

63. 時 time, o'clock   とき   時々〔ときどき〕 sometimes

    ジ   何時〔なんじ〕 What time?

    一時間〔いちじかん〕 one hour

64. 間 between,   あいだ   学校〔がっこう〕と 家〔いえ〕の 間

    among,   between school and my house.

    interval   カン   時間〔じかん〕 time

    一時間〔いちじかん〕 one hour

65. 分 minute   わ(かる)   分かりません。I do not understand.

    フン   二分〔にふん〕 two minutes

    プン   六分〔ろっぷん〕 six minutes

    ブン   半分〔はんぶん〕 a half

66.	正	correct	ただ（しい）	正しいです is correct
			ショウ	お正月〔しょうがつ〕New Year
				正田〔しょうだ〕さん
67.	家	house	いえ	大きい　家 a big house
			カ	家族(ぞく) family
68.	々	[pluralizer]		時々〔ときどき〕sometimes
				木々〔きぎ〕trees
				山々〔やまやま〕mountains
				日々〔ひび〕days
				人々〔ひとびと〕people
				家々〔いえいえ〕houses

9課

69.	白	white	しろ	白い　シャツ a white shirt
				白木屋〔しろきや〕 *Shirokiya* department store
			ハク	白人〔はくじん〕Caucasian
70.	百	hundred	ヒャク	百人〔ひゃくにん〕100 people
			ビャク	三百〔さんびゃく〕300
			ピャク	六百〔ろっぴゃく〕600
				八百〔はっぴゃく〕800
71.	千	thousand	セン	二千〔にせん〕2,000
				八千〔はっせん〕8,000
			ゼン	三千〔さんぜん〕3,000
72.	万	ten thousand	マン	一万〔いちまん〕10,000
				十万〔じゅうまん〕100,000
				百万〔ひゃくまん〕one million
73.	方	person [polite]	かた	あの　方 that person [polite]
		alternative	ホウ	この　方が　好きです。I like this better.
				両方(りょう)〔りょうほう〕both

74. 玉	ball, coin	たま	玉田〔たまだ〕さん
			玉川〔たまかわ〕さん
			玉城〔たましろ〕さん
		だま	お年玉〔としだま〕 New Year's monetary gift
			十円玉〔じゅうえんだま〕￥10 coin
			目玉〔めだま〕 eyeball
75. 国	country	くに, ぐに	どこの　国 Which country?
			国本〔くにもと〕さん
		コク, ゴク	外国〔がいこく〕 foreign country
			韓国〔かんこく〕 Korea
			中国〔ちゅうごく〕 China
76. 安	cheap	やす（い）	安い　本〔やすい　ほん〕a cheap book
			安田〔やすだ〕さん
77. 高	expensive, high	たか（い）	高い　家〔たかい　いえ〕an expensive house
			高田〔たかた/たかだ〕さん
			高山〔たかやま〕さん
			高木〔たかき/たかぎ〕さん
		コウ	高校〔こうこう〕 high school
			高校生〔こうこうせい〕 high school student

10課

78. 牛	cow	うし	牛が　いる。There are cows.
		ギュウ	牛肉〔ぎゅうにく〕 beef
			牛乳〔ぎゅうにゅう〕 milk (cow)
79. 半	half	ハン	半分〔はんぶん〕a half
			五時半〔ごじはん〕5:30 (time)
*3. 手	hand	て	大きい　手 big hands
		シュ	バスケット選手 basketball player

			☆	上手〔じょうず〕skillful
				下手〔へた〕unskillful
80.	友	friend	とも	友達〔ともだち〕friend
				友子〔ともこ〕さん
81.	帰	return	かえ（る）	家へ 帰る〔うちへ かえる〕return home
82.	待	wait	ま（つ）	待って 下さい。 Please wait.
83.	持	have, hold	も（つ）	持って います。 I have it.
84.	米	rice	こめ	米を 買〔か〕う buy rice
				米屋 rice store
85.	番	number	バン	一番〔いちばん〕No. 1
86.	事	matter	こと	どんな 事 What kind of things?
			ごと	仕事〔しごと〕job
			ジ	食事〔しょくじ〕meal
				大事〔だいじ〕important
				事務所〔じむしょ〕office

| 11課 |

87.	雨	rain	あめ	雨が ふって います。 It is raining.
88.	電	electricity	デン	電話 telephone
				電気 electricity
				電車 electric train
89.	天	heaven	テン	天ぷら *tenpura*
				天どん *tenpura donburi*
90.	気	spirit	キ	天気〔てんき〕weather
				病気 illness
				合気道 *aikido*
				お気の毒に。 I'm sorry. [sympathy]
91.	会	meet	あ（う）	会いましょう。 Let's meet.
			カイ	会社〔かいしゃ〕company

473

社会〔しゃかい〕 social studies; society

教会〔きょうかい〕 church

92. 話 talk　はな（す）　話して　下さい。 Please speak.

はなし　お話〔はなし〕 story

ばなし　昔話〔むかしばなし〕 folk tale

ワ　電話〔でんわ〕 telephone

会話〔かいわ〕 conversation

93. 売 sell　う（る）　売って　いますか。 Are they selling?

94. 読 read　よ（む）　本を　読む read a book

13課

95. 右 right　みぎ　右手〔みぎて〕 right hand

右目〔みぎめ〕 right eye

右耳〔みぎみみ〕 left ear

右田〔みぎた〕さん

96. 左 left　ひだり　左手〔ひだりて〕 left hand

左目〔ひだりめ〕 left eye

左耳〔ひだりみみ〕 left ear

97. 入 put in　い（れる）　入れて　下さい。 Please put it in.

enter　はい（る）　入って　下さい。 Please enter.

いり　入口〔いりぐち〕 entrance

98. 物 thing　もの　食べ物〔たべもの〕 food

飲み物 drink

建物 building

着物 kimono (things to wear)

買い物 shopping

読み物〔よみもの〕 things to read

ブツ　動物 animal

動物園 zoo

漢字　　474

99.	名	name	な	名前 name
			メイ	有名〔ゆうめい〕 famous
100.	前	front, before	まえ	名前〔なまえ〕 name
				家の　前〔いえの　まえ〕 front of the house
				前田〔まえだ〕さん
				前川〔まえかわ〕さん
			ゼン	午前〔ごぜん〕 a.m.
101.	戸	door	と	戸を　閉めて　下さい。Please close the door.
				戸田〔とだ〕さん
				戸口〔とぐち〕さん
				戸川〔とがわ〕さん
			ど	木戸〔きど〕さん
102.	所	place	ところ	しずかな　所 a quiet place
			どころ	田所〔たどころ〕さん
			ショ	住所〔じゅうしょ〕 address
				事務所〔じむしょ〕 office
103.	近	near	ちか（い）	近い　所〔ちかい　ところ〕 a nearby place
				川近〔かわちか〕さん

| 14課 |

104.	立	stand	た（つ）	立って　下さい。Please stand.
			リツ	起立〔きりつ〕。Stand up.
105.	作	make	つく（る）	作って　下さい。Please make (it).
			サク	作文 composition
				作田〔さくだ〕さん
				作本〔さくもと〕さん
106.	肉	meat	にく	肉を　食べる〔にくを　たべる〕 eat meat
				牛肉〔ぎゅうにく〕 beef
				豚肉〔ぶたにく〕 pork

鳥肉〔とりにく〕chicken

焼き肉〔やきにく〕*yakiniku*

筋肉〔きんにく〕muscle

107.	魚	fish	さかな	
108.	多	many	おお（い）	人が　多いです。There are many people.
			タ	多分〔たぶん〕probably
109.	少	few	すく（ない）	人が　少ないです。There are few people.
			すこ（し）	少し　食べました。I ate a little.
110.	古	old	ふる（い）	古い　車〔ふるい　くるま〕old car
				古川〔ふるかわ〕さん
				古本〔ふるもと〕さん
				古田〔ふるた〕さん
111.	新	new	あたら（しい）	新しい　本〔あたらしい　ほん〕a new book
			シン	新聞〔しんぶん〕newspaper
				新幹線〔しんかんせん〕bullet train

15課

112.	才	~ years old	サイ	十六才〔じゅうろくさい〕16 years old
113.	心	heart, mind	こころ	心が　きれいです good-hearted person
			シン	心配しないで　下さい。Please do not worry.
114.	思	think	おも（う）	いいと　思います。I think it is good.
115.	休	rest, absent	やす（む）	学校を　休んで　います is absent from school
				お休み holiday, day off
116.	買	buy	か（う）	買いたいです。I want to buy it.
				買い物〔かいもの〕shopping
117.	早	early	はや（い）	早い　is early
				早見〔はやみ〕さん
				早川〔はやかわ〕さん

漢字

118. 自   oneself   ジ   自分〔じぶん〕の車 one's own car

                                        自動車〔じどうしゃ〕car

                                        自転車〔じてんしゃ〕bicycle

                                        自由〔じゆう〕free

119. 犬   dog   いぬ   白い 犬〔しろい いぬ〕 a white dog

120. 太   fat   ふと（る）   太って います is fat

121. 屋   store   や   本屋〔ほんや〕bookstore

                                        パン屋 bakery

                                        白木屋〔しろきや〕 *Shirokiya* department store

                                        部屋〔へや〕room

JAPANESE-ENGLISH & ENGLISH-JAPANESE WORD LIST

Abbreviations of Grammatical References

A		い Adjective: *atsui, takai, shiroi*
Adv		Adverb: *totemo, amari, sukoshi*
C		Copula: *desu, de, na*
D		Derivative
	Da	Adjectival Derivative: *-tai*
	Dv	Verbal Derivative: *masu, mashoo, masen*
Exp		Expression
N		Noun
	Na	な Adjective: *kirei, joozu, suki, yuumei*
	Nd	Dependent Noun: *-doru, -han*
	Ni	Interrogative Noun: *dare, doko, ikura*
	N	Noun: *hana, kuruma, enpitsu*
PN		Pre-Noun: *donna, kono, ano*
P		Particle: *de, e, ni*
Pc		Clause Particle: *kara, ga*
SI		Sentence Interjective: *anoo, eeto*
SP		Sentence Particle: *ka, yo, ne, nee*
V		Verb
	V1	Verb (group) 1: *ikimasu, hanashimasu, nomimasu*
	V2	Verb (group) 2: *tabemasu, nemasu, imasu*
	V3	Verb (group) 3 [irregular verb]: *kimasu, shimasu*

Japanese	Volume-Lesson #	Word type	English
<A>			
Aa ああ	2-13	SI	Oh!
abunai あぶない＝危ない	2-4	A	(is) dangerous
abura あぶら＝油	2-14	N	oil
achira あちら	2-5	N	over there [polite equiv. of あそこ]
	2-9	N	that one over there [polite equiv. of あれ]
agemasu あげます	1-15	V2	(to) give (to equal)
ai あい＝愛	2-15	N	love, affection
aida あいだ＝間	2-2	N	between
aishite iru あいしている＝愛している	2-15	V1	(to be in) love
aisukuriimu アイスクリーム	2-4	N	ice cream
aji あじ＝味	2-14	N	taste, flavor
aka あか＝赤	1-5	N	red
akachan あかちゃん＝赤ちゃん	2-2	N	baby
akai あかい＝赤い	1-6	A	(is) red
akarui あかるい＝明るい	2-11	A	(is) bright
Akemashite omedetoo (gozaimasu).	2-7	Exp	[New Year's greeting]
あけましておめでとうございます＝明けましておめでとうございます			
akeru あける＝開ける	1-13	V2	(to) open
akete kudasai あけてください	1-2	Exp	Please open.
＝開けて下さい			
aki あき＝秋	1-12	N	autumn, fall
amai あまい＝甘い	2-14	A	(is) sweet
amari + Neg. あまり + Neg.	1-5	Adv	(not) very
ame あめ＝雨	1-1	N	rain
ame あめ＝飴	1-2	N	candy
amerika アメリカ	1-3	N	U.S.
amerikajin アメリカじん＝アメリカ人	1-3	N	U.S. citizen
ana あな＝穴	2-11	N	hole
anata あなた	1-2	N	you
anatano あなたの＝あなたの	1-2	N	yours
ane あね＝姉	1-3	N	(my) older sister
ani あに＝兄	1-3	N	(my) older brother
ano ～ あの ～	1-2	PN	that ～ over there
anoo . . . あのう . . .	1-2	SI	let me see . . . well . . .
anzen あんぜん＝安全	2-4	Na	(is) safe
ao あお＝青	1-5	N	blue
	2-4	N	green [traffic lights]
aoi あおい＝青い	1-6	A	(is) blue
arau あらう＝洗う	2-7	V1	(to) wash

are あれ	1-1	N	that one over there
Arigatoo. ありがとう。	1-1	Exp	Thank you.
Arigatoo gozaimashita. ありがとうございました。 =有難うございました。	2-9	Exp	Thank you very much. [used after one has received something, or after a deed has been done.]
Arigatoo gozaimasu. ありがとうございます	1-1	Exp	Thank you very much.
aru ある	1-10	V1	there is (inanimate object)
	1-11	V1	have
aru ~ ある ~	2-11	PN	(a) certain ~
(place で) arubaito(o) suru アルバイト(を)する	2-2	V3	(to) work part-time (at ~)
aruku あるく=歩く	1-7	V1	(to) walk
asa あさ=朝	1-4	N	morning
asagohan あさごはん=朝御飯	1-4	N	breakfast
asatte あさって=明後日	1-11	N	(the) day after tomorrow
ashi あし=脚	1-6	N	leg
ashi あし=足	1-6	N	foot
ashita あした=明日	1-4	N	tomorrow
asobu あそぶ=遊ぶ	1-15	V1	(to) play, amuse [not used for sports & music]
asoko あそこ	1-2	N	over there
atama あたま=頭	1-6	N	head
atarashii あたらしい=新しい	1-10	A	(is) new
atatakai あたたかい=暖かい	1-14	A	(is) warm
ato ~ あと~=後~	2-10	PN	~ more
(~no) ato de (~の) あとで=(~の) 後で	1-12	P+N+P	after ~
atsui あつい=暑い	1-1	A	(is) hot [temperature]
atsui あつい=厚い	2-14	A	(is) thick
atsuku あつく=厚く	2-14	Adv	thick
atsuku suru あつくする=熱くする	2-14	V3	(to) make hot, (to) heat
(place で) (person に) au あう=会う	1-12	V1	(to) meet (someone) (at a place)
<B>			
baggu バッグ	2-3	N	bag
Baibai. バイバイ。	1-14	Exp	Good bye.
ban ばん=晩	1-4	N	evening
-ban -ばん=-番	2-10	Nd	Number -
bangohan ばんごはん=晩御飯	1-4	N	dinner, supper
-banme -ばんめ=-番目	2-13	Nd	[in order]
Banzai! ばんざい！=万歳！	2-10	Exp	Hurray!
baree(booru) バレー(ボール)	1-5	N	volleyball
basho ばしょ=場所	2-10	N	place, location
basu バス	1-7	N	bus

basuketto(booru) バスケット(ボール)	1-5	N	basketball
basutei バスてい＝バス停	2-13	N	bus stop
beddo ベッド	1-10	N	bed
bengoshi べんごし＝弁護士	1-3	N	lawyer
benkyoo (o) suru べんきょう(を)する＝勉強(を)する			
	1-4	V3	(to) study
bentoo べんとう＝弁当	1-14	N	box lunch
bideo ビデオ	1-4	N	video
biiru ビール	2-4	N	beer
bijutsu びじゅつ＝美術	1-11	N	art
bijutsukan びじゅつかん＝美術館	2-13	N	art museum
binboo びんぼう＝貧乏	2-11	Na	poor
boku ぼく＝僕	1-1	N	I [used by males]
bokutachi ぼくたち＝僕達	1-12	N	we [used by males]
boorupen ボールペン	1-2	N	ballpoint pen
booshi ぼうし＝帽子	1-2	N	cap, hat
buta ぶた＝豚	1-10	N	pig
butaniku ぶたにく＝豚肉	2-14	N	pork
byooin びょういん＝病院	1-3	N	hospital
byooki びょうき＝病気	1-12	N	illness, sickness

\<C\>

chairo ちゃいろ＝茶色	1-5	N	brown
chairoi ちゃいろい＝茶色い	1-6	A	(is) brown
chakuseki ちゃくせき＝着席	1-1	Exp	Sit.
- chan - ちゃん	2-2	Nd	[Used instead of - さん when addressing or referring to young, small or cute animals or children.]
chichi ちち＝父	1-3	N	(my) father
chichi no hi ちちのひ＝父の日	1-15	N	Father's Day
chigau ちがう＝違う	2-2	V1	(is) wrong, (to) differ
chiimu チーム	1-12	N	team
chiisai ちいさい＝小さい	1-6	A	(is) small
chika ちか＝地下	2-9	N	basement
chikai ちかい＝近い	1-10	A	(is) near, close
chikaku ちかく＝近く	2-2	N	vicinity, nearby
chikara ちから＝力	2-11	N	power, strength, ability
chikatetsu ちかてつ＝地下鉄	1-7	N	subway
Chikoku desu. ちこくです。＝遅刻です。	1-1	Exp	(He/She) is tardy, late.
chippu チップ	2-5	N	tip
chizu ちず＝地図	2-13	N	map
chokoreeto チョコレート	2-5	N	chocolate
chotto ちょっと	1-4	Adv	a little [more informal than すこし]

Chotto matte kudasai. ちょっとまってください。＝ちょっと待って下さい。
　　　　　　　　　　　　　　　　　1-1　Exp　Please wait a minute.
Chotto ukagaimasu ga . . . ちょっとうかがいますが . . .
　　　　　　　　　　　　　　　　　2-13　Exp　I have a question.
chuugaku ちゅうがく＝中学　　　　　1-3　N　　intermediate school
chuugaku ichinensei ちゅうがくいちねんせい＝中学一年生
　　　　　　　　　　　　　　　　　1-3　N　　seventh grader
chuugaku ninensei ちゅうがくにねんせい＝中学二年生
　　　　　　　　　　　　　　　　　1-3　N　　eighth grader
chuugaku sannensei ちゅうがくさんねんせい＝中学三年生
　　　　　　　　　　　　　　　　　1-3　N　　freshman, ninth grader
chuugakusei ちゅうがくせい＝中学生　1-3　N　　intermediate school student
chuugoku ちゅうごく＝中国　　　　　1-3　N　　China
chuugokugo ちゅうごくご＝中国語　　1-4　N　　Chinese language
chuumon (o) suru ちゅうもん(を)する＝注文(を)する
　　　　　　　　　　　　　　　　　2-5　V3　　(to) order
(Go)chuumon wa. ごちゅうもんは。＝御注文は。
　　　　　　　　　　　　　　　　　2-5　Exp　What is your order? May I take your order?
chuushajoo ちゅうしゃじょう＝駐車場　2-13　N　　parking lot

\<D\>

da だ　　　　　　　　　　　　　　　2-11　C　　[plain form of a copula です]
- dai - だい＝ - 台　　　　　　　　　10-3　Nd　[counter for mechanized goods]
daidokoro だいどころ＝台所　　　　2-14　N　　kitchen
daigaku だいがく＝大学　　　　　　1-12　N　　college, university
daigakusei だいがくせい＝大学生　　1-12　N　　college student
daiji だいじ＝大事　　　　　　　　1-12　Na　important
daijoobu だいじょうぶ＝大丈夫　　　1-12　Na　all right
daikirai だいきらい＝大嫌い　　　　1-5　Na　dislike a lot, hate
daisuki だいすき＝大好き　　　　　1-5　Na　like very much, love
daitai だいたい　　　　　　　　　　2-5　Adv　generally
dakara だから　　　　　　　　　　　2-11　SI　Therefore [Informal]
～dake ～だけ　　　　　　　　　　　2-3　Nd　only ～
dame だめ　　　　　　　　　　　　　1-2　Na　no good
dansu ダンス　　　　　　　　　　　1-5　N　　dance, dancing
dare だれ＝誰　　　　　　　　　　　1-3　Ni　who?
Dashite kudasai. だしてください。＝出して下さい。
　　　　　　　　　　　　　　　　　1-2　Exp　Please turn in.
dasu だす＝出す　　　　　　　　　　1-13　V1　(to) turn in, hand in
　　　　　　　　　　　　　　　　　2-4　V1　　(to) extend out, submit, take out
(gomi o) dasu ゴミをだす＝ゴミを出す　2-7　V1　(to) take out (the garbage)
datta だった　　　　　　　　　　　2-11　C　　[plain form of a copula でした]
[tool] de で　　　　　　　　　　　　1-14　P　　by, with, on, in [tool particle]
(place) de で (+ action verb)　　　　1-4　P　　at, in (a place)

J-E　　　　　　　　　　　482

de で	1-14	C	[Te form of copula です]
(counter) de で	1-14	P	[totalizing particle]
(reason) de で	2-6	P	because of (reason)
(~ no naka ~のなか＝~の中) de で	2-9	P	among ~
~ de で	2-9	P	between, among
(transportation) de で	1-7	P	by (transportation facility)
deguchi でぐち＝出口	2-13	N	exit
(place を/から) dekakeru でかける＝出かける			
	2-4	V2	(to) leave, go out (from a place)
(~が) dekimashita できました＝出来ました			
	2-14	V2	(~ is) ready, (~ is) done
(~ が) dekiru できる＝出来る	2-6	V2	(be) able to do ~
Demo でも	1-4	SI	But [used at the beginning of a sentence]
densha でんしゃ＝電車	1-7	N	electric train
denwa でんわ＝電話	1-4	N	telephone
denwa o kakeru でんわをかける＝電話をかける			
	2-6	V2	(to) make a phone call
denwabangoo でんわばんごう＝電話番号	1-15	N	telephone number
depaato デパート	1-7	N	department store
(shiai ni) deru (しあいに)でる＝(試合に)出る			
	2-10	V2	(to) participate in a (sports) game
(place を) deru でる＝出る	2-4	V2	(to) leave (a place)
-deshoo でしょう [falling intonation]	2-7	C	probably ~
-deshoo でしょう [rising intonation]	2-7	C	Isn't it ~?
desu です	1-1	C	am, is, are
Desukara ですから	2-11	SI	Therefore [formal]
Dewa では	1-14	Exp	Well then [formal]
dezaato デザート	2-14	N	dessert
dezain デザイン	2-9	N	design
- do - ど＝-度	2-6	Nd	- degree(s), - time(s)
doa ドア	1-10	N	door
dochira どちら	2-5	Ni	where? [polite equiv. of どこ]
	2-9	Ni	which (one of two)? [polite]
dochiramo + neg. どちらも + neg.	2-9	N	neither, not either
doitsu ドイツ	1-3	N	Germany
doitsugo ドイツご＝ドイツ語	1-4	N	German language
dokidoki suru ドキドキする	2-10	V3	(is) excited, (is) nervous
doko どこ	1-3	Ni	where?
dokoemo + neg. どこへも + neg.	7-5	Ni+P	(not to) anywhere
dokusho どくしょ＝読書	1-5	N	reading
donna ~ どんな~	1-5	PN	what kind of ~?
dono - どの -	1-13	Nd	which ~?
donogurai どのぐらい	2-6	Ni	about how long/far/often?

Donogurai arimasu ka. どのぐらい　ありますか。	2-13	Exp	How far is it? [distance]
Donogurai desu ka. どのぐらいですか。	2-13	Exp	How long/far is it?
Donogurai kakarimasu ka. どのぐらい　かかりますか。			
	2-13	Exp	How long does it take? [time]
Doo desu ka. どうですか。	1-11	Exp	How is it? [informal]
Doo shimashita ka. どうしましたか。	1-12	Exp	What happened?
doobutsuen どうぶつえん＝動物園	2-13	N	zoo
Doo itashimashite. どういたしまして。	1-1	Exp	You are welcome.
Doomo どうも。	1-1	Exp	Thank you.
dooshite? どうして?	1-11	Ni	why?
Doozo kochira e. どうぞこちらへ。	2-5	Exp	This way, please.
Doozo yoroshiku. どうぞ　よろしく。	1-1	N	Nice to meet you.
doraibaa ドライバー	2-4	N	driver
dore どれ	1-13	Ni	which one?
	2-9	Ni	which one (of three or more)?
- doru - ドル	1-13	Nd	- dollar(s)
dotchi どっち	2-9	Ni	which (one of two)? [informal]
doyoobi どようび＝土曜日	1-7	N	Saturday

<E>

e え＝絵	1-5	N	painting, drawing
(place) e へ	1-7	P	to (place)
Ee ええ	1-1	SI	Yes [informal]
Eeto . . . ええと . . .	1-2	SI	Let me see . . . Well . . .
eiga えいが＝映画	1-5	N	movie
eigakan えいがかん＝映画館	2-3	N	movie theater
eigo えいご＝英語	1-4	N	English
eki えき＝駅	2-13	N	train station
emu-saizu エムサイズ	1-14	N	medium (size)
- en - えん＝ - 円	1-13	Nd	- yen
enjinia エンジニア	1-3	N	engineer
enpitsu えんぴつ＝鉛筆	1-2	N	pencil
enpitsukezuri えんぴつけずり＝鉛筆削り	1-10	N	pencil sharpener
erai えらい＝偉い	2-11	A	(is) great (person)
eru-saizu エルサイズ	1-14	N	large (size)
esu-saizu エスサイズ	1-14	N	small (size)
E えっ	2-11	SI	Huh?

<F>

fooku フォーク	1-14	N	fork
fukitobasu ふきとばす＝吹き飛ばす	2-11	V1	(to) blow away
fuku ふく＝服	2-3	N	clothing
Fukuoka ふくおか＝福岡	2-1	N	Fukuoka
fukuro ふくろ＝袋	2-9	N	(paper) bag
- fun - ふん＝ - 分	1-7	Nd	- minute(s)

fune ふね＝船	1-7	N	boat, ship
furaidopoteto フライドポテト	1-14	N	french fries
furansu フランス	1-3	N	France
furansugo フランスご＝フランス語	1-4	N	French language
furu ふる＝降る	2-7	V1	(rain, snow) fall
furui ふるい＝古い	1-10	A	(is) old (not for person's age)
futago ふたご＝双児	2-15	N	twin
futari ふたり＝二人	1-3	N	two (persons)
futatsu ふたつ＝二つ	1-2	N	two [general counter]
futoru ふとる＝太る	1-6	V1	to gain weight
futotte imasu ふとっています＝太っています	1-6	V1	(is) fat
futsuka ふつか＝二日	1-11	N	(the) second day of the month
futtobooru フットボール	1-5	N	football
fuusen ふうせん＝風船	1-15	N	balloon
fuyu ふゆ＝冬	1-12	N	winter

<G>

(Sentence) ga... が...	2-6	Ps	[Softens the statement.]
(Sentence 1) ga が、(Sentence 2)	1-5	Pc	(S1), but (S2)
(subject) ga が	1-7	P	[subject particle]
gaikokugo がいこくご＝外国語	1-11	N	foreign language
gakkoo がっこう＝学校	1-3	N	school
gakusei がくせい＝学生	1-3	N	student [college]
gamu ガム	2-3	N	gum
ganbaru がんばる＝頑張る	1-12	V1	(to) do one's best
Ganbatte. がんばって。＝頑張って。	1-12	V1	Good luck.
gareeji ガレージ	1-10	N	garage
garigari ガリガリ	2-11	Adv	chew away, gnaw [onomatopoetic]
- gatsu umare - がつうまれ＝ - 月生まれ	1-3	Nd	born in (- month)
～ gawa ～がわ＝～側	2-13	Nd	(～) side
geemu ゲーム	1-15	N	game
geemu o suru ゲームをする	1-15	V3	(to) play a game
geki げき＝劇	2-12	N	(stage) play
geki o suru げきをする＝劇をする	2-12	V3	(to) give/put on a (stage) play
(o)genki (お)げんき＝(お)元気	1-1	Na	fine, healthy [polite]
(O)genki desu ka. おげんきですか。＝お元気ですか。			
	1-1	Exp	How are you?
getsuyoobi げつようび＝月曜日	1-7	N	Monday
gin ぎん＝銀	2-15	N	silver
giniro ぎんいろ＝銀色	1-5	N	silver (color)
ginkoo ぎんこう＝銀行	2-2	N	bank
gitaa ギター	1-5	N	guitar
go ご＝五	1-1	N	five
go-juu ごじゅう＝五十	1-1	N	fifty

gochisoo (o) suru ごちそう(を)する	2-5	V3	(to) treat (someone)
Gochisoosama ごちそうさま＝御馳走様	1-14	Exp	[after a meal]
gogatsu ごがつ＝五月	1-3	N	May
gogo ごご＝午後	1-7	N	p. m.
gohan ごはん＝ご飯	1-4	N	(cooked) rice
gokiburi ごきぶり	1-10	N	cockroach
gomi ごみ	1-2	N	rubbish
gomibako ごみばこ＝ごみ箱	1-10	N	trash can
- goro - ごろ	1-7	Nd	about (time)
gorufu ゴルフ	1-5	N	golf
goryooshin ごりょうしん＝御両親	2-2	N	(someone else's) parents [polite]
gozen ごぜん＝午前	1-7	N	a. m.
guai ga warui ぐあいがわるい＝具合が悪い	2-6	A	condition is bad, feel sick
～ gurai ～ぐらい	1-13	Nd	about ～ [Not used for time.]
gurei グレイ	1-5	N	grey
gyuuniku ぎゅうにく＝牛肉	2-14	N	beef
gyuunyuu ぎゅうにゅう＝牛乳	1-4	N	(cow's) milk

<H>

ha は＝歯	1-6	N	tooth
hachi はち＝八	1-1	N	eight
hachijuu はちじゅう＝八十	1-1	N	eighty
hachigatsu はちがつ＝八月	1-3	N	August
haha はは＝母	1-3	N	(my) mother
haha no hi ははのひ＝母の日	1-15	N	Mother's Day
Hai doozo. はい、どうぞ。	1-2	Exp	Here, you are.
Hai. はい。	1-3	Exp	Yes. [used in response to roll call]
	1-6	SI	Yes
Hai, chiizu. はい、チーズ。	1-15	Exp	Say, "Cheese."
Hai, piisu. はい、ピース。	1-15	Exp	Say, "Peace."
(place に) hairu はいる＝入る	2-4	V1	(to) enter (a place)
(something が) hajimaru はじまる＝始まる	2-10	V1	(something will) begin, start
hajime ni はじめに＝始めに	2-14	Adv	(at the) beginning
Hajimemashite. はじめまして。	1-1	Exp	How do you do?
Hajimemashoo. はじめましょう。＝始めましょう。			
	1-4	Exp	Let's begin.
(something を) hajimeru はじめる＝始める	2-10	V2	(someone will) start, begin (something)
hajimete はじめて＝始めて	2-7	N	(for the) first time
hako はこ＝箱	2-9	N	box
haku はく＝履く	2-3	V1	(to) wear [below the waist]
- han - はん＝ - 半	1-7	Nd	- half
hana はな＝花	1-10	N	flower
hana はな＝鼻	1-6	N	nose
hanabi o suru はなびをする＝花火をする	2-7	V3	(to do) fireworks

hanashichuu はなしちゅう＝話し中	2-6	Exp	line is busy
hanasu はなす＝話す	1-4	V1	(to) speak, talk
hanaya はなや＝花屋	1-13	N	flower shop
hanbaagaa ハンバーガー	1-14	N	hamburger
hanbun ni はんぶんに＝半分に	2-14	Adv	(in) half
harau はらう＝払う	2-5	V1	(to) pay
hare はれ＝晴れ	2-7	N	clear (weather)
haru はる＝春	1-12	N	spring
(o) hashi (お)はし＝(お)箸	1-14	N	chopsticks
hashi はし＝橋	2-13	N	bridge
hashiru はしる＝走る	1-12	V1	(to) run
hatachi はたち＝二十歳	1-3	N	twenty years old
(place で) hataraku はたらく＝働く	2-2	V1	work (at ～)
hatsuka はつか＝二十日	1-11	N	(the) twentieth day of the month
hayai はやい＝早い	1-7	A	(is) early
Hayaku. はやく。＝速く。	1-4	Exp	Hurry!
hayaku はやく＝早く	1-12	Adv	early [used with a verb]
hayaku はやく＝速く	2-4	Adv	fast, quickly
(Dic./NAI) hazu desu はずです	2-6	Nd	I expect that he/she will do/will not do. He/She is expected to do/not to do.
hen へん＝変	2-6	Na	strange, weird, unusual
hen へん＝辺	2-13	N	area
heta へた＝下手	1-5	Na	unskillful, (be) poor at
heya へや＝部屋	1-10	N	room
hi ひ＝日	1-15	N	day
hidari ひだり＝左	2-2	N	left side
hidoi ひどい＝酷い	1-11	A	(is) terrible
higashi ひがし＝東	2-1	N	east
hige ひげ＝髭	1-6	N	beard, moustache
- hiki - ひき＝ - 匹	1-10	Nd	[counter for small animals]
hikooki ひこうき＝飛行機	1-7	N	airplane
hiku ひく＝弾く	2-6	V1	(to) play (a string instrument)
hikui ひくい＝低い	1-6	A	(is) short (height)
hima ひま＝暇	2-15	Na	(is) free (time)
hiroi ひろい＝広い	1-10	A	(is) wide, spacious
Hiroshima ひろしま＝広島	2-1	N	Hiroshima
(o)hiru (お)ひる＝(お)昼	1-4	N	daytime
hirugohan ひるごはん＝昼御飯	1-4	N	lunch
hito ひと＝人	1-10	N	person
hitori ひとり＝一人	1-3	N	one (person)
hitorikko ひとりっこ＝一人っ子	2-15	N	only child
hitotsu ひとつ＝一つ	1-2	N	one [general counter]
～ hodo + Neg. ほど + Neg.	2-9	P	(not) as ～ as

hoka ほか	2-9	N	other
Hoka ni nani ka. ほかになにか。＝ほかに何か。	2-5	Exp	Anything else?
Hokkaidoo ほっかいどう＝北海道	2-1	N	Hokkaido
hon ほん＝本	1-2	N	book
Honshuu ほんしゅう＝本州	2-1	N	Honshu
hontoo ほんとう＝本当	1-3	N	true
Hontoo desu ka. ほんとうですか。＝本当ですか。	2-3	Exp	(Is it) true/real?
hontoo ni ほんとうに＝本当に	2-3	Adv	really, truly
honya ほんや＝本屋	1-13	N	bookstore
(〜 の) hoo ほう＝方	2-9	N	alternative
hoomuruumu ホームルーム	1-11	N	homeroom
hoomusutei o suru ホームステイをする	2-2	V3	do a homestaty
(something が) hoshii ほしい＝欲しい	1-11	A	want (something)
hottodoggu ホットドッグ	1-14	N	hotdog
hyaku ひゃく＝百	1-1	N	hundred
hyaku-man ひゃくまん＝百万	1-13	N	(one) million
<I>			
- i - い＝- 位	2-15	Nd	[rank]
ichi いち＝一	1-1	N	one
ichiban いちばん＝一番	2-9	Adv	the most
ichigatsu いちがつ＝一月	1-3	N	January
ichigo いちご＝苺	2-14	N	strawberry
ie いえ＝家	2-2	N	house
ii いい	1-2	A	(is) good
Ii desu nee. いいですねえ。	1-11	Exp	How nice! [on a future event]
Iie いいえ	1-1	SI	No [formal]
Iie, kekkoo desu. いいえ、けっこうです。	1-14	Exp	No, thank you.
Ikaga desu ka. いかがですか。＝如何ですか。	1-13	Ni	how about 〜? [Polite form of どうですか]
ike いけ＝池	1-10	N	pond
ikemasen いけません	2-3	V2	won't do, must not do
iku いく＝行く	1-7	V1	(to) go
(o)ikura (お)いくら	1-13	Ni	how much?
ikutsu いくつ	1-2	Ni	how many? [general counter]
(o)ikutsu (お)いくつ	1-3	Ni	how old?
ima いま＝今	1-3	N	now
iru いる	1-10	V2	there is (animate object)
imooto いもうと＝妹	1-3	N	(my) younger sister
imootosan いもうとさん＝妹さん	1-3	N	(someone's) younger sister
inu いぬ＝犬	1-10	N	dog
Irasshaimase. いらっしゃいませ。	2-5	Exp	Welcome.
irassharu いらっしゃる [いらっしゃいます]	2-6	V1	(to) exist, be (for animate) [polite equiv. of います]

(〜に) ireru いれる＝入れる	2-9	V2	(to) put in 〜
iriguchi いりぐち＝入口	2-13	N	entrance
iro いろ＝色	1-5	N	color
iroiro いろいろ	2-9	Na	various
iru いる＝要る	1-14	V1	need
isha いしゃ＝医者	1-3	N	(medical) doctor [informal]
isogashii いそがしい＝忙しい	1-7	A	(is) busy
issho ni いっしょに＝一緒に	1-4	Adv	together
isshookenmei いっしょうけんめい＝一生懸命	2-11	Adv	(with one's) utmost effort
isu いす＝椅子	1-10	N	chair
Itadakimasu. いただきます。	1-14	Exp	[before a meal]
itai いたい＝痛い	1-12	A	(is) painful, sore
itoko いとこ	1-15	N	cousin
itokonnyaku いとこんにゃく＝糸こんにゃく	2-14	N	shredded *konnyaku* [grey or transparent tuber root gelatin]
itsu いつ	1-7	Ni	when?
itsuka いつか＝五日	1-11	N	(the) fifth day of the month
itsumo いつも	1-4	Adv	always
itsutsu いつつ＝五つ	1-2	N	five [general counter]
iu いう＝言う	1-13	V1	(to) say
iya(tt) いや(っ)	2-11	SI	No [stronger negation than いいえ]
iyaringu イヤリング	2-3	N	earrings
<J>			
Ja じゃ	1-14	Exp	Well then [informal]
jaketto ジャケット	1-13	N	jacket
jama じゃま＝邪魔	1-6	Na	hindrance, nuisance, is in the way
- ji - じ＝- 時	1-7	Nd	- o'clock
jibun じぶん＝自分	2-15	N	oneself
jidoosha じどうしゃ＝自動車	1-7	N	car, vehicle
jikan じかん＝時間	2-10	N	time
- jikan - じかん＝- 時間	2-6	Nd	- hour(s)
jikoshookai(o) suru じこしょうかい(を)する＝自己紹介(を)する			
	2-2	V3	(to) do a self-introduction
jimusho じむしょ＝事務所	1-10	N	office
jinja じんじゃ＝神社	2-7	N	shrine (Shinto)
jisho じしょ＝辞書	1-2	N	dictionary
jitensha じてんしゃ＝自転車	1-7	N	bicycle
jiyuu じゆう＝自由	2-3	Na	free, liberal
jogingu ジョギング	1-5	N	jogging
joodan じょうだん＝冗談	2-10	N	(a) joke
joozu じょうず＝上手	1-5	Na	skillful, (be) good at
jugyoo じゅぎょう＝授業	1-11	N	class, instruction
juu じゅう＝十	1-1	N	ten

juu-go じゅうご=十五	1-1	N	fifteen
juu-hachi じゅうはち=十八	1-1	N	eighteen
juu-ichi じゅういち=十一	1-1	N	eleven
juu-ku じゅうく=十九	1-1	N	nineteen
juu-kyuu じゅうきゅう=十九	1-1	N	nineteen
juu-man じゅうまん=十万	1-13	N	hundred thousand
juu-nana じゅうなな=十七	1-1	N	seventeen
juu-ni じゅうに=十二	1-1	N	twelve
juu-roku じゅうろく=十六	1-1	N	sixteen
juu-san じゅうさん=十三	1-1	N	thirteen
juu-shi じゅうし=十四	1-1	N	fourteen
juu-shichi じゅうしち=十七	1-1	N	seventeen
juu-yokka じゅうよっか=十四日	1-11	N	(the) fourteenth day of the month
juu-yon じゅうよん =十四	1-1	N	fourteen
juugatsu じゅうがつ=十月	1-3	N	October
juuichigatsu じゅういちがつ=十一月	1-3	N	November
juunigatsu じゅうにがつ=十二月	1-3	N	December
juusho じゅうしょ=住所	1-15	N	address
juusu ジュース	1-4	N	juice
<K>			
ka か	1-1	SP	[question particle]
kabe かべ=壁	2-11	N	wall
kaburu かぶる	2-3	V2	(to) wear [on or draped over the head]
kado かど=角	2-4	N	corner
kaeru かえる=帰る	1-7	V1	(to) return (to a place)
kaesu かえす=返す	2-5	V1	(to) return (something)
kafeteria カフェテリア	1-4	N	cafeteria
kagaku かがく=科学	1-11	N	science
- kagetsu - かげつ= - か月	2-6	Nd	- month(s)
kagi かぎ=鍵	2-4	N	key
kaimono かいもの=買い物	1-7	N	shopping
kaimono (o) suru かいもの(を)する=買い物(を)する	1-7	V3	(to) shop
kaisha かいしゃ=会社	1-7	N	company
kaishain かいしゃいん=会社員	1-3	N	company employee
kakaru かかる	2-9	V1	(to) require, to take (time)
kakeru かける	2-3	V2	(to) wear [glasses]
kaku かく=書く	1-4	V1	(to) write
(えを) kaku かく=描く	2-15	V1	(to) draw, paint a picture
kakusu かくす=隠す	2-11	V1	(to) hide (something)
kamaimasen かまいません	2-3	V1	(I) do not mind if . . .
kamera カメラ	1-15	N	camera
kami かみ=紙	1-2	N	paper
kami (no ke) かみ(のけ)=髪(の毛)	1-6	N	hair

kamoku かもく＝科目	1-11	N	subject
(gamu o) kamu （ガムを）かむ	2-3	V1	(to) chew gum
kanashii かなしい＝悲しい	1-11	A	(is) sad
(o)kane（お）かね＝(お)金	1-2	N	money
(o)kanemochi（お）かねもち＝(お)金持ち	2-11	N	rich person
(o)kanjoo（お）かんじょう＝(お)勘定	2-5	N	(a) check, bill
kankoku かんこく＝韓国	1-3	N	Korea
kankokugo かんこくご＝韓国語	1-4	N	Korean language
kansha (o) suru かんしゃ（を）する＝感謝（を）する	2-15	V3	(to) appreciate, thank
kao かお＝顔	1-6	N	face
～kara ～から	1-11	P	from ～
～kara ～made ～から ～まで	2-13	P	from ～ to ～
(sentence) kara から	11-4	Pc	because ～ , since ～ , ～ so
karada からだ＝体	1-6	N	body
karai からい＝辛い	2-14	A	(is) salty, (is) spicy
kareeraisu カレーライス	2-5	N	curry rice
kariru かりる＝借りる	2-3	V2	(to) borrow, (to) rent (from)
kasu かす＝貸す	1-14	V1	(to) lend, (to) rent (to)
～kata ～かた＝ ～方	1-10	Nd	person [polite form of ひと]
(Verb stem +) kata かた＝方	2-14	N	how to do ～
katazukeru かたづける＝片付ける	2-14	V2	(to) clean up, put away
katsu かつ＝勝つ	1-12	V1	(to) win
Katta! Katta! かった！かった！＝勝った！勝った！	2-10	Exp	(We) won! (We) won!
kau かう＝買う	1-13	V1	(to) buy
kawa かわ＝川	1-7	N	river
kawaii かわいい＝可愛い	1-6	A	(is) cute
Kawaisoo ni. かわいそうに＝可愛そうに	1-12	Exp	How pitiful.
Kawarimashita かわりました。＝代わりました。	2-6	Exp	It's me. [lit., We've changed over.]
kawaru かわる＝代わる	2-6	V1	(to) change over
kayoobi かようび＝火曜日	1-7	N	Tuesday
kaze かぜ＝風邪	1-12	N	(a) cold
kaze かぜ＝風	2-7	N	wind
kaze o hiku かぜをひく＝風邪を引く	2-6	V1	(to) catch a cold
kazoku かぞく＝家族	1-3	N	(my) family
(go)kazoku（ご）かぞく＝(御)家族	1-3	N	(someone's) family
～kedo けど	2-6	Pc	Although ～
keikan けいかん＝警官	2-4	N	police officer
(person と) kekkon (o) suru けっこん（を）する＝結婚（を）する	2-2	V3	(is) married (to ～)
kenka (o) suru けんか（を）する＝喧嘩（を）する	2-4	V3	(to) fight
～keredo けれど	2-6	Pc	Although ～
kesa けさ＝今朝	1-12	N	this morning

keshigomu けしごむ＝消しゴム	1-2	N	eraser [rubber]
kesshite + Neg. けっして＋ Neg.	2-4	Adv	never
ki き＝木	1-10	N	tree
ki o tsukeru きをつける＝気をつける	2-3	V2	(to be) careful
kibishii きびしい＝厳しい	1-6	A	(is) strict
kiiro きいろ＝黄色	1-5	N	yellow
kiiroi きいろい＝黄色い	1-6	A	(is) yellow
kikoemasen きこえません＝聞こえません	1-2	V2	cannot hear
kikoemasu きこえます＝聞こえます	1-2	V2	can hear
(something が) kikoeru きこえる＝聞こえる	2-3	V2	～ can be heard
kiku きく＝聞く	1-4	V1	(to) listen, hear
(person に) kiku きく＝聞く	2-3	V1	(to) ask someone
kimochi ga ii きもちがいい＝気持ちがいい	2-14	A	(is) pleasant, comfortable
kimochi ga warui きもちがわるい＝気持ちが悪い	2-14	A	(is) unpleasant, uncomfortable
kin きん＝金	2-15	N	gold
kiniro きんいろ＝金色	1-5	N	gold (color)
(O)kinodoku ni. (お)きのどくに。＝(お)気の毒に。	2-6	Exp	I am sorry. [Sympathy - formal]
kinoo きのう＝昨日	1-4	N	yesterday
kinyoobi きんようび＝金曜日	1-7	N	Friday
kippu きっぷ＝切符	1-15	N	ticket
kirai きらい＝嫌い	1-5	Na	dislike
kirei きれい	1-6	Na	pretty, clean, neat, nice
kirei ni suru きれいにする	2-14	V3	(to) make clean, (to) clean
kirisutokyoo キリストきょう＝キリスト教	2-7	N	Christianity
Kiritsu. きりつ。＝起立。	1-1	Exp	Stand.
kiru きる＝切る	2-14	V1	(to) cut, slice
kiru きる＝着る	2-3	V2	(to) wear [above the waist or on the entire body]
kisoku きそく＝規則	2-3	N	rule, regulation
kissaten きっさてん＝喫茶店	1-13	N	coffee shop
kita きた＝北	2-1	N	north
kitanai きたない	1-6	A	dirty, messy
- ko - こ＝- 個	2-5	Nd	[general counter]
kochira こちら	1-3	N	this one [polite equiv. of これ to introduce a person]
	2-5	N	here [polite equiv. of ここ]
	2-9	N	this one [polite equiv. of これ]
kodomo こども＝子供	1-10	N	child
koe こえ＝声	1-6	N	voice
koko ここ	1-2	N	here
kokonoka ここのか＝九日	1-11	N	(the) ninth day of the month
kokonotsu ここのつ＝九つ	1-2	N	nine [general counter]
kokoro こころ＝心	1-6	N	heart

komu こむ＝込む	2-13	V1	(to) get crowded
konban こんばん＝今晩	1-7	N	tonight
Konban wa. こんばんは。＝今晩は。	1-7	Exp	Good evening.
konbini コンビニ	2-13	N	convenience store
konde iru こんでいる＝込んでいる	2-13	V1	(is) crowded
kongetsu こんげつ＝今月	1-12	N	this month
konkuuru コンクール	2-15	N	competition [music]
Konnichi wa. こんにちは。	1-1	Exp	Hello. Hi.
kono naka de このなかで＝この中で	2-9	PN+N+P	among these
kono ～ この ～	1-2	PN	this ～
konpyuutaa コンピューター	1-4	N	computer
konsaato コンサート	15-2	N	concert
konshuu こんしゅう＝今週	1-11	N	this week
Koobe こうべ＝神戸	2-1	N	Kobe
kooen こうえん＝公園	2-2	N	park
koohii コーヒー	1-4	N	coffee
kookoo こうこう＝高校	1-3	N	high school
kookoo ichinensei こうこういちねんせい＝高校一年生	1-3	N	sophomore, tenth grader
kookoo ninensei こうこうにねんせい＝高校二年生	1-3	N	junior, eleventh grader
kookoo sannensei こうこうさんねんせい＝高校三年生	1-3	N	senior, twelfth grader
kookoosei こうこうせい＝高校生	1-3	N	high school student
koora コーラ	1-4	N	cola (drink)
koosaten こうさてん＝交差点	2-13	N	intersection
kooshuudenwa こうしゅうでんわ＝公衆電話	2-13	N	public phone
kootsuujiko こうつうじこ＝交通事故	2-4	N	traffic accident
koppu コップ	1-14	N	cup
kore これ	1-1	N	this one
korekara これから	1-14	SI	from now on
(time) koro ころ	1-7	Nd	about (time)
koshoo こしょう＝胡椒	2-14	N	black pepper
kotae こたえ＝答え	2-2	N	answer
kotaeru こたえる＝答える	2-2	V2	(to) answer
koto こと＝事	1-5	N	thing [intangible]
kotoba ことば＝言葉	2-15	N	words, language
kotoshi ことし＝今年	1-15	N	this year
kowai こわい＝恐い	2-4	A	(is) scary
ku く＝九	1-1	N	nine
kubi くび＝首	1-6	N	neck
kuchi くち＝口	1-6	N	mouth
kudamono くだもの＝果物	2-14	N	fruit
(～を)kudasai ください＝下さい	1-2	Exp	please give me ～.
kugatsu くがつ＝九月	1-3	N	September
kumo くも＝雲	2-11	N	cloud

kumori くもり＝曇り	2-7	N	cloudy (weather)
kuni くに＝国	2-9	N	country, nation
kuraberu くらべる＝比べる	2-9	V2	(to) compare
~kurai ～くらい	1-13	Nd	about ～ [not for time]
kurai くらい＝暗い	2-11	A	(is) dark
kurasu クラス	1-11	N	class, instruction
kurejitto kaado クレジットカード	2-9	N	credit card
kureru くれる	1-15	V2	(to) give (to me or to my family)
kurisumasu クリスマス	2-7	N	Christmas
kurisumasukaado クリスマスカード	2-7	N	Christmas card
kurisumasutsurii クリスマスツリー	2-7	N	Christmas tree
kuro くろ＝黒	1-5	N	black
kuroi くろい＝黒い	1-6	A	(is) black
kuru くる＝来る	1-7	V3	(to) come
kuruma くるま＝車	1-7	N	car, vehicle
kusuri くすり＝薬	1-12	N	medicine
kutsu くつ＝靴	1-13	N	shoes
kutsushita くつした＝靴下	2-3	N	socks
kuukoo くうこう＝空港	2-13	N	airport
kyandii キャンディ	2-5	N	candy
kyanpu キャンプ	1-7	N	camp
kyonen きょねん＝去年	1-15	N	last year
kyoo きょう＝今日	1-4	N	today
kyoodai きょうだい＝兄弟	1-3	N	(my) sibling(s)
kyookai きょうかい＝教会	2-7	N	church
kyookasho きょうかしょ＝教科書	1-2	N	textbook
kyooshitsu きょうしつ＝教室	1-10	N	classroom
Kyooto きょうと＝京都	2-1	N	Kyoto
kyuu ni きゅうに＝急に	2-4	Adv	suddenly
kyuu きゅう＝九	1-1	N	nine
kyuu-juu きゅうじゅう＝九十	1-1	N	ninety
kyuukyuusha きゅうきゅうしゃ＝救急車	2-4	N	ambulance
Kyuushuu きゅうしゅう＝九州	2-1	N	Kyushu

<M>

maamaa まあまあ	1-5	Adv	"so, so"
machi まち＝町	2-13	N	town
machigaeru まちがえる＝間違える	2-6	V2	(to) make a mistake
mada + Aff. まだ + Aff.	2-2	Adv	still
mada + Neg. まだ + Neg.	1-14	Adv	(not) yet
Mada desu. まだです。	1-14	Exp	Not yet.
~ made ～まで	1-11	P	to ～; until ～
(time) made ni までに	2-10	P	by (a certain time)
mado まど＝窓	1-10	N	window

～mae ～まえ＝ ～前	1-7	Nd	before ～
mae まえ＝ 前	1-3	N	before
mae まえ＝ 前	2-2	N	front
(～no) mae ni （～の）まえに＝（～の）前に	1-12	P+N+P	before ～
(place で/を) magaru まがる＝曲がる	2-4	V1	(to) turn at/along (place)
-mai -まい＝-枚	1-2	Nd	[counter for flat objects]
mainen まいねん＝毎年	1-15	N	every year
mainichi まいにち＝毎日	1-4	N	everyday
maishuu まいしゅう＝毎週	1-11	N	every week
maitoshi まいとし＝毎年	1-15	N	every year
maitsuki まいつき＝毎月	1-12	N	every month
makeru まける＝負ける	1-12	V2	(to) lose
(ichi)man （いち）まん＝(一)万	1-13	N	ten thousand
-masen ka -ませんか	1-7	Dv	won't you do ～? [invitation]
-mashoo -ましょう	1-7	Dv	let's do ～. [suggestion]
massugu まっすぐ	2-13	Adv	straight
mata また＝又	1-10	Adv	again
(Ja) mata ato de. (じゃ)またあとで。	1-14	Exp	(Well,) see you later.
Mata doozo. またどうぞ。	2-9	Exp	Please come again.
matsu まつ＝待つ	1-13	V1	(to) wait
mazu まず	2-14	SI	first of all
mazui まずい	1-13	A	(is) unappetizing, is tasteless
me め＝目	1-6	N	eye
megane めがね＝眼鏡	2-3	N	eyeglasses
menyuu メニュー	2-5	N	menu
michi みち＝道	2-4	N	street, road, way
midori みどり＝緑	1-5	N	green
miemasen みえません＝見えません	2-1	V2	cannot see
miemasu みえます＝見えます	2-1	V2	can see
(something が) mieru みえる＝見える	2-3	V2	～ can be seen
migi みぎ＝右	2-2	N	right side
mijikai みじかい＝短い	1-6	A	(is) short [not for height]
mikka みっか＝三日	11-1	N	(the) third day of the month
mimi みみ＝耳	1-6	N	ear
minami みなみ＝南	2-1	N	south
minasan みなさん＝皆さん	1-15	N	everyone [polite]
minna みんな＝皆	1-15	N	everyone
miru みる＝見る	1-4	V2	(to) watch, look, see
(Verb TE form +) miru みる	2-5	Dv	try to (do)
miruku ミルク	1-4	N	(cow's) milk
(o)mise (お)みせ＝(お)店	1-13	N	store
miseru みせる＝見せる	1-13	V2	(to) show
Misete kudasai. みせてください。＝見せて下さい。	1-2	Exp	Please show.

(o)misoshiru (お)みそしる＝(お)味噌汁	2-5	N	soup flavored with *miso*
Mite kudasai. みてください。＝見て下さい。	1-2	Exp	Please look.
mittsu みっつ＝三つ	1-2	N	three [general counter]
(o)miyage (お)みやげ＝(お)土産	2-9	N	souvenir gift
(o)mizu (お)みず＝(お)水	1-4	N	water
～mo ～も (+ Aff.)	1-3	P	too, also
～mo ～も (+ Neg.)	1-3	P	either
(counter) mo も	2-6	P	as many/long as ～
mochiron もちろん	2-6	SI	of course
mokuyoobi もくようび＝木曜日	1-7	N	Thursday
mon もん＝門	2-3	N	gate
mondai もんだい＝問題	2-6	N	problem
mono もの＝物	1-5	N	thing [tangible]
moo (+ Aff.) もう＋ Aff.	1-14	Exp	already
moo (ippai) もう(いっぱい)＝もう(一杯)	1-14	Adv	(one) more (cup)
moo + Neg. もう＋ Neg.	2-2	Adv	(not) any more
moo ichido もういちど＝もう一度	1-1	Adv	one more time
moo sugu もうすぐ	1-15	Adv	very soon
morau もらう	1-15	V1	(to) receive, get from
Moshi moshi. もしもし。	2-6	Exp	Hello. (on the phone)
motsu もつ＝持つ	2-2	V1	(to) have, hold, carry
motte iku もっていく＝持って行く	2-7	V1	(to) take (thing)
motte kaeru もってかえる＝持って帰る	2-7	V1	(to) take/bring (thing) back home
motte kuru もってくる＝持って来る	2-7	V3	(to) bring (thing)
motto もっと	2-9	Adv	more
muika むいか＝六日	1-11	N	(the) sixth day of the month
(person を) mukae ni iku むかえにいく＝迎えに行く			
	2-10	V1	(to) go to pick up (person)
(person を) mukae ni kaeru むかえにかえる＝迎えに帰る			
	2-10	V1	(to) return to pick up (person)
(person を) mukae ni kuru むかえにくる＝迎えに来る			
	2-10	V3	(to) come to pick up (someone)
mukashibanashi むかしばなし＝昔話	2-11	N	folk tale
mukashimukashi むかしむかし＝昔々	2-11	N	long, long ago
mukoo むこう＝向こう	2-13	N	other side, beyond
murasaki むらさき＝紫	1-5	N	purple
mushiatsui むしあつい＝蒸し暑い	1-1	A	(is) hot and humid
(o)musubi (お)むすび	1-14	N	riceball
musuko むすこ＝息子	2-11	N	(own) son
musukosan むすこさん＝息子さん	2-11	N	(someone else's) son
musume むすめ＝娘	2-11	N	(own) daughter, young lady
musumesan むすめさん＝娘さん	2-11	N	(someone else's) daughter, young lady [polite]

muttsu むっつ＝六つ	1-2	N	six [general counter]
muzukashii むずかしい＝難しい	1-11	A	(is) difficult

<N>

nabe なべ＝鍋	2-14	N	pot, pan
～nado ～など	1-15	Nd	～ etc.
nagai ながい＝長い	1-6	A	(is) long
Nagoya なごや＝名古屋	2-1	N	Nagoya
Naha なは＝那覇	2-1	N	Naha
naifu ナイフ	1-14	N	knife
naka なか＝中	2-2	N	inside
-nakereba narimasen -なければなりません	2-5	Dv	have to (do), should (do)
naku なく＝泣く	2-15	V1	(to) cry
-nakutemo iidesu -なくてもいいです	2-5	Dv	do not have to (do), no need to (do)
nama tamago なまたまご＝生卵	2-14	N	raw egg
namae なまえ＝名前	1-3	N	name
(o)namae おなまえ＝御名前	1-3	N	(someone's) name [polite]
nan なん＝何	1-1	Ni	what?
nan-bai なんばい＝何杯	1-14	Ni	how many cups?
nan-gatsu なんがつ＝何月	1-3	Ni	what month?
nan-nensei なんねんせい＝何年生	1-3	N	what grade?
nan-nichi なんにち＝何日	1-11	Ni	(the) what day of the month?
nan-nin なんにん＝何人	1-3	Ni	how many people?
nan-sai なんさい＝何歳, 何才	1-3	Ni	how old?
nan-satsu なんさつ＝何冊	1-15	Ni	how many [bound objects]?
nan-yoobi なんようび＝何曜日	1-7	Ni	what day of the week?
nana なな＝七	1-1	N	seven
nana-juu ななじゅう＝七十	1-1	N	seventy
nanatsu ななつ＝七つ	1-2	N	seven [general counter]
nanbiki なんびき＝何匹	1-10	Ni	how many [small animals]?
nanbon なんぼん＝何本	1-10	Ni	how many [long cylindrical objects]?
nandai なんだい＝何台	1-10	Ni	how many [mechanized goods]?
nandomo なんども＝何度も	2-6	Adv	many times
Nani o sashiagemashoo ka. なにをさしあげましょうか。＝何を差し上げましょうか。			
	2-9	Exp	May I help you?
nani なに＝何	1-1	Ni	what?
nani-jin なにじん＝何人	1-3	Ni	what nationality?
nanigo なにご＝何語	1-4	Ni	what language?
naniiro なにいろ＝何色	1-5	N	what color?
nanika なにか＝何か	2-15	N	something
nanimo (+ Neg.) なにも＝何も (+ Neg.)	1-4	Ni+P	(not) anything
nanji なんじ＝何時	1-7	Ni	what time?
nanoka なのか＝七日	1-11	N	(the) seventh day of the month
nanwa なんわ＝何羽	1-10	Ni	how many [birds]?

napukin ナプキン		1-14	N	napkin
Nara なら＝奈良		2-1	N	Nara
narau ならう＝習う		2-2	V1	(to) learn
nareetaa ナレーター		2-11	N	narrator
narimasen なりません		2-5	V1	(it) won't do
(〜に) naru なる		2-12	V1	(to) become 〜
naruhodo なるほど		2-11	Exp	Indeed! I see!
natsu なつ＝夏		1-12	N	summer
naze なぜ		1-11	Ni	why?
(sentence +) ne ね		1-6	SP	isn't it? [sentence ending particle]
(o)nedan （お）ねだん＝（お）値段		2-9	N	price
nekkuresu ネックレス		2-3	N	necklace
neko ねこ＝猫		1-10	N	cat
nemui ねむい＝眠い		1-12	A	(is) sleepy
nengajoo ねんがじょう＝年賀状		2--7	N	New Year's card
neru ねる＝寝る		1-7	V2	(to) sleep, go to bed
- nen - ねん＝ - 年		1-15	Nd	- year
- nen(kan) - ねんかん＝ - 年間		2-6	Nd	- year(s)
netsu ねつ＝熱		1-12	N	fever
nezumi ねずみ＝鼠		1-10	N	mouse
〜 ni 〜 に		2-6	P	per 〜
(place) ni に (+ direction verb)		1-7	P	to (place)
(place) ni に (+ existence verb)		1-10	P	in, at (place)
〜 ni 〜 〜 に〜		2-5	P	〜 and 〜 (as a set)
(specific time) ni に		1-7	P	at (specific time)
(activity) ni に		1-7	P	for (activity)
ni に＝二		1-1	N	two
ni-juu にじゅう＝二十		1-1	N	twenty
- nichi - にち＝ - 日		1-11	Nd	day of the month
- nichi(kan) - にち（かん）＝- 日(間)		2-6	Nd	- day(s)
nichiyoobi にちようび＝日曜日		1-7	N	Sunday
nigate にがて＝苦手		1-5	Na	(be) weak in
nigatsu にがつ＝二月		1-3	N	February
(o)nigiri （お）にぎり		1-14	N	riceball
nigirizushi にぎりずし＝握り鮨		2-5	N	*sushi* rice shaped in bite-sized rectangles topped with fish, roe, shellfish, vegetables or egg
nihon にほん＝日本		1-3	N	Japan
nihongo にほんご＝日本語		1-4	N	Japanese language
(-wa) nihongo de nan to iimasu ka (-は)にほんごでなんといいますか		1-1	Exp	How do you say 〜 in Japanese?
nihonjin にほんじん＝日本人		1-3	N	Japanese citizen
nijuu-yokka にじゅうよっか＝二十四日		1-11	N	(the) twenty fourth day of the month

nikoniko ニコニコ	2-15	Adv	smilingly [onomatopoetic]
nikuudon にくうどん＝肉うどん	2-5	N	*udon* topped with beef
- nin - にん＝ - 人	1-3	Nd	[counter for people]
nioi におい＝臭い	2-7	N	smell, fragrance
nishi にし＝西	2-1	N	west
～ni tsuite ～について	2-2	P+V	about
～niwa にわ＝庭	1-10	N	garden, yard
no の	1-3	P	[possessive and descriptive particle]
nodo のど＝喉	1-6	N	throat
Nodo ga karakara desu. のどがカラカラです。＝喉がカラカラです。			
	1-14	Exp	I am thirsty.
Nodo ga kawakimashita. のどがかわきました。＝喉が渇きました。			
	1-14	Exp	I got thirsty.
nomimono のみもの＝飲み物	1-5	N	(a) drink
nomu のむ＝飲む	1-4	V1	(to) drink
	1-12	V1	take (medicine)
nooto ノート	1-2	N	notebook
(vehicle に) noru のる＝乗る	2-4	V1	(to) ride
<O>			
o を	2-4	P	through, along
obaasan おばあさん	1-3	N	grandmother, elderly woman
obasan おばさん	1-15	N	aunt, middle aged woman
oboeru おぼえる＝覚える	2-6	V2	(to) memorize
ocha おちゃ＝お茶	1-4	N	tea
Ohayoo. おはよう。	1-1	Exp	Good morning. (Informal)
Ohayoo gozaimasu. おはようございます。	1-1	Exp	Good morning. (Formal)
ohisama おひさま＝お日様	2-11	N	sun [polite]
oishasan おいしゃさん＝御医者さん	1-3	N	(medical) doctor [polite form of いしゃ]
oishii おいしい＝美味しい	1-13	A	(is) delicious
ojiisan おじいさん	1-3	N	grandfather, elderly man
ojisan おじさん	1-15	N	uncle, man
okaasan おかあさん＝お母さん	1-3	N	(someone's) mother
Okinawa おきなわ＝沖縄	2-1	N	Okinawa
okiru おきる＝起きる	1-7	V2	(to) wake up, get up
okoru おこる＝怒る	2-15	V1	(to become) angry
oku おく＝置く	2-5	V1	(to) put, leave
okuru おくる＝送る	2-7	V1	(to) send, mail
Omedetoo gozaimasu. おめでとうございます	1-15	Exp	Congratulations.
omoshiroi おもしろい＝面白い	1-11	A	(is) interesting
omou おもう＝思う	2-11	V1	(to) think
onaji おなじ＝同じ	2-9	N	same
onaka おなか＝お腹	1-6	N	stomach

Onaka ga ippai desu. おなかがいっぱいです＝お腹が一杯です

| | | | 1-14 | Exp | (I am) full. |

Onaka ga pekopeko desu. おなかがペコペコです。＝お腹がペコペコです。

| | | | 1-14 | Exp | I am hungry. |

Onaka ga sukimashita. おなかがすきました。＝お腹が空きました。

			1-14	Exp	I got hungry.
ondo おんど＝温度			2-7	N	(weather) temperature
oneesan おねえさん＝お姉さん			1-3	N	(someone's) older sister
Onegaishimasu. おねがいします。＝御願いします。		1-1	Exp	Please. [request]
ongaku おんがく＝音楽			1-5	N	music
oniisan おにいさん＝お兄さん			1-3	N	(someone's) older brother
onna おんな＝女			1-10	N	female
onna no hito おんなのひと＝女の人			1-10	N	woman, lady
onna no ko おんなのこ＝女の子			1-10	N	girl
ooen (o) suru おうえん(を)する＝応援(を)する		2-10	V3	(to) cheer
ooi おおい＝多い			1-11	A	(are) many, much
ookii おおきい＝大きい			1-6	A	(is) big
orenji (iro) オレンジいろ＝オレンジ色			1-5	N	orange (color)
(vehicle から／を) oriru おりる＝降りる		2-4	V2	(to) get off (vehicle)
Osaka おおさか＝大坂			2-1	N	Osaka
oshieru おしえる＝教える			2-4	V2	(to) teach
oshimai おしまい			2-11	N	(the) end
osoi おそい＝遅い			1-7	A	(is) late
osoku おそく＝遅く			1-12	Adv	late

Osoku narimashita. おそくなりました。＝遅くなりました。

			2-14	Exp	Sorry to be late.
Osuki desu ka. おすきですか。＝お好きですか。	2-9	Exp	Do you like it? [polite]
otaku おたく＝お宅			2-6	N	(someone's) house, residence [polite]
otoko おとこ＝男			1-10	N	male
otoko no hito おとこのひと＝男の人			1-10	N	man
otoko no ko おとこのこ＝男の子			1-10	N	boy
otona おとな＝大人			2-14	N	adult
otoosan おとうさん＝お父さん			1-3	N	(someone's) father
otooto おとうと＝弟			1-3	N	(my) younger brother
otootosan おとうとさん＝弟さん			1-3	N	(someone's) younger brother
otoshidama おとしだま＝お年玉			2-7	N	money received mainly by children from adults at New Year's
ototoi おととい＝一昨日			1-11	N	(the) day before yesterday
otsuri おつり＝お釣			2-9	N	change (from a larger unit of money)
owari ni おわりに＝終わりに			2-14	Adv	(at the) end
Owarimashoo. おわりましょう。＝終わりましょう。	1-4	Exp	Let's finish.
(〜が) owaru おわる＝終わる			2-10	V1	(something) finish, end
(〜を) owaru おわる＝終わる			2-10	V1	(someone will) finish (something)

oyako donburi おやこどんぶり＝親子丼	2-5	N	chicken and egg over a bowl of steamed rice
oyogu およぐ＝泳ぐ	1-15	V1	(to) swim

<P>

-paasento -パーセント	2-5	Nd	percent
paatii パーティー	1-7	N	party
- pai - ぱい＝ - 杯	1-14	Nd	cupful, glassful, bowlful, spoonful
pan パン	1-4	N	bread
pantsu パンツ	1-13	N	pants
pasupooto パスポート	2-3	N	passport
patokaa パトカー	2-4	N	patrol car
piano ピアノ	1-5	N	piano
piasu ピアス	2-3	N	pierced earrings
pikunikku ピクニック	1-7	N	picnic
pinku ピンク	1-5	N	pink
piza ピザ	1-14	N	pizza
- pon - ぽん＝ - 本	1-10	Nd	[counter for long cylindrical objects]
potetochippu ポテトチップ	2-4	N	potato chips
purezento プレゼント	1-15	N	present
puuru プール	1-10	N	pool

<R>

raamen ラーメン	2-5	N	Chinese noodle soup
raigetsu らいげつ＝来月	1-12	N	next month
rainen らいねん＝来年	1-15	N	next year
raishuu らいしゅう＝来週	1-11	N	next week
raisukaree ライスカレー	2-5	N	curry rice
rajio ラジオ	1-4	N	radio
Rei. れい。＝礼。	1-1	Exp	Bow.
reji レジ	2-5	N	cash register
renshuu (o) suru れんしゅう(を)する＝練習(を)する	1-12	V3	(to) practice
repooto レポート	1-4	N	report, paper
resutoran レストラン	1-7	N	restaurant
rikon (o) suru りこん(を)する＝離婚(を)する	2-15	V3	(to) divorce
rokkaa ロッカー	1-10	N	locker
roku ろく＝六	1-1	N	six
roku-juu ろくじゅう＝六十	1-1	N	sixty
rokugatsu ろくがつ＝六月	1-3	N	June
rusu るす＝留守	2-6	N	(is) not at home
ryokoo りょこう＝旅行	1-7	N	trip, traveling
ryokoo (o) suru りょこう(を)する＝旅行(を)する	1-7	V3	(to) travel
ryoo りょう＝寮	2-2	N	dormitory
ryoohoo りょうほう＝両方	2-9	N	both
ryoori (o) suru りょうり(を)する＝料理(を)する	2-7	V3	(to) cook

ryooshin りょうしん＝両親	2-2	N	(own) parents
<S>			
Saa . . . さあ . . .	2-9	SI	Well . . . [Used when one is unsure of an answer.]
does not know			
- sai - さい＝ - 才, - 歳	1-3	Nd	[counter for age]
saifu さいふ＝財布	2-5	N	wallet
saizu サイズ	1-14	N	size
sakana さかな＝魚	1-10	N	fish
(o)sake (お)さけ＝(お)酒	2-14	N	rice wine, liquor in general
sakkaa サッカー	1-5	N	soccer
samui さむい＝寒い	1-1	A	(is) cold (temperature)
- san - さん	1-1	Nd	Mr./Mrs./Ms.
san さん＝三	1-1	N	three
san-juu さんじゅう＝三十	1-1	N	thirty
sandoitchi サンドイッチ	1-14	N	sandwich
sangatsu さんがつ＝三月	1-3	N	March
sangurasu サングラス	2-3	N	sunglasses
sanpo (o) suru さんぽ(を)する＝散歩(を)する	2-15	V3	(to) take a walk
Sapporo さっぽろ＝札幌	2-1	N	Sapporo
(o)sara おさら＝お皿	1-14	N	plate, dish
sarada サラダ	1-14	N	salad
(superior ni に) sashiageru さしあげます＝差し上げます	2-9	V2	(to) give (to a superior)
satoo さとう＝砂糖	2-14	N	sugar
- satsu - さつ＝ - 冊	1-15	Nd	[counter for bound objects]
Sayoonara. さようなら。	1-1	Exp	Good-bye.
se(i) せ(い)＝背	1-6	N	height
seeru(chuu) セール中	2-9	N	(for) sale
seetaa セーター	2-3	N	sweater
seifuku せいふく＝制服	2-3	N	(school) uniform
seiseki せいせき＝成績	1-11	N	grade
seito せいと＝生徒	1-3	N	student [non-college]
sekai せかい＝世界	2-9	N	world
semai せまい＝狭い	1-10	A	(is) narrow, small (room)
sen せん＝千	1-13	N	thousand
Sendai せんだい＝仙台	2-1	N	Sendai
sengetsu せんげつ＝先月	1-12	N	last month
sensei せんせい＝先生	1-1	N	teacher, Mr./Mrs./Ms./Dr.
senshu せんしゅ＝選手	2-10	N	(sports) player
senshuu せんしゅう＝先週	1-11	N	last week
sentaku (o) suru せんたく(を)する＝洗濯(を)する	2-7	V3	(to do) laundry
- sento - セント	1-13	Nd	- cent(s)
shakai しゃかい＝社会	1-11	N	social studies
shashin しゃしん＝写真	1-2	N	photo

shatsu シャツ	1-13	N	shirt
shi し＝四	1-1	N	four
shi し＝市	2-9	N	city
shiai しあい＝試合	1-12	N	(sports) game
shichi しち＝七	1-1	N	seven
shichi-juu しちじゅう＝七十	1-1	N	seventy
shichigatsu しちがつ＝七月	1-3	N	July
shigatsu しがつ＝四月	1-3	N	April
(o)shigoto（お）しごと＝（お）仕事	1-3	N	job
shiitoberuto o suru シートベルトをする	2-4	V3	(to) wear a seat belt
shikaru しかる＝叱る	2-15	V1	(to) scold
Shikashi しかし	2-15	SI	However [Formal equivalent of でも]
Shikata ga arimasen/nai. しかたがありません／ない。＝仕方がありません／ない。			
	2-6	Exp	(It) cannot be helped.
shiken しけん＝試験	1-2	N	exam
Shikoku しこく＝四国	2-1	N	Shikoku
shima しま＝島	2-9	N	island
suru する	1-4	V3	(to) do
(something に) suru する	2-5	V3	(to) decide on ～
(verb TE) shimau しまう	2-11	V1	(to) do ～ completely [regret, criticism]
shimeru しめる＝閉める	1-13	V2	(to) close
Shimete kudasai. しめてください。＝閉めて下さい。	1-1	Exp	Please close.
shinbun しんぶん＝新聞	1-4	N	newspaper
shingoo しんごう＝信号	2-4	N	traffic lights
shinu しぬ＝死ぬ	1-12	V1	(to) die
shinpai (o) suru しんぱい（を）する＝心配（を）する	2-4	V3	(to) worry
shinseki しんせき＝親戚	1-15	N	relatives
shio しお＝塩	2-14	N	salt
shiokarai しおからい＝塩辛い	2-14	A	(is) salty
shirimasen しりません＝知りません	1-2	V1	do not know
shiro しろ＝白	1-5	N	white
shiroi しろい＝白い	1-6	A	(is) white
shita した＝下	2-2	N	under, below
shitsumon しつもん＝質問	2-2	N	question
shitsumon (o) suru しつもん（を）する＝質問（を）する	2-2	V3	(to) ask a question
shitte iru しっている＝知っている	2-2	V1	know
shizuka しずか＝静か	1-6	Na	quiet
shizuka ni suru しずかにする＝静かにする	1-13	V3	(to) quiet down
Shizukani shite kudasai. しずかにしてください＝静かにして下さい			
	1-2	Exp	Please be quiet.
shokuji しょくじ＝食事	1-7	N	meal, dining

shokuji (o) suru しょくじ(を)する＝食事(を)する	1-7	V3	(to) dine, have a meal
(o)shoogatsu (お)しょうがつ＝(お)正月	2-7	N	New Year
shookai (o) suru しょうかい(を)する＝紹介(を)する	2-2	V3	(to) introduce
shoomeisho しょうめいしょ＝証明書	2-3	N	I. D.
shoorai しょうらい＝将来	2-14	N	future
shootesuto しょうテスト＝小テスト	1-2	N	quiz
shootopantsu ショートパンツ	2-3	N	shorts
shootsu ショーツ	2-3	N	shorts
shufu しゅふ＝主婦	1-3	N	housewife
shukudai しゅくだい＝宿題	1-2	N	homework
shumi しゅみ＝趣味	1-5	N	hobby
shuu しゅう＝州	2-9	N	state
- shuukan - しゅうかん＝- 週間	2-6	Nd	- week(s)
shuumatsu しゅうまつ＝週末	1-11	N	weekend
soba そば＝傍	2-2	N	by, nearby
sochira そちら	2-5	N	there [polite equiv. of そこ]
	2-9	N	that one [polite equiv. of それ]
sokkusu ソックス	2-3	N	socks
soko そこ	1-2	N	there
sono ~ その ~	1-2	PN	that ~
sono koro そのころ＝その頃	2-10	PN+N	around that time
sono toki そのとき＝その時	2-15	N	at that time
(Stem form +) soo desu -そうです	2-5	SI	looks ~
Soo desu nee . . . そうですねえ. . .	1-5	Exp	Let me see . . .
Soo desu. そうです。	1-1	Exp	It is.
Soo desu ka. そうですか。	1-3	Exp	Is that so?
Soo dewa arimasen. そうではありません。	1-1	Exp	It is not so. [formal]
Soo ja arimasen. そうじゃありません。	1-1	Exp	It is not so. [informal]
sooji (o) suru そうじ(を)する＝掃除(を)する	2-7	V3	(to) clean up
sore それ	1-1	N	that one
Soredake desu. それだけです。	2-5	Exp	That's all.
Sorekara それから	1-7	SI	And then
Soreni それに	1-11	SI	Moreover, Besides
Soretomo それとも	1-6	SI	(Question 1). Or (Question 2)
Sore wa ii kangae desu. それはいいかんがえです。＝それはいい考えです。			
	2-10	Exp	That is a good idea.
Soshite そして	1-3	SI	And [Used at the beginning of a sentence.]
soto そと＝外	1-10	N	outside
su す＝酢	2-14	N	vinegar
subarashii すばらしい＝素晴らしい	1-13	A	(is) wonderful
- sugi - すぎ＝ - 過ぎ	1-7	Nd	after ~
(Stem form +) sugiru すぎる＝過ぎる	2-14	V2	too ~

sugoi すごい＝凄い	1-13	A	(is) terrible, terrific
suiei すいえい＝水泳	1-5	N	swimming
suite iru すいている	2-13	V1	(is) not crowded, (is) empty
suiyoobi すいようび＝水曜日	1-7	N	Wednesday
sukaato スカート	2-3	N	skirt
suki すき＝好き	1-5	Na	like
sukiyaki すきやき＝鋤焼き	2-14	N	*sukiyaki*
sukoa スコア	2-10	N	score
sukoshi すこし＝少し	1-4	Adv	a little [formal]
	1-10	Adv	a few, a little
suku すく	2-13	V1	(to) get empty, be empty
sukunai すくない＝少ない	1-11	A	is few, little
sukuurubasu スクールバス	2-4	N	school bus
Sumimasen. すみません	1-1	Exp	Excuse me.
	1-13	Exp	Excuse me. (to get attention)
(place に) sumu すむ＝住む	2-2	V1	live (in 〜)
sunakkubaa スナックバー	1-4	N	snack bar
supein スペイン	1-3	N	Spain
supeingo スペインご＝スペイン語	1-4	N	Spanish language
supiido o dasu スピードをだす＝出す	2-4	V1	(to) speed
supootsu スポーツ	1-5	N	sports
suppai すっぱい＝酸っぱい	2-14	A	(is) sour
supuun スプーン	1-14	N	spoon
suru する	2-3	V3	(to) wear [accessories]
Suruto すると	2-13	SI	Thereupon
sushiya すしや＝寿司屋	1-13	N	*sushi* shop/bar
(gomi o) suteru (ごみを)すてる	2-3	V2	(to) litter, (to) throw away (garbage)
Sutoresu ga ippai desu. ストレスがいっぱいです。	2-6	Exp	(is) very stressed
sutoroo ストロー	1-14	N	straw
(tabako o) suu (たばこを)すう	2-3	V1	(to) smoke cigarettes
suugaku すうがく＝数学	1-11	N	math
suupaa スーパー	1-13	N	super market
suwaru すわる＝座る	1-13	V1	(to) sit
Suwatte kudasai. すわってください。＝座って下さい。			
	1-2	Exp	Please sit.
suzushii すずしい＝涼しい	1-1	A	(is) cool [temperature]
<T>			
tabako たばこ	2-3	N	tobacco, cigarettes
taberu たべる＝食べる	1-4	V2	(to) eat
tabemono たべもの＝食べ物	1-5	N	food
tabun たぶん＝多分	2-7	Adv	probably
- tachi - たち＝ - 達	1-12	Nd	[suffix for animate plurals]
tadashii ただしい＝正しい	2-2	A	(is) correct

(Verb stem +) tai -たい	1-12	Da	want (to do)
〜 tai 〜　〜たい〜＝〜対 〜	2-10	PN	〜 to 〜, 〜 vs. 〜
taihen たいへん＝大変	1-11	Na	hard, difficult
taiiku たいいく＝体育	1-11	N	P.E.
taiikukan たいいくかん＝体育館	2-10	N	gym
taipu (o) suru タイプ(を)する	1-4	V3	(to) type
taitei たいてい＝大抵	1-4	Adv	usually
takai たかい＝高い	1-6	A	(is) tall
	1-13	A	(is) expensive
takusan たくさん＝沢山	1-10	Adv	a lot, many
takushii タクシー	1-7	N	taxi
tamago たまご＝卵	2-14	N	egg
tama ni たまに	2-15	Adv	occasionally, once in a while
(o)tanjoobi (お)たんじょうび＝(お)誕生日	1-11	N	birthday
tanoshii たのしい＝楽しい	1-11	A	(is) fun, enjoyable
(〜を)tanoshimi ni shite imasu (-を)たのしみにしています＝(-を)楽しみにしています			
	1-15	Exp	I am looking forward to (something).
tasukeru たすける＝助ける	2-15	V2	(to) rescue, (to) help
tatemono たてもの＝建物	1-10	N	building
tatsu たつ＝立つ	1-13	V1	(to) stand
Tatte kudasai. たってください。＝立って下さい。	1-2	Exp	Please stand.
te て＝手	1-6	N	hand
(o)tearai (お)てあらい＝(お)手洗い	1-10	N	bathroom, restroom
teeburu テーブル	1-2	N	table
teepu テープ	1-4	N	tape
tegami てがみ＝手紙	1-4	N	letter
tekisuto テキスト	1-2	N	textbook
- ten - てん＝ - 点	2-10	Nd	- point(s)
tenisu テニス	1-5	N	tennis
(o)tenki (お)てんき＝(お)天気	1-1	N	weather
(o)tera (お)てら＝(お)寺	2-7	N	temple (Buddhist)
terebi テレビ	1-4	N	T.V.
terebigeemu テレビゲーム	1-5	N	video game
tetsudau てつだう＝手伝う	2-7	V3	(to) help
tiishatsu Tシャツ	2-3	N	T-shirt
tisshu ティッシュ	1-2	N	tissue
to (issho ni) と(いっしょに)	1-4	P	with (person)
(quotation) to と	2-11	P	[quotation particle]
to と	1-3	P	and [used between two nouns]
to と＝戸	1-10	N	door
(o)toire (お)トイレ	1-10	N	bathroom, restroom
tokei とけい＝時計	1-13	N	watch, clock
〜toki 〜とき＝〜時	2-15	N	time, when 〜

tokidoki ときどき＝時々	1-4	Adv	sometimes
tokoro ところ＝所	2-2	N	place
Tokorode ところで	2-3	SI	By the way
tokui とくい＝得意	1-5	Na	(be) strong in, can do well
toku ni とくに＝特に	2-2	Adv	especially
Tokyo とうきょう＝東京	2-1	N	Tokyo
(place で/に) tomaru とまる＝止まる	2-4	V1	(to) stop
tomodachi ともだち＝友達	1-4	N	friend
tonari となり＝隣	2-2	N	next to
Tondemonai. とんでもない。	2-11	Exp	How ridiculous! That's impossible!
tonkatsu とんかつ＝豚カツ	2-5	N	pork cutlet
too とお＝十	1-2	N	ten [general counter]
tooi とおい＝遠い	1-10	A	(is) far
tooka とおか＝十日	1-11	N	(the) tenth day of the month
tooku とおく＝遠く	2-2	N	far away
toori とおり＝通り	2-13	N	street, avenue
tootoo とうとう	2-11	Adv	finally, at last [after much effort]
toraberaazu chekku トラベラーズチェック	2-9	N	traveler's check
toranpu トランプ	1-5	N	(playing) cards
(thing を) tori ni iku とりにいく＝取りに行く	2-10	V1	(to) go to pick up (thing)
(thing を) tori ni kaeru とりにかえる＝取りに帰る	2-10	V1	(to) return to pick up (thing)
(thing を) tori ni kuru とりにくる＝取りに来る	2-10	V3	(to) come to pick up (thing)
tori とり＝鳥	1-10	N	bird
toru とる＝取る	1-15	V1	(to) take, get
toriniku とりにく＝鳥肉	2-14	N	chicken (meat)
toshi o totte iru としをとっている＝年を取っている	1-6	V1	(is) old (person's, animal's age)
toshokan としょかん＝図書館	1-4	N	library
totemo とても	1-5	Adv	very
tsugi つぎ＝次	1-11	N	next
tsugi ni つぎに＝次に	2-14	Adv	next
tsuitachi ついたち＝一日	1-11	N	(the) first day of the month
tsukaremashita つかれました＝疲れました	1-12	V2	(got) tired
tsukarete imasu つかれています＝疲れています	1-12	V2	(is) tired
(object を thing に) tsukeru つける	2-14	V2	(to) dip (object in thing)
(place に) tsuku つく＝着く	2-4	V1	(to) arrive (at a place)
tsukue つくえ＝机	1-10	N	desk
tsukurikata つくりかた＝作り方	2-14	N	how to make
tsukuru つくる＝作る	1-15	V1	(to) make
tsumaranai つまらない	1-11	A	(is) boring, uninteresting
tsumetai つめたい＝冷たい	1-14	A	cold (to the touch)
(Dic./NAI) tsumori desu つもりです	2-6	Nd	plan to do/do not plan to do
tsurete iku つれていく＝連れて行く	2-7	V1	(to) take (animate)
tsurete kaeru つれてかえる＝連れて帰る	2-7	V1	(to) take/bring (animate) back home

tsurete kuru つれてくる＝連れて来る	2-7	V3	(to) bring (animate)
(place に) tsutomeru つとめる＝勤める	2-2	V2	(is) employed (at ～)
tsuyoi つよい＝強い	1-12	A	(is) strong
\<U\>			
uchi うち	1-4	N	house
udon うどん	2-5	N	thick white noodles in broth
ue うえ＝上	2-2	N	on, top
(thing が) ugoku うごく＝動く	2-11	V1	(thing to) move
ukagau うかがう＝伺う	2-13	V1	(to) ask [polite equiv. of 聞く]
(place で) umareru うまれる＝生まれる	2-2	V2	(be) born (in ～)
umi うみ＝海	1-7	N	beach, ocean, sea
Un うん	2-4	SI	Yes [informal]
undoo うんどう＝運動	2-10	N	sports
undoo (o) suru うんどう(を)する＝運動(を)する	2-10	V3	(to) exercise
undoogutsu うんどうぐつ＝運動靴	2-10	N	sports shoes
undoojoo うんどうじょう＝運動場	2-10	N	athletic field
unten (o) suru うんてん(を)する＝運転(を)する	2-3	V3	(to) drive
untenmenkyo うんてんめんきょ＝運転免許	2-3	N	driver's license
untenshu うんてんしゅ＝運転手	2-4	N	driver
ureshii うれしい＝嬉しい	1-11	A	(is) glad, happy
uru うる＝売る	2-9	V1	(to) sell
urusai うるさい	1-6	A	(is) noisy
ushiro うしろ＝後ろ	2-2	N	back, behind
uso うそ＝嘘	2-10	N	(a) lie
Uso deshoo. うそでしょう。	2-10	Exp	Are you kidding? Are you serious?
usui うすい＝薄い	2-14	A	(is) thin
usuku うすく＝薄く	2-14	Adv	thin
uta うた＝歌	1-5	N	song, singing
utau うたう＝歌う	1-15	V1	(to) sing
utsukushii うつくしい＝美しい	1-10	A	(is) beautiful
Uun う～ん	2-5	SI	Yummm . . .
Uun ううん	2-4	SI	No [informal]
\<W\>			
-wa -わ＝-羽	1-10	Nd	[counter for birds]
wa は	1-1	P	[particle marking the topic of the sentence]
Waa わあ	1-13	SI	Wow!
waakushiito ワークシート	1-2	N	worksheet
wakai わかい＝若い	1-6	A	(is) young
wakaru わかる＝分かる	1-2	V1	(to) understand
wanpiisu ワンピース	2-3	N	dress
warau わらう＝笑う	2-15	V1	(to) smile, laugh
warui わるい＝悪い	1-6	A	(is) bad

wasureru わすれる＝忘れる	1-14	V2	(to) forget
(place を) wataru わたる＝渡る	2-13	V1	(to) cross, go over
watashi わたし＝私	1-1	N	I (used by anyone informally)
watashino わたしの＝私の	1-2	N	mine
watashitachi わたしたち＝私達	1-12	N	we
weitaa ウェイター	2-5	N	waiter
weitoresu ウェイトレス	2-5	N	waitress
wookuman ウォークマン	1-4	N	walkman

\<Y\>

(N1) ya や (N2)	1-15	P	(N1) and (N2), etc.
yakiniku やきにく＝焼肉	2-5	N	meat grilled on fire
yakitori やきとり＝焼き鳥	2-5	N	grilled skewered chicken
yakyuu やきゅう＝野球	1-5	N	baseball
yama やま＝山	1-7	N	mountain
yaru やる	1-15	V2	(to) give (to inferior)
yasai やさい＝野菜	2-14	N	vegetable
yasashii やさしい＝易しい	1-11	A	(is) easy
yasashii やさしい＝優しい	1-6	A	(is) nice, kind
yasete iru やせている＝痩せている	1-6	V2	(is) thin
yasui やすい＝安い	1-13	A	(is) cheap
(o)yasumi (お)やすみ＝(お)休み	1-7	N	day off, vacation
(o)yasumi desu (お)やすみです＝(お)休みです	1-1	Exp	(is) absent
yasumijikan やすみじかん＝休み時間	1-11	N	(a) break
yasumu やすむ＝休む	1-12	V1	(to) rest
(～を) yasumu やすむ＝休む	1-12	V1	(be) absent (from ～)
Yattaa. やったあ。	2-10	Exp	We did it!
yattsu やっつ＝八つ	1-2	N	eight [general counter]
(sentence) yo よ	1-6	SP	you know [sentence ending particle]
yoi よい＝良い	1-6	A	(is) good
Yokatta desu nee. よかったですねえ。＝良かったですねえ。	1-11	Exp	How nice! [on a past event]
yokka よっか＝四日	1-11	N	(the) fourth day of the month
yoku よく	1-4	Adv	well, often
Yoku dekimashita. よくできました。＝良く出来ました。	1-2	Exp	Well done.
yomu よむ＝読む	1-4	V1	(to) read
yon よん＝四	1-1	N	four
Yonde kudasai. よんでください。＝読んで下さい。	1-2	Exp	Please read.
yon-juu よんじゅう＝四十	1-1	N	forty
yooka ようか＝八日	1-11	N	(the) eighth day of the month
～yori ～より	2-9	P	more than ～
yoru よる＝夜	1-4	N	night
(place に) yoru よる＝寄る	2-10	V1	(to) stop by, drop by (a place)

yottsu よっつ＝四つ	1-2	N	four [general counter]
yowai よわい＝弱い	1-12	A	(is) weak
yoyaku (o) suru よやく(を)する＝予約(を)する	2-5	V3	(to) make reservations
yubi ゆび＝指	1-6	N	finger, toe
yubiwa ゆびわ＝指輪	2-3	N	ring
yuka ゆか＝床	2-4	N	floor
yuki ゆき＝雪	2-7	N	snow
yukkuri ゆっくり	1-1	Adv	slowly
yunifoomu ユニフォーム	2-10	N	(sports) uniform
yuube ゆうべ	1-12	N	last night
yuubinkyoku ゆうびんきょく＝郵便局	2-13	N	post office
yuugata ゆうがた＝夕方	1-4	N	late afternoon, early evening
yuumei ゆうめい＝有名	1-10	Na	famous
yuushoo suru ゆうしょうをする＝優勝をする	2-10	V3	(to) win a championship

<Z>

Zannen deshita nee. ざんねんでしたねえ。＝残念でしたねえ。	1-11	Exp	How disappointing! [on a past event]
Zannen desu ga ... ざんねんですが 残念ですが ...	2-6	Exp	Sorry, but ...
Zannen desu nee. ざんねんですねえ。＝残念ですねえ。	1-11	Exp	How disappointing! [on a future event]
zarusoba ざるそば	2-5	N	buckwheat noodle dish
zasshi ざっし＝雑誌	1-4	N	magazine
zehi ぜひ＝是非	2-7	Adv	by all means, definitely
zeikin ぜいきん＝税金	2-9	N	tax
zenbu ぜんぶ＝全部	1-14	N	everything
zenbu de ぜんぶで＝全部で	1-14	N	for everything
zenzen (+ Neg.) ぜんぜん＝全然	1-5	Adv	(not) at all
zettai ni ぜったいに＝絶対に	2-3	Adv	absolutely
zubon ズボン	2-3	N	pants
zutto ずっと	2-9	Adv	by far
	2-15	Adv	throughout, all the time

ENGLISH-JAPANESE WORD LIST

English	Volume-Lesson #	Word type	Japanese
<A>			
ability	2-11	N	ちから＝力
(be) able to do ～	2-6	V2	(～が) できる＝出来る[できます]
about (time)	1-7	Nd	～ころ, ～ごろ
about how long/far/often?	2-6	Ni	どのぐらい
about ～ [topic]	2-2	P+V	～について
about ～ [Not used for time]	13-4	Nd	～くらい, ～ぐらい
(be) absent (from ～)	12-2	V2	(～を)やすむ＝休む[やすみます]
(He/She is) absent.	1-4	Exp	(お)やすみです＝(お)休みです
absolutely	2-3	Adv	ぜったいに＝絶対に
address	1-15	N	じゅうしょ＝住所
adult	2-14	N	おとな＝大人
affection	2-15	N	あい＝愛
after (an event)	1-12	P+N+P	～のあとで＝ ～の後で
after (time)	1-7	Nd	～すぎ＝ ～過ぎ
again	1-10	Adv	また＝又
～ago	2-15	Nd	～まえ＝～前
airplane	7-4	N	ひこうき＝飛行機
airport	2-13	N	くうこう＝空港
all right	1-12	Na	だいじょうぶ＝大丈夫
all the time	2-15	Adv	ずっと
along	2-4	P	を
already	14-1	Exp	もう(+aff.)
alternative	2-9	N	(～の) ほう＝方
Although ～	2-6	Pc	～けど, ～けれど
always	1-4	Adv	いつも
a. m.	1-7	N	ごぜん＝午前
ambulance	2-4	N	きゅうきゅうしゃ＝救急車
among ～	2-9	P	(～のなか＝～の中) で
among these	2-9	PN+N+P	このなかで＝この中で
amuse [not used for sports & music]	1-15	V1	あそぶ＝遊ぶ[あそびます]
(Noun1) and (Noun2), etc.	1-15	P	(N1) や (N2) など
and [used between two nouns]	1-3	P	と
And [used only at the beginning of a sentence]	1-3	SI	そして
～ and ～ (as a set)	2-5	P	～に～
And then	1-7	SI	それから
(to become) angry	2-15	V1	おこる＝怒る[おこります]
answer	2-2	N	こたえ＝答え
(to) answer	2-2	V2	こたえる＝答える[こたえます]
(not) any more	2-2	Adv	もう+ Neg.

Anything else?	2-5	Exp	ほかになにか。＝ほかに何か。
(not) anything	1-4	Ni+P	なにも＝何も＋Neg.
(not to) anywhere	1-7	Ni+P	どこへも＋Neg.
(to) appreciate	2-15	V3	かんしゃ(を)する＝感謝(を)する [かんしゃ(を)します]
approximately	2-6	Adv	だいたい
April	1-3	N	しがつ＝四月
area	2-13	N	へん＝辺
around that time	2-10	PN+N	そのころ＝その頃
(to) arrive (at a place)	2-4	V1	(place に) つく＝着く[つきます]
art	1-11	N	びじゅつ＝美術
art museum	2-13	N	びじゅつかん＝美術館
as many/long as ～	2-6	P	(counter) も
(not) as ～ as	2-9	P	～ほど (＋ Neg.)
ask [polite equiv. of 聞く]	2-13	V1	うかがう＝伺う[うかがいます]
(to) ask a question	2-2	V3	しつもん(を)する＝質問(を)する [しつもん(を)します]
(to) ask (someone)	2-3	V1	(person に) きく＝聞く[ききます]
at (location) [with existence verb]	1-10	P	に [with existence verb]
at (place) [with action verb]	1-4	P	で [with action verb]
at (specific time)	1-7	P	(specific time) に
(not) at all	1-5	Adv	ぜんぜん＝全然＋Neg.
at last [after much effort]	2-11	Adv	とうとう
at that time	2-15	N	そのとき＝その時
athletic field	2-10	N	うんどうじょう＝運動場
August	1-3	N	はちがつ＝八月
aunt	1-15	N	おばさん
autumn	1-12	N	あき＝秋
avenue	2-13	N	とおり＝通り
<B>			
baby	2-2	N	あかちゃん＝赤ちゃん
back	2-2	N	うしろ＝後ろ
(is) bad	1-6	A	わるい＝悪い
bag	1-2	N	バッグ
(paper) bag	2-9	N	ふくろ＝袋
balloon	1-15	N	ふうせん＝風船
ballpoint pen	1-2	N	ボールペン
bank	2-2	N	ぎんこう＝銀行
baseball	1-5	N	やきゅう
basement	2-9	N	ちか＝地下
basketball	1-5	N	バスケット(ボール)
bathroom	1-10	N	(お)トイレ, (お)手洗い
be (for animate) [polite equiv. of います]	2-6	V1	いらっしゃる [いらっしゃいます]

beach	1-7	N	うみ＝海
beard	1-6	N	ひげ＝髭
(is) beautiful	1-10	A	うつくしい＝美しい
because	1-11	Pc	(reason) から
because of (noun)	2-6	P	(noun) で
become ～	2-12	V1	(～ に) なる [なります]
bed	1-10	N	ベッド
beef	2-14	N	ぎゅうにく＝牛肉
beer	2-4	N	ビール
before	1-3	N	まえ＝前
before (not time)	1-12	P+N+P	～のまえに＝ ～の前に
before (time)	1-7	Nd	～まえ＝ ～前
begin (something)	1-4	V2	(～ を) はじめる＝始める [はじめます]
(at the) beginning	2-14	Adv	はじめに＝始めに
(something) begins	2-10	V1	(～ が) はじまる＝始まる [はじまります]
behind	2-2	N	うしろ＝後ろ
below	2-2	N	した＝下
Besides [used at the beginning of a sentence]	1-11	SI	それに
between [comparison]	2-9	P	～で
between [location]	2-2	N	あいだ＝間
beyond	2-13	N	むこう＝向こう
bicycle	1-7	N	じてんしゃ＝自転車
big	1-6	A	おおきい＝大きい
bill	2-5	N	(お)かんじょう＝(お)勘定
bird	1-10	N	とり＝鳥
birthday	1-11	N	(お)たんじょうび＝(お)誕生日
black	1-5	N	くろ＝黒
(is) black	1-6	A	くろい＝黒い
(to) blow away	2-11	V1	ふきとばす＝吹き飛ばす [ふきとばします]
blue	1-5	N	あお＝青
(is) blue	1-6	A	あおい＝青い
boat	1-7	N	ふね＝船
body	1-6	N	からだ＝体
book	1-2	N	ほん＝本
bookstore	1-13	N	ほんや＝本屋
boring	1-11	A	つまらない
(be) born (in ～)	2-2	V2	(place で)うまれる＝生まれる [うまれます]
born in (month)	1-3	Nd	- がつうまれ＝ - 月生まれ
(to) borrow	2-3	V2	かりる＝借りる [かります]
both	2-9	N	りょうほう＝両方
Bow.	1-1	Exp	れい＝礼
bowlful	1-14	Nd	- ぱい＝ - 杯
box	2-9	N	はこ＝箱

box lunch	1-14	N	べんとう＝弁当
boy	1-10	N	おとこのこ＝男の子
bread	1-4	N	パン
(a) break	1-11	N	やすみじかん＝休み時間
breakfast	1-4	N	あさごはん＝朝御飯
bridge	2-13	N	はし＝橋
(is) bright	2-11	A	あかるい＝明るい
(to) bring (animate)	2-7	V3	つれてくる＝連れて来る [つれてきます]
(to) bring (thing)	2-7	V3	もってくる＝持って来る [もってきます]
brown	1-5	N	ちゃいろ＝茶色
(is) brown	1-6	A	ちゃいろい＝茶色い
buckwheat noodle dish	2-5	N	ざるそば
building	1-10	N	たてもの＝建物
bus stop	2-13	N	バスてい＝バス停
bus	1-7	N	バス
(is) busy	1-7	A	いそがしい＝忙しい
but	1-5	Pc	(sentence 1) が, (sentence 2)
But [used at the beginning of the sentence.]	1-4	SI	でも
(to) buy	1-13	V1	かう＝買う [かいます]
by	2-2	N	そば＝傍
by (a certain time)	2-10	P	(time) までに
by (tool)	1-4	P	(tool) で
by (transportation facility)	1-7	P	(transportation) で
by all means	2-7	Adv	ぜひ＝是非
by far	2-9	Adv	ずっと
By the way	2-3	SI	ところで
<C>			
cafeteria	1-4	N	カフェテリア
camera	1-15	N	カメラ
camp	1-7	N	キャンプ
～ can be heard	1-2	V2	(～ が) きこえる＝聞こえる [きこえます]
～ can be seen	1-2	V2	(～ が) みえる＝見える [みえます]
can do well	1-5	Na	とくい＝得意
candy	1-2	N	あめ＝飴, キャンディ
(It) cannot be helped.	2-6	Exp	しかたがありません/ない。 ＝仕方がありません/ない。
cannot hear	1-2	V2	きこえません＝聞こえません
cannot see	1-2	V2	みえません＝見えません
cap, hat	2-3	N	ぼうし＝帽子
car	1-7	N	くるま＝車, じどうしゃ＝自動車
(playing) cards	1-5	N	トランプ
(to be) careful	2-3	V2	きをつける＝気をつける [きをつけます]
(to) carry	2-2	V1	もつ＝持つ [もちます]

cash register	2-5	N	レジ
cat	1-10	N	ねこ＝猫
(to) catch a cold	2-6	V1	かぜをひく＝風邪を引く [ひきます]
cent(s)	1-13	Nd	‐セント
(a) certain 〜	2-11	PN	ある 〜
chair	1-10	N	いす＝椅子
change (from a larger unit of money)	2-9	N	おつり＝お釣
(to) change over	2-6	V1	かわる＝代わる [かわります]
(is) cheap, inexpensive	1-13	A	やすい＝安い
(a) check, bill	2-5	N	(お)かんじょう＝(お)勘定
(to) cheer	2-10	V3	おうえん(を)する＝応援(を)する [おうえん(を)します]
chew away	2-11	Adv	ガリガリ
(to) chew gum	2-3	V1	(ガムを)かむ[かみます]
chicken (meat)	2-14	N	とりにく＝鳥肉
chicken and egg over a bowl of steamed rice	2-5	N	おやこどんぶり＝親子丼
child	1-10	N	こども＝子供
China	1-3	N	ちゅうごく＝中国
Chinese language	1-4	N	ちゅうごくご＝中国語
Chinese noodle soup	2-5	N	ラーメン
chocolate	2-5	N	チョコレート
chopsticks	1-14	N	(お)はし＝(お)箸
Christianity	2-7	N	キリストきょう＝キリスト教
Christmas	2-7	N	クリスマス
Christmas card	2-7	N	クリスマスカード
Christmas tree	2-7	N	クリスマスツリー
church	2-7	N	きょうかい＝教会
cigarettes	2-3	N	たばこ
city	2-9	N	し＝市
class	1-11	N	じゅぎょう＝授業, クラス
classroom	1-10	N	きょうしつ＝教室
(to) clean	2-14	V3	きれいにする[きれいにします]
(is) clean	1-6	Na	きれい
(to) clean up	2-7	V3	そうじ(を)する＝掃除(を)する [そうじ(を)します]
(to) clean up, put away	2-14	V2	かたづける＝片付ける[かたづけます]
clear (weather)	2-7	N	はれ＝晴れ
clock, watch	1-13	N	とけい＝時計
(to) close	1-13	V2	しめる＝閉める[しめます]
(Please) close.	1-2	Exp	しめてください＝閉めて下さい
close, near	1-10	A	ちかい＝近い
clothing	2-3	N	ふく＝服
cloud	2-11	N	くも＝雲

cloudy (weather)	2-7	N	くもり＝曇り
cockroach	1-10	N	ごきぶり
coffee	1-4	N	コーヒー
coffee shop	1-13	N	きっさてん＝喫茶店
cola (drink)	1-4	N	コーラ
(is) cold (to the touch)	1-14	A	つめたい＝冷たい
(is) cold (temperature)	1-1	A	さむい＝寒い
(a) cold	1-12	N	かぜ＝風邪
college	1-12	N	だいがく＝大学
college student	1-12	N	だいがくせい＝大学生
color	1-5	N	いろ＝色
(to) come	1-7	V3	くる＝来る[きます]
(to) come to pick up (someone)	2-10	V3	(person を) むかえにくる＝迎えに来る[むかえにきます]
(to) come to pick up (thing)	2-10	V3	(thing を) とりにくる＝取りに来る[とりにきます]
(is) comfortable	2-14	A	きもちがいい＝気持ちがいい
company	1-7	N	かいしゃ＝会社
company employee	1-3	N	かいしゃいん＝会社員
(to) compare	2-9	V2	くらべる＝比べる[くらべます]
competition [music]	2-15	N	コンクール
computer	1-4	N	コンピューター
concert	1-15	N	コンサート
condition is bad	2-6	A	ぐあいがわるい＝具合が悪い
Congratulations.	1-15	Exp	おめでとうございます。
convenience store	2-13	N	コンビニ
(to) cook	2-7	V3	りょうり(を)する＝料理(を)する[りょうり(を)します]
cool [temperature]	1-1	A	すずしい＝涼しい
corner	2-4	N	かど＝角
(is) correct	2-2	A	ただしい＝正しい
country	2-9	N	くに＝国
cousin	1-15	N	いとこ
credit card	2-9	N	クレジットカード
(to) cross (over) ～	2-13	V1	(～を) わたる＝渡る[わたります]
(is) crowded	2-13	V1	こんでいる＝込んでいる[こんでいます]
(to get) crowded	2-13	V1	こむ＝込む[こみます]
(to) cry	2-15	V1	なく＝泣く[なきます]
cup	1-14	N	コップ
cupful	1-14	Nd	-ぱい＝-杯
curry rice	2-5	N	カレーライス, ライスカレー
(to) cut	2-14	V1	きる＝切る[きります]
cute	1-6	A	かわいい＝可愛い

\<D\>

English	Lesson	Type	Japanese
dance	1-5	N	ダンス
dancing	1-5	N	ダンス
(is) dangerous	2-4	A	あぶない＝危ない
(is) dark	2-11	A	くらい＝暗い
(own) daughter	2-11	N	むすめ＝娘
(someone else's) daughter	2-11	N	むすめさん＝娘さん
day	1-15	N	ひ＝日
day(s)	2-6	Nd	-にち(かん)＝-日(間)
(the) day after tomorrow	1-11	N	あさって＝明後日
(the) day before yesterday	1-11	N	おととい＝一昨日
day of the month	1-11	Nd	-にち＝-日
day off	1-7	N	(お)やすみ＝(お)休み
daytime	1-4	N	(お)ひる＝(お)昼
December	1-3	N	じゅうにがつ＝十二月
decide on ～	2-5	V3	(something に) する[します]
definitely	2-7	Adv	ぜひ＝是非
- degree(s)	2-6	Nd	- ど＝- 度
(is) delicious	1-13	A	おいしい＝美味しい
department store	1-7	N	デパート
design	2-9	N	デザイン
desk	1-10	N	つくえ＝机
dessert	2-14	N	デザート
dictionary	1-2	N	じしょ＝辞書
(to) die	1-12	V1	しぬ＝死ぬ[しにます]
(to) differ	2-2	V1	ちがう＝違う[ちがいます]
(is) different	2-9	V1	ちがう＝違う[ちがいます]
(is) difficult	1-11	A	むずかしい＝難しい
difficult, hard	1-11	Na	たいへん＝大変
(to) dine, have a meal	1-7	V3	しょくじをする＝食事をする [しょくじをします]
dining	1-7	N	しょくじ＝食事
dinner	1-4	N	ばんごはん＝晩御飯
(to) dip (object in thing)	2-14	V2	(object を thing に) つける[つけます]
(is) dirty	1-6	A	きたない
dish	1-14	N	(お)さら＝(お)皿
dislike	1-5	Na	きらい＝嫌い
dislike a lot	1-5	Na	だいきらい＝大嫌い
(to) divorce	2-15	V3	りこん(を)する＝離婚(を)する [りこん(を)します]
(to) do	1-4	V3	する[します]
(to) do ～ completely [regret]	2-11	V1	(verb TE) しまう[しまいます]

do a homestaty	2-2	V3	ホームステイをする[ホームステイをします]
do a self-introduction	2-2	V3	じこしょうかい(を)する＝自己紹介(を)する[じこしょうかい(を)します]
do not have to (do)	2-5	Dv	-なくてもいいです
do not know	1-2	V1	しりません＝知りません
(I) do not mind if . . .	2-3	V1	かまいません
do one's best	1-12	V1	がんばる＝頑張る[がんばります]
Do you like it? [polite]	2-9	Exp	おすきですか。＝お好きですか。
(medical) doctor	1-3	N	いしゃ＝医者
(medical) doctor [polite form of いしゃ]	1-3	N	おいしゃさん＝御医者さん
dog	1-10	N	いぬ＝犬
dollar(s)	1-13	Nd	－ドル
(～ is) done	2-14	V2	(～が) できました＝出来ました
door	1-10	N	ドア, と＝戸
dormitory	2-2	N	りょう＝寮
(to) draw	2-15	V1	(えを) かく＝描く[かきます]
drawing	1-5	N	え＝絵
dress	2-3	N	ワンピース
(to) drink	1-4	V2	のむ＝飲む[のみます]
(a) drink	1-5	N	のみもの＝飲み物
(to) drive	2-3	V3	うんてん(を)する＝運転(を)する[うんてん(を)します]
driver	2-4	N	うんてんしゅ＝運転手, ドライバー
driver's license	2-3	N	うんてんめんきょ＝運転免許
(to) drop by (a place)	2-10	V1	(place に) よる＝寄る[よります]

<E>

ear	1-6	N	みみ＝耳
early	2-4	Adv	はやく＝早く
(is) early	1-7	A	はやい＝早い
early [used with a verb]	1-12	Adv	はやく＝早く
early evening	1-4	N	ゆうがた＝夕方
earrings	2-3	N	イヤリング
east	2-1	N	ひがし＝東
(is) easy	1-11	A	やさしい＝易しい
(to) eat	1-4	V2	たべる＝食べる[たべます]
egg	2-14	N	たまご＝卵
eight	1-1	N	はち＝八
eight [general counter]	1-2	N	やっつ＝八つ
eighteen	1-1	N	じゅうはち＝十八
(the) eighth day of the month	1-11	N	ようか＝八日
eighth grader	1-3	N	ちゅうがくにねんせい＝中学二年生

English	Lesson	Type	Japanese
eighty	1-1	N	はちじゅう＝八十
(not) either	2-9	N	どちらも＋Neg.
elderly man	1-3	N	おじいさん
elderly woman	1-3	N	おばあさん
electric train	1-7	N	でんしゃ＝電車
eleven	1-1	N	じゅういち＝十一
eleventh grader	1-3	N	こうこうにねんせい＝高校二年生
(is) employed (at ～)	2-2	V2	(place に) つとめる＝勤める[つとめます]
(is) empty	2-13	V1	すいている[すいています]
(to get) empty	2-13	V1	すく[すきます]
(something) ends	2-10	V1	(～が) おわる＝終わる[おわります]
(the) end	2-11	N	おしまい
(at the) end	2-14	Adv	おわりに＝終わりに
engineer	1-3	N	エンジニア
English language	1-4	N	えいご＝英語
(is) enjoyable	1-11	A	たのしい＝楽しい
(to) enter (a place)	2-4	V1	(place に) はいる＝入る[はいります]
entrance	2-13	N	いりぐち＝入口
eraser [rubber]	1-2	N	けしごむ＝消しゴム
especially	2-2	Adv	とくに＝特に
(N1 and N2) etc.	1-15	Nd	(N1) や (N2) など
evening	1-4	N	ばん＝晩
every month	1-12	N	まいつき＝毎月
every week	1-11	N	まいしゅう＝毎週
every year	1-15	N	まいとし＝毎年, まいねん＝毎年
everyday	1-4	N	まいにち＝毎日
everyone	1-15	N	みんな＝皆
everyone [polite]	1-15	N	みなさん＝皆さん
everything	1-14	N	ぜんぶ＝全部
exam	1-2	N	しけん＝試験
(is) excited	2-10	V3	ドキドキする[ドキドキします]
Excuse me. (apology)	1-1	Exp	すみません
Excuse me. (to get attention)	1-13	Exp	すみません
(to) exercise	2-10	V3	うんどう(を)する＝運動(を)する [うんどう(を)します]
(to) exist	2-6	V1	いらっしゃる [いらっしゃいます]
exit	2-13	N	でぐち＝出口
(I) expect that he/she will do/will not do. He/She is expected to do/not to do	2-6	Nd	(Dic./NAI) はずです
(is) expensive	1-13	A	たかい＝高い
eye	1-6	N	め＝目
eyeglasses	1-2	N	めがね＝眼鏡

<F>

English			Japanese
face	1-6	N	かお=顔
(rain, snow) fall	2-7	V1	ふる=降る[ふります]
fall (season)	1-12	N	あき=秋
(my) family	1-3	N	かぞく=家族
(someone's) family	1-3	N	ごかぞく=御家族
famous	1-10	Na	ゆうめい=有名
(is) far	1-10	A	とおい=遠い
far away	2-2	N	とおく=遠く
fast	2-4	Adv	はやく=速く
(is) fat	1-6	V1	ふとっている=太っている [ふとっています]
(my) father	1-3	N	ちち=父
(someone's) father	1-3	N	おとうさん=お父さん
Father's Day	1-15	N	ちちのひ=父の日
February	1-3	N	にがつ=二月
feel sick	2-6	A	ぐあいがわるい=具合が悪い
female, woman	1-10	N	おんな=女
fever	1-12	N	ねつ=熱
(a) few	1-10	Adv	すこし=少し
(is) few	1-11	A	すくない=少ない
fifteen	1-1	N	じゅうご=十五
(the) fifth day of the month	1-11	N	いつか=五日
fifty	1-1	N	ごじゅう=五十
(to) fight	2-4	V3	けんか(を)する=喧嘩(を)する [けんか(を)します]
finally	2-11	Adv	とうとう
fine, healthy	1-1	Na	(お)げんき=(お)元気
finger	1-6	N	ゆび=指
(to) finish	1-1	V	おわります=終わります
(something) finishes	2-10	V1	(〜が)おわる=終わる[おわります]
(to do) fireworks	2-7	V3	はなび(をする)=花火(をする)
(the) first day of the month	1-11	N	ついたち=一日
first of all	2-14	SI	まず
(for the) first time	2-7	N	はじめて=始めて
fish	1-10	N	さかな=魚
five	1-1	N	ご=五
five [general counter]	1-2	N	いつつ=五つ
flavor	2-14	N	あじ=味
floor	2-4	N	ゆか=床
flower	1-10	N	はな=花
flower shop	1-13	N	はなや=花屋
folk tale	2-11	N	むかしばなし=昔話

food	1-5	N	たべもの＝食べ物
foot	1-6	N	あし＝足
football	1-5	N	フットボール
for (activity)	1-7	P	(activity) に
for everything	1-14	N	ぜんぶ＝全部で
foreign language	1-11	N	がいこくご＝外国語
(to) forget	1-14	V2	わすれる＝忘れる[わすれます]
fork	1-14	N	フォーク
forty	1-1	N	よんじゅう＝四十
four	1-1	N	し＝四, よん＝四
four [general counter]	1-2	N	よっつ＝四つ
fourteen	1-1	N	じゅうし＝十四, じゅうよん＝十四
(the) fourteenth day of the month	1-11	N	じゅうよっか＝十四日
(the) fourth day of the month	1-11	N	よっか＝四日
fragrance	2-7	N	におい＝臭い
France	1-3	N	フランス
(is) free	2-3	Na	じゆう＝自由
(is) free (time)	2-15	Na	ひま＝暇
french fries	1-14	N	フライドポテト
French language	1-4	N	フランスご＝フランス語
freshman (9th grader)	1-3	N	ちゅうがくさんねんせい＝中学三年生
Friday	1-7	N	きんようび＝金曜日
friend	1-4	N	ともだち＝友達
from ～	1-11	P	～から
from now on	1-14	SI	これから
from ～ to ～	2-13	P	～から～まで
front	1-2	N	まえ＝前
fruit	2-14	N	くだもの＝果物
Fukuoka	2-1	N	ふくおか＝福岡
(I am) full.	1-14	Exp	おなかがいっぱいです。 ＝お腹が一杯です。
(is) fun	1-11	A	たのしい＝楽しい
future	2-14	N	しょうらい＝将来
<G>			
game	1-15	N	ゲーム
(sports) game	1-12	N	しあい＝試合
garage	1-10	N	ガレージ
garden	1-10	N	にわ＝庭
gate	2-3	N	もん＝門
generally	2-5	Adv	だいたい
German language	1-4	N	ドイツご＝ドイツ語
Germany	1-3	N	ドイツ
(to) get	2-6	V1	とる＝取る[とります]

(to) get/receive from ～	1-15	V1	～から/に もらう[もらいます]
(to) get off (vehicle)	2-4	V2	(vehicle から/を)おりる＝降りる[おります]
(to) get up	1-7	V2	おきる＝起きる[おきます]
girl	1-10	N	おんなのこ＝女の子
(to) give (to equal)	1-15	V2	あげる[あげます]
(to) give (to inferior)	1-15	V2	やる[やります]
(to) give (to speaker or to speaker's family)	1-15	V2	くれる[くれます]
(to) give (to a superior)	2-9	V2	(superior に) さしあげる＝差し上げる[さしあげます]
(is) glad	1-11	A	うれしい＝嬉しい
glassful	1-14	Nd	- はい, - ばい, - ぱい＝ - 杯
gnaw [onomatopoetic]	2-11	Adv	ガリガリ
(to) go	1-7	V1	いく＝行く[いきます]
(to) go out (from a place)	2-4	V2	(place を/から)でかける＝出かける[でかけます]
(to) go over	2-13	V1	(～を) わたる＝渡る[わたります]
(to) go to bed	1-7	V2	ねる＝寝る[ねます]
(to) go to pick up (person)	2-10	V1	(person を)むかえにいく＝迎えに行く[むかえにいきます]
(to) go to pick up (something)	2-10	V1	(thing を)とりにいく＝取りに行く[とりにいきます]
gold (color)	1-5	N	きんいろ＝金色
gold	2-15	N	きん＝金
golf	1-5	N	ゴルフ
(is) good	1-2	A	いい, よい＝良い
(be) good at	1-5	Na	じょうず＝上手
Good-bye. [Formal]	1-1	Exp	さようなら。
Good-bye. [Informal]	1-14	Exp	バイバイ
Good evening.	1-7	Exp	こんばんは＝今晩は
Good luck.	1-12	Exp	がんばって＝頑張って
Good morning. [Formal]	1-1	Exp	おはようございます。
Good morning. [Informal]	1-1	Exp	おはよう。
grade	1-11	N	せいせき＝成績
grandfather	1-3	N	おじいさん
grandmother	1-3	N	おばあさん
(is) great (person)	2-11	A	えらい＝偉い
green	1-5	N	みどり＝緑
green [traffic lights]	2-2	N	あお＝青
grey	1-5	N	グレイ
grilled skewered chicken	2-5	N	やきとり＝焼き鳥
guitar	1-5	N	ギター
gum	2-3	N	ガム

gym	2-10	N	たいいくかん＝体育館
<H>			
hair	1-6	N	かみ(のけ)＝髪(の毛)
(in) half	2-14	Adv	はんぶんに＝半分に
-half	1-7	Nd	-はん＝-半
hamburger	1-14	N	ハンバーガー
hand	1-6	N	て＝手
(is) happy	1-11	A	うれしい＝嬉しい
Happy New Year!	2-7	Exp	あけましておめでとうございます ＝明けましておめでとうございます
(is) hard (difficult)	1-11	Na	たいへん＝大変
hat	2-3	N	ぼうし＝帽子
hate	1-5	Na	だいきらい＝大嫌い
(to) have	1-11	V1	ある
(to) have, hold, carry	2-2	V1	もつ＝持つ[もちます]
have to (do)	2-5	Dv	-なければなりません
head	1-6	N	あたま＝頭
healthy	1-1	Na	(お)げんき＝(お)元気
(to) hear	1-4	V1	きく＝聞く[ききます]
heart	1-6	N	こころ＝心
(to) heat	2-14	V3	あつくする＝熱くする[あつくします]
height	1-6	N	せ(い)＝背
Hello. Hi.	1-1	Exp	こんにちは。
Hello. [telephone]	2-6	Exp	もしもし
(to) help	2-7	V3	てつだう＝手伝う[てつだいます]
(to) help, rescue	2-15	V2	たすける＝助ける[たすけます]
Here.	1-3	Exp	はい。
here	1-2	N	ここ
here [polite equiv. of ここ]	1-2	N	こちら
Here, please (take it).	1-2	Exp	はい、どうぞ。
(to) hide (something)	2-11	V1	かくす＝隠す[かくします]
high school	1-3	N	こうこう＝高校
high school student	1-3	N	こうこうせい＝高校生
hindrance	1-6	Na	じゃま＝邪魔
Hiroshima	2-1	N	ひろしま＝広島
hobby	1-5	N	しゅみ＝趣味
Hokkaido	2-1	N	ほっかいどう＝北海道
(to) hold	2-2	V1	もつ＝持つ[もちます]
hole	2-11	N	あな＝穴
homeroom	1-11	N	ホームルーム
homework	1-2	N	しゅくだい＝宿題
Honshu	2-1	N	ほんしゅう＝本州
hospital	1-3	N	びょういん＝病院

(is) hot and humid	1-1	A	むしあつい＝蒸し暑い
(is) hot [temperature]	1-1	A	あつい＝暑い
hotdog	1-14	N	ホットドッグ
-hour(s)	2-6	Nd	-じかん＝-時間
house [building]	2-2	N	いえ＝家
house, home	1-4	N	うち
(someone's) house [polite]	2-6	N	おたく＝お宅
housewife	1-3	N	しゅふ＝主婦
how? [Polite exp. of どう]	1-13	Ni	いかが？
How are you?	1-1	Exp	おげんきですか。＝お元気ですか。
How disappointing! [on a future event]	1-11	Exp	ざんねんですねえ。＝残念ですねえ。
How disappointing! [on a past event]	1-11	Exp	ざんねんでしたねえ。＝残念でしたねえ。
How do you do?	1-1	Exp	はじめまして。
How do you say ～ in Japanese?	1-2	Exp	～はにほんごでなんといいますか ＝～は日本語で何と言いますか。
How far is it? [distance]	2-13	Exp	どのぐらい　ありますか。
How is it? [informal]	1-11	Exp	どうですか。
How long does it take? [time]	2-13	Exp	どのぐらい　かかりますか。
How long/far is it?	2-13	Exp	どのぐらいですか。
how many [birds]?	1-10	Ni	なんわ＝何羽
how many [bound objects]?	1-15	Ni	なんさつ＝何冊
how many [long cylindrical objects]?	1-10	Ni	なんぼん＝何本
how many [mechanized goods]?	1-10	Ni	なんだい＝何台
how many [small animals]?	1-10	Ni	なんびき＝何匹
how many cups?	1-14	Ni	なんばい＝何杯
how many people?	1-3	Ni	なんにん＝何人
how many? [general counter]	1-2	Ni	いくつ
how much? [price]	1-13	Ni	おいくら
How nice! [on a future event]	1-11	Exp	いいですねえ。
How nice! [on a past event]	1-11	Exp	よかったですねえ。
how old? [age]	1-3	Ni	なんさい＝何歳, 何才, (お)いくつ
How pitiful.	1-12	Exp	かわいそうに。＝可愛そうに。
How ridiculous!	2-11	Exp	とんでもない。
how to do ～	2-14	N	(Verb stem) かた＝方
how to make	2-14	N	つくりかた＝作り方
However [Formal expression of でも]	2-15	SI	しかし
Huh?	2-11	SI	えっ
hundred	1-1	N	ひゃく＝百
hundred thousand	1-13	N	じゅうまん＝十万
(I am) hungry.	1-14	Exp	おなかがペコペコです。 ＝お腹がペコペコです。
(I got) hungry.	1-14	Exp	おなかがすきました。 ＝お腹が空きました。

Hurray!	2-10	Exp	ばんざい！＝万歳！
Hurry!	1-1	Exp	はやく＝速く
<I>			
I (used by anyone informally)	1-1	N	わたし＝私
I (used by males)	1-1	N	ぼく＝僕
I have a question.	2-13	Exp	ちょっとうかがいますが…
I see!	2-11	Exp	なるほど
ice cream	2-4	N	アイスクリーム
I. D.	2-3	N	しょうめいしょ＝証明書
illness	1-12	N	びょうき＝病気
important	1-12	Na	だいじ＝大事
in (location)	1-10	P	(location) に
in (place) [with action verb]	1-4	P	(place) で [with action verb]
in [tool particle]	1-4	P	(tool) で
(is) in the way	1-6	Na	じゃま＝邪魔
Indeed!	2-11	Exp	なるほど
inside	2-2	N	なか＝中
(is) interesting	1-11	A	おもしろい＝面白い
intermediate school	1-3	N	ちゅうがく＝中学
intermediate school student	1-3	N	ちゅうがくせい＝中学生
intersection	2-13	N	こうさてん＝交差点
(to) introduce	2-2	V3	しょうかい(を)する＝紹介(を)する
(It) is not so. [formal]	1-1	Exp	そうではありません
(It) is not so. [informal]	1-1	Exp	そうじゃありません
island	2-9	N	しま＝島
Isn't it 〜 ?	2-7	C	-でしょう [rising intonation]
isn't it? [sentence ending particle]	1-6	SP	ね
(Yes,) it is.	1-1	Exp	そうです。
It's me.	2-6	Exp	かわりました。＝代わりました。
			[used on the telephone]
<J>			
jacket	1-13	N	ジャケット
January	1-3	N	いちがつ＝一月
Japan	1-3	N	にほん＝日本
Japanese citizen	1-3	N	にほんじん＝日本人
Japanese language	1-4	N	にほんご＝日本語
job	1-3	N	(お)しごと＝(お)仕事
jogging	1-5	N	ジョギング
(a) joke	2-10	N	じょうだん＝冗談
juice	1-4	N	ジュース
July	1-3	N	しちがつ＝七月
June	1-3	N	ろくがつ＝六月
junior (in high school)	1-3	N	こうこうにねんせい＝高校二年生

<K>

key	2-4	N	かぎ＝鍵
(Are you) kidding?	2-10	Exp	うそでしょう。
(is) kind	1-6	A	やさしい＝優しい
kitchen	2-14	N	だいどころ＝台所
knife	1-14	N	ナイフ
(to) know	2-2	V1	しっている＝知っている[しっています]
(do not) know	1-1	V1	しりません＝知りません
Kobe	2-1	N	こうべ＝神戸
Korea	1-3	N	かんこく＝韓国
Korean language	1-4	N	かんこくご＝韓国語
Kyoto	2-1	N	きょうと＝京都
Kyushu	2-1	N	きゅうしゅう＝九州

<L>

lady	1-10	N	おんなのひと＝女の人
language	2-15	N	ことば＝言葉
large size	1-14	N	エルサイズ
last month	1-12	N	せんげつ＝先月
last night	1-12	N	ゆうべ
last week	1-11	N	せんしゅう＝先週
last year	1-15	N	きょねん＝去年
(is) late	1-7	A	おそい＝遅い
late	1-12	Adv	おそく＝遅く
late afternoon	1-4	N	ゆうがた＝夕方
(to) laugh	2-15	V1	わらう＝笑う[わらいます]
(to do) laundry	2-7	V3	せんたく(を)する＝洗濯(を)する[せんたく(を)します]
lawyer	1-3	N	べんごし＝弁護士
(to) learn	2-2	V1	ならう＝習う[ならいます]
(to) leave (a place)	2-4	V2	(place を) でる＝出る[でます]
(to) leave (something)	2-5	V1	おく＝置く[おきます]
left side	2-2	N	ひだり＝左
leg	1-6	N	あし＝脚
(Please) lend me.	1-14	V1	かしてください＝貸して下さい
Let me see . . .	2-1	SI	ええと..，あのう..，そうですねえ..
Let's begin.	1-1	Exp	はじめましょう＝始めましょう
Let's do 〜. [suggestion]	1-4	Dv	-ましょう
Let's finish.	1-1	Exp	おわりましょう＝終わりましょう
letter	1-4	N	てがみ＝手紙
liberal	2-3	Na	じゆう＝自由
library	1-4	N	としょかん＝図書館
(a) lie	2-10	N	うそ＝嘘
like	1-5	Na	すき＝好き

like very much	1-5	Na	だいすき=大好き
line is busy	2-6	Exp	はなしちゅう=話し中
liquor (in general)	2-14	N	(お)さけ=(お)酒
(to) listen	1-4	V1	きく=聞く[ききます]
(Please) listen.	1-2	Exp	きいてください=聞いて下さい
(to) litter	2-3	V2	（ごみを）すてる[すてます]
(a) little [formal]	1-4	Adv	すこし=少し
(a) little [more colloquial than すこし]	1-4	Adv	ちょっと
(is a) little, few	1-11	A	すくない=少ない
(to) live (in ～)	2-2	V1	(place に)すむ=住む[すみます]
location	2-10	N	ばしょ=場所
locker	1-10	N	ロッカー
(is) long	1-6	A	ながい=長い
long ago	2-11	N	むかしむかし=昔々
(to) look	1-4	V2	みる=見る[みます]
(Please) look.	1-2	Exp	みてください=見て下さい
(I am) looking forward to ～.	1-15	Exp	(～を)たのしみにしています。 =(～を)楽しみにしています。
looks ～	2-5	SI	(stem)そうです
(to) lose	1-12	V2	まける=負ける[まけます]
(a) lot	1-10	Adv	たくさん=沢山
love	2-15	N	あい=愛
love, like very much	1-5	Na	だいすき=大好き
(to be in) love	2-15	V1	あいしている=愛している[あいしています]
lunch	1-4	N	ひるごはん=昼御飯
<M>			
magazine	1-4	N	ざっし=雑誌
(to) mail	2-7	V1	おくる=送る[おくります]
(to) make	1-15	V1	つくる=作る[つくります]
(to) make clean	2-14	V3	きれいにする[きれいにします]
(to) make a mistake	2-6	V2	まちがえる=間違える[まちがえます]
(to) make a phone call	2-6	V2	でんわをかける＝電話をかける[でんわ(を)かけます]
(to) make reservations	2-5	V3	よやく(を)する=予約(を)する[よやく(を)します]
male	1-10	N	おとこ=男
man	1-10	N	おとこのひと=男の人
	1-15	N	おじさん
(are) many	1-11	A	おおい=多い
many, a lot (+ verb)	1-10	Adv	たくさん=沢山
many times	2-6	Adv	なんども＝何度も
map	2-13	N	ちず＝地図
March	1-3	N	さんがつ=三月

(to) marry	2-2	V3	(person と) けっこん(を)する[けっこん(を)します]
math	1-11	N	すうがく=数学
May I help you?	2-9	N	なにをさしあげましょうか。＝何を差し上げましょうか。
May	1-3	N	ごがつ=五月
meal	1-7	N	しょくじ=食事
(have a) meal	1-7	V3	しょくじをする=食事をする[しょくじ(を)します]
meat grilled on fire	2-5	N	やきにく=焼肉
medicine	1-12	N	くすり=薬
medium (size)	1-14	N	エムサイズ
(to) meet	1-12	V1	あう=会う[あいます]
(to) meet someone	2-3	V1	(person に) あう=会う[あいます]
(to) memorize	2-6	V2	おぼえる=覚える[おぼえます]
menu	2-5	N	メニュー
(is) messy	1-6	A	きたない
(cow's) milk	1-4	N	ぎゅうにゅう=牛乳, ミルク
(one) million	1-13	N	ひゃくまん=百万
mine	1-2	N	わたしの=私の
-minute(s)	1-7	Nd	-ふん=-分
Monday	1-7	N	げつようび=月曜日
money	1-2	N	(お)かね=(お)金
money received mainly by children from adults at New Year's			
	2-7	N	おとしだま=お年玉
-month(s)	2-6	Nd	-かげつ=-か月
～ more	2-10	PN	あと～=後 ～
more	2-9	Adv	もっと
(one) more (cup)	1-14	Adv	もう(いっぱい)=もう(一杯)
more than ～	2-9	P	～より
Moreover	1-11	SI	それに
morning	1-4	N	あさ=朝
(the) most	2-9	Adv	いちばん=一番
(my) mother	1-3	N	はは=母
(someone's) mother	1-3	N	おかあさん=お母さん
Mother's Day	1-15	N	ははのひ=母の日
mountain	1-7	N	やま=山
mouse	1-10	N	ねずみ=鼠
moustache	1-6	N	ひげ=髭
mouth	1-6	N	くち=口
(thing) move	2-11	V1	(thing が)うごく=動く[うごきます]
movie	1-5	N	えいが=映画
movie theater	2-3	N	えいがかん=映画館

Mr./Mrs./Ms.	1-1	Nd	-さん
Mr./Mrs./Ms./Dr. (teacher, doctor, statesman)	1-1	N	せんせい＝先生
(are) much	1-11	A	おおい＝多い
music	1-5	N	おんがく＝音楽
must not do	2-3	V2	いけません

<N>

Nagoya	2-1	N	なごや＝名古屋
Naha	2-1	N	なは＝那覇
name	1-3	N	なまえ＝名前
(someone's) name	1-3	N	おなまえ＝御名前
napkin	1-14	N	ナプキン
Nara	2-1	N	なら＝奈良
narrator	2-11	N	ナレーター
(is) narrow, small [a place]	1-10	A	せまい＝狭い
nation	2-9	N	くに＝国
(is) near	1-10	A	ちかい＝近い
nearby	2-2	N	ちかく＝近く, そば＝傍
neat	1-6	Na	きれい
neck	1-6	N	くび＝首
necklace	2-3	N	ネックレス
need ～	1-14	V1	(～が)いる＝要る[いります]
neither	2-9	N	どちらも＋Neg.
never + Neg.	2-4	Adv	けっして＋Neg.
(is) new	1-10	A	あたらしい＝新しい
New Year	2-7	N	(お)しょうがつ＝(お)正月
New Year's card	2-7	N	ねんがじょう＝年賀状
newspaper	1-4	N	しんぶん＝新聞
next	1-11	N	つぎ＝次
	2-2	N	となり＝隣
	2-14	Adv	つぎに＝次に
next month	1-12	N	らいげつ＝来月
next week	1-11	N	らいしゅう＝来週
next year	1-15	N	らいねん＝来年
(is) nice, kind	1-6	A	やさしい＝優しい
nice, pretty	1-6	Na	きれい
Nice to meet you.	1-1	Exp	どうぞよろしく。
night	1-4	N	よる＝夜
nine	1-1	N	く＝九, きゅう＝九
nine [general counter]	1-2	N	ここのつ＝九つ
nineteen	1-1	N	じゅうく＝十九, じゅうきゅう＝十九
ninety	1-1	N	きゅうじゅう＝九十
(the) ninth day of the month	1-11	N	ここのか＝九日
ninth grader	1-3	N	ちゅうがくさんねんせい＝中学三年生

No [formal]	1-1	SI	いいえ
No [informal]	2-4	SI	ううん
No [stronger negation than いいえ.]	2-11	SI	いや(っ)
no good	1-2	Na	だめ
no need to (do)	2-5	Dv	-なくてもいいです
No, thank you.	1-14	Exp	いいえ、けっこうです。
(is) noisy	1-6	A	うるさい
north	2-1	N	きた＝北
nose	1-6	N	はな＝鼻
(is) not at home	2-6	N	るす＝留守
(is) not crowded	2-13	V1	すいている[すいています]
not yet	1-14	Exp	まだです
notebook	1-2	N	ノート
November	1-3	N	じゅういちがつ＝十一月
now	1-3	N	いま＝今
nuisance	1-6	Na	じゃま＝邪魔
number -	2-10	Nd	-ばん＝-番
(is) nervous	2-10	V3	ドキドキする[ドキドキします]

\<O\>

occasionally	2-15	Adv	たまに
ocean	1-7	N	うみ＝海
-o'clock	1-7	Nd	-じ＝-時
October	1-3	N	じゅうがつ＝十月
of course	2-6	SI	もちろん
office	1-10	N	じむしょ＝事務所
often	1-4	Adv	よく
Oh!	2-13	SI	ああ
oil	2-14	N	あぶら＝油
Okinawa	2-1	N	おきなわ＝沖縄
(is) old (age)	1-6	V1	としをとっている＝年を取っている[としをとっています]
old (not for person's age)	1-10	A	ふるい＝古い
(my) older brother	1-3	N	あに＝兄
(someone's) older brother	1-3	N	おにいさん＝お兄さん
(my) older sister	1-3	N	あね＝姉
(someone's) older sister	1-3	N	おねえさん＝お姉さん
on, top	2-2	N	うえ＝上
once in a while	2-15	Adv	たまに
one	1-1	N	いち＝一
one (person)	1-3	N	ひとり＝一人
one [general counter]	1-2	N	ひとつ＝一つ
one more time	1-1	Adv	もういちど＝もう一度
oneself	2-15	N	じぶん＝自分

only ~	2-3	Nd	ーだけ
only child	2-15	N	ひとりっこ＝一人っ子
open	1-13	V2	あける＝開ける[あけます]
(Please) open.	1-2	Exp	あけてください＝開けて下さい
Or	1-6	SI	それとも
orange (color)	1-5	N	オレンジいろ＝オレンジ色
(to) order	2-5	V3	ちゅうもん(を)する＝注文(を)する[ちゅうもん(を)します]
(What is your/May I take your) order?	2-5	Exp	ごちゅうもんは。＝御注文は。
Osaka	2-1	N	おおさか＝大坂
other	2-9	N	ほか
other side	2-13	N	むこう＝向こう
outside	1-10	N	そと＝外
over there	1-2	N	あそこ
over there [polite equiv. of あそこ]	2-5	N	あちら
<P>			
P.E.	1-11	N	たいいく＝体育
p. m.	1-7	N	ごご＝午後
(is) painful	1-12	A	いたい＝痛い
(to) paint (a picture)	2-15	V1	(えを) かく＝描く[かきます]
painting	1-5	N	え＝絵
pan	2-14	N	なべ＝鍋
pants	1-13	N	パンツ [Used by younger people.]
	2-3	N	ズボン
paper	1-2	N	かみ＝紙
paper (report)	1-4	N	レポート
(own) parents	1-2	N	りょうしん＝両親
(someone else's) parents	1-2	N	ごりょうしん＝御両親
park	2-2	N	こうえん＝公園
parking lot	2-13	N	ちゅうしゃじょう＝駐車場
(to) participate in a (sports) game	2-10	V2	(しあいに)でる＝(試合に)出る[でます]
party	1-7	N	パーティー
passport	2-3	N	パスポート
patrol car	2-4	N	パトカー
(to) pay	2-5	V1	はらう＝払う[はらいます]
pencil	1-2	N	えんぴつ＝鉛筆
pencil sharpener	1-10	N	えんぴつけずり＝鉛筆削り
pepper (black)	2-14	N	こしょう＝胡椒
per ~	2-6	P	～に
- percent	2-5	Nd	ーパーセント
person	1-10	N	ひと＝人
person [polite form of ひと]	1-10	Nd	ーかた＝ー方
photo	1-2	N	しゃしん＝写真

piano	1-5	N	ピアノ
picnic	1-7	N	ピクニック
pierced (earrings)	2-3	N	ピアス
pig	1-10	N	ぶた＝豚
pink	1-5	N	ピンク
pizza	1-14	N	ピザ
place	2-2	N	ところ＝所
place, location	2-10	N	ばしょ＝場所
plan to do/do not plan to do	2-6	Nd	(Dic./NAI) つもりです
plate	1-14	N	おさら＝お皿
(to) play a game	1-15	V3	ゲームをする[ゲームをします]
(to) play (a string instrument)	2-6	V1	ひく＝弾く[ひきます]
(to) play (for fun)	1-15	V1	あそぶ＝遊ぶ[あそびます]
(to) play (sports)	1-15	V3	する[します]
(stage) play	2-12	N	げき＝劇
(to give/put on a stage) play	2-12	V3	げきをする＝劇をする[げきをします]
(sports) player	2-10	N	せんしゅ＝選手
(is) pleasant	2-14	A	きもちがいい＝気持ちがいい
Please. [request]	1-1	Exp	おねがいします＝御願いします
(Here) please (take it).	1-2	Exp	はい、どうぞ
Please come again.	2-9	Exp	またどうぞ。
Please give me ～.	1-2	Exp	～をください＝～を下さい
- point(s) [score]	2-10	Nd	-てん＝-点
police officer	2-4	N	けいかん＝警官
pond	1-10	N	いけ＝池
pool	1-10	N	プール
poor	2-11	Na	びんぼう＝貧乏
(be) poor at, unskillful	1-5	Na	へた＝下手
pork	2-14	N	ぶたにく＝豚肉
pork cutlet	2-5	N	とんかつ＝豚カツ
post office	2-13	N	ゆうびんきょく＝郵便局
pot	2-14	N	なべ＝鍋
potato chips	2-4	N	ポテトチップ
power	2-11	N	ちから＝力
(to) practice	1-12	V3	れんしゅう(を)する＝練習(を)する[れんしゅうをします]
(a) present	1-15	N	プレゼント
(is) pretty	1-6	Na	きれい
price	2-9	N	(お)ねだん＝(お)値段
probably	2-7	Adv	たぶん＝多分
probably ～	2-7	C	-でしょう [falling intonation]
problem	2-6	N	もんだい＝問題
public phone	2-13	N	こうしゅうでんわ＝公衆電話

purple	1-5	N	むらさき＝紫
(to) put	2-5	V1	おく＝置く[おきます]
(to) put away	2-14	V2	かたづける＝片付ける[かたづけます]
(to) put in ～	2-9	V2	(～ に)いれる＝入れる[いれます]

<Q>

question	2-2	N	しつもん＝質問
quickly	2-4	Adv	はやく＝速く
quiet	1-6	Na	しずか＝静か
(to) quiet down	1-13	V3	しずかにする＝静かにする[しずかにします]
(Please be) quiet.	1-2	Exp	しずかにしてください。 ＝静かにして下さい。
quiz	1-2	N	しょうテスト＝小テスト

<R>

radio	1-4	N	ラジオ
rain	1-1	N	あめ＝雨
raw egg	2-14	N	なまたまご＝生卵
(to) read	1-4	V1	よむ＝読む[よみます]
(Please) read.	1-2	Exp	よんでください＝読んで下さい
reading	1-5	N	どくしょ＝読書
(～ is) ready	2-14	V2	(～ が)できました＝出来ました
really	2-3	Adv	ほんとうに＝本当に
(to) receive	1-15	V1	もらう[もらいます]
red	1-5	N	あか＝赤
(is) red	1-6	A	あかい＝赤い
regulation	2-3	N	きそく＝規則
relatives	1-15	N	しんせき＝親戚
(to) rent (from)	2-3	V2	かりる＝借りる[かります]
report, paper	1-4	N	レポート
(to) require	2-9	V1	かかる[かかります]
(to) rescue	2-15	V2	たすける＝助ける[たすけます]
residence	2-6	N	おたく＝お宅
(to) rest	1-12	V1	やすむ＝休む[やすみます]
restaurant	1-7	N	レストラン
restroom	1-10	N	(お)トイレ, (お)てあらい＝(お)手洗い
(to) return (something)	2-5	V1	かえす＝返す[かえします]
(to) return to pick up (person)	2-10	V1	(person を)むかえにかえる＝迎えに帰る [むかえにかえります]
(to) return (to a place)	1-7	V1	かえる＝帰る[かえります]
(to) return to pick up (thing)	2-10	V1	(thing を)とりにかえる＝取りに帰る[とり にかえります]
(cooked) rice	1-4	N	ごはん＝ご飯
riceball	1-14	N	おむすび, おにぎり
rice wine	2-14	N	(お)さけ＝(お)酒

rich person	2-11	N	(お)かねもち＝(お)金持ち
(to) ride	2-4	V1	(vehicle に)のる＝乗る[のります]
right (side)	2-2	N	みぎ＝右
ring	2-3	N	ゆびわ＝指輪
river	1-7	N	かわ＝川
road	2-4	N	みち＝道
room	1-10	N	へや＝部屋
rubbish	1-2	N	ごみ
rule	2-3	N	きそく＝規則
(to) run	1-12	V1	はしる＝走る[はしります]
<S>			
(is) sad	1-11	A	かなしい＝悲しい
(is) safe	2-4	Na	あんぜん＝安全
salad	1-14	N	サラダ
(for) sale	2-9	N	セール中
salt	2-14	N	しお＝塩
(is) salty	2-14	A	からい＝辛い, しおからい＝塩辛い
same	2-9	N	おなじ＝同じ
sandwich	1-14	N	サンドイッチ
Sapporo	2-1	N	さっぽろ＝札幌
Saturday	1-7	N	どようび＝土曜日
(to) say	1-13	V1	いう＝言う[いいます]
Say, "cheese."	1-15	Exp	はい、チーズ。
Say, "peace."	1-15	Exp	はい、ピース。
(is) scary	2-4	A	こわい＝恐い
school	1-3	N	がっこう＝学校
school bus	2-4	N	スクールバス
science	1-11	N	かがく＝科学
(to) scold	2-15	V1	しかる＝叱る[しかります]
score	2-10	N	スコア
sea	1-7	N	うみ＝海
(the) second day of the month	1-11	N	ふつか＝二日
(to) see	1-4	V2	みる＝見る[みます]
(Well then,) see you later.	1-14	Exp	(じゃ)またあとで。
(to) sell	2-9	V1	うる＝売る[うります]
(to) send	2-7	V1	おくる＝送る[おくります]
Sendai	2-1	N	せんだい＝仙台
(high school) senior	1-3	N	こうこうさんねんせい＝高校三年生
September	1-3	N	くがつ＝九月
seven	1-1	N	しち＝七, なな＝七
seven [general counter]	1-2	N	ななつ＝七つ
seventeen	1-1	N	じゅうしち, じゅうなな＝十七
(the) seventh day of the month	1-11	N	なのか＝七日

seventh grader	1-3	N	ちゅうがくいちねんせい＝中学一年生
seventy	1-1	N	ななじゅう,しちじゅう＝七十
Shikoku	2-1	N	しこく＝四国
ship	1-7	N	ふね＝船
shirt	1-13	N	シャツ
shoes	1-13	N	くつ＝靴
(to) shop	1-7	V3	かいものをする＝買い物をする[かいものをします]
shopping	1-7	N	かいもの＝買い物
(is) short (height)	1-6	A	ひくい＝低い
(is) short [not for height]	1-6	A	みじかい＝短い
shorts	2-3	N	ショーツ, ショートパンツ
should (do)	2-5	Dv	-なければなりません
(to) show	1-13	V2	みせる＝見せる[みせます]
(Please) show.	1-2	Exp	みせてください＝見せて下さい
shredded *konnyaku*	2-14	N	いとこんにゃく＝糸こんにゃく
shrine (Shinto)	2-7	N	じんじゃ＝神社
(my) sibling(s)	1-3	N	きょうだい＝兄弟
sickness	1-12	N	びょうき＝病気
～ side	2-13	Nd	～がわ＝～側
silver	2-15	N	ぎん＝銀
silver color	1-5	N	ぎんいろ＝銀色
since (reason)	1-11	Pc	(reason) から
(to) sing	1-15	V1	うたう＝歌う[うたいます]
singing	1-5	N	うた＝歌
Sit. [ceremony]	1-4	Exp	ちゃくせき＝着席
(to) sit	1-13	V1	すわる＝座る[すわります]
(Please) sit.	2-2	Exp	すわってください＝座って下さい
six	1-1	N	ろく＝六
six [general counter]	1-2	N	むっつ＝六つ
sixteen	1-1	N	じゅうろく＝十六
(the) sixth day of the month	1-11	N	むいか＝六日
sixty	1-1	N	ろくじゅう＝六十
size	1-14	N	サイズ
skillful	1-5	Na	じょうず＝上手
skirt	2-3	N	スカート
(to) sleep	1-7	V2	ねる＝寝る[ねます]
(is) sleepy	1-12	A	ねむい＝眠い
(to) slice	2-14	V1	きる＝切る[きります]
slowly	1-1	Adv	ゆっくり
(is) small	1-6	A	ちいさい＝小さい
(is) small, narrow	1-10	A	せまい＝狭い
small size	1-14	N	エスサイズ
smell	2-7	N	におい＝臭い

(to) smile	2-15	V1	わらう＝笑う[わらいます]
smilingly [onomatopoetic]	2-15	Adv	ニコニコ
(to) smoke (cigarettes)	2-3	V1	(たばこを)すう[すいます]
snack bar	1-4	N	スナックバー
snow	2-7	N	ゆき＝雪
(Is that) so?	1-3	Exp	そうですか。
(sentence 1,) so (sentence 2).	1-11	Pc	(reason) から、 (result)
so, so	1-5	Adv	まあまあ
soccer	1-5	N	サッカー
social studies	1-11	N	しゃかい＝社会
socks	2-3	N	くつした＝靴下, ソックス
something	2-15	N	なにか＝何か
sometimes	1-4	Adv	ときどき＝時々
(own) son	2-11	N	むすこ＝息子
(someone else's) son	2-11	N	むすこさん＝息子さん
song	1-5	N	うた＝歌
sophomore, 10th grader	1-3	N	こうこういちねんせい＝高校一年生
(is) sore	1-12	A	いたい＝痛い
Sorry, but . . .	2-6	Exp	ざんねんですが 残念ですが...
(I am) sorry. [sympathy - formal]	2-6	Exp	(お)きのどくに。＝(お)気の毒に。
Sorry to be late.	2-14	Exp	おそくなりました。＝遅くなりました。
soup flavored with *miso*	2-5	N	(お)みそしる＝(お)味噌汁
(is) sour	2-14	A	すっぱい＝酸っぱい
south	2-1	N	みなみ＝南
souvenir gift	2-9	N	(お)みやげ＝(お)土産
(is) spacious	1-10	A	ひろい＝広い
Spain	1-3	N	スペイン
Spanish language	1-4	N	スペインご＝スペイン語
(to) speak	1-4	V1	はなす＝話す[はなします]
(to) speed	2-4	V1	スピードをだす＝出す[だします]
(is) spicy	2-14	A	からい＝辛い
spoon	1-14	N	スプーン
spoonful	1-14	Nd	-はい／-ぱい／-ばい＝-杯
sports	1-5	N	スポーツ
	2-10	N	うんどう＝運動
sports shoes	2-10	N	うんどうぐつ＝運動靴
spring	1-12	N	はる＝春
(to) stand	1-13	V1	たつ＝立つ[たちます]
(Please) stand.	1-2	Exp	たってください＝立って下さい
Stand. [ceremony]	1-1	Exp	きりつ＝起立
(someone) starts (something)	2-10	V2	(〜を)はじめる＝始める[はじめます]
(something) starts	2-10	V1	(〜が)はじまる＝始まる[はじまります]
state	2-9	N	しゅう＝州

(to) extend out	2-4	V1	だす＝出す[だします]
still	2-2	Adv	まだ + Aff.
stomach	1-6	N	おなか＝お腹
(to) stop by	2-10	V1	(place に)よる＝寄る[よります]
(to) stop (at a place)	2-4	V1	(place で/に)とまる＝止まる[とまります]
store	1-13	N	(お)みせ＝(お)店
straight	2-13	Adv	まっすぐ
strange, unusual	2-6	Na	へん＝変
straw	1-14	N	ストロー
strawberry	2-14	N	いちご＝苺
street, avenue	2-13	N	とおり＝通り
street, road	2-4	N	みち＝道
strength	2-11	N	ちから＝力
(is very) stressed	2-6	Exp	ストレスがいっぱいです。
(is) strict	1-6	A	きびしい＝厳しい
(is) strong	1-12	A	つよい＝強い
(be) strong in	1-5	Na	とくい＝得意
student [college]	1-3	N	がくせい＝学生
student [non-college]	1-3	N	せいと＝生徒
(to) study	1-4	V3	べんきょうする＝勉強(を)する [べんきょう(を)します]
subject	1-12	N	かもく＝科目
(to) submit	2-4	V1	だす＝出す[だします]
subway	1-7	N	ちかてつ＝地下鉄
suddenly	2-4	Adv	きゅうに＝急に
sugar	2-14	N	さとう＝砂糖
sukiyaki	2-14	N	すきやき＝鋤焼き
summer	1-12	N	なつ＝夏
sun [polite]	2-11	N	おひさま＝お日様
Sunday	1-7	N	にちようび＝日曜日
sunglasses	2-3	N	サングラス
supermarket	1-13	N	スーパー
supper	1-4	N	ばんごはん＝晩御飯
sushi shop/bar	1-13	N	すしや＝寿司屋
sweater	2-3	N	セーター
(is) sweet	2-14	A	あまい＝甘い
(to) swim	1-15	V1	およぐ＝泳ぐ[およぎます]
swimming	1-5	N	すいえい＝水泳
<T>			
table	2-5	N	テーブル
(to) take	1-15	V1	とる＝取る[とります]
(to) take (animate)	2-7	V1	つれていく＝連れて行く[つれていきます]
(to) take (medicine)	1-12	V1	のむ＝飲む[のみます]

(to) take (something)	2-7	V1	もっていく＝持って行く[もっていきます]
(to) take (time)	2-9	V1	かかる[かかります]
(to) take/bring (animate) back home	2-7	V1	つれてかえる＝連れて帰る[つれてかえります]
(to) take/bring (thing) back home	2-7	V1	もってかえる＝持って帰る[もってかえります]
(to) take a walk	2-15	V3	さんぽ(を)する＝散歩(を)する[さんぽ(を)します]
(to) take out	2-4	V1	だす＝出す[だします]
(to) take out (the garbage)	2-7	V3	ごみをだす＝ごみを出す[だします]
(to) talk	1-4	V1	はなす＝話す[はなします]
(is) tall	1-6	A	たかい＝高い
tape	1-4	N	テープ
(He/She is) tardy, late.	1-1	Exp	ちこくです＝遅刻です
taste, flavor	2-14	N	あじ＝味
tax	2-9	N	ぜいきん＝税金
taxi	1-7	N	タクシー
tea	1-4	N	おちゃ＝お茶
(to) teach	2-4	V2	おしえる＝教える[おしえます]
teacher	1-1	N	せんせい＝先生
team	1-12	N	チーム
telephone	1-4	N	でんわ＝電話
telephone number	1-15	N	でんわばんごう＝電話番号
(weather) temperature	2-7	N	おんど＝温度
temple (Buddhist)	2-7	N	(お)てら＝(お)寺
ten	1-1	N	じゅう＝十
ten [general counter]	1-2	N	とお＝十
tennis	1-5	N	テニス
ten thousand	1-13	N	(いち)まん＝(一)万
(the) tenth day of the month	1-11	N	とおか＝十日
tenth grader	1-3	N	こうこういちねんせい＝高校一年生
(is) terrible	1-11	A	ひどい＝酷い
(is) terrific	1-13	A	すごい＝凄い
textbook	1-2	N	きょうかしょ＝教科書,テキスト
(to) thank	2-15	V3	かんしゃ(を)する＝感謝(を)する[かんしゃ(を)します]
Thank you.	1-1	Exp	どうも,ありがとう。
Thank you very much.	1-1	Exp	ありがとうございます。
Thank you very much. [used after one has received something]			
	1-2	Exp	ありがとうございました。＝有難うございました。
That is a good idea.	2-10	Exp	それはいいかんがえです。＝それはいい考えです。

English	Lesson	Type	Japanese
that ~	1-2	PN	その～
that ~ over there	1-2	PN	あの～
that one	1-1	N	それ
that one [polite equiv. of それ]	2-9	N	そちら
that one over there	1-1	N	あれ
that one over there [polite equiv. of あれ]	2-9	N	あちら
That's all.	2-5	Exp	それだけです。
That's impossible!	2-11	Exp	とんでもない（です）。
there	1-2	N	そこ
there [polite equiv. of そこ]	2-5	N	そちら
there is (animate object)	1-10	V2	いる＝居る[います]
there is (inanimate object)	1-10	V1	ある＝有る[あります]
Therefore [Formal]	2-11	SI	ですから
Therefore [Informal]	2-11	SI	だから
Thereupon	2-13	SI	すると
thick	2-14	Adv	あつく＝厚く
(is) thick	2-14	A	あつい＝厚い
thick white noodles in broth	2-5	N	うどん
thin	2-14	Adv	うすく＝薄く
(is) thin	2-14	A	うすい＝薄い
(is) thin (person)	1-6	V2	やせている＝痩せている[やせています]
thing [intangible]	1-5	N	こと＝事
thing [tangible]	1-5	N	もの＝物
(to) think	2-11	V1	おもう＝思う[おもいます]
(the) third day of the month	1-11	N	みっか＝三日
(I am) thirsty.	1-14	Exp	のどがカラカラです。
(I got) thirsty.	1-14	Exp	のどがかわきました。＝喉が渇きました。
thirteen	1-1	N	じゅうさん＝十三
thirty	1-1	N	さんじゅう＝三十
this ~	1-2	PN	この ～
this month	1-12	N	こんげつ＝今月
this morning	1-12	N	けさ＝今朝
this one	1-1	N	これ
this one [polite equiv. of これ]	1-3	N	こちら
This way, please.	2-5	Exp	どうぞこちらへ。
this week	1-11	N	こんしゅう＝今週
this year	1-15	N	ことし＝今年
thousand	1-13	N	せん＝千
three	1-1	N	さん＝三
three [general counter]	1-2	N	みっつ＝三つ
throat	1-6	N	のど＝喉
through ~	2-4	P	～を
throughout	2-15	Adv	ずっと

(to) throw away (garbage)	2-3	V2	(ごみを)すてる[すてます]
Thursday	1-7	N	もくようび＝木曜日
ticket	1-15	N	きっぷ＝切符
time	2-10	N	じかん＝時間
～time	2-15	N	～とき＝～時
-time(s)	2-6	Nd	-ど＝-度
tip	2-5	N	チップ
(I got) tired.	1-12	Exp	つかれました。＝疲れました。
(I am) tired.	1-12	Exp	つかれています。＝疲れています。
tissue	1-2	N	ティッシュ
to ～	2-13	P	～まで
(from ～) to ～	1-11	P	(～から) ～まで
to (place)	1-7	P	(place) へ, (place) に
～ to ～ (score)	2-10	PN	～たい～＝～対～
tobacco	2-3	N	たばこ
today	1-4	N	きょう＝今日
toe	1-6	N	ゆび＝指
together	1-4	Adv	いっしょに＝一緒に
Tokyo	2-1	N	とうきょう＝東京
tomorrow	1-4	N	あした＝明日
tonight	1-7	N	こんばん＝今晩
too ～	2-14	V2	(stem+)すぎる＝(stem+)過ぎる[すぎます]
tooth	1-6	N	は＝歯
top	2-2	N	うえ＝上
town	2-13	N	まち＝町
traffic accident	2-4	N	こうつうじこ＝交通事故
traffic lights	2-4	N	しんごう＝信号
train station	2-13	N	えき＝駅
trash can	1-10	N	ごみばこ＝ごみ箱
(to) travel	1-7	V3	りょこうをする＝旅行をする[りょこう(を)します]
traveler's check	2-9	N	トラベラーズチェック
traveling	1-7	N	りょこう＝旅行
(to) treat (someone) to a meal	2-5	V3	ごちそう(を)する＝御馳走(を)する[ごちそう(を)します]
tree	1-10	N	き＝木
trip	1-7	N	りょこう＝旅行
true	1-3	N	ほんとう＝本当
(Is it) true/real?	2-3	Exp	ほんとうですか。＝本当ですか。
truly	2-3	Adv	ほんとうに＝本当に
try to (do)	2-5	Dv	(-て) みる[みます]
T-shirt	2-3	N	Tシャツ
Tuesday	1-7	N	かようび＝火曜日

(to) turn at/along (place)	2-4	V1	(place で/を) まがる＝曲がる[まがります]
(to) turn in, hand in	1-13	V1	だす＝出す[だします]
(Please) turn in.	1-2	Exp	だしてください＝出して下さい
T.V.	1-4	N	テレビ
twelfth grader	1-3	N	こうこうさんねんせい＝高校三年生
twelve	1-1	N	じゅうに＝十二
(the) twentieth day of the month	1-11	N	はつか＝二十日
twenty	1-1	N	にじゅう＝二十
(the) twenty fourth day of the month	1-11	N	にじゅうよっか＝二十四日
twenty years old	1-3	N	はたち＝二十歳
twin(s)	2-15	N	ふたご＝双児
two	1-1	N	に＝二
two [general counter]	1-2	N	ふたつ＝二つ
two (persons)	1-3	N	ふたり＝二人
(to) type	1-4	V3	タイプ(を)する[タイプ(を)します]

<U>

udon topped with beef	2-5	N	にくうどん＝肉うどん
(is) unappetizing, tasteless	1-13	A	まずい
uncle	1-15	N	おじさん
(is) uncomfortable	2-14	A	きもちがわるい＝気持ちが悪い
under	2-2	N	した＝下
(to) understand	1-1	V1	わかる＝分かる[わかります]
uniform	2-3	N	せいふく＝制服
(sports) uniform	2-10	N	ユニフォーム
(is) uninteresting	1-11	A	つまらない
university	1-12	N	だいがく＝大学
(is) unpleasant	2-14	A	きもちがわるい＝気持ちが悪い
unskillful	1-5	Na	へた＝下手
unusual	2-6	Na	へん＝変
U.S.	1-3	N	アメリカ
U.S. citizen	1-3	N	アメリカじん＝アメリカ人
usually	1-4	Adv	たいてい＝大抵
(with one's) utmost effort	2-11	Adv	いっしょうけんめい＝一生懸命

<V>

vacation	1-7	N	(お)やすみ＝(お)休み
various	2-9	Na	いろいろ
vegetable	2-14	N	やさい＝野菜
vehicle	1-7	N	くるま＝車, じどうしゃ＝自動車
very	1-5	Adv	とても
very soon	1-15	Adv	もうすぐ
(not) very	1-5	Adv	あまり ＋ Neg.
vicinity	2-2	N	ちかく＝近く
video	1-4	N	ビデオ

English	Lesson	Type	Japanese
video game	1-5	N	テレビゲーム
vinegar	2-14	N	す＝酢
voice	1-6	N	こえ＝声
volleyball	1-5	N	バレー(ボール)
～ vs. ～	2-10	PN	～たい～＝～対～

<W>

English	Lesson	Type	Japanese
(to) wait	1-13	V1	まつ＝待つ[まちます]
(Please) wait a minute.	1-1	Exp	ちょっとまってください。 ＝ちょっと待って下さい。
waiter	2-5	N	ウェイター
waitress	2-5	N	ウェイトレス
(to) wake up	1-7	V2	おきる＝起きる[おきます]
(to) walk	1-7	V1	あるく＝歩く[あるきます]
walkman	1-4	N	ウォークマン
wall	2-11	N	かべ＝壁
wallet	1-2	N	さいふ＝財布
want (something)	1-11	A	(something が)ほしい＝欲しい
want (to do)	1-12	Da	(verb stem form) -たい
(is) warm	1-14	A	あたたかい＝暖かい
(to) wash	2-7	V1	あらう＝洗う[あらいます]
(a) watch	1-13	N	とけい＝時計
(to) watch	1-4	V2	みる＝見る[みます]
water	1-4	N	(お)みず＝(お)水
we	1-12	N	わたしたち＝私達
we [Used by males.]	1-12	N	ぼくたち＝僕達
We did it!	2-10	Exp	やったあ！
(be) weak in	1-5	Na	にがて＝苦手
(is) weak	1-12	A	よわい＝弱い
(to) wear [above the waist or on the entire body]	2-3	V2	きる＝着る[きます]
(to) wear [accessories]	2-3	V3	する[します]
(to) wear [below the waist]	2-3	V1	はく＝履く[はきます]
(to) wear [glasses]	2-3	V2	(めがねを)かける[かけます]
(to) wear [on or draped over the head]	2-3	V2	かぶる[かぶります]
(to) wear a seat belt	2-4	V3	シートベルトをする[します]
weather	1-1	N	(お)てんき＝(お)天気
Wednesday	1-7	N	すいようび＝水曜日
-week(s)	2-6	Nd	-しゅうかん＝-週間
weekend	1-11	N	しゅうまつ＝週末
weird	2-6	Na	へん＝変
Welcome.	2-5	Exp	いらっしゃいませ。
(You are) welcome.	1-1	Exp	どういたしまして。
well	1-4	Adv	よく

Well . . . [Used when one does not know or is unsure of the answer.]

| | 2-9 | SI | さあ... |

Well . . . [Used when one is unsure of the answer]

	2-1	SI	ええと... あのう...
Well done.	1-2	Exp	よくできました。=良く出来ました。
Well then [formal]	1-14	Exp	では
Well then [informal]	1-14	Exp	じゃ
west	2-1	N	にし=西
what?	1-1	Ni	なに=何, なん=何
what color?	1-5	N	なにいろ=何色
(the) what day of the month?	1-11	Ni	なんにち=何日
what day of the week?	1-7	Ni	なんようび=何曜日
what grade?	1-3	N	なんねんせい=何年生
What happened?	1-12	Exp	どうしましたか。
what kind of 〜?	1-5	PN	どんな〜
what language?	1-4	Ni	なにご=何語
what month?	1-3	Ni	なんがつ=何月
what nationality?	1-3	Ni	なにじん=何人
what time?	1-7	Ni	なんじ=何時
when?	1-7	Ni	いつ
where?	1-3	Ni	どこ
where? [polite equiv. of どこ]	2-5	Ni	どちら
which 〜?	1-13	Nd	どの〜
which (one of two)? [informal]	2-9	Ni	どっち
which (one of two)? [polite]	2-9	Ni	どちら
which one (of three or more)?	1-13	Ni	どれ
white	1-5	N	しろ=白
(is) white	1-6	A	しろい=白い
who?	1-3	Ni	だれ=誰
why?	1-11	Ni	なぜ, どうして
(is) wide	1-10	A	ひろい=広い
(to) win	1-12	V1	かつ=勝つ
(to) win a championship	2-10	V3	ゆうしょうをする=優勝をする[ゆうしょう(を)します]
wind	2-7	N	かぜ=風
window	1-10	N	まど=窓
winter	1-12	N	ふゆ=冬
with (person)	1-4	P	(person)と(いっしょに)
with (tool)	1-4	P	(tool) で
woman	1-10	N	おんなのひと=女の人
woman (middle-aged)	1-15	N	おばさん
(We) won! (We) won!	2-10	Exp	かった！かった！=勝った！勝った！
(is) wonderful	1-13	A	すばらしい=素晴らしい

won't do	2-3	V2	いけません
(it) won't do	2-5	V1	なりません
Won't you do ～? [invitation]	7-1	Dv	-ませんか
words	2-15	N	ことば＝言葉
(to) work (at ～)	2-2	V1	(place で) はたらく＝働く[はたらきます]
(to) work part-time (at ～)	2-2	V3	(place で) アルバイト(を)する[します]
worksheet	1-2	N	ワークシート
world	2-9	N	せかい＝世界
(to) worry	2-4	V3	しんぱい(を)する＝心配(を)する[しんぱい(を)します]
Wow!	1-13	SI	わあ
(to) write	1-4	V1	かく＝書く[かきます]
(Please) write.	1-2	Exp	かいてください＝書いて下さい
(is) wrong	2-2	V1	ちがう＝違う[ちがいます]

<Y>

(a) yard	1-10	N	にわ＝庭
-year	1-15	Nd	-ねん＝-年
-year(s) (duration)	2-6	Nd	-ねんかん＝-年間
yellow	1-5	N	きいろ＝黄色
(is) yellow	1-6	A	きいろい＝黄色い
yen	1-13	Nd	-えん＝-円
Yes [formal]	1-1	SI	はい
Yes [informal]	2-4	SI	うん
Yes [less formal than はい]	1-1	SI	ええ
yesterday	1-4	N	きのう＝昨日
you	1-2	N	あなた
You are welcome.	1-1	Exp	どういたしまして。
you know [sentence ending particle]	1-6	SP	よ
(is) young	1-6	A	わかい＝若い
young lady [informal]	2-11	N	むすめ＝娘
young lady [polite]	2-11	N	むすめさん＝娘さん
(my) younger brother	1-3	N	おとうと＝弟
(someone's) younger brother	1-3	N	おとうとさん＝弟さん
(my) younger sister	1-3	N	いもうと＝妹
(someone's) younger sister	1-3	N	いもうとさん＝妹さん
yours	1-2	N	あなたの＝あなたの
Yummm . . .	2-5	SI	う～ん

<Z>

| zoo | 2-13 | N | どうぶつえん＝動物園 |

かんじ

1	一 いち, ひと (つ)	二 に, ふた (つ)	三 さん, みっ (つ)	四 し, よん, よっ (つ)	五 ご, いっ (つ)			
	六 ろく, むっ (つ)	七 なな, しち, なな (つ)	八 はち, やっ (つ)	九 きゅう, く, ここの (つ)	十 じゅう, とお			
	日 に, にち, ひ, び, か	月 がつ, げつ	火 か	水 みず, すい	木 き, もく	金 かね, きん	土 ど	
2 課	口 くち, ぐち	目 め	人 ひと, にん, じん	本 もと ほん, ぽん, ぼん	今 いま こん	年 とし, ねん	私 わたし, わたくし	曜 よう
3 課	上 うえ	下 した, くだ (さい)	大 おお (きい) たい, だい	小 ちい (さい), しょう	夕 ゆう	何 なに, なん	中 なか, ちゅう	外 そと, がい
4 課	行 い (く), こう	来 き (ます), く (る), こ (ない), らい	子 こ	車 くるま, しゃ	学 がく, がっ	校 こう	見 み (る)	良 よ (い)	食 た (べる), しょく
5 課	川 かわ, がわ	山 やま, さん	出 で (る) だ (す)	先 せん	生 う (まれる), せい	父 ちち, とう	母 はは, かあ	毎 まい	書 か (く), しょ
6 課	手 て	耳 みみ	門 もん	聞 き (く), ぶん	女 おんな	好 す (き)	田 た, だ	男 おとこ	
7 課	言 い (う)	語 ご	寺 てら, でら じ	時 とき, じ	間 あいだ, かん	分 わ (かる) ふんぷん, ぶん	正 ただ (しい), しょう	家 いえ, か	々 [repeat]

545

9課	白 しろ, はく	百 ひゃく, びゃく, ぴゃく	千 せん, ぜん	万 まん	方 かた, がた, ほう	玉 たま, だま	国 くに, ぐに こく, ごく	安 やす (い)	高 たか (い), こう	
10課	牛 うし, ぎゅう	半 はん	*手 て, しゅ	友 とも	帰 かえ (る)	待 ま (つ)	持 も (つ)	米 こめ	番 ばん	事 こと, ごと, じ
11課	雨 あめ	電 でん	天 てん	気 き	会 あ (う), かい	話 はな (す), はなし、 ばなし, わ	売 う (る)	読 よ (む)		
13課	右 みぎ	左 ひだり	入 い (れる), はい (る), いり	物 もの, ぶつ	名 な, めい	前 まえ, ぜん	戸 と, ど	所 ところ, どころ しょ, じょ	近 ちか (い)	
14課	立 た (つ), りつ	作 つく (る) ・さく	肉 にく	魚 さかな	多 おお (い), た	少 すく (ない), すこ (し)	古 ふる (い)	新 あたら (しい), しん	*生 う (まれ る), せい, なま	
15課	才 さい	心 こころ, しん	思 おも (う)	休 やす (み)	買 か (う)	早 はや (い)	自 じ	犬 いぬ	太 ふと (る)	屋 や

＊ Previously introduced.

Verb Conjugations

	NAI form	MASU form	Dic. form	Potential	TE form	TA form	NAKATTA form
	informal, neg., nonpast	formal, nonpast	informal, nonpast	(Group 2 verb) L.10		informal, past	informal, neg., past
I. Group 1 Verbs							
み	のまない nomanai	のみます nomimasu	のむ nomu	のめる nomeru	のんで nonde	のんだ nonda	のまなかった nomanakatta
に	しなない shinanai	しにます shinimasu	しぬ shinu	しねる shineru	しんで shinde	しんだ shinda	しななかった shinanakatta
び	あそばない asobanai	あそびます asobimasu	あそぶ asobu	あそべる asoberu	あそんで asonde	あそんだ asonda	あそばなかった asobanakatta
い	かわない kawanai	かいます kaimasu	かう kau	かえる kaeru	かって katte	かった katta	かわなかった kawanakatta
ち	またない matanai	まちます machimasu	まつ matsu	まてる materu	まって matte	まった matta	またなかった matanakatta
り	かえらない kaeranai	かえります kaerimasu	かえる kaeru	かえれる kaereru	かえって kaette	かえった kaetta	かえらなかった kaeranakatta
	＊ない * nai	あります arimasu	ある aru		あって atte	あった atta	＊なかった * nakatta
き	かかない kakanai	かきます kakimasu	かく kaku	かける kakeru	かいて kaite	かいた kaita	かかなかった kakanakatta
	いかない ikanai	いきます ikimasu	いく iku	いける ikeru	＊いって * itte	＊いった * itta	いかなかった ikanakatta
ぎ	およがない oyoganai	およぎます oyogimasu	およぐ oyogu	およげる oyogeru	およいで oyoide	およいだ oyoida	およがなかった oyoganakatta
し	はなさない hanasanai	はなします hanashimasu	はなす hanasu	はなせる hanaseru	はなして hanashite	はなした hanashita	はなさなかった hanasanakatta
II. Group 2 Verbs							
- e	たべない tabenai	たべます tabemasu	たべる taberu	たべられる taberareru	たべて tabete	たべた tabeta	たべなかった tabenakatta
□	みない minai	みます mimasu	みる miru	みられる mirareru	みて mite	みた mita	みなかった minakatta
Special verbs: おきます get up, かります borrow, おります get off, できます can do							
III. Group 3 Irregular verbs							
する (do)	しない shinai	します shimasu	する suru	できる dekiru	して shite	した shita	しなかった shinakatta
くる (come)	こない konai	きます kimasu	くる kuru	こられる korareru	きて kite	きた kita	こなかった konakatta

＊Exceptional form.

547

REFERENCES

Hello Japan. Tokyo: メイクフレンズ・フォー・ジャパン・キャンペーン事務局, 1994

Japan: An Illustrated Encyclopedia. Tokyo: Kodansha Ltd., 1993

Japanese In Modules Book 1 & Book 2. Tokyo: ALC Press Inc., 1993

JTB's Illustrated Book Series. Tokyo: Nihon Kootsuukoosha Shuppan Jigyookyoku

Joya, Mock. *Things Japanese*. Tokyo: Tokyo News Service, 1960

Kawashima, Masaru. 漢字をおぼえる辞典.. Tokyo: Obunsha, 1975

Makino, Seiichi and Tsutsui, Michio. *A Dictionary of Basic Japanese Grammar*. Tokyo: The Japan
    Times, 1998

Nagara, Susumu. *Japanese For Everyone*. Tokyo: Gakken Co. Ltd., 1991

Sato, Esther and Sakihara, Jean. *Japanese Now*, Vols. 1 - 4. Honolulu: University of Hawaii Press,
    1982

Shokyu Nihongo. Tokyo: Tokyo Gaikokugo Daigaku Fuzoku Nihongo Gakkoo, 1994

Seki, Kiyo and Yoshiki, Hisako. *Nihongo Kantan*. Tokyo: Kenkyuusha, 1988

書の年賀状. Tokyo: 日貿出版社, 1989

スクールカット図典学校生活編 & 家庭生活編. Tokyo: 東陽出版, 1997

Tohsaku, Yasu-Hiko. *Yookoso*. New York McGraw-Hill, 1994

Young, John and Nakajima-Okano, Kimiko. *Learn Japanese: New College Text*, Vols. 1 - 4.
    Honolulu: University of Hawaii Press, 1985

藤堂方式／小学生版漢字なりたち辞典, 藤堂明保監修教育社編, Tokyo: 教育社, 1997